WALKS WITH OUR LORD THROUGH JOHN'S GOSPEL

Walks with Our Lord Through John's Gospel

by

Erling C. Olsen

Author of

"Meditations in the Psalms"
"Focusing the Bible on Current Problems"

VOLUME I

SECOND EDITION

ZONDERVAN PUBLISHING HOUSE
GRAND RAPIDS, MICHIGAN

COPYRIGHT MCMXLI BY
ERLING C. OLSEN

PUBLISHED BY
ZONDERVAN PUBLISHING HOUSE
EIGHT FORTY-SEVEN OTTAWA AVE., N.W.
GRAND RAPIDS, MICHIGAN

DEDICATION

To three lovely girls
ALICE KIRBY OLSEN, *my wife*,
CLARE KIRBY OLSEN, *our first*,
CAROL KIRBY OLSEN, *our second*.

PREFACE

IN the first epistle of all those which he wrote to be included in the sacred canon of scripture, the Apostle Paul told the Thessalonians that he was continually remembering their "labor of love." All things that have any permanent value and result in definite blessing cost hard labor—when that labor is done in love, because of love, as the outflow of love, the result is infinitely richer, and in some mysterious way, bears the very characteristics of the one who has brought the result into being.

This new work of my dear friend, Mr. Erling C. Olsen, seems to me to be born not of one love, but of four. First, he has a great love for his Lord and Saviour Jesus Christ: Christ is here in these vividly warm pages not the subject of theological discussion, not just some great person of the ancient past, nor even the intangible ideal of a mystical life, but the ever-present, redeeming, strengthening Son of God, who walks at our side, who is our Divine Friend, who is indeed the glorious Lord of our life.

Secondly, the author has a passionate love for the Word of God. Again and again in my own mind I have, as I have known him these last ten years, been compelled to compare Mr. Olsen to Sir Robert Anderson—because, in the midst of a strenuous business career, he has had time, and sees that he *does* have time, to dig deeply into the treasures of the great storehouse of Divine Truth. No Christian can be with Mr. Olsen anywhere, on a train, walking to a meeting, in his office, enjoying luncheon or sitting about the fireplace in his home, but that he is aware of this great love for the Word of God.

In the third place, Mr. Olsen has a great love for the souls of men. Some gifted men seem to have a longing to see souls saved only while they are engaged in the fascinating, sacred work of preaching to large assemblies of people. My dear friend who has written these pages will quickly talk to an elevator boy about his soul, or gladly spend time in conversing with some unsaved business friend about the things of God. Jewish merchants, financiers, aged widows, college students troubled with doubts, his own dear little daughter (the baby not quite yet), thousands of people everywhere, know that this man cares for their souls.

Finally, our friend loves the writings of great men: the amount of reading he does is simply amazing. That is one reason why all of his messages are always so fresh, so remarkably illustrated with contemporary anecdotes and timely statements.

As to this particular book—when I finished reading its pages as they came from the printer, this is what I became convinced of anew—there is not another layman anywhere in America, and very, very few ministers on our continent (less than the fingers of one's two hands) who could produce such a work as this. My own opinion is this, that no layman in the English world today, week after week, year after year, is so clearly, so winsomely, so courageously, so authoritatively, interpreting the Word of God, in all its breadth and depth and variety of teachings, as the author of these messages. Mr. Olsen, it is true, has a gift from God for this kind of work—but he is forever stirring up that gift which is within him, and these messages are the result of incessant toil, day and night—but always "the labor of love."

By these pages Mr. Olsen reveals what radio messages *ought* to be: he rebukes us all by making us ashamed we have not gone and done likewise, as far as our ability would permit; he rekindles in all our hearts a greater love for Jesus Christ and His Eternal Word.

It is a privilege, an honor deeply appreciated to be allowed to write this Preface; it is a greater privilege to know as one of the choicest friends I will ever have on this earth, the one from whose abundant and radiant life these messages have sprung.

May God use this volume for all the years that remain until our Lord returns, to the edification of the Body of Christ, and the completion of His Church.

WILBUR M. SMITH, D. D.

Moody Bible Institute,
Chicago, Ill.

AUTHOR'S PREFACE

ONCE a man writes a book—they say he must write another. But neither "Meditations in the Psalms" (now in its second printing) nor "Walks with our Lord through John's Gospel" can be called the author's work. If it were not for two eternal Books—"The Psalms" and "The Gospel according to St. John" there never would have been these volumes. And if others had not contributed (knowingly or unknowingly) to these works, they would hardly warrant printing. No less than 125 books or people have been quoted throughout these "Walks." The only thing that can be said to have belonged to the author were the many long hours of work that were expended—but what intelligent Christian would call any time his own time? The Psalmist said, "my times are in thy hand."

Something needs to be said however.

First, these "Walks" were suggested by a friend whose fellowship in the Gospel (mostly by letter—seeing he is a missionary in Manchukuo) has been a great blessing from God. Edwin J. Tharp, thank you and God bless you.

Secondly, these one hundred "Walks" were given as radio talks over WMCA in New York and WIP in Philadelphia, each Sunday morning at 9 o'clock for a period of two years. I believe it can be said that God has been pleased to add His blessing to these radio Walks and Talks.

Thirdly, (to be homiletical) will scholars and preachers please remember these "Walks" were primarily prepared for the common people, who "heard Him gladly."

I must confess that my own soul has been fed as I have labored over the re-editing of these "Walks" in preparation for printing. How unfathomable is the Word of God! May it please our Lord to use this effort to the salvation of souls—to the building up of believers —and to His glory.

Erling C. Olsen

Scarsdale, New York
November, 1941.

TABLE OF CONTENTS

Walk No.	Title	Chapter	Verses	Page
1	Before Genesis—What?	I	1-5	11
2	The Pre-Incarnation Glory of Christ	I	1-5	16
3	A Man Sent From God	I	6-13	22
4	The Incarnation	I	14-18	28
5	The Greatest Man Born of Woman	I	19-28	35
6	The Lamb of God	I	29-34	41
7	As Jesus Walked	I	35-42	48
8	In the Steps of Saint Philip	I	43-51	55
9	His First Miracle	II	1-11	63
10	The First Temple Purge	II	13-22	69
11	"Ye Must Be Born Again"	III	1-5	77
12	Self-Made, Un-Made, New-Made	III	1-15	83
13	The Greatest Verse in the Bible	III	16	90
14	The Gift of God	III	16	98
15	The Open Door in John 3:16	III	16	104
16	Will God Condemn A Man Who Has Never Heard About Christ?	III	17-21	108
17	John the Baptist's Swan Song	III	22-36	114
18	A Trek Through Samaria	IV	1-6	121
19	An Enticer Becomes An Evangelist	IV	7-29	126
20	The Power of a Testimony	IV	30-42	132
21	Sickness—A Tragedy Or a Blessing	IV	44-54	139
22	The Clinic and the Angel of Bethesda	V	1-15	147
23	What Jesus Claimed For Himself	V	16-27	153
24	The Two Resurrections	V	28-30	159
25	The Witnesses and the Summation	V	30-47	166
26	Christ and the Anti-christ	V	30-47	170
27	The Economic Problem in the Hands of the Lord Jesus	VI	1-14	177
28	Why Do Christian People Have Trouble?	VI	15-21	184
29	Seeking For Jesus	VI	22-29	190
30	True Bread	VI	30-42	195
31	The Hard Sayings of Jesus	VI	51-58	200
32	The Sovereign Will and Grace of God and the Free Will of Man	VI	37-65	206
33	The Christ Men Thought They Knew	VII	1-30	211
34	Never Man Spake Like This Man	VII	37-53	217
35	Snooping Religionists	VII / VIII	53 / 1-11	223
36	The Light of the World	VIII	12-28	229
37	The Tragedy of Mistaken Parentage	VIII	31-45	235
38	The Unanswerable Challenge	VIII	45-51	241
39	The Incomparable I Am	VIII	51-59	247
40	The Seeing Eye—The Blind Man's Friend	IX	1-7	254
41	The Neighbour's Therefore	IX	8-34	260
42	The First Ex-Communicant	IX	35-41	265
43	Sheep Stealers in Shepherd's Clothes	X	1-6	272
44	The More Abundant Life	X	7-12	279
45	One Flock and One Shepherd	X	14-18	285
46	The Supernaturalism of Jesus	X	19-21	291
47	A Plain Answer to a Perplexing Problem	X	25-30	297
48	The Final Apologetic of Jesus	X	34-42	303
49	How God Makes Our Disappointments His Appointments	XI	1-6	310
50	Conqueror Over Death and Decay!	XI	7-44	316

TABLE OF CONTENTS

Walk No.	Title	Chapter	Verses	Page
51	The Irresistible Force of a Silent Testimony	XI	45-54	322
52	The Breaking of The Alabaster Box	XII	1-11	329
53	"Behold the World Is Gone After Him"	XII	12-19	335
54	God's Other Bible	XII	20-26	341
55	Glorifying God When Troubled	XII	27-33	348
56	The First Blackout in Palestine	XII	34-41	354
57	The Treachery of Intellectual Faith	XII	42-50	361
58	The Bowing of a Sovereign	XIII	1-20	368
59	The Fifth Column Member of the Twelve	XIII	21-35	375
60	The Cure for Troubled Hearts	XIII / XIV	36-38 / 1-4	382
61	Preaching Prophecy or Prophesying—Which?	XIV	1-4	389
62	The Testimony of Jesus	XIV	6-14	397
63	The Character and Ministry of the Holy Spirit	XIV	16-21	405
64	The Lord's Bequest	XIV	25-31	411
65	The Three Kinds of Church Members	XV	1-14	417
66	Abiding in Christ	XV	1-14	424
67	Apostolic Succession, Apostolic Preaching and Apostolic Reception	XV	15-25	429
68	The Presence and Ministry of the Holy Spirit in the World	XV / XVI	26-27 / 1-11	437
69	The Supreme Ministry of the Supreme Spirit	XVI	12-15	445
70	The Autobiography of Jesus	XVI	16-33	451
71	With Christ in the Inner Sanctuary	XVII	1-3	459
72	The Glory and the Gift of His Work	XVII	4-6	466
73	God and the World	XVII	6-9	474
74	"Divine Communism"	XVII	10	480
75	The Security and the Unity of the Believer	XVII	11-13	484
76	Sanctification: What It Is and What It Is Not	XVII	14-19	491
77	The Forgotten Note in Modern Evangelism	XVII	20-23	497
78	Sharing Christ's Glory	XVII	22-26	504
79	Satan's Hour	XVIII	1-11	510
80	A Cold Night	XVIII	12-27	516
81	The Man Who Asked the Most Questions	XVIII	28-38	523
82	Barabbas Or Jesus	XVIII / XIX	38-40 / 1-5	530
83	Pilate's Dilemma	XIX	6-11	536
84	No King But Caesar	XIX	12-15	543
85	The Crucifixion	XIX	16-22	549
86	The Seamless Robe	XIX	23-24	555
87	The Mother of Jesus	XIX	25-27	563
88	The Knowledge of Jesus Our Lord	XIX	28	571
89	The Man Who Died with a Psalm on His Lips	XIX	29-30	577
90	The Blood and the Water	XIX	31-37	584
91	The Funeral Service of Jesus	XIX	38-42	591
92	Why the Cross	XIX		597
93	What the First Visitors Saw the First Easter Sunday	XX	1-10	604
94	The First to See the Risen Christ	XX	11-18	610
95	"The Charter of the Christian Church"	XX	19-23	614
96	The Answer to a Doubting Thomas	XX	24-29	621
97	The Divine Proof Book	XX	30-31	627
98	The God Who Waits On His People	XXI	1-14	634
99	Simon Peter	XXI	15-19	639
100	In the Care of God	XXI	18-25	645

Walk One

BEFORE GENESIS—WHAT?

IN a letter from my esteemed friend, Edwin J. Tharp, in Manchukuo, a man true to all the fine traditions of that great army of Christian missionaries beginning with the Apostle Paul, he suggested that I "take a walk with our Lord through the Gospel of John and notice how our Lord did His most effective work with individuals." That is exactly what we intend doing in this series of studies.

Most of us like crowds. Certainly a preacher likes a crowd. There is nothing quite so inspiring to him as to have the meeting place filled to the rafters. But I think every preacher will also agree that his most effective work has been done with individuals, particularly during the course of private interviews. I am not discounting mass evangelism nor great spiritual revivals where multitudes are swept into the kingdom of God. But, apart from a definite promise concerning the nation of Israel, who we are told will be born in a day, God has usually dealt with individuals, rarely with a whole race or a multitude of people. One can be in a vast audience listening to one man preach under the power of God's Spirit and he can shut out completely every other person in that audience and be face to face with his Lord. That is a miracle of the Holy Spirit's working upon an individual soul.

So, as we begin our series of "walks with our Lord" through this magnificent Gospel of John, I trust that each of us may come to experience a personal walk with our Lord.

We shall consider a Man Who was a Jew, depicted in a book written by a Jew. The book is a miracle of literature—written by one who at no prior time gave any evidence of the possession of literary skill, indeed he did not even take a course in short story writing. He was a stout-hearted man, a son of thunder. His hands were brawny. He was a fisherman associated with his father in the fishery business. Yet he produced what no literary genius has ever been able to create. He magnificently obscures himself, not even so much as once mentioning his own name. He has superbly presented the only perfect character even portrayed within the pages of a book. No wonder someone has suggested, that if no such Person as Jesus ever existed, then we must fall down before four men, Matthew, Mark, Luke and John, and worship them for presenting and depicting such a character. Incidentally these men, while presenting a faultless character, have not been silent about their own sins and frailties.

The Person of Christ

There is something about the matchless Person of Jesus of Nazareth that knows no clime nor race. He meets the need of every man! In the turmoil of the hour in which we live, it is a blessing to note that an increasing number of voices are being heard drawing men back to the Person of Jesus Christ. After nineteen hundred years this Man, Christ Jesus, a Jew according to the flesh, still lives in the pages of human history as *the* outstanding character, towering above all others who ever walked this earth.

This fact is all the more remarkable when we consider that He was born in an obscure town, of peasant parentage, and for the major part of His earthly life lived in Nazareth, a city of no reputation. During those years He was practically unheard of, except for a brief period of three days when He was in Jerusalem in the Temple, entering into the privileges that become a Jewish lad's upon reaching the age of twelve. Then suddenly, when He was about thirty years of age, His personality and ministry electrified the coasts of Judæa. Everyone was excited. They all began chatting with each other. They asked, "Do the rulers know indeed that this is the very Christ?"

He became a problem. The common people heard Him gladly: the religious leaders were unable to comprehend Him. And then, about three years later, although all agreed that "never man spake like this man," He was taken and led as a criminal outside the walls of the city and there crucified by a band of Roman soldiers amid a howling mob. Two wealthy members of the Sanhedrin buried Him. One of them had spent an evening with this Man, introducing his conversation by saying, "Rabbi, *we* know (I do not think Nicodemus used the editorial *"we"* when he said *"we know."* I believe he meant the Sanhedrin) that thou art a teacher come from God . . . " How did they know? He added, "for no man can do these miracles that thou doest, except God be with him." That statement therefore from a contemporary of Christ Jesus ought to carry weight with every one.

This Man, was buried in a rich man's tomb, in the garden part of his estate. And, it is the testimony of more than five hundred witnesses that He broke the jaws of death and arose from the dead on the third day, as He promised He would. Forty days later He led a small band of His followers to the Mount of Olives and while conversing with them there, like Elijah of old He was taken up into the heavens.

That briefly comprises the life on this earth of the Man we are about to consider and with Whom we shall walk through the familiar scenes of His ministry in the land of Palestine. He is the most unique character this world has ever considered. No man compares with Him. Man can only be contrasted to Him.

It is the testimony of the New Testament that this Man is God manifest in flesh. It is important that we examine His claims and the claims that are advanced for Him in the Scriptures. If He be God manifest in flesh, then it is incumbent upon every one to acknowledge His Lordship. If He be not God manifest in flesh, we who have placed our faith in Him are guilty of idolatry, and unless we repent we are doomed for time and eternity; and Jesus of Nazareth becomes the world's greatest imposter. There can be no middle ground. He is either one or the other. It makes no difference therefore what we are, whether "Barbarian, Scythian, bond nor free," whether wise or unwise, whether heathen or churchman; we must face the question that Pilate raised "What shall I do then with Jesus which is called Christ?" There is no such thing as brushing aside Jesus Christ or refusing to consider Him or excusing one's self on the ground of one's "bringing up." There never was a day in the history of the world when the choice has so narrowed as it has in this day. For this civilization it is either Christ—or ruin! We have gone too far—we cannot turn back—we are at the brink of the precipice. I repeat, for this civilization it is either Christ—or ruin, while for the individual it is salvation or damnation.

The Book Itself and Its Purpose

It is a trite thing to say, but it needs to be said just here: there are four Gospels, two of which were written by Apostles, while the other two were written by men who were not members of "the twelve." Many believe that Mark collaborated with Peter in the preparation of his Gospel. Luke, in the opening verses of his Gospel, tells us he received his material "from above." Each is equally inspired by the

Spirit of God, and any critical examination will reveal perfect harmony between all four, although each presents a specific viewpoint of the Man Whom we shall consider. Until recently, it has been thought that John's Gospel was the last of the four to be written and that it was penned by John when he was an aged man. A very short time ago one scholar suggested that we might have to change our view as to the time the book was written. In fact this authority believes it was written shortly after the crucifixion of Christ. But as a matter of fact, it does not make any difference *when* it was written, though I think there is much to support the traditional view that it was penned by the Apostle when he was an old man.

The Gospel of John has probably been more used by the Holy Spirit in bringing men and women to a knowledge of the Lord than any other New Testament book. Every Christian loves John's Gospel. I do not know how many Bibles I have used in the course of the years. Invariably I discard a Bible every few years and begin afresh with a new one, for with myriads of others, I have made extensive notes in the margins of my Bibles. It is both a good and a bad practice. It is good for it familiarizes one with the Bible. It is bad when it prevents one from enjoying a fresh viewpoint of a specific portion. The Bible I am now using gives evidence that John's Gospel has been referred to and read more diligently and more frequently than any other part of the Bible. It is always the most soiled part of my Bibles, and if you do not misunderstand me, the *dirtiest* page in my Bible is the page on which the 3rd chapter of John is printed—I mean dirty from use!

We learn from the 20th chapter of this Gospel that John wrote with two purposes in mind. This is what he said:

> "And many other signs truly did Jesus in the presence of his disciples, which are not written in this book:
> "But these are written, that ye might believe that Jesus is the Christ, the Son of God; and that believing ye might have life through his name."

Therefore, the Holy Spirit guided the mind and the pen of the Apostle so that he culled out of the ministry of our Lord those sayings and acts which particularly manifested His deity. With the evidence, he has skillfully interwoven the gospel message which declares that by simply believing, men have life through His name.

There is only one other book which begins like this book. Every Jew, every Christian, and every Gentile who is acquainted with the

Bible immediately recognizes the similarity between the opening statement of this Gospel with the opening verse of the first book of the Bible. In Genesis we read the most matchless scientific statement that ever has been put into language. In Hebrew it contains only seven words, in English it has ten words: "In the beginning God created the heaven and the earth." There is more in these few words than in all the volumes that have been written on geology, cosmogony, evolution, and all allied subjects.

The Gospel of John opens:

> "In the beginning was the Word, and the Word was with God, and the Word was God.
> "The same was in the beginning with God.
> "All things were made by him; and without him was not any thing made that was made.
> "In him was life; and the life was the light of men.
> "And the light shineth in darkness; and the darkness comprehended it not."

Moses, when he took up his pen to write the book of Genesis, was carried away by the Spirit of God to an indeterminate hour in the history of the world, to the beginning, when God created the heaven and the earth. John was carried away by the same Spirit to an era, earlier far, than that which introduces the book of Genesis, even before God created the heaven and the earth, to the very beginning, an age no mind can comprehend or understand. "In the beginning was the Word, and the Word was with God, and the Word was God." Since it is true that Genesis 1:1 is the most matchless scientific expression that has ever been put in print concerning the beginning of this universe, so the first verse of John's Gospel is the most magnificent declaration in human language describing the infinite God.

The Prologue of the Book

The very first phrase of the first verse of this Gospel stamps it as having been written by the same Spirit Who guided the pen of Moses when he wrote the first statement in the Bible. Men who have been critical students of literature know that it is possible to determine the authorship of a book even when the author's name is not given. Each man has a style of his own. Again and again it crops out like the watermark in a sheet of paper. An author cannot hide his own personality. So in Holy Writ the pen was John's and the pen was Moses', but the Author was the Holy Spirit—that is the way He writes. No man could write an introduction to a book like the first verse of this

Gospel. The most spiritual minds of the ages have examined it microscopically and yet its depths cannot be fathomed.

"In the beginning!" When? "In the beginning." When was that? "In the beginning." What was in the beginning? "The Word." What is the Word? The Greek word in the text is *logos*. It means: thought, concept, idea, expression, word. Our spoken or written word is the expression of our thoughts. We could not know what is in each other's heart and mind if we did not use words to clothe our thoughts. If you please, our word is the visibility of our thoughts and inmost being. So *is* the *Word* in relation to the infinite, invisible God.

But note the following statement "and the Word was with God." Here we have a clear distinction between the Word and God. If the first verse of John's Gospel read—In the beginning was the Word and the Word was God—it would be like two legs of a tripod—it could not stand. It required a trinity of phrases to reveal the perfection of deity. So we read, "In the beginning was the Word, and the Word was with God, and the Word was God." We will later observe that John declared that the Word was none other than Jesus Christ. So, in the beginning, our Lord was the expression of the mind and the heart of God. And He was *with* God always from the beginning. He was not inferior to God, for He *was* God. And He was in the beginning—*with* God. What a matchless statement concerning this magnificent Person, the Jew, Jesus of Nazareth. Since He is risen and ascended on high, we children of the dust may walk with Him and talk with Him along life's way!

Walk Two

THE PREINCARNATION GLORY OF CHRIST

SINCE we are to walk with our Lord through this Gospel, it is imperative that we know something about His "antecedents." When one undertakes to write a biography of another, he not only examines the man's life from all available sources, but he looks into the antecedents of the man—perchance there is something in his background that will account for his life and work. That is exactly what the Holy Spirit has superbly done in the prologue of this Gospel. With the fewest of words, yet every one a gem, we learn everything we need to know of the background of Jesus of Nazareth, thus enabling us to more fully understand His ministry on earth.

We have already observed one of the watermarks of the Holy Spirit by which we determined that it was the same Spirit Who guided the pen of Moses and that of John. Here is another of the watermarks of the Holy Spirit. I have already used four times as many words in introducing this study as the Holy Spirit used in John's Gospel to introduce our Lord. The Holy Spirit never seeks to be heard for His much speaking. He never wastes words. A Master wrote the opening verses of John's Gospel.

The other evening in our home we had a visit from a gentleman who is Chinese by birth, but a Christian by new birth. He amused our little girl by drawing a fish. With just eight strokes of the pencil he perfectly pictured a fish and fascinated the mind of that little youngster. With a few strokes of the pen, the Holy Spirit has magnificently presented the matchless Person of Jesus Christ in His pre-incarnation glory. We stand in awe before such a portrait.

The opening two verses reveal three things to us concerning Christ. First, that He *as* "the Word" was the very expression of God, and as such, was in the beginning; second, that He *was with* God, a separate and distinct personality; and third, that He was God; and all this was in the beginning with God.

In the next three verses is summarized the work and ministry of our Lord prior to His coming as a babe to Bethlehem's manger. First, we are told that all things were made by Him; second, that without Him was not anything made that was made. Greek scholars tell us that the words used by John are emphatic. Translated literally, John wrote "Without Him was not *one single thing* made that was made." Third, we read that in Him was life, and what is more, His life was the light of men; then, the light shineth in darkness; and finally, a miracle—the darkness was impotent to comprehend the light.

Has God a Son?

Let me now come to the heart of our subject for this study. Has God a Son? How could God have a Son? Is Jesus Christ His Son? No questions of greater importance could be asked about Jesus of Nazareth. All three were raised in a single question by a group of

Pharisees who asked our Lord "Who art thou?" His answer was "Even the same that I said unto you from the beginning."

It is generally conceded that the oldest book of the Bible is Job. In it we have a revelation of the earliest philosophies of men, the purest wisdom, and the most profound questions. That sorely perplexed man in the land of Uz who feared God and eschewed evil and who was perfect and upright, lost everything in a day. As his perplexities increased, a few friends gathered to "comfort" him. So great was Job's grief that his friends sat on the ground speechless for seven days and seven nights. Job finally encouraged them to speak, but again and again he broke in to answer their questions, to justify himself, and to give expression to the deepest anguish of the human soul. Said Job of God, "Oh that I knew where I might find him! that I might come even to his seat! I would order my cause before him, and fill my mouth with arguments." For, said Job, ". . . he (God) is not a man, as I am, that I should answer him, and we should come together in judgment. Neither is there any daysman (redeemer) betwixt us, that might lay his hand upon us both." Thus at the very cradle of human civilization, there existed in the breast of man the desire to know God, Who only could be known through One, equal with God, Who could lay His one hand upon God and His other upon man.

Again in the 30th chapter of the book of Proverbs we have the words of a prophet, one Agur, the son of Jakeh. In the 4th verse of that chapter we read these words: "Who hath ascended up into heaven, or descended? who hath gathered the wind in his fists? who hath bound the waters in a garment? who hath established all the ends of the earth? what is his name, and what is his son's name, if thou canst tell?" Undoubtedly Agur understood that God had a son.

Now let us go back to the first words that appear in the Bible. "In the beginning *God* created the heaven and the earth." The name for God in that verse, as every scholar knows, is the Hebrew word *Elohim*. *Elohim* is a uni-plural noun. Thus without an injustice to the text, the first verse of Genesis could be translated "In the beginning *Gods* created the heaven and the earth." Later in the same chapter of Genesis we observe the record of a conversation between the members of the Godhead. Genesis 1:26: "And God said, Let *us* make man in *our* image, after *our* likeness . . ." With whom could that conversation have been held? Certainly it necessitated an equal Who possessed the image and likeness of God. Who could it be but His Son? Here we have a plural pronoun used three times by God in a single verse. Whom did God address when He said, "Let *us* make man in *our* image, after *our* likeness"? In whose image was man to be made? Whose likeness should man manifest? Certainly God talked to someone. John 1:3 tells us that One was the Lord Jesus, for we learn there that all things were made by Him and without Him was not a single thing made that was made.

Thus our questions have been answered. Has God a Son? Could God have a Son? Is Jesus Christ His Son? For fear some may feel that insufficient testimony has been exhibited to sustain the point made, we shall examine another passage.

It is axiomatic that in the eyes of two or three witnesses, a matter is established. We have already called three witnesses, Job, Moses, and Agur. Now we shall call Isaiah, the chief of the major prophets. In the 9th chapter of his prophecy, verses 6 and 7 we read, "For unto us a child is born, unto us a son is given: and the government shall be upon his shoulder: and his name shall be called Wonderful, Counsellor, The mighty God, The everlasting Father, The Prince of Peace." Now notice what else he had to say about Him: "Of the increase of his government and peace there shall be no end, upon the throne of David, and upon his kingdom, to order it, and to establish it with judgment and with justice from henceforth even for ever." Knowing full well that the prophecy seemed utterly impossible of fulfillment, Isaiah added these words: "The zeal (or the zealousness) of the LORD of hosts will perform this."

There have been scholars who have suggested that the verb in verse 6 of this prophecy is in the past tense; that it should be translated, "For unto us a child *was* born, unto us a son *was* given." They have therefore concluded that the prophecy cannot possibly refer to Jesus of Nazareth because He was not born until seven hundred years later. We ask: Of whom then was the prophet speaking? Of himself? Of course the answer is No. Who is it then? The suggestion has been made that it was Hezekiah, the great reformer. Let us look at Hezekiah. Did anyone ever call him by such names as these "Wonderful, Counsellor, The mighty God, The everlasting Father, The Prince of Peace"? If Hezekiah had taken these titles unto himself, or if any had ascribed these titles to him, they would have been guilty of blasphemy. Nowhere in Holy Writ is a single one of these titles ascribed to Hezekiah nor can we find where any man or group of men bestowed these titles upon him, or for that matter, upon any other man.

"*His* name," Isaiah said, "shall be called Wonderful . . ." Who in the Bible is called "Wonderful"? We shall soon find out. In the 13th chapter of the book of Judges we have the record of a man of the Danites whose name was Manoah, whose wife failed to bear him a child. One day the angel of the Lord appeared unto the woman and promised that she would give birth to a son. In so doing, the angel made some remarkable statements regarding this son. The woman came and told her husband saying: "A man of God came unto me, and his countenance was like the countenance of an angel of God, very terrible: but I asked him not whence he was, neither told he me his name . . ." Then she revealed to her husband the promise of this man of God. Manoah intreated the Lord, and said, "O my Lord, let the man of God which thou didst send come again unto us, and teach us what we shall do unto the child that shall be born." And God answered his prayer.

The angel of God came again the second time, and Manoah met him and conversed with him as a man talks with a man. Manoah desired to show him hospitality, thus prayed him to stay while a kid was made ready for him. The man of God said, No, I cannot remain: if you wish to offer a burnt offering, you must offer it unto the Lord. To this Manoah answered "What is thy name, that when thy sayings come to pass we may do thee honour?" And the angel of the Lord said unto him, "Why askest thou thus after my name, seeing it is *Wonderful*[*]?" So Manoah took a kid with a meat offering and offered it upon a rock unto the Lord; and the angel, the record says, "did wonderously . . . For it came to pass when the flame went up toward heaven from off the altar, that the angel of the Lord ascended in the flame of the altar. And Manoah and his wife looked on."

What would you have done if you were that man or that woman? You would have done exactly as they did. They fell on their faces to the ground, and Manoah said unto his wife, "We shall surely die, because we have seen God." The word for God that Manoah used was *El* which is the singular form of *Elohim*. Only God is entitled to the name *Wonderful!*

---

[*] The Authorized translation is *secret*, but the original Hebrew word is *Wonderful*.

Again this child, this son, is also called in Isaiah's prophecy "The mighty God (The mighty *Elohim*), The everlasting Father, The Prince of Peace." Again, only God is entitled to these names!

The Light—Shining in Darkness

It is the testimony of the writer of this Gospel that in Christ is life and His life was the light of men.

The fact that men cannot comprehend that statement is another testimony to the truth of this book, for it immediately adds, "And the light shineth in darkness; and the darkness *comprehended* (apprehended R. V.) it not." I like S. D. Gordon's comment on this portion of Scripture. He said, "Both are rather large words, larger in English than John would use. John loved to use simple language. Yet there is help even in these English words. Comprehended is a mental word. It means to take hold of with your mind, to understand. Apprehend is a physical word. It means to take up with your hands. You cannot comprehend Jesus. That is just the simple, plain fact. You may have a fine mind. It may have been well schooled and trained. You may have dug into all the books on the subject . . . you may have spent a lifetime at it. But at the end, there is immensely more of Jesus that you don't understand than the part you do understand. You've touched the smaller part only, just the edges. You cannot take Jesus in with your mind simply. The one is too big and the other too limited for that particular process."

But I hasten to add that verses 3 and 5 of the 1st chapter of John's Gospel which we have been looking at, do not refer to the ministry of Jesus of Nazareth on earth. They refer to the ministry of the Son of God from the time of the Creation spoken of in Genesis 1:1 up to the time when the virgin gave birth to a child in Bethlehem. In other words, these statements refer to His preincarnation ministry.

In connection with the statement that Christ, as the Light, was not comprehended by the darkness, F. B. Meyer has given a soul-searching word. He said "There are two methods by which darkness is produced. One by absence of light; the other by loss of sight. It is dark when the sun sets—it is also dark when the eye is blind. And the darkness mentioned in this verse is not the first but the second." The "Son" was shining in those days though not as perfectly as now. "But the light shone amid blind and darkened hearts, which could not comprehend it. Although men knew God, 'they glorified him not as God, neither were thankful; and as a result they became vain in their reasonings and their senseless heart was darkened.' We, therefore, as well as they, are a family, born blind; a race stricken with blindness ... a vault like that in which the dead are buried, around which the sunlight plays whilst not one beam can enter. Such is the picture of our race. 'The light shineth in darkness.'"

None of the ancient prophets, sages or patriarchs ever saw as clearly the Person of Christ as did the writer of this Gospel when he wrote "... we beheld his glory, the glory as of the only begotten of the Father ..."

Moses spoke with God as a man speaks with his friend, but he yearned to see the face of God. Who would not? But it was not given to Moses to see God's face. God made provision for him in the cleft of a rock, hid him there, and allowed His glory to pass by and then, for a flash of a moment, God gave Moses to see His back parts. "But," said God, "no man shall see my face and live."

The face of God is manifested only in the incarnation of Jesus Christ. That is the testimony of the Word of God.

WALK THREE

A MAN SENT FROM GOD

FOR the third walk "with our Lord through the Gospel of John" we shall commence reading from verse 6 of the 1st chapter, to and including verse 13.

> "There was a man sent from God, whose name was John.
> "The same came for a witness, to bear witness of the Light, that all men through him might believe.
> "He was not that Light, but was sent to bear witness of that Light.
> "That was the true Light, which lighteth every man that cometh into the world.
> "He was in the world, and the world was made by him, and the world knew him not.
> "He came unto his own, and his own received him not.
> "But as many as received him, to them gave he power to become the sons of God, even to them that believe on his name:
> "Which were born, not of blood, nor of the will of the flesh, nor of the will of man, but of God."

Literature cannot boast of a more beautiful presentation of a man than that which we have in the 6th verse of this chapter: "There was a man sent from God, whose name was John." Our Lord witnessed concerning him that "Among them that are born of women there hath not risen a greater than John the Baptist..." If you do not mind, he was a minister's son who made good, for his father was a priest.

John was a plain man, his raiment was of camel's hair and he had a leathern girdle about his loins. His diet was limited to locusts and wild honey. Except for a few words concerning his conception and birth we know nothing about him until one day he entered the wilderness of Judæa with a message that electrified the whole countryside. All Jerusalem went out to hear him and all Judæa and all the regions round about Jordan. He had one message: "Repent ye: for the kingdom of heaven is at hand." This man was "sent from God." Others have been given the title, "A man of God." They were known by their character and their ministry as men of God. But John was "sent from God." He was given a specific and limited ministry. He came for a witness, to bear witness of the Light, that all through Him might believe. The Scriptures carefully guard against the exaltation of a man who may be used by God. Therefore, the Holy Spirit immediately added, "He was not that Light, but was sent to bear witness of that Light." The "Light" was our Lord Jesus Christ. "In him was life; and the life was the light of men." Since ". . . the light shineth in darkness; and the darkness comprehended it not," God sent a man to bear witness of "the Light" that all through Him might believe.

The Place of a Man of God

Now we come to a most important subject. We shall call it "The place of men in the economy of God." In the Old Testament God ordained a priesthood. Only the High Priest could enter the innermost sanctuary and commune with God as the representative of the people. We are apt to assume that the arrangement was intended to be permanent whereas in fact it ceased when Jesus Christ died on the cross. At that time, an unseen hand rent the veil of the temple from the top to the bottom thus ending the priesthood. The High Priest who ministered in the temple symbolized or typified our Lord Jesus Christ. In the New Testament there is only one mediator between God and man, "the man Christ Jesus. . . ."

There are "men of God" in this world at the present time. They are men who by virtue of their ministry and the character of their lives have indelibly stamped upon them the title, "A man of God." What is the God-ordained place of such a man in the economy of God at this time? Well, let's look at John! "There was a man sent from God, whose name was John. The same came for a witness. . . ." That is all John came for and that is all any man of God is ordained to do in this day. He is only a witness. He is not the Light, He is come to bear witness of the Light. John came to herald our Lord's coming and to bear witness to Him as the Light of the world, that all through Him might believe. John was not that Light, the Scripture is careful to say. Later our Lord called John a shining light but the word which He used means *a little candle*. We are only candles. We are here to bear witness in the night to the Light of this world Who is none other than Jesus Christ.

Neither is the church "the light of this world." What crimes have been committed by the church in the name of Jesus Christ! As the individual believer is "a candle light in this world" so the church can be likened to the moon, which does not possess light of itself but reflects the light of the sun. Jesus Christ is the "true Light, which lighteth every man that cometh into the world."

"... The Light of the World ..."

Our Lord was the Light of the world even before He came as a babe in Bethlehem's manger, for the Scriptures read: "He *was* in the world, and the world *was* made by him, and the world knew him not." He was always in the world. Every man who has ever been born into this world received light from the only One Who is the Light of this world, Jesus Christ the Son of God. Not a single man on this earth, be he ever so steeped in heathenism, is without light. In the breast of every man there has been placed a God-consciousness so that every man is absolutely without excuse. Something inbred and inborn in man tells him there is a God. No man was ever born an atheist. Atheists are not born—they are "self-made" men. The Bible declares "the fool hath said in his heart, there is no God." If there had never been a Bible there still would be no excuse for a man to be an atheist, for every atheist was born with the same light with which any other man was born. There is nothing wrong with the revelation of God but there is something radically wrong with men. It is not a question of the absence of light: there is plenty of light but men have refused it.

What a testimony it is to the blackness of the human heart, the human conscience, and the human mind that it was necessary for God to send a man, born of the dust of the earth, to go before His Son to direct other men's attention to the fact that this Son of God is the Light of the world. We know nothing comparable to it. If we turn on the light in a room the darkness disappears: but not so when Jesus Christ came into this world. Think of it—He, the Light of the world, He Who made the sun and the astronomical system that illuminates this earth, heats it and warms it, though it be one of the smaller suns that were made by Him—when He came required a man to tell the rest of us that He is the Light of the world!!

Note, will you, the world-wide extent of the ministry of Christ. "He was in the *world,* and the *world* was made by him, and the *world* knew him not." Thus our Lord's ministry and influence prior to His coming was world-wide. It still is, though He no longer prays for the world as we learn from the 17th chapter of this Gospel.

Some men have used the phrase "limited atonement" in speaking about the death of Christ. They suggest that it is quite true to say that Jesus Christ died for the world, but that more specifically Jesus Christ died for the church, for those who are His own in this world. No, my friend, the extreme opposite is the case. There is no such thing in the Bible as a "limited atonement." The Apostle John was used by the Lord to refute the suggestion. In the 2nd verse of the 2nd chapter of his First Epistle, John contradicts such an idea. There we learn that our Lord Jesus Christ is "the propitiation for *our* sins . . ." That of course refers to a limited group of people, those who have received the Lord Jesus Christ as Savior. But lest we become exalted in our own mind, the Holy Spirit immediately added "and not for our's only, but also for the sins of the whole world."

To Bethlehem

Now let us walk with our Lord to Bethlehem. "He came unto his own . . ." Oh yes, Israel occupied and still occupies a unique place before God in this world. Our Lord was not a Gentile, He was not an Aryan, He was a minister of the circumcision, as the Scripture puts it. He was a Jew, He was an Israelite, and "He came unto his own." Just as the world did not know our Lord prior to His incarnation, even so Israel failed to recognize Him at His coming, for ". . . his own received him not." And now notice —we read in verse 12, "But as many as received him . . ." How thankful we should be for the *buts* that are in Scripture. God is never defeated. It undoubtedly was a disappointment that our Lord was not received by His own, "*But* as many as received him, to them gave he power (or right) to become the children of God, even to them that believe on his name: Which were born, not of blood, nor of the will of the flesh, nor of the will of man, but of God."

Recently, I heard the familiar voice of a man who is an outstanding leader in modern Christendom. He was talking of the value of a "good heritage." That is something worthwhile—to be born well, to be born into a good family! This man went on to say that a good heritage requires a good environment. Yes, that too is nice! It is great to be born with a silver spoon in your mouth. It is wonderful to have a splendid ancestry, one that you can trace back to the Mayflower. But don't go too far back for you will find a common origin. Yes, it is nice to be well born and well bred! I do not deprecate it. Human culture is a fine thing. A good environment is more to be desired than an unhealthy one. But this leader of "ancient modernism" in Christendom went on to say that even with both a good environment and a good heritage, we come sometimes to the place where we are almost overwhelmed by temptation. What then? His suggestion was to "accept responsibility!"

Now let us look at what the Word of God suggests. "He came unto his own . . ." We learned a moment ago who His own were. "But as many as accepted responsibility, to them gave He the right to become the children of God?" Oh no! "But as many as *received him* (Jesus Christ, the Light of the world) to them gave he the right to become the children of God, even to them that believe on his name." That's it. To assure us that this has nothing to do with environment or heritage, we read "Which were born, not of blood, nor of the will of the flesh, nor of the will of man, but of God." We were born the first time of flesh and of blood and of the will of man. We must be born the second time by the will of God. The Bible says that men are born again by believing the record that God has given concerning His Son. What a Gospel, what a message for a world in darkness!

A short time ago the world was lulled to sleep by a false philosophy which found a ready echo in many pulpits. We were told that the world was getting better, and every day in every way, man was becoming better and better. But alas! The world has suddenly become conscious of the fact that we have been living in a fool's paradise. No informed man believes that philosophy now.

What's Wrong with the Church?

Recently a full page advertisement, paid by the United States News, appeared in a number of the country's newspapers. The article was entitled "The New Idolatry" taken from the recent speech by Anthony Eden. It was written by David Lawrence, the well known newspaper columnist. It was a call to the people to go back to prayer and to God. Imagine the impotency of the church in this country when a newspaper columnist must call the nation back to God and to prayer. Let me quote a sentence or two of what Mr. Lawrence has to say about the church. "The Church has for two decades wondered why it had so often been subordinated, why its usefulness has seemed at times to be questioned if not nullified in a world of sin. The Church has been groping, too, even as you and I." But we ask—Why has the church lost its power? I think I know the answer.

For the past two or three decades there has been an insistent boring at the foundations of Christianity by those who professed to be its friends. Men in pulpits, men in theological seminaries, men in high places in religious circles, wolves in sheep's clothing, who after boring at the foundations, finally became bold and openly denied the virgin birth of Christ, the deity of our Lord Jesus Christ, the inspiration of the Scriptures, the sacrificial death of Christ, the atoning work of our Lord, the bodily resurrection of

Christ: indeed they shook the very foundations from under some men. They exalted man and pulled Christ down to the level of a mere man. Now these same men stand aghast as they observe the superstructure of this civilization reeling like a drunken sailor. Now they are alarmed. They are even telling us what America's greatest need is! They are putting their shoulders together in an attempt to hold up the superstructure, when the need is to repair the foundations. When faith in the Bible is destroyed, the wild passions of men are fanned into a flame. The Scriptures go so far as to say, "If the foundations be destroyed, what can the righteous do?"

Possibly what this world needs is a new voice, the voice of a John the Baptist, the voice of a John Wesley, or the voice of a D. L. Moody. Let him be a young man like John if need be, who was in his early thirties, only let him be "a man sent from God." May God send the man! When he comes he will come with a message about which there will be no uncertain sound. He will not tickle men's ears, he will preach to their hearts. He will come with the same message which the 1st chapter of John's Gospel brings to us. "But as many as received him (Christ), to them gave he (God) power (or the right) to become the sons (or children) of God, even to them that believe on his name: Which were born, not of blood, nor of the will of the flesh, nor of the will of man, but of God." True, there are many voices being heard throughout the land today, faithfully proclaiming Christ and Him crucified—but alas, how few hear the Word.

We in this generation need a Holy Spirit revival. Better still, we need the coming of our Lord Jesus Christ to right the wrongs of this world and to set up His universal kingdom of peace and of righteousness! God speed the day!

Walk Four

THE INCARNATION

THERE are no accidents with God. With Him, everything is planned to the minutest detail—He is never ahead of time—He is never late—He is always on time. Thus it is written in Galatians

4:4, "But when the *fulness* of the time was come, God sent forth his Son, made of a woman, made under the law . . ." Our Lord was not late. He came in the fulness of the time. When He comes the second time He will not be late either. He will come on time.

It is striking how expressions develop that really have no basis in Scripture. For example, many Christians use the phrase "if He tarry," in referring to our Lord. There is nothing in the Word of God to justify such a statement. The Bible tells us the opposite in Hebrews 10:37, where we read: "For yet a little while, and he that shall come will come, and will not tarry." It may be given to us to *tarry until He comes;* in fact, in the closing chapter of this Gospel, after our Lord had announced by what death Peter "should glorify God," Peter pointing to John asked, "Lord, and what shall this man do?" Our Lord answered, "If I will that he tarry till I come, what is that to thee? follow thou me." No, God is always on time, though we may tarry.

For our present study we shall consider verses 14 to 18.

> "And the Word was made flesh, and dwelt among us, (and we beheld his glory, the glory as of the only begotten of the Father,) full of grace and truth.
> "John bare witness of him, and cried, saying, This was he of whom I spake, He that cometh after me is preferred before me: for he was before me.
> "And of his fulness have all we received, and grace for grace.
> "For the law was given by Moses, but grace and truth came by Jesus Christ.
> "No man hath seen God at any time; the only begotten Son, which is in the bosom of the Father, he hath declared him."

When we considered the opening verse of this Gospel, "In the beginning was the Word, and the Word was with God, and the Word was God," I suggested that it was the most matchless expression in human language as to "the Person of God." We also learned that the Greek word *logos* means thought, idea, concept, the very expression of one's being. That is what the Word was. In verse 14 we read: "And the Word was made flesh, and dwelt among us. . ." At least that is the way it appears in our Authorized Version; but in the Greek there are not two words, *was made,* there is only one word which means *became,* so what John actually wrote was this: "And the Word *became* flesh."

The Word was in the beginning and was with God and was God; that Word, the visibility of God, the very expression of God, *became* flesh. A mystery you say! Yes, but why not marvel rather at its majestic simplicity—for do we know anything about God that is not a mystery?

"The Word Became Flesh . . ."

The whole of God's revelation to man is embodied in these four words "the Word became flesh." That statement takes us to a manger connected with an inn in the city of Bethlehem, the least of the provinces of Judæa. As we in our minds bend over the manger together with the shepherds, to look into the face of a little babe, we stand in awe and worship, remembering that it is written "the Word became flesh." We handle the child, touch his hands and his feet. We touch something tangible: Flesh! We feel the warmth of the blood flowing through the veins of that little body. And then, as we peer into his eyes, we remember certain things that were revealed to the mother of that child, who is by our side as we linger at the manger, as for example, this word, "The Holy Ghost shall come upon thee, and the power of the Highest shall overshadow thee: therefore. . ." I repeat—"therefore," because the Holy Spirit shall come upon thee, and the power of the Almighty God shall overshadow thee: *"therefore also that holy thing which shall be born of thee shall be called the Son of God."* That is exactly what the angel said about the body which we by faith are touching and feeling ". . . *that holy thing* which shall be born of thee shall be called the Son of God."

We are on holy ground, therefore one must take his shoes from off his feet; but in that remarkable statement of the angel we are privileged to look into a mystery—to understand that the power of the Almighty God was present in the womb of a virgin to protect a child about to be born, so that under no circumstances could the body become contaminated in the slightest degree with anything remotely touching human frailty and human sin. That which was to be born was called by the angel "that holy thing," because the Word which was with God and was God and is God, became flesh. Mystery! Yes indeed, but not so much of a mystery as it is "just like God," or God-like—in fact the Bible uses that very term in speaking of this event. It calls it "the mystery (or the unfolding) of *godliness.*"

It is simply wonderful how the Holy Spirit in four words not only declared a positive truth, but also refuted every false notion held by every conceivable "ism" regarding the Person and work of Jesus Christ. There is not an unscriptural view held by any concerning the Person of Christ but which is fully answered in these four words.

Let me give a few examples. There are those who say that Jesus Christ was only a man. This passage refutes them—"the *Word* became flesh. . ." There are those who insist that our Lord laid aside His deity during His earthly ministry and thus was only a man. This passage refutes them—"the *Word became* flesh," He is still the Word, He is still God. Again, there are those who insist that He did not become the Son of God until He was anointed and baptized by John the Baptist. This passage, only four words, refutes them too, for as we look at the child in the manger, we remember that it is written, "the Word (the personality of God, the One Who was always in the beginning, the Word Who was with God and Who was God) the Word *became flesh*." When? At the manger. I repeat, there is not a false "ism" nor a strange theory concerning the Person of Jesus Christ which is not refuted in these four words by the Spirit of God. No one but the Holy Spirit could write four such words. John could not, but the Holy Spirit did. We stand in awe not only before the Person of Christ, but before the Holy Spirit Who wrote these words.

God—Man

Dr. F. B. Meyer whom we have already referred to in one of our previous messages, carries a comment worth quoting. "Open the golden compasses of thought to measure, if it be possible, the distance between these two extremes, *the Word* and *flesh*. The Word, the eternal and ever-blessed Son of God; the fellow of Jehovah; able to utter God because Himself God; through whom all things were made. Flesh, a frail and transitory fabric woven from dust, and designed to return to dust; limited to time and space; comprehending, as it does so evidently, not only the human body, but the entire human nature of which the flesh is the outward and visible embodiment. What verb shall unite extremes so infinitely removed? What link is there for these two?"

How I wish I could express the thoughts that travel through my mind as I think on these two extremes: God—expressed by "the

Word," in all His matchless deity and glory; His omnipotence; His omnipresence; all the qualities that God possesses, the Word possesses. Flesh—look at this little "thing" we call flesh. Transport yourselves to the top of the Empire State Building. Look at the size of a man as he walks the streets. "Flesh" describes that man. What extremes! God—flesh. How will the two be united? I think of good Bishop J. Taylor Smith whose memory is a benediction to my heart and mind. I once heard him tell how one day, standing in an open field with a cane in his hand, he moved a stone. As he did so, a number of ants crawled from under the stone. Then he looked down and gazed at the ants. They began to run hither and yon, seeking a place of safety. He asked himself, How could I convey to these ants that I do not mean to harm them, that I wish to do them good? How could I convey my love and affection for them? As he looked upon those ants he concluded that there was but one way for him to speak to ants in a language they could understand. It would be necessary for him, while retaining all of his human faculties, to become an ant, to become like them, and then to express in their own language his affection and love for them.

That is exactly what God has done in Christ. That *is* the Gospel. The Word, the visibility of God, the very expression of God, all that we will ever get to know about God, our Lord Jesus was, throughout all the ages of eternity. He became flesh, and by that little word *became* He united God with man. Do not misunderstand; there is more in that word *became* than the incarnation. All of the ministry of Christ, His death, His resurrection, His present exaltation at the right hand of God the Father, all is embodied in that word *became*. What condescension! It is impossible for us to fathom it. God became flesh. Why did "the Word" become "flesh"? I answer, In order that "flesh" might become like "the Word."

God's Word vs. Satan's Word

Satan was a creature of a very high order. He brought the worship of all creation to God. It appears from Satan's statement to Eve that he probably knew that God had a prepared plan long before this earth was re-created that Jesus Christ was to become man, in order that man might be raised in Him to be Godlike. The cross was not an accident with God, it was in His plan. Satan came to the woman in the Garden of Eden, and after having placed a doubt in her mind concerning the word of God, he put forth his lie, which was half truth and half lie, the most dangerous and subtle thing in the world. He said "Ye shall not surely die: For God doth know that in the day ye eat thereof, then your eyes shall be opened, and ye shall *be as gods,* knowing good and evil." Do you observe the contrary philosophy of Satan? He suggested—Violate God's word and you will become like God; whereas the Gospel message is—Believe God's word and you will become like Christ.

Therefore, the Word became flesh that we sinners, creatures of the dust, limited by flesh, may some day be transformed into the glorious image of His Son, to be like Him, to manifest His glory throughout all the ages of eternity. All this is ours because God, in the Person of Jesus Christ, *became* flesh.

Now notice what more is written concerning the incarnation: "... the Word became flesh, and dwelt (or tabernacled) among us..." It would have been wonderful for God to become man so that in one body could reside the God-man, the man Christ Jesus, and yet the Son of God. That would have been a wonderful thing in itself. But that is only the beginning of the Gospel. The Bible goes on to tell us that this One, the Word Who became man, *"dwelt* among us." In the Old Testament, one of His names is Immanuel, meaning "God with us" so that it is not only the Lord *becoming* flesh, but *tabernacling* with us. And now notice what John wrote in a parenthesis—but what a parenthesis, "(and we beheld his glory, the glory as of the only begotten of the Father)." If you cannot see that glory, it is because you are blinded. If men can look up into the face of Jesus Christ and not see the glory of God abiding upon His face, it is because the god of this age (Satan) has "blinded the minds of them which believe not, lest the light of the glorious gospel of Christ, who is the image of God, should shine unto them."

"His Fulness"

But let us continue to walk with our Lord in this Gospel. "John bare witness of him, and cried, saying, This was he of whom I spake, He that cometh after me is preferred before me: for he was before me." John the Baptist came first—our Lord followed; but in a more real sense, our Lord was first. He was "preferred before me:" said John, "for he was before me." John added, "... of his fulness have all we received, and grace for grace. For the law was given by Moses, but grace and truth came by Jesus Christ." I have never heard a man expound this portion of Scripture in a way to satisfy my heart. I certainly cannot do it. They are human words to be sure, but they convey God's thoughts. "His fulness." What an expression! Shall we say that it is the fulness of His grace and character? Yes, it is all of that, but it is more than that. ". . . of his fulness have all we received, and grace for grace." A better translation would be "grace upon grace." There is no limit to grace; it is grace upon grace. We cannot measure the grace of God, it is too boundless to be measured. We shall have to wait until we get to glory before we find out what grace means; and, when we get there, we will discover it is just one continuous outpouring of His grace—grace upon grace.

Let us continue in this Word. ". . . the law was given by Moses, but grace and truth came by Jesus Christ." Moses was a great man of God, one of the greatest that ever lived. He symbolizes everything that the Old Testament contains. John wrote ". . . the law was given by Moses. . ." Yes, that is correct. Moses received the law of the Ten Commandments, likewise the law of the sacrifices. But contrast the law with grace and truth. Grace and truth are like Siamese twins, they cannot be separated. God's grace always operates through truth and righteousness, ". . . grace and truth came by Jesus Christ." By the way, this is the first time in this Gospel that John mentions Christ's name. Previously he spoke of Him under the title "the Word," but here he reveals Him as Jesus Christ. Just as it is impossible to separate grace and truth, so the Son of God and the Son of Man are indivisible, they are one. He did not cease to be the Son of God when He became the Son of Man. When that fact is borne in mind the vapors of contradiction with which men have shrouded the 18th verse of this 1st chapter disappear and it emerges as a great truth that becomes clearer than a sea of crystal. He, the Son of God and God the Son, was, is and always will be in the bosom of the Father. He has manifested the heart of God, indeed, He is the bosom of God. He is still in the bosom of the Father, though He also is the Son of Man, Whom we can see and touch and through Whom the Father is revealed to us. He is God's gift to the world.

WALK FIVE

THE GREATEST MAN BORN OF WOMAN

FOR a long time I was unable to appreciate why our Lord said, "Among them that are born of women there hath not risen a greater than John the Baptist. . ." But if our "Walks with our Lord through the Gospel of John" have accomplished nothing else so far, they have at least made me appreciate the person and the ministry of this remarkable young man. I think I now understand why our Lord said he was so great, though He immediately added for our encouragement, "notwithstanding he that is least in the kingdom of heaven is greater than he."

We will consider the ministry of John the Baptist, particularly as it is related for us in the 1st chapter of this Gospel. We shall examine a few verses describing an interview which took place on the day preceding our Lord's introduction into His public ministry. Commencing with verse 19 we read:

> "And this is the record of John, when the Jews sent priests and Levites from Jerusalem to ask him, Who art thou?
> "And he confessed, and denied not; but confessed, I am not the Christ.
> "And they asked him, What then? Art thou Elias? And he saith, I am not. Art thou that prophet? And he answered, No.
> "Then said they unto him, Who art thou? that we may give an answer to them that sent us. What sayest thou of thyself?
> "He said, I am the voice of one crying in the wilderness, Make straight the way of the Lord, as said the prophet Esaias.
> "And they which were sent were of the Pharisees.
> "And they asked him, and said unto him, Why baptizest thou then, if thou be not that Christ, nor Elias, neither that prophet?
> "John answered them, saying, I baptize with water: but there standeth one among you, whom ye know not;
> "He it is, who coming after me is preferred before me, whose shoe's latchet I am not worthy to unloose.
> "These things were done in Bethabara beyond Jordan, where John was baptizing."

A period of six weeks had elapsed since John baptized Jesus. Prior to this baptism John had appeared in the wilderness of Judæa preaching, "Repent ye: for the kingdom of heaven is at hand." How long he preached we do not know, probably not more than a year or two years at the most. But how that man could preach! When he saw the best people coming, the Pharisees, the Sadducees, and the leaders of the people, he said, "O generation of vipers, who hath warned you to flee from the wrath to come?" Imagine a preacher doing that today in any of our fashionable churches!

John the Baptist preached a message of judgment. Here are some of the things he said,

> "And now also the axe is laid unto the root of the trees: therefore every tree which bringeth not forth good fruit is hewn down, and cast into the fire.
> "I indeed baptize you with water unto repentance: but he that cometh after me is mightier than I, whose shoes I am not worthy to bear: he shall baptize you with the Holy Ghost, and with fire:
> "Whose fan is in his hand, and he will throughly purge his floor, and gather his wheat into the garner; but he will burn up the chaff with unquenchable fire."

There is no doubt that the Baptist was a "hell fire" preacher. He was a young man. When he began to preach he was not thirty years of age. He was six months older than our Lord, and, he was a cousin of the Christ. Except for the recognition given to the Lord by John when both were yet in the wombs of their mothers, there is no *record* that either saw the other until the day Jesus of Nazareth, going from Galilee to Jordan, suffered John to baptize him. Whether they met or not, we do know that it was not until the moment when John baptized Jesus that he knew Jesus to be the Son of God. We will have more to say about that in our next study. For the moment we shall observe that John's message was exclusively one of judgment; of calling men to repentance because a tremendous event was at hand.

John said, ". . . the kingdom of heaven is at hand." To his hearers that meant only one thing. The phrase is taken from the 2nd chapter of the prophecy of Daniel, where we learn of a kingdom which the "God of heaven" shall set up on the earth. Therefore, when John the Baptist came preaching: "Repent ye: for the kingdom of heaven is at hand" every listener was filled with a spirit of expectancy, for since the kingdom was at hand the king must also be at hand.

Up to the time John baptized our Lord Jesus he saw only one coming of Christ. Like all the other prophets John was unable to reconcile the two seemingly contradictory lines of prophecy found in the Old Testament concerning the Messiah. One tells of His humiliation, His death, His sufferings and disappointments, and the other of His kingliness, His rule, His reign, His glory, and the exaltation of the nation. John observed these, but was unable to reconcile them. He did not know that there would be a period, now already extending almost two thousand years, between the first coming of Christ and His second coming. He was only aware of one event so that up to the hour when he baptized Christ, he spoke of the things that would put the people in preparation for the second coming of Christ. Later on, he saw something else. We will have more to say about that also, in our next study.

With the possible exception of Jonah, John was the most powerful preacher who ever lived. Jonah only preached one sermon—but that sermon caused a whole city to repent. He was a man of one sermon. John preached continuously for possibly a period of two years. Let's look at his audience. In the 5th verse of the 3rd chapter of Matthew's Gospel we learn that all the people of Jerusalem, and of Judæa, and of the region round about Jordan went out to hear him. If you please, he was a layman, the greatest lay preacher this world has ever seen. Let me remind you again that he was only a young man, in his late twenties or just thirty. No wonder our Lord said there was none greater born of women.

Incidentally, a word in passing to young people. John of course was a chosen vessel called of God, but what God can do through one man, he can do through another if that person will yield himself completely to the domination of God's Holy Spirit. It is impossible to yield a life to the Lord at too early an age. God values old saints, He loves them intensely; but do not think for a moment that He is uninterested in young people. Jesus Christ was a young man. He died at an age too young for a man to be considered a candidate for the Presidency of the United States. He was a *young* man. Indeed at that time the writer of this Gospel, John the Apostle, was also a very young man. Many believe He was in his early twenties or possibly in his late teens, when he first came in contact with the Lord Jesus Christ.

When a young layman makes such a stir by his preaching as did John the Baptist, you can be sure that the "Federation of Professional Preachers" sits up and takes notice. Probably in the beginning they were uninterested. They might have referred to him as a stripling or an "upstart"—but the crowd followed and clung to him. Multitudes were baptized by him. The influence of that young man's preaching was so tremendous that finally the "Union" decided they had better send a delegation to check up on him. He hadn't a card in either the A. F. of L. or the C. I. O.! He was just a plain, ordinary unordained layman—but called of God, ordained, and anointed by God, filled and energized by the Holy Spirit. We learn from the 19th verse of the 1st chapter of John's Gospel, that priests and Levites were sent from Jerusalem to ask John, "Who art thou?" It was the Sanhedrin, "the Federation," if you please, that sent the delegation to "the Baptist." They wanted to know who he was. No one had "laid hands" on him. He had not been educated at the feet of a Gamaliel or in any of the leading seminaries of his day. His father was a priest to be true; his parents were godly people; undoubtedly they had saturated his mind with the Word of God so that John was familiar with every portion of the Old Testament. He was a prophet. He caused even kings to quake before his word.

Testimony of Josephus About John

Let me quote a passage from Josephus about the ministry of John. Josephus was a contemporary of the Apostle Paul, born a few years after the death of Christ. He is considered one of, if not *the greatest*, of Jewish historians. He was also a military commander. His great work "The Jewish Antiquities" covers in twenty books the history of that people from the creation of the world to the outbreak of the war with Rome. Josephus makes only one reference to Jesus of Nazareth and some consider it to be spurious. He of course was not a follower of the Christ. Evidently what our Lord said about John is true for Josephus could not avoid referring to him. Let me quote what he wrote as translated by Alfred Edersheim. "But to some of the Jews it appeared that the destruction of Herod's army came from God, and, indeed, as a just punishment on account of what had been done to John, who was surnamed The Baptist. For Herod ordered him to be killed, who was a good man and had called upon the Jews to exercise virtue, both as to righteousness toward one another and piety toward God, and so come to baptism. For so would the baptising be acceptable to Him (God) if they made use of it, not for the putting away (remission, expiation) of some sins, but for the purification of the body after the soul had been previously cleansed by righteousness. And when others came in crowds, for they were exceedingly moved by hearing these words, Herod, fearing lest such influence of his over the people might lead to some rebellion, for they seemed ready to do anything by his counsel, deemed it best, before any new movement should happen through him, to put him to death, rather than when a change in affairs (revolution) had come he might have to repent the mischief into which he had fallen when it should be too late." Ant. xviii—5.

From this reference by Josephus we learn several things. First, that John was an historic character. Second, that he was held in great esteem by the people. Third, that he was a powerful preacher whose influence was tremendous. Fourth, that he had a baptism, and that this baptism was related to the matter of sin and its forgiveness or purification. Fifth, that the great crowds which flocked to hear him, were deeply moved by his preaching. Finally, that John the Baptist was executed by Herod, though Josephus said it was because he feared that the preaching of the Baptist might issue in a new movement or revolution against himself (Herod), since the people "seemed ready to do anything by his (John's) counsel." We of course know from Holy Writ that it was John's uncompromising preaching against sin which led to his own execution. But here is a testimony from a contemporary writer that stamps the record of the Scripture to be true in its salient points concerning the ministry of John the Baptist, a young man, about thirty years of age.

The Interview

Now notice what this Gospel tells us took place when John was interviewed. Here was a delegation of venerable gentlemen with long grey beards and scrolls of the Scriptures under their arms, their garments indicating who were priests and who were Levites. They opened by saying, We are a committee sent from the Sanhedrin: we have only one question to ask you—"Who art thou?" And now hear John's response. "And he confessed, and denied not; but confessed, I am not the Christ." Well, said they, "if you are not the Christ, of whom the Old Testament witnesses, who then?—are you Elijah?" God promised He would send Elijah back before that great and notable day of the Lord should come. So they asked John, "Art thou Elias?" John answered, "No." Well, "Art thou that prophet?" to whom Moses referred when he said that a Prophet like unto him would God raise up, and unto Him should they hearken. Again John answered, "No."

Notice that John refused to volunteer a single thing or elaborate upon his answers. He answered their questions, that was all. That is all a good witness ever does! John was an excellent witness. A Christian is a witness. That is all that any of us are called to be—simply a witness to the Lord Jesus Christ. The delegates were pretty well "stumped" by this time. They had run through the whole gamut of celebrated names, and to them all, John had answered "No." In desperation they asked, "Who art thou? that we may give an answer to them that sent us. What sayest thou of thyself?" To this John answered with these marvelous words, "I am the voice of one crying in the wilderness, Make straight the way of the Lord, as said the prophet Isaiah." This prophecy is found in the 3rd verse of the 40th chapter of Isaiah. There is no doubt that John *knew his Isaiah.* We ought to know it also. It is one of the great books of the Old Testament. Someone has called it the "fifth Gospel."

John said, "I am the voice of one crying in the wilderness . . ." John's answer, therefore, inferred, I am nothing in myself, I am only a mouthpiece—I am a mouthpiece for God so that He can speak His word through me—the word that I speak is a re-echo of the word that the Prophet Isaiah spoke seven hundred years previously: "I am the voice of one crying in the wilderness, Make straight the way of the Lord."

John's Background

There is something interesting about this answer when we consider John's background. John's father was a priest. His name was Zacharias and John's mother's name was Elizabeth. John was their only child. He was a miracle baby, for he was born when both parents were well stricken in years. In the course of the religious rites of the day it fell upon Zacharias to minister in the priest's office. His lot was to burn incense when he went into the temple, while the people stood without, praying. Suddenly an angel of the Lord appeared on the right side of the altar. When the aged priest saw him he was troubled and fear fell upon him but the angel said unto him:

> "Fear not, Zacharias: for thy prayer is heard; and thy wife Elisabeth shall bear thee a son, and thou shalt call his name John.
> "And thou shalt have joy and gladness; and many shall rejoice at his birth.
> "For he shall be great in the sight of the Lord, and shall drink neither wine nor strong drink; and he shall be filled with the Holy Ghost, even from his mother's womb."

The angel had more to say about John but we quote enough for our purpose. Zacharias answered, "Whereby shall I know this? for I am an old man, and my wife well stricken in years." The angel revealed himself and said, "I am Gabriel, that stand in the presence of God; and am sent to speak unto thee, and to shew thee these glad tidings. And, behold, *thou shalt be dumb, and not able to speak,* until the day that these things shall be performed, because thou believest not my words, which shall be fulfilled in their season." The Bible declares, "For if the word spoken by angels was stedfast, and every transgression and disobedience received a just recompense of reward; How shall we escape, if we neglect so great salvation; which at the first began to be spoken by the Lord, and was confirmed unto us by them that heard him. . ."

Zacharias doubted the word of Gabriel. He immediately suffered the loss of his voice. Such being the case, what about men who refuse to believe the testimony of God concerning our Lord Jesus Christ?

The people wondered what was detaining Zacharias in the temple but they marveled more when upon coming out of the temple they discovered that he was *speechless.* He immediately departed to his home until the appointed time when the child was born. His friends wanted to call the child by his father's name. But Zacharias beckoned for a paper and wrote down the name by which the child was to be called. At that very moment *his voice* was restored. Is it not interesting that the boy, whose father *lost* his voice, because he refused to believe the promise of the angel should later say of himself, "I am the *voice* of one crying in the wilderness"?

WALK SIX

THE LAMB OF GOD

HAVING answered the question "Who art thou?" put to John the Baptist by the delegation sent from the Sanhedrin, by saying he was "the voice of one crying in the wilderness, Make straight the way of the Lord . . ." John was immediately confronted with a second and last question, this time from the Pharisees, who were the ritualists of the day. They asked, "Why baptizest thou then, if thou be not that Christ, nor Elias, neither that prophet?" It was an unheard of thing for a young man to institute a religious rite. John was an unordained man. Though he was never ordained by men, he was *fore*ordained of God to preach. No man has a commission to preach unless he has been ordained of God. No Christian is faithful to God unless he is a witnessing Christian, but God has not called all Christians to be preachers. From the 4th chapter of Ephesians we learn that the risen Lord gave gifts to men. Then, the Lord gave these gifted men to the whole body of the church. Some were called apostles, some prophets, some evangelists, some pastors and teachers. Only men chosen by the Lord and gifted by the Lord have a call to preach.

The Signs of a Call

There are two methods for determining whether a man has been called and endowed by the Lord. First, his ministry will give evidence of the possession of a gift, and second, his demeanor will further attest the fact that he has been called.

Consider the ministry of John the Baptist from these two angles. There can be no question that John's ministry indicated that he possessed a gift. He was called of the Lord; the effects of his preaching demonstrated this. But notice his behavior. His humility manifested itself in his answers to the questions that were addressed to him. First, he said he was not the Light, but was sent to bear witness of the Light. Second, he was not the sun, he was but a burning candle; he was not the Master, he was only a voice. Dr. F. B. Meyer has well said: "This humility is as rare as it is fascinating. We are all so apt to use our relationship to Christ as a means of enhancing our own importance, and attracting attention. Though we formally ascribe supremacy to our Lord, we are elated when our name is on every lip and our work in every thought, even though we should never have been heard of had it not been for the Lord. But there was nothing of this in John."

May the Lord give us more men like John, men who are burning candles witnessing to the Light, but who are humble before God and man. The extent of the humility of John is beautifully expressed in verses 26 and 27 of this chapter. John answered the Pharisees saying, "I baptize with water: but there standeth one among you, whom ye know not; He it is, who coming after me is

THE GOSPEL OF JOHN — CHAPTER I, VERSES 29-34   43

preferred before me, whose shoe's latchet I am not worthy to unloose." His response is illuminating when we consider that the Rabbis have said "every office which a servant should do for his master, a scholar should perform for his teacher, except to loose his sandal-thong." But John said he was unworthy to do even that. God grant that we may have a similar vision of the majesty of Christ.

THE DAY FOLLOWING

As we commence reading from verse 29 it is apparent that the delegation from the Sanhedrin remained over to the following day. Let us read what took place at that time.

> "The next day John seeth Jesus coming unto him, and saith, Behold the Lamb of God, which taketh away the sin of the world.
> "This is he of whom I said, After me cometh a man which is preferred before me: for he was before me.
> "And I knew him not: but that he should be made manifest to Israel, therefore am I come baptizing with water.
> "And John bare record, saying, I saw the Spirit descending from heaven like a dove, and it abode upon him.
> "And I knew him not: but he that sent me to baptize with water, the same said unto me, Upon whom thou shalt see the Spirit descending, and remaining on him, the same is he which baptizeth with the Holy Ghost.
> "And I saw, and bare record that this is the Son of God."

If the preceding day could be called the day of John's interrogation, then this day can be called the day of John's greatest triumph. Our Lord had just returned from the wilderness where He successfully met and mastered Satan. Almost immediately ". . . John seeth Jesus coming unto him, and saith, Behold the Lamb of God, which taketh away the sin of the world." Turning to the scribes and Pharisees who had been sent to interview him, John said, "This is he of whom I said, After me cometh a man which is preferred before me: for he was before me. *And I knew him not:* but that he should be made manifest to Israel, therefore am I come baptizing with water." Of that day John bare record and said, "I saw the Spirit descending from heaven like a dove, and it *abode upon him.*" Because of two important facts in that statement, John reiterated, *"And I knew him not:* but he that sent me to baptize with water, the same said unto me, Upon whom thou shalt see the Spirit descending, and *remaining on him,* the same is he which baptizeth with the Holy Ghost." John continued and said, "I saw, and bare record that this is the Son of God." That had taken place when John baptized Jesus some forty days earlier.

Coming to Christ and Christ Coming to Us

As we examine this testimony we should contrast verse 29 with verse 12 of this 1st chapter. In verse 12 we read, "But as many as received him (Christ), to them gave he power to become the sons of God, even to them that believe on his name . . ." That verse teaches that a man must receive Christ. It contains the same message which our Lord addressed to the people when He said, *"Come unto me,* all ye that labour and are heavy laden, and I will give you rest." No man therefore will have rest in his soul, or know what salvation means, or experience an intimate family relationship with God unless he first comes to Jesus Christ and receives Him as his personal Savior. That is essential. But notice what we read in verse 29. There it is not the sinner *coming to Christ:* it is *Christ coming to the sinner.* ". . . John seeth Jesus coming unto him . . ." That is wonderful, condescending grace upon the part of the Son of God. Consider the majesty of Christ. Then look at this man, born of woman. Great though he was, he was only a child of the dust. Yet the Son of God is seen coming to him. Before a man comes to Christ, Christ comes to that man. God is always presented in the Bible as seeking the lost.

We who have received Christ as our Saviour may not have known when we received Him that He first sought us, but as we have grown in grace and in the knowledge of the Lord Jesus, we have been overwhelmingly convinced that had He not first sought us we should never have come to Him. It is not in man, dead in trespasses and sins, to even so much as be able to open an eye and behold Christ. Therefore even the most brilliant unregenerate men, with the keenest of minds, listening to the simplest of gospel messages, cannot comprehend or understand the Gospel. These men are both spiritually dead and spiritually blind. They must first have a miracle transpire in their lives which can only be wrought by the Son of God. Then there must be an operation performed on their eyes.

In connection with Christ's coming to a man, the picture presented in the 3rd chapter of the Book of Revelation, verse 20, is most interesting. There our Lord speaks and says, "Behold, I stand at the door, and knock . . ." In order to stand and knock, Christ had to come down to man, and having come, He stands at the door, knocking. The door, of course, is the door of man's heart. Our Lord speaks to the sinner: ". . . if any man hear my voice, and open the door, I will *come in to him,* and will sup with him, and he with me." Here is divine grace. The Son of God first knocks. When the door is opened to Him, He comes in and sups with the sinner ere the sinner sups with the Son of God. It is an honor to receive an invitation to dine with a king: it is a greater honor to have a king come as a guest to your table. What is more, the King of Glory will never invite us to sit with him at the table of bounty in the heavens unless we first invite Him to dine with us in our hearts. How can one consider such condescending grace, without exclaiming "Thanks be unto God for His indescribable gift"? Small wonder that the Apostle Paul said, ". . . God forbid that I should glory, save in the cross of our Lord Jesus Christ . ."

"Behold the Lamb of God"

When John saw Jesus coming unto him, undoubtedly there was a great crowd of people gathered about him, including the delegation from the Sanhedrin. He presented Christ to them all and said, "Behold the Lamb of God, which taketh away the sin of the world." When John first began preaching, he saw only the coming of Christ in judgment. He did not talk about the *Lamb.* He talked about the *Lion.* He did not know that before our Lord could enter into the office of the Lion of the tribe of Judah, it was necessary for Him to perform the work of the Lamb of God. But between the day when John baptized our Lord and the day when he presented Him to the multitude as the Lamb of God, something had transpired. During that forty-day period, the Holy Spirit showed John some amazing things. A cross loomed between the time where he was standing and the coming of Christ *in judgment.* He then understood that before Christ could reign in righteousness and kingly glory, God had to do something about man's sin. In other words, Christ had to be a Savior before He could be a King. John now saw clearly the purpose of the coming of Christ. He ceased to proclaim judgment. He presented a Savior and talked about grace. He said: "Behold the Lamb of God, which taketh away the sin of the world." But the Holy Spirit revealed something more of Christ's ministry. Up to that time, John understood that our Lord's manifestation was limited to Israel, therefore he said, ". . . I knew him not: but that he should be made *manifest to Israel,* therefore am I come baptizing with water." But now John understood that the extent of our Lord's ministry was world-wide—"Behold the Lamb of God, which taketh away *the sin of the world.*"

The "Lamb of God" is a wonderful title. Abraham first used it in conversation with his son Isaac when he said, "My son, God will provide himself a lamb for a burnt offering . . ." And indeed He did. Therefore, when God did provide the Lamb, John said, "Behold the Lamb of God . . ." John did not call attention to the character of Christ, wonderful as that is. He did not call attention to the words of Christ, though the words of Christ are wonderful. He did not call attention to the law of Christ or the example of Christ, wonderful though His law and His example are. He went to the heart of the purpose of Christ's coming and said, "Behold the Lamb of God, which taketh away the sin of the world." No one will ever behold the face of Jesus Christ unless he first beholds Him as the Lamb of God. There simply is no use talking about His character, His words, His works, His example, His life—ere we receive Him as our Savior. The gospel begins at Calvary where Christ, as the Lamb of God, died for our sins. What is more, no believer will ever get away from nor ever grow so far in grace as to rise to a place where he will get beyond contemplation of Christ as the Lamb of God. Even in the glory we will sing of the Lamb that was slain.

One thing more. John was given a sign by God whereby he would know who was the anointed of God. The sign was the Spirit of God, Who would descend in the form of a dove and abide upon the anointed One at the time of the baptism. John said, "I saw the Spirit descending from heaven like a dove, and it abode upon him." Throughout the Scriptures one of the symbols of the Holy Spirit has been the dove, the peaceful, brooding bird. This symbolism is simply wonderful. Our Lord was surrounded by water. He had come to John to be baptized by him. Suddenly the heavens opened and the Spirit in the form of a dove descended upon the Son of God. The dove had been looking for a place where he could rest his feet. He had never found one on earth heretofore. He now found a resting place. So the dove abode upon the head of Christ. The scene resembles the flood. Noah had opened the window of the ark to let a dove out, so that he could determine if the waters had subsided. But the dove returned for he found no resting place for his feet. The earth was still covered with water. But here was One who had stood in the midst of the water upon Whom the dove could find a resting place. The dove abode upon Him.

The Holy Spirit's ministry is manifested in two ways. Sometimes He reveals Himself in a quiet, harmless, peaceful, brooding ministry so beautifully symbolized by the dove. But the moment the Holy Spirit rested upon our Lord Jesus Christ, He manifested His other method of ministry. He is not only a brooding dove. He is a dynamic force. So we read in St. Mark's Gospel ". . . immediately the spirit driveth him (Jesus) into the wilderness." It appeared as if the Holy Spirit had waited for centuries to anoint the One Who could meet and conquer Satan. Here He was—the man Christ Jesus. Without a moment's hesitation, immediately, the Spirit literally drove Him into the wilderness to be tested by Satan. Of course, the Holy Spirit knew our Lord was more than a match for Satan and would conquer him. There never was a question in the mind of the Spirit concerning the ability of our Lord to meet all the fiery darts of the wicked one. Our Lord Jesus Christ was sinless, therefore sin never appealed to Him.

The Holy Spirit is a dynamic power as well as a harmless, brooding dove. We need power today. The only power that can meet Satan is the power in which our Lord Jesus Christ met him, the power of God's Holy Spirit. The Bible says it is "Not by might, nor by power, but by my spirit. . . ."

Without Money

An advertisement appeared in the New York papers January 7, 1939, announcing a series of meetings intended to help the individual attain spiritual power. The meetings were to be conducted by a number of leading ministers, but as I read I noticed that the series, which would take ten evenings, required that a fee of two dollars be paid for the course. Before one could know anything about spiritual power one evidently had to have the power of two

American dollars to permit one to know how to be able to attain spiritual power. But when we turn the pages of our Bible, we observe two passages. On one occasion a man offered to give the Apostles money saying, "Give me also this *power*, that on whomsoever I lay hands, he may receive the Holy Ghost. But Peter said unto him, Thy money perish with thee, because thou hast thought that the gift of God may be purchased with money." One cannot buy the power of God's Holy Spirit with money, whether it be two dollars or two billion dollars. Now listen to the words of the Prophet Isaiah: "Ho, every one that thirsteth, come ye to the waters, and he that hath no money; come ye, buy, and eat; yea, come, buy wine and milk *without* money and *without* price."

Wine makes the heart of man glad. Wine is a symbol of the joy of fellowship with God which comes by the presence of the Holy Spirit in the life of a believer. A joyous heart makes for good digestion but the prophet offered not only wine but milk. Milk strengthens the bones and makes fat the flesh. Milk is a symbol of strength and of power. Come, said the prophet, buy "without money and without price." We must come just as we are. And, coming in faith, believing we may buy without money and without price the power of God's Holy Spirit so that He may dominate our lives.

Walk Seven

AS JESUS WALKED

OUR previous studies have all been of an introductory character. Now we actually begin our Walks with our Lord through the familiar scenes of His earthly ministry. Everything that had taken place previously was in preparation for this moment.

When my friend Edwin J. Tharp gave me the title for this series, he asked me specifically to observe that our Lord did His most effective work with individuals. Now we shall get our first glimpse of the great Physician in His individual soul clinic ministry. Beginning with verse 35, we read:

THE GOSPEL OF JOHN — CHAPTER I, VERSES 35-42

> "Again the next day after John stood, and two of his disciples;
>
> "And looking upon Jesus as he walked, he saith, Behold the Lamb of God!
>
> "And the two disciples heard him speak, and they followed Jesus.
>
> "Then Jesus turned, and saw them following, and saith unto them, What seek ye? They said unto him, Rabbi, (which is to say, being interpreted, Master,) where dwellest thou?
>
> "He saith unto them, Come and see. They came and saw where he dwelt, and abode with him that day: for it was about the tenth hour.
>
> "One of the two which heard John speak, and followed him, was Andrew, Simon Peter's brother.
>
> "He first findeth his own brother Simon, and saith unto him, We have found the Messias, which is, being interpreted, the Christ.
>
> "And he brought him to Jesus. And when Jesus beheld him, he said, Thou art Simon the son of Jona: thou shalt be called Cephas, which is by interpretation, A stone."

Here is the divine record of the second day of our Lord's public ministry. The first day John presented Him to the multitude and cried, "Behold the Lamb of God, which taketh away the sin of the world." The next day John stood and two of his disciples. While they stood, the three of them looked upon Jesus *as He walked.*

THE POWER AND HUMILITY OF THE PRINCE OF PREACHERS

Let's stop a moment, to examine this wonderfully Holy Spirit drawn picture. As far as I know, no one has put this scene on canvas. Would that some gifted artist would paint it, placing in the background a picture of John with a great multitude about him, presenting to them a great Person. In the foreground would be the scene of the following day with John standing alone while his two disciples moved toward Jesus *as He walked.* The background scene would represent the climax of John's ministry. It was the last time John spoke to a crowd. He was such a remarkable preacher that multitudes subjected themselves to great inconvenience in order to hear him. He did not speak in an auditorium, he did not speak in a city, he did not preach in the temple, he did not preach over the radio. He preached under an open sky *in the wilderness*—and the people went out to hear him. No man since has exercised such power over a people in his ministry as did John the Baptist. There have been men whose influence was great, who spoke to crowds; but invariably they went where the crowd was. But the crowd went where John was. At the climax of John's ministry, he lost his crowd. *He is the only man who lost a crowd because the people believed what he preached.* What a remarkable person was this young man, John the Baptist.

There are men, faithful as far as the truth of the gospel is concerned, but who make use of their personalities and their gifts to gather people about themselves. John used his gift, his personality, and his power to gather people about Christ. He said, "Behold the Lamb of God, which taketh away the sin of the world." There was so much sincerity in the man's message that the crowd got the point. They left John and followed Jesus. Would that men of God today understood that the zenith of their ministry is reached when they lead a soul *to* Christ! Sirs, permit a *layman* to suggest—leave that soul with Him; don't put a tag on him, don't call him yours. He is Christ's. Leave him with the Lord. No man was ever left with the Lord but he came away a new man in Christ. Furthermore, cease speaking of the pulpit as *your* pulpit and the church in which you minister *your* church. It is *His* pulpit and *His* church.

The disciples of John also observed that John lost his crowd, for on a later occasion they said, "Rabbi, he that was with thee beyond Jordan, to whom thou barest witness, behold, the same baptizeth, and all . . . come to him." They thought he would show a spirit of jealousy, but John answered, "A man can receive nothing, except it be given him from heaven. Ye yourselves bear me witness, that I said, I am not the Christ, but that I am sent before him. He that hath the bride is the bridegroom: but the friend of the bridegroom, which standeth and heareth him, rejoiceth greatly because of the bridegroom's voice: this my joy therefore is fulfilled." We will have more to say about this when we come to the 3rd chapter of this Gospel. But John continued and said, "He must increase, but I must decrease." Greek scholars tell us that the words which John used, translated *increase* and *decrease*, are not static words but they imply a continuance of the trend, so that John actually said, "He must keep on *increasing* and I must keep on *decreasing.*"

There is no end to the exaltation and the increase of glory which becomes our Lord Jesus Christ. Likewise, as far as a faithful servant of God is concerned, this side of the glory, there is no such thing as getting to the place where he is so humble that he cannot be more humble. A Christian must go on decreasing. No ministry will ever have the *full* power of the Holy Spirit resting upon it, as long as the man who ministers seeks to exalt himself; but in the measure which he decreases in his own estimation, our Lord will increase in majesty and glory in the minds and the hearts of those who hear the message. Our Lord also expressed the same principle to the Apostle Paul when He said, "... my strength is made perfect in weakness."

One more thought about John before we *look* at our Lord. The experiences that John had were amazing! He went up like a skyrocket and came down even more quickly than he went up. He lost his crowd overnight. He went down so far that he landed in a dungeon and had his head cut off on the executioner's block. While in prison, he was greatly encumbered with difficulties and conflicting emotions, so that his faith began to waiver. Some Christians are annoyed when they hear of another believer in the throes of distressing doubts and clouds of disappointments. They mistakenly think that unless the sun is always shining on one's pathway, a man is out of fellowship with God. But as William Blane so beautifully wrote,

> "Ceaseless sunshine makes the desert
> Constant heat the burning sand;
> Winter's snows make healthy climate,
> Summer rains the fertile land;
> And do not our light afflictions,
> Like the rain and like the snow,
> Keep our souls from being deserts,
> Where no heavenly fruit could grow?"

If you are experiencing a period of perplexity, God has a word for you, a most comforting word. At times one is apt to think that one's experiences and disappointments are greater than the disappointments and sorrows of any other person. But look at John the Baptist. I do not know of any man (except possibly Job) who had such an experience as he, certainly not in the spiritual realm, for being faithful to one's calling.

The only comparable experience that I know, but which is in an entirely different realm and for the opposite reason, involved a man whose name was in every newspaper a short time ago. He was a cultured, refined gentleman, who traveled in the finest society circles, who was educated in the cream of universities, possessed of a splendid physique, a proud man, but a man's man, he had everything that men, as men, call desirable. But how quickly that man fell! He fell from the top of the social ladder, to the bottom. Indeed he went farther than the bottom, he went right through to the basement and landed in a cell with convicts. My reference to this gentleman is not in a pharisaical vein. God forbid. "He that is without sin . . . let him first cast a stone . . ." I sympathize deeply with that man. In a letter, to which I received a courteous response, I suggested that there was only one Person in all the world Who could help him in his distress— our Lord Jesus Christ.

John went from the pinnacle of preaching success clear down the ladder. He went below the last rung of the ladder and landed as a dejected, disappointed, sorrowful young man in a prison. While there, our Lord did not once visit him. He did not even send a disciple to encourage him. He left John alone in a prison cell. So great was John's depression of mind that he finally could not resist any longer. He sent two of his disciples to Jesus to ask, "Art thou he that should come, or do we look for another?" You will recall the answer our Lord gave. He said, Go and tell John "these things;" but before you go, let Me show you "these things" so you can tell John that you have both *seen* and *heard*. So our Lord performed many miracles in the presence of those two disciples. They saw the blind receive their sight; they saw the lame walk; they saw lepers cleansed by a spoken word. They observed that the deaf heard; they even saw the dead raised up; and then their attention was called to one thing that is peculiar alone to God's Gospel: our Lord said ". . . and the poor have the gospel preached to them." Talk about comparative religions! Yes, compare them with each other; you can only contrast them with the Gospel. No religion in this world ever had a message for the poor. It is only the Gospel that has a message for them. So our Lord said to them: Go and tell John these things and carry this little word from Me to him, ". . . blessed is he, whosoever shall not be offended in me." We are not told that the message encouraged John's heart and faith, but I am certain it did. I am sure he went as happily and as resignedly to the executioner's block as John and Betty Stam went to their death in China.

The greatest honor that a child of God can render to his Lord is never to be offended in Him, irrespective of difficulties and circumstances. Who knows but that they may emanate from the same source as those Job experienced. God help us to say with that great patriarch, "Though he slay me, yet will I trust . . . him . . ."

"As He Walked"

We have spent much time with John the Baptist. He deserves it. Now let's *look* at Jesus. John had only two disciples with him that morning. They *stood* with him. They must have chatted about the things that had happened the day before. Suddenly they saw our Lord. They fastened their eyes upon Him. There were six eyes attracted to Him that day. They looked upon Jesus *"as He walked."* Our studies, you remember, are *Walks with our Lord* through this Gospel. Here our Lord is seen *"as He walked."* No man ever walked as our Lord walked.

I once walked with a friend. It was a brisk walk, as we were to meet another gentleman, a friend of both. Our mutual friend had gone on ahead, we were following behind, hurrying to catch up with him. The friend by my side turned to me and said as we observed this gentleman about fifty yards away, "Every time I see John walk I see his father; he acts like his father, walks like his father; he is his father all over." Incidentally my friend had thus given expression to a great truth of the Gospel. We who believe in the Lord Jesus Christ as our Savior do not walk much like Him now, but there will come a day when we will walk as He walked. Then the world will say concerning us that we are children of the Son and that we walk like our Lord.

Our Lord walked like His Father. He manifested His Father. He so perfectly represented His Father, that He could say at the close of His ministry, ". . . he that hath seen me hath seen the Father . . ." Let us take a look at Him; but we must *stand still* if we are to look at Christ. This hustle-bustle world of today rushes by and pays no attention to Christ. If we are to know Him, we will have to stop and look at Him as those three men looked that day.

In our last study, we said that there simply is no use talking about the life of Christ ere we receive Him as our Savior. John, though a young man, pressed that truth upon his two disciples. As they watched our Lord walk he turned to them and said, "Behold the *Lamb* of God!"

The life of our Lord Jesus Christ is the greatest condemnation this world has ever witnessed. If our Lord had only lived a life, He would have condemned the world, but He died a death that justified the sinner. Therefore the Gospel begins at the cross, never at the manger. The Gospel begins, ". . . Christ died for our sins according to the scriptures . . ." The life of our Lord Jesus Christ is not a saving influence, though it was the life of Christ that gave value to His death. But the life of our Lord, apart from His death, will never get a soul within the portals of heaven.

There was something about the voice of John that had in it the nature of a command. The two disciples understood him thoroughly. They left him and walked toward Jesus. They left John standing alone. They followed Jesus. If you please, they *beheld* Him. Any man who really *beholds* Him must necessarily *follow* Him also.

IN THE CLINIC

Our Lord turned and saw them following, then addressed them: "What seek ye?" The two men answered—I paraphrase their answer—they said: We are not seeking *anything*—we are not looking for a *what*—we are seeking a *Person*. "Rabbi . . ." said they, "where dwellest *thou?*" Our Lord gave them the Gospel invitation. They are wonderful, ringing words: "Come and see." "They came and saw where he dwelt, and abode with him that day . . ." Undoubtedly they were fascinated by the Person of Christ. We are given the name of one of these disciples. It was Andrew, Simon Peter's brother. We are not given the name of the other. It probably was John, the writer of this Gospel.

One can always tell when a man has salvation, or to use other words, when he knows the Lord Jesus Christ, by his immediate actions after getting in touch with the Lord. The first thing Andrew did was to find his brother Simon. So, surely did John—but Andrew was the first to lead another (his brother) to Christ. He did not argue with Peter, he did not reason with him, he told him some good news. He said: "We have found the Messiah—we have found the Christ."

From what we know of Peter's later history, he was no man with whom to argue. Andrew knew his brother perfectly. He brought him to *the Jesus clinic* and put him into the hands of the great Physician. When our Lord beheld him, He said to Peter, "Thou art Simon the son of Jona: thou shalt be called Cephas, which is by interpretation, A stone."

The world has placed a halo around the heads of the disciples, but they were men of like passions with us. They were stumbling, faltering men, but men who *knew* the Savior. We usually speak of Peter as St. Peter. Peter has more names in the Scripture than any other

THE GOSPEL OF JOHN — CHAPTER I, VERSES 43-51

disciple. When our Lord saw him, He said: Thou art Simon the son of Jona: I am going to change your name: from now on you shall be called Cephas. John tells us, ignorant Gentiles, that Cephas means a *stone* or a *rock*. If he lived today, in these United States, Peter's name before he had come in contact with the Christ would have been *Simon Johnson* (a good Scandinavian name) but our Lord changed his name to *Simon Stone*.

Every man who has ever come to Christ has been given a new name. Previously he was a sinner; now he is a saint. Previously he was a child of this world; now he is a child of God. When one enters into a new family, he is entitled to a new name. If you are a believer in the Lord, some day He will give you your new name.

If you know Christ and have a Peter in your family, take your brother Peter and lead him to the Lord. Get him to see the glory of God upon the face of Jesus Christ, even as you have come to see it. That's the test of Christian discipleship, it is the test of *our walk* with the Lord Jesus.

Walk Eight

IN THE STEPS OF SAINT PHILIP

THERE are a number of days in the first chapter of the Gospel according to St. John. Some refer to ages prior to our Lord's incarnation, and others to days following His induction into His public ministry. We are now to consider what transpired on the second day of our Lord's acts or ministry, the third day since John called Him "The Lamb of God."

The inspired record reads,

> "The day following Jesus would go forth into Galilee, and findeth Philip, and saith unto him, Follow me.
> "Now Philip was of Bethsaida, the city of Andrew and Peter.
> "Philip findeth Nathanael, and saith unto him, We have found him, of whom Moses in the law, and the prophets, did write, Jesus of Nazareth, the son of Joseph.
> "And Nathanael said unto him, Can there any good thing come out of Nazareth? Philip saith unto him, Come and see.
> "Jesus saw Nathanael coming to him, and saith of

> him, Behold an Israelite indeed, in whom is no guile!
> "Nathanael saith unto him, Whence knowest thou me? Jesus answered and said unto him, Before that Philip called thee, when thou wast under the fig tree, I saw thee.
> "Nathanael answered and saith unto him, Rabbi, thou art the Son of God; thou art the King of Israel.
> "Jesus answered and said unto him, Because I said unto thee, I saw thee under the fig tree, believest thou? thou shalt see greater things than these.
> "And he saith unto him, Verily, verily, I say unto you, Hereafter ye shall see heaven open, and the angels of God ascending and descending upon the Son of man."

During the preceding day our Lord had interviewed two of the disciples of John. One, Andrew by name, immediately went out to find his brother and brought him to Jesus. During that day's ministry Christ did not seek men; men sought our Lord. On the second day of His public ministry, our Lord went out to seek men. Thus we read in verse 43: "The day following Jesus would go forth into Galilee, and findeth Philip, and saith unto him, Follow me."

Accompanying Christ

Philip was the first man who was invited by our Lord to follow Him. Many since have followed in the steps of Philip. The word *follow* is an arresting word. Observe that our Lord was going forth into Galilee. He had a purpose, as we learn from the 2nd chapter, for making that trip. It was the Spring season and the Passover was nigh at hand. Before going to Jerusalem, He was invited to a marriage feast. Evidently He felt free or was urged to bring several guests, and so He went out and found Philip and suggested that he also accompany Him to the marriage. That is the meaning of the word *follow*—"accompany me," or as Dr. G. Campbell Morgan put it, "Come and travel with me."

Some people like to be alone most of the time. Our Lord loved to be alone in the night but invariably delighted in having company during the day season. Therefore, He said to Philip, "Accompany me" or "Travel with me." He knew that Philip had to be dealt with differently from the two men with whom He had spent the preceding day. We are not told what conversations took place between the Lord and the two disciples of John. All we know is that they wanted to see where He dwelt and that our Lord invited them to "Come and see." The master Physician so thoroughly and perfectly revealed Himself to those disciples that they knew they had found the Messiah.

On this second day our Lord again is seen in the soul clinic. He knew that what Philip required more than anything else was to walk by His side. When we consider who this Physician is—the Lord of Glory, the Creator of the universe, the visibility of God, then it is astounding that a man is invited to walk alongside of the Lord. For years I labored under the impression that the word *follow* meant only to follow *after* our Lord. But I am now satisfied that He not only invites us to follow after Him; He wants us also to walk by His side, even as He wants to walk by our side. He does not want us to lag behind nor to go before. He wants to walk by our side and to have us accompany Him as He accompanies us.

The Spirit of God has not been pleased to tell us what took place when our Lord and Philip walked together. But we do know that Philip was convinced who Jesus was by merely walking by His side. Some of us make a great mistake in believing that men are convinced by argumentation and disputation. Our Lord was the master soul-winner. He knew how to deal with men. He knew the spot that was diseased. What's more He had the healing balm of Gilead.

So Philip accompanied our Lord. We know little about Philip from the inspired record but what we do read is most revealing. We will touch upon those things as we come to them in this study of John's Gospel. At this time we want to be occupied with what this portion of the Scripture tells us about Philip. It reads: "Now Philip was of Bethsaida, the city of Andrew and Peter." Our Lord had quite a few Bethsaidans in His company of the twelve. I enjoy Dr. Ironside's comment on *the twelve* in his new book on First Corinthians, which is the work of a real master. He says: "The earlier followers of the Lord Jesus Christ were, with very few exceptions, men from the lower walks of life: fishermen, tax-collectors, Galilean peasants! Judas was the only 'gentleman' in the entire apostolic band. He was from Judea, the bursar of the little company, and he turned traitor." How true! It is evident that our Lord knew men and knew to whom He could commit Himself. Philip was of Bethsaida. That may not mean much to some of us today, but if Philip lived in New York City and we wanted to describe a man of Philip's type and background, we would say that Philip came from the Fulton Fish Market Section of New

York City. Bethsaida means "fishtown." How interesting that our Lord should go down to fishtown to get several of His choicest disciples and invite them to accompany Him to a wedding.

The Bible pictures man under many symbols. One of them is a *fish*. Our Lord later suggested to His disciples, who were fishermen by trade, that if they would accompany Him He would make them fishers of men. If you please, what the Lord plans to do with us is to take us out of the slave or fish market and take us to a wedding feast in His Father's house. What's more, He wants us to sit down at the table with Him as His bride.

When our Lord chose His disciples, He did not go to the religious leaders of His day; He went to the hard-boiled brawny fishermen and rough politicians of Matthew's type. Could it be that even today our Lord's choicest disciples are in *unexpected* places? But our Lord did not make a mistake when He went to Judea and called a "gentleman" by the name of Judas. He did so in order that the Scriptures might be fulfilled. What gentlemen need to know is that they are sinners as much as anybody else. There is one who can handle that matter delicately—He is the Physician Himself! We think it is our business to convict men of sin, whereas that is one of the ministries of the Holy Spirit.

A Balanced Experience

From the 45th verse we learn that the walk which our Lord had with Philip was broken in order to search for a friend, as we read: "Philip findeth Nathanael, and saith unto him, We have found him, of whom Moses in the law, and the prophets, did write, Jesus of Nazareth, the son of Joseph." Here is the earliest Christianity in action. From it we learn that it was never the intention of the Lord to make His followers mystics but workers. On a later occasion He said, ". . . look on the fields; for they are white already to harvest." "The harvest truly is plenteous, but the labourers are few; Pray ye therefore the Lord of the harvest, that he will send forth *labourers* into his harvest."

To avoid an unhealthy, lop-sided Christian experience, one must maintain a balance between devotion and service. All service and no devotion is as bad as all devotion and no service. Alone, each tends to abnormality. We need to accompany our Lord, we need to be with Him and enjoy His presence, indeed, His companionship. But our

> "Rabbi, thou art the Son of God; thou art the King of Israel.
>
> "Jesus answered and said unto him, Because I said unto thee, I saw thee under the fig tree, believest thou? thou shalt see greater things than these.
>
> "And he saith unto him, Verily, verily, I say unto you, Hereafter ye shall see heaven open, and the angels of God ascending and descending upon the Son of man."

Here is a wonderful revelation. Nathanael saw two aspects of our Lord's ministry, or two phases of His character. He saw Him as the Son of God and as the King of Israel. Our Lord wished him to see another phase of His character and ministry and so He said "Hereafter ye shall see heaven open, and the angels of God ascending and descending upon the *Son of man.*" Our Lord was the first to refer to Himself as the Son of man. It is a title He loved to use in order that men might understand that He understood them. Some day the heavens will open and the angels of God will ascend and descend upon the *Son of man.* There will be close intercourse between heaven and earth. The angels of God will be the ministering servants in the economy of the Kingdom of God fig tree, I saw thee." Nathanael knew it was utterly impossible, from where our Lord stood, for Him to have seen him with natural eyesight. It was quite evident that the Lord knew everything about Nathanael. First, He said Nathanael was an Israelite. Second, He knew the kind of person he was: an Israelite in whom there was no guile. And third, He knew where he was: he was under the fig tree and it was *there* our Lord saw him. Dr. F. B. Meyer beautifully comments that "the tree has never grown which could conceal a soul from the eye of Jesus."

The Great Physician

Let's bring the application of this truth to our hearts. The Lord knows us by name. He knows our character. He knows where we are sitting and where we live. What's more, He sees us this moment and every moment. When no one else can see us, He does and can. There is not a thing hid from His eyes! Whatever our name or character, our whereabouts, whatever we might be—He knows! I have already referred to our Lord as "the great Physician." Here we see Him again working in His soul clinic. He has no scientific apparatus, He does not even have an X-ray machine or a fluoroscope, but His eye can see into every part of our being. He can look through us in broad daylight or in the night season. He knows our case history without examining the records. But best of all, He knows the remedy for our sin.

When it was evident to Nathanael that our Lord possessed fluoroscopic eyes, Nathanael confessed and said, "Rabbi, thou art the Son of God; thou art the King of Israel." It did not take our Lord long, in dealing with Nathanael, to lead him to a knowledge of Himself. But let us notice particularly a practice which our Lord invariably followed in His ministry as the Physician of the soul. Before He applied the remedy, He diagnosed the case. In other words, He stripped a man naked before He revealed His glory to that man. To put it in other language, He convinced the man of his sin before He presented Himself as the Savior of sinners. He proved that the man was lost—for only lost people can be saved. So, when He had revealed to Nathanael that He knew him, then it was that our Lord revealed Himself to Nathanael, so that he saw Him clearly. Nathanael did not then ask ". . . Can any good thing come out of Nazareth?" He bowed before Him and said,

When the Holy Spirit *speaks,* which of course is *revelation,* He never once makes the mistake of suggesting that Jesus is the son of Joseph.

One would not expect Philip to be a Doctor of Sacred Theology after spending only a part of one day with our Lord. He was still a babe in Christ. And babes in Christ are apt to make mistakes and say strange things, just as children say strange things. My little girl was talking with her mother the other day about the Lord. My wife sought to make plain the fact that the Lord Jesus Christ is in the glory by His Father and yet He is inside the heart of the individual who receives Him. Our little three-year-old turned to her mother and asked, "Mommie, will you open me up so I can see the Lord?" The fact of the matter is, many of us who have known the Lord for years must confess that we evidence so little of His indwelling, that we would have to be opened up to let the world know that Christ really lives in us.

What we find in verse 45 was all that Philip knew of the Lord on that day. The fact of the matter is that even after he had walked three years with Him he had not grown very much for it was then that he said to the Lord, ". . . shew us the Father, and it sufficeth us." How true it is that these men were men of like passions with us, apt to make mistakes except when the Holy Spirit guarded them and caused them to write by revelation and inspiration.

Nathanael was somewhat of a skeptic. He must have shrugged his shoulder as he said: ". . . Can any good thing come out of Nazareth?" While I have never been to Nazareth, friends of mine have. They tell me that it is still a dirty, unattractive, little town. How wonderful is the grace of God that our Lord should have lived in Nazareth and been brought up there. If you please, this world is an enlarged Nazareth. It is a dirty place, full of sin, and vileness, and dirt, and filth. But our Lord grew up in Nazareth and was unspotted by the filth of the town, and a Christian can walk in this world unspotted, if he walks in company with his Lord.

Fortunately for Philip, he did not know enough of our Lord to argue about Him. He simply invited Nathanael to "Come and see." Nathanael was an honest skeptic for he came along with Philip. And the Scripture says that when Jesus saw Nathanael coming to Him He said, "Behold an Israelite indeed, in whom is no guile! Nathanael saith unto him, Whence knowest thou me? Jesus answered and said unto him, Before that Philip called thee, when thou wast under the

Lord will never object if in our walk with Him we turn to Him and say—excuse me Lord, while I go over and talk to so-and-so—as we suddenly think of or see a friend who does not yet know the Christ. Thus Philip, I think, excused himself. He either thought of Nathanael, or he knew where Nathanael was to be on that day. Some authorities have suggested that this second day was a Sunday, the first day of the week. If so, how perfect that the Lord's day, the first day of the week, should be devoted to two things; devotion to the Lord and seeking the lost.

So Philip went to find Nathanael. And when he found him, he said: *"We* have found him. . ." That would lead us to believe that in addition to Philip accompanying our Lord that day, there were also Peter and Andrew and possibly John. How much these disciples learned during one interview with the Lord! The thing that impressed the two disciples who met the Lord on the previous day, and which also impressed Philip on this day, was the Person of Jesus Christ. Andrew said to his brother, "We have found the *Messias* . . ." Philip said to Nathanael, "We have found *him* . . ." Christianity is a *Person;* it is not a thing. It is not even a religious system: we have made it that. In the final analysis, Christianity is a Person, Jesus Christ. Eternal life is the knowledge of a Person. Our Lord said, ". . . this is life eternal, that they might know thee the only true God, and Jesus Christ, whom thou hast sent." Philip said, "We have found *him,* of whom Moses in the law, and the prophets, did write. . ." Philip knew that the whole of the Old Testament is concerned with a Person. From the beginning of Genesis to the end of Malachi, all of the writers present the coming one, the Messiah, the Son of David. Philip said, "We have found him . . . Jesus of Nazareth, the son of Joseph." Ah, say some critics, here is evidence that the early disciples were not much concerned about the virgin birth of Christ. Even Philip called him "the son of Joseph."

While at the recent Founders Week Conference of the Moody Bible Institute, I heard an excellent address by Dr. Harry Rimmer, of Duluth, Minn. He touched on the subject of "Inspiration and Revelation." Most people think they are one and the same, but they are not. Here in verse 45 we have inspiration not revelation. Inspiration means that this is exactly what Philip said to Nathanael. The Holy Spirit recorded it accurately, word for word, through John, many years later.

WALK NINE

HIS FIRST MIRACLE

"WISDOM is justified of her children." In addressing a multitude, commenting upon Himself and His ministry in contrast with John the Baptist and his ministry, our Lord said:

> ". . . whereunto shall I liken this generation? It is like unto children sitting in the markets, and calling unto their fellows,
> "And saying, We have piped unto you, and ye have not danced; we have mourned unto you, and ye have not lamented.
> "For John came neither eating nor drinking, and *they say,* He hath a devil.
> "The Son of man came eating and drinking, and *they say,* Behold a man gluttonous and a winebibber, a friend of publicans and sinners. But wisdom is justified of her children."

In this walk we are to consider our Lord as guest at a wedding feast in Cana of Galilee when "He here adorned and beautified it with His presence." The record is reduced by the divine penman into eleven short verses. This and every preceding generation, in attempting to understand its message, have demonstrated that they were and are like "children sitting in the markets, and calling unto their fellows . . . We have piped unto you, and ye have not danced; we have mourned unto you, and ye have not lamented." But if we believe, as I do from the very bottom of my heart and with all the powers of my mind, that the Bible is the inerrant, inspired Word of God and that Jesus Christ is the Son of God, and God the Son, then this incident which introduced the miracle workings of the Son of God and the Son of Man, presents a challenge that, to say the least, is arresting.

We read:

> "And the third day there was a marriage in Cana of Galilee; and the mother of Jesus was there:
> "And both Jesus was called, and his disciples, to the marriage.
> "And when they wanted wine, the mother of Jesus saith unto him, They have no wine.

"Jesus saith unto her, Woman, what have I to do with thee? mine hour is not yet come.

"His mother saith unto the servant, Whatsoever he saith unto you, do it.

"And there were set there six waterpots of stone, after the manner of the purifying of the Jews, containing two or three firkins apiece.

"Jesus saith unto them, Fill the waterpots with water. And they filled them up to the brim.

"And He saith unto them, Draw out now, and bear unto the governor of the feast. And they bare it.

"When the ruler of the feast had tasted the water that was made wine, and knew not whence it was: (but the servants which drew the water knew;) the governor of the feast called the bridegroom,

"And saith unto him, Every man at the beginning doth set forth good wine; and when men have well drunk, then that which is worse: but thou hast kept the good wine until now.

"This beginning of miracles did Jesus in Cana of Galilee, and manifested forth his glory; and his disciples believed on him."

I never tire of asserting that the Bible is a wonderful book. No man knows enough to criticize it, to take it apart, to contradict it, or to use the "King's penknife" in deleting from it that which is supposedly inaccurate and incorrect. From whatever viewpoint the Book is microscopically examined, its beauties increase, its accuracy is attested to and its message becomes crystal clear. The Bible anticipates objections; it foretells the future; it broadcasts on every page an authoritative, "Thus saith the Lord." Whether it be science or history or revelation or life or death or any other thing, whenever this Book touches upon or in any way discusses them, it is as accurate and sure as the daily rising of the sun.

The Holy Spirit evidently anticipated that many books would be written about Jesus of Nazareth and that the fantastic ideas of men would creep into these writings. Therefore, by a simple, brief and seemingly undesigned comment, the Holy Spirit gives the lie to every book that has ever been written about the Person of Jesus during the silent years of His life in Nazareth. We read in the 11th verse, "This *beginning* of miracles did Jesus. . ." All the books that purport to tell of miraculous things which He did in His childhood and adolescence and prior to this wedding feast are pure fabrications. He never wrought a miracle in all those years. He lived in Nazareth unrecognized, but He grew in wisdom and in stature before God and man. Here we have the record of the *first* miracle which He performed. We are told that the miracle was a sign, and through it, He manifested His glory and His disciples believed on Him.

No human being, in presenting a Messiah, would have assumed for a moment that the thing to do to manifest His glory would be, to have Him change water into wine at a wedding feast. As far as a religious character is concerned, a wedding would have been the last place in the world that we would have put a Messiah. As for changing water into wine—it would have been utterly unthinkable. We would have chosen an æsthete and with all the imagination of a Hollywood producer we would have had Him enter the scene by the route that was suggested by *Satan, the first movie producer and operator* (Luke 4:5) when he took our Lord into the Holy City and set Him on a pinnacle of the temple. You will remember he suggested that if He be the Son of God, He should cast Himself down, for immediately upon doing so, the angels would take charge concerning Him, and their hands would have held Him up, lest He should dash His foot against a stone; and the world would have shouted "Hail to the Messiah!" But as the natural mind cannot comprehend spiritual things, so God never follows in the channels of the natural man's thinking. Every detail of our Lord's life was pre-arranged by His Father. Every word that He spoke was given to Him by His Father. He said, "I have not spoken of myself, but the Father which sent me, he gave me a commandment, what I should say, and what I should speak."

Now let's look at the incident. It was on the third day from the time He started to go forth into Galilee, which would be the sixth day since John stood and announced to the multitude, "Behold the Lamb of God, which taketh away the sin of the world." Undoubtedly there were many people at the wedding feast. Strange as it may seem, we have the names or the titles of all the moving and leading participants in the wedding, except the bride. Here was one wedding where the bride was not the chief attraction! In fact, she is not even mentioned. That in itself is noteworthy. In our generation, as soon as the strains of Lohengrin are played, every eye and every mind is possessed of only one picture and one thought: "Here comes the *bride!*" Can it be that the Holy Spirit was teaching us that in *that* day, when the marriage supper of the Lamb shall take place, all eyes will be centered upon the Bridegroom, not the bride. The bride will have been granted robes of fine linen, clean and white, but the chief attraction will be the Lord Jesus Christ, even as He proved to be at the wedding feast in Cana of Galilee.

In this record, the Holy Spirit calls attention to several things and several people. First, we have the mother of Jesus. Second, Jesus Himself. Third, His disciples. Fourth, the sudden discovery that they were without further wine. Then our attention is called to a conversation that ensued between the mother of Jesus and the Lord; then the instructions of His mother to the servants; then the command of our Lord to the servants; the comment of the ruler of the feast; and finally, the bridegroom himself. Did I neglect to suggest the wine that Jesus made?

The Virgin Mary

Let us first consider the mother of Jesus. Hitherto our Lord was subject to Mary His mother, and to Joseph. We neither have the time nor is this the place to enter into a discussion of the events that led up to the birth of our Lord; sufficient to say that in the eyes of many people there was always a cloud over the mother of Jesus. There is no indication however that she at any time rebelled against it, though she well knew that if the world only knew, the cloud of "suspicion" would lift and they would recognize the "Shechinah" cloud of glory, for it was the power of the Almighty that overshadowed her. Dr. G. Campbell Morgan gives expression to a most suggestive thought when he said ". . . that the Virgin Mother went through life under suspicion, because there are some things which cannot be interpreted to common carnal humanity. And now the thought of her heart was,—Oh if only He would show something and prove!" And so the mother of Jesus said unto Him, "They have no wine." But He said unto her, "Woman, what have I to do with thee? mine hour is not yet come." There has been much debate by scholars as to the root meaning of the word translated *woman*. Yet it seems clear that the word means *woman*. That there was rebuke in the answer is also clear, but did He mean disrespect? It is unthinkable. Dr. Harris Gregg is the author of a suggestion that may be the answer to the problem. He suggests that Jesus could have paid Mary no higher compliment than He did when He addressed her, "Woman," for He used the very language of Scripture. It is written in Genesis 3:15 that the seed of the *woman* should bruise the serpent's head. He thereby doubly assured Mary that He was the promised seed and that she was the *woman* of Genesis 3:15. Hitherto there had been the closest human association: now she must step back while He steps forward. From now on, the arena is to be occupied with but two persons, the seed of the woman and the seed of the serpent: Christ and Satan. Stripped of all the "extras," the stage is to be occupied by two personalities only, Christ and antichrist. Men line up with either one or the other. Neutrality is out of all possible consideration here.

The phrase "mine hour is not yet come" is understood as we follow its usage throughout the Gospel of John. We shall not take the time, now, to note each reference to it, but invite you to examine these for yourself. Sufficient to say that "the hour" to which our Lord referred is that one when He was nailed to the cross. It was the hour when He triumphed over the seed of the serpent.

The Chief Wedding Guest

Now look at our Lord Jesus Christ. To some it is a strange thing that He should have attended a wedding; and yet a more careful examination of the Person of Christ would convince all that it was a most appropriate place for Him to have been. Did not our Lord institute marriage, and does not marriage symbolize the perfect union that exists between the Lord and His people? "For this cause shall a man leave his father and mother, and shall be joined unto his wife, and they two shall be one flesh. This is a great mystery: (said the Apostle Paul) but I speak concerning Christ and the church." Evidently our Lord felt perfectly at home at this wedding feast. Indeed, was He not the first to attend a wedding; was He not the first to give away a bride? After the Lord God had made woman from the side of Adam, He brought her unto the man. In Genesis 5:1-2 we read: "This is the book of the generations of Adam. In the day that God created man, in the likeness of God made he him: Male and female created he them; and blessed them, and called their name Adam, in the day when they were created." Dr. Morgan says, "I once heard Dan Crawford reading that chapter at Northfield say 'please note that He called their name Adam, not the Adamses.'"

The Lord's presence did not put a damper on the joy of the wedding in Cana of Galilee. No one seemed to be uncomfortable in His presence. Oh, that men would understand that our God loves them, that Jesus Christ is God and in every sense of the word, the Son of Man as well. He still meets every emergency, whether it be in the field of sorrow or in the realm of joy. It is wonderful to have the Savior with us at a sick bed. It is equally wonderful to have the Lord as the center of the joys of our life.

The Servants and the Wine

Mary was a wise mother. After our Lord's comment to her, she simply told the servants "whatsoever he saith unto you, do." Many have called this, and rightly so, the gospel according to the Virgin Mary. Would God that men would heed her gospel, "Whatsoever he saith unto you, do." Mary's answer infers, Ask no questions, seek no help from me—"Whatsoever he saith unto you, do."

The scene then shifts to the servants and to the waterpots that were set after the manner of the purifying of the Jews. We are told there were six waterpots, each containing two or three firkins apiece. A firkin is about 9 gallons. That would mean there were between 18 and 27 gallons in each waterpot. Multiplied by six, makes a total of between 108 and 162 gallons. Now, say some smart wine merchants and their inebriate sort, What a feast! 108 to 162 gallons of wine after the guests had already well drunk! If these scoffers had known anything about the setting in an Eastern Hebrew home, they would not have found occasion to gloat over the *amount* of water that our Lord turned into wine.

We are specifically told that the waterpots were set *after the manner of the purifying of the Jews*. No guest would have expected a drink of water from those waterpots. The water was there for purifying (or washing) purposes. It would have been an unheard of thing and would have caused a riot if the servants had drawn the water from the waterpots and poured out their contents into glasses, only to have it turn into wine.

The waterpots were undoubtedly empty or nearly empty, because of the washings that had been performed upon the arrival of the guests. So our Lord instructed the servants to fill the waterpots with water. We are told that in obedience they filled them to the brim. These were wonderful servants—they did exactly as they were told. When John the Baptist rebelled against baptizing our Lord, Jesus said, "Suffer it to be so now: for thus it becometh us to fulfill all righteousness." Before men can enjoy the wine of heaven (which is fellowship with God) all righteousness must be fulfilled. These waterpots symbolized that truth. Thus our Lord said to the servants, "Fill the waterpots with water." It was then that He said to the servants, "Draw out now. . ." The use of this same word in the 4th chapter confirms the view that it means going to a well and drawing water. They did not go to the waterpots, they went to the well from which they had previously filled the waterpots.

As the servants poured the water, it changed to the purest wine. No one knows how much wine was made that evening by our Lord.

We know that everyone present knew that a miracle had taken place. The miracle manifested forth our Lord's glory and His disciples were confirmed in their faith in Him.

Ordinarily our Lord takes one year to change water into wine in the fruitful vineyard, as every husbandman knows. But that night it required no time nor even a vine. The spiritual import of the miracle is its greatest message. Our Lord Himself is the vine. Only as we live in Him do we enjoy the wine of heaven. Our Lord begets joy in the hearts and lives of those who trust in Him. It is worthy of note that the first miracle Moses performed after his work began was to turn water into blood—our Lord turned water into wine.

Walk Ten

THE FIRST TEMPLE PURGE

AFTER our Lord had performed His first miracle, which revealed His glory, we learn that He went down to Capernaum. His company of disciples was beginning to show some growth. We read that He "and his mother, and his brethren, and his disciples" went to Capernaum, and there they continued "not many days." Our Lord had already gathered five disciples about Him: Andrew, Peter, Philip, Nathanael and John. The influence which our Lord exercised over His disciples was so strong that each gave up his business and his former associates. They broke every tie that linked them to the past. Now that they had cast in their lot with the Lord Jesus, there was no such thing as turning back. I am afraid that we do not appreciate, or value, nor even understand the command of our Lord "Follow Me." Embracing Christ meant a radical change in the lives of His disciples; so radical that their whole outlook on life, their walk in life, and their relationship to life were entirely changed. Incidentally, that's exactly what conversion means. When a man confesses Christ, that confession should involve a definite break with the old life. If we know who our Lord Jesus really is, there would never be a question as to what our relationship should be to former ties.

After spending a little time in Capernaum, our Lord continued His journey and went up to Jerusalem. Here is the divine record:

> "And the Jews' passover was at hand, and Jesus went up to Jerusalem,
> "And found in the temple those that sold oxen and sheep and doves, and the changers of money sitting:
> "And when he had made a scourge of small cords, he drove them all out of the temple, and the sheep, and the oxen; and poured out the changers' money, and overthrew the tables;
> "And said unto them that sold doves, Take these things hence; make not my Father's house an house of merchandise.
> "And his disciples remembered that it was written, The zeal of thine house hath eaten me up.
> "Then answered the Jews and said unto him, What sign shewest thou unto us, seeing that thou doest these things?
> "Jesus answered and said unto them, Destroy this temple, and in three days I will raise it up.
> "Then said the Jews, Forty and six years was this temple in building, and wilt thou rear it up in three days?
> "But he spake of the temple of his body.
> "When therefore he was risen from the dead, his disciples remembered that he had said this unto them; and they believed the scripture, and the word which Jesus had said."

The portion records our Lord's first purification of the temple at Jerusalem. It was not long before that same crowd of thieves returned to the temple. Reformation in government usually lasts just about as long as reformation in an individual's life and as reformation in the temple procedure proved to last. The human

THE GOSPEL OF JOHN — CHAPTER II, VERSES 13-22   71

heart is so sinful that it would take eternal vigilance to prevent a recurrence of a bad situation.

But I must add something, which a few years ago would not have been necessary, but present circumstances have made it imperative as we are living in a day when the vilest emotions of the human breast are manifested in hatred and persecution that matches, if not surpasses, anything that this world has known in bygone days. You will note we read in verse 13, *"the Jews'* passover was at hand . . ." Verse 18: "Then answered *the Jews* and said unto him . . ." Verse 20: "Then said *the Jews* . . ." This is a divine record; therefore it cannot be purged. In each of these instances, as in the majority of occasions where the term is used in the Gospel of John, it was not the *people* to whom the writer referred; it was the religious *leaders* of the people. The people gladly heard our Lord. The common people crowded about Him. Their leaders feared to lay hands upon our Lord because the common people held Him in such high esteem. We should clearly differentiate between the leaders of a people and the people themselves. While leaders are expected to represent the people, innumerable instances can be gathered from history, contemporary as well as ancient, to prove that their leaders were not in sympathy with the people nor the people in sympathy with their leaders.

There was a hierarchy in Israel at that time which debauched the sanctuary and besmirched the worship of Jehovah by a traffic in sheep and oxen, thus making the temple, instead of a house of worship, a den of thieves. It was for that reason our Lord walked into the temple, unobtrusively, and without any blaring of trumpets, drove out the sheep and the oxen and them that sold them, and overturned the tables of the money changers. And, in justification of His purge He said: "Take these things hence; make not my Father's house an house of merchandise."

THE CHURCH OF THE BINGO

Now let's say something to Christians—I mean Christendom. Many people read the record of the Gospels and develop a spirit of pharisaical pride, saying, We do not sell oxen and sheep and doves in our temples, nor do we have money changers in our sanctuaries. Indeed? Let's see. The other day I was driving along a road when I saw a huge electric sign containing one word

"Bingo." Of course it was a church (although it is a misnomer to call it that). Do you think for one moment if our Lord were here physically, He would do differently in such "churches" than He did when He visited the temple? Do you think He would not turn over the tables and drive out of the church those who have made it a center for gambling? Unregenerate man has never touched any divine instrument for worship without defiling the instrument.

Our Lord's attitude toward the temple is interesting. When He entered the first time He spoke of it as His "Father's house." It still was. When He walked out of it the last time, He said to the religious leaders of the people, "*your* house is left unto you desolate." Many a building erected for the worship of the Lord, where the Gospel of the grace of God was preached in the power of God's Holy Spirit, is now used for any and every other purpose but that for which it was built. Now do not take refuge behind the fact that *your* church does not have a Bingo party. How about cake sales, and suppers, and bazaars, and bridge parties—anything to raise money except in the manner in which the Holy Spirit has directed that the work of the Lord should be supported.

Now let's look at exactly what happened. Here was a high day in Israel's history. The passover was about to be celebrated. The leaders of the people had so mutilated it that it had ceased to be a feast of the Lord. That was a fearful state of affairs. A multitude of people were on their way to Jerusalem. There was only one place to worship, and that was in the temple. Sacrifices had to be offered; individuals had to be redeemed; and the only money acceptable within the grounds of the temple, was temple money. Those who lived outside the environs of Jerusalem had to change their money in order to have the proper coins for redemption purposes. Needless to say, the money changers charged a good commission, in fact, all that the traffic would bear! The "district leaders" were well taken care of so that the money changers proceeded unmolested in their nefarious task. It is amazing what kind of a God some people think the Lord is! We act as if He were a politician, and that He could be appeased by money or offerings or services. It is repellent to an honest man to suggest that God can be bought! And yet, multitudes of so-called professing Christians act as if that were not only possible, but absolutely necessary.

It is a matter of passing interest to know that this very temple was destroyed by the Romans under Titus about forty years after our Lord had attempted to purge it. The Scripture says, "My spirit shall not always strive with man . . ." God gives man an opportunity to repent. He sends warnings and visitations. When these are not heeded, there is nothing left for God but to exercise Himself in judgment.

We should also take notice of the particular place where our Lord found this traffic in oxen and sheep and money changing. Certainly it was not in the Sanctuary. Even those leaders had that much sense of propriety! The word translated *temple* in John 2:14, where we learn that Jesus found in the temple those that sold oxen, etc., is not the word for the sanctuary. It is a word that describes "the court of the Gentiles within the temple precinct." In the eyes of God, that part was as important and holy as the Holy of Holies. "It was always God's intention that through Israel, blessing should come upon all the nations." The leaders on this occasion had lost sight of that ministry and had converted the court of the Gentiles into a commercial mart. When our Lord came into the court and noticed the desecration, He made a scourge of small cords and with burning zeal He drove them all out of the temple and poured out the changers' money and overthrew the tables. Remember our Lord then was only a young man, thirty years of age. This part of the temple was crowded with animals and peoples. Yet the Lord drove out the animals, cleared the precinct of the money changers and poured out the money to the floor. Our Lord did that single-handed, with the use of a scourge made of small cords. He did not need *storm troopers* nor the aid of a single bodyguard. Sinners become cowards in the presence of the holy God about to exercise His righteous zeal.

It was after the purge had taken place that the religious rulers began to speak, but not until then. For the moment they were silenced. They knew that the traffic they had sanctioned was an unholy one. For it they had no defense. But, as New York's alert District Attorney recently remarked in his address to the jury in the now famous Hines case, "when a man has no defense, he attacks the Prosecutor." So these men began an attack against the zealous prophet of Nazareth. It, of course, took them a little time to compose themselves, but when they did, they said to Him,

"What sign shewest *thou* unto *us,* seeing that thou doest these things?" To this our Lord answered—"Destroy this temple . . ." and now He used an entirely different word. He used the word meaning *sanctuary.* "Destroy this sanctuary, and in three days I will raise it up." Of course our Lord spoke in a parable. And, the parable proved to be an enigma to them; in fact, it was an enigma to the disciples also. It was not until after His resurrection that they understood Him. So the leaders said: Absurd! Forty and six years was this temple in building and wilt thou rear it up in three days?—There is no evidence that our Lord answered their second foolish question.

The Church in Thy House

Now then, let's make some spiritual applications, from this event in the ministry of Christ, which will be of help in our individual lives. Christendom speaks of a building set apart for worship and preaching as a church. No man should take exception to that, of course; but it is well to bear in mind that the New Testament never speaks of a *building* as a church. It sometimes speaks of "the church that is in their house" as for instance in 1st Corinthians 16:19 Paul wrote: ". . . Aquila and Priscilla salute you much in the Lord, with the church that is in their house." Thus the New Testament clearly distinguishes between a house and a church. The church which gathered in the house of Aquila and Priscilla was a company of people. The word *church* in the Greek means "called out ones." Brick and mortar do not make a church. We call it that, but strictly speaking it is the individual believers as they come together in the name of the Lord who are collectively referred to, in the Scriptures as "the church."

Our Lord, at the time of this purification of the temple, made an application of the word *temple* which is of interest. The rulers thought He was speaking of Herod's temple, which was a magnificent and awe-inspiring structure; when, in fact, He was speaking of His own body.

Now let me address specifically you who have confessed Jesus Christ as your Savior. In 1st Corinthians 6:19 Paul wrote to those recently converted Christians, "What? know ye not that your body is the temple of the Holy Spirit which is in you, which ye have of God . . ." And again in his second letter, chapter 6 verse 16, he wrote, ". . . ye are the temple of the living God." Therefore the body of every individual who has received Christ becomes the temple of God. On the authority of the Word of God, Jesus Christ the risen Lord dwells in a believer's body. What makes his body a sanctuary? The answer is simple—the presence of God. The religious leaders in our Lord's day would never have countenanced any commercial traffic in the sanctuary proper. They knew that it was the holy place because there God met the representative of His people. The presence of God made it the sanctuary. Now then, we who have confessed Jesus Christ as our Savior, we have Christ in us. He lives within our breasts; our bodies therefore have become the temples of the Holy Spirit. He lives in us by His Spirit. Therefore, He makes these bodies of ours sanctuaries.

Glorifying God in Our Body

The Pharisees on this occasion made the mistake of assuming that God was less interested in the outer court than He was in the sanctuary proper. There are multitudes of Christians who believe the same, or at least, practice that same principle in their lives. Oh yes, Christ is the center of the life on the Lord's Day, when we gather together with other people of like mind and have fellowship with them in the Lord and worship Him. But do we ever stop to seriously think that these hands of ours, these eyes, these feet, and every part of our body becomes a holy instrument seven days each week by virtue of the presence of Jesus Christ in our lives? What do we do with our hands, our eyes, our feet? Do we permit them to become defiled by sinful traffic of one sort or another? Have we overlooked the fact that every part of our being should be holy, seeing that every part is sanctified by the presence of the Holy Spirit within our hearts? The Bible urges us, as we are bought with a price, to glorify God in our body and in our spirit which are God's. The Lord Jesus by His Spirit has come in to make our heart His dwelling-place. As we cannot go anywhere in this world without our heart, therefore, we must take Him everywhere we go.

If Christians understood this great fact and believed it, we would have a revival in this country overnight, and the world would wonder what had happened to Christians. The reason this world is not much concerned about Christians is due to the fact that they live like the world. If Christians walked as they ought to walk, they would stir up a mighty spiritual awakening. Men and women everywhere would want to partake of the same life of which we have partaken, the life of the risen Lord.

I have met Christians who are unhappy—they lack a joyous countenance. You never see them at a prayer meeting. They have no ringing testimony. Sometimes I have been asked by people of this type, "What is wrong with my Christian experience?" The answer is found in this portion of Scripture, particularly in our Lord's words. Did you ever stop to consider that a home is the expression of unity between two people? You have never heard of a happy home where a wife and husband were not on speaking terms. Neither have you ever known of a Christian being happy except he is in fellowship and communion with the Lord, and where every member of his body functions as a unity, expressing the fact that his body is the temple of God. Our Lord said, "make not my Father's house an house of merchandise." Neither should we lend our bodies to any purpose that does not glorify God.

The thing that our Lord did, and the word which He spoke on that day, angered and bewildered His enemies, but confirmed the faith of His disciples; not only their faith in the Lord, but also their faith in the Word of God. Jesus Christ cuts across the life of every individual who has ever heard about Him; what He has done and what He has said. Our Lord either bewilders and angers a man or He confirms him in his faith in Him and in the Scriptures.

Walk Eleven

"YE MUST BE BORN AGAIN"

PROFESSOR Stalker has given expression to an arresting fact when he said, "Jesus never had a house of His own to which He could invite people." Yet in our Walks with our Lord, as we come to the 3rd chapter of St. John's Gospel, we discover that here was a place where our Lord could give an interview to a seeking soul. It was a night scene, one of the few in the Gospels in which our Lord was found in company with another, for almost invariably our Lord was alone in the night seasons. It would be a fascinating study to consider the night life of Jesus.

The setting of this chapter is simply exquisite. It was the Passover season. Our Lord was in Jerusalem. It was His first Passover visit to the city since He began His public ministry. It was the spring season of the year. It must have been a balmy night. Later that evening our Lord made use of a gentle breeze that was stirring to illustrate a deep spiritual truth. At Jerusalem, where the crowds gathered to celebrate and commemorate the Passover, our Lord wrought many signs. As a result, "many believed in his name, when they saw the miracles which he did. But Jesus did not commit himself unto them . . ." It is to be regretted that our translators have given us two English words to express the same Greek word. We read "many *believed* in his name" and again, "Jesus did not *commit* himself unto them." The words *believe* and *commit* are identical in the Greek, so that we might safely say "many believed in his name when they saw the miracles which he did. But Jesus did not believe in them." Or "many trusted in his name . . . but Jesus did not trust himself unto them."

How and What to Believe

That leads us to an important subject. How should a man believe or what should he believe? Someone has suggested that there are more than 57 varieties of professing Christians. One can hardly blame an unsaved man for wondering whom and what he is to believe. The New Testament does not suggest or even intimate that one is saved by *joining* a church, or that it is essential that one join the right church in order to be saved. Even in the Apostle's day disintegration had already manifested itself so that some said they were of Paul, some of Peter, and others of Apollos, and some, refusing to own the name of an Apostle, suggested that they were of Christ. The cardinal fact of the Christian faith is Christ Himself; and whether a man spends eternity with the Lord or spends it in hell depends on his relationship to Christ. It is not sufficient that he merely believes in His name: there is more to it than that—it depends upon the *kind* of faith he possesses. Here were people of whom the Scripture witnessed that they believed in His name when they saw the miracles which He did. But our Lord had no confidence in them, therefore He did not commit Himself unto them. Thus it is possible to believe in His name and yet have no relationship with Him.

You say, Who then can be saved? That's a good question. We will observe the answer before we complete our consideration of this portion of Scripture. Note that these people did not believe in Christ, they merely believed in *His name*. They were attracted to Him by the miracles which He wrought. By the way, notice something else. The Scripture says, they "believed in his name, when they *saw* the miracles . . ." Today we have some who do not believe that our Lord performed miracles—and yet they call themselves Christians! Here was a group of people who believed that He performed miracles; they saw them. But even the seeing of miracles did not beget saving faith in their hearts.

These people were enamored with our Lord. They were ready to acknowledge His Kingship and His Messiahship, but our Lord knew what was in them. He knew how shallow was their faith. Thus He did not have faith in them nor did He commit Himself unto them.

We read in the Scriptures that "faith cometh by hearing, and hearing by the word of God." Faith cannot be born any other way. Men are not saved by touching stories or by having their emotions moved or by seeing a display of the miraculous. Men are saved because they hear the voice of the Son of God; and hearing, they believe.

Note one further statement concerning our Lord which appears in the last verses of the 2nd chapter. Not only did Jesus refuse to commit Himself unto them because He knew men, but what's more, He "needed not that any should testify of man: for he knew what was *in* man."

A Teacher Come From God?

But there was a man, a Pharisee named Nicodemus, a ruler of the Jews, to whom our Lord did commit Himself. This man, just as all the others, had seen the miracles which our Lord did. So he said to our Lord, "Rabbi, we know that thou art a teacher come from God: for no man can do these miracles that thou doest, except God be with him."

Let's look at this man for a moment. We know something of his character, a little of his position, and considerable of his determination. He was not satisfied to be one of the mob; therefore he came to our Lord by night. Whether any of the disciples were present, I do not know: probably they were. Our Lord did not have a house into which He could invite Nicodemus, but He must have had some place where He could be found. He is always where the seeking sinner is to be found. You never have to go far if you are really seeking. This man *came*. He *came to Jesus*. He came *alone*. He did not even require a disciple to introduce him. You do not have to go to anybody; you may go directly to Christ even as did this man. No one can save but Christ.

Now notice the compliment Nicodemus paid our Lord. He said, "we know that thou art a teacher come from God: for no man can do these miracles that thou doest, except God be with him." Incidentally that's the extent of the ability of the human heart to comprehend Christ. It is not within the scope of the intellect to comprehend Jesus Christ as the Son of God. The best that can be said for Him from the humanist viewpoint is that He was a teacher come from God and that God was with Him.

We are living in a day of shallow thinking and superficial decisions. If Nicodemus lived today he would be accepted for church membership in ninety-nine out of a hundred churches. Indeed, you would probably find him in the ministry. But our Lord told him he had to be born again; that he was both blind and spiritually lame. Nicodemus had no life, even though he did say some complimentary things about Jesus Christ. As Nicodemus examined our Lord, he concluded first, that He was a teacher; second, that He was a teacher come from God; third, that His miracles evidenced His commission; and finally, that it was impossible to conceive of a man doing the things that our Lord did except God be with him. A man did say *all* of these things about Christ—and still he was dead in trespasses and sins. Nicodemus had faith in Christ but not the kind of faith that is the gift of God.

Some men have suggested that this is just a wrangle about words for it appears to them that there is only a shade of difference between the language of a true believer and that of a mere professor. The cross which will forever lighten the glory, casts a shadow over the eternal abode of the wicked dead. The Person of Jesus Christ is a savour of life unto life to them that believe, but He is also a savour of death unto death to those who do not believe. The cross not only manifested the love and righteousness of God, but there the wrath of God was revealed from heaven against all who hold down the truth in unrighteousness. In this particular case, the difference between the true and the false was evidenced by the use of a single pronoun. Nicodemus said to Christ, God is *with you*. The Bible says that in Christ, God is *with us*. Nicodemus believed that God was with Christ, but as he was spiritually blind he could not see that God was with *him*, standing right by his side in the Person of Jesus Christ, because Jesus Christ is God. When a man perceives that revelation, he falls down before our Lord as Thomas did and confesses, "My Lord and my God."

The Imperative of the Christ

I trust I have made clear the tremendous difference between admiring Jesus and worshipping Him. Incidentally, that's the difference between a merely religious person and a saved man. Nicodemus was a remarkable character. No man could lift a finger of accusation against him. He was a rich man, but he did not gain his possessions through questionable means. He was a highly respected and respectable man. Yet the first thing our Lord said to him was this: "Verily, verily, I say unto thee, Except a man be born again, he cannot see the kingdom of God." These are the words of our Lord. They are so singularly plain that an attempt

The Gospel of John — Chapter III, Verses 1-15

to expound them beclouds them. Our Lord said "Except"—Nicodemus said "How?" Our Lord said "Must"—Nicodemus still said "How?"

There is a story told of Dr. Reuben A. Torrey, one of the great evangelists of the past generation. One day he was preaching in Chicago for another pastor. At the close of the service, the minister came to him and said, "I have a young man in my congregation who wishes to be a minister. I would like you to have a talk with him." So he brought the young man to Dr. Torrey. The young fellow proved to have one of the cleanest, finest, most open faces Dr. Torrey had ever seen. He looked into the face of that young man and said, "Your pastor says you wish to enter the ministry." "Yes, I do," was the reply. "Well," said Dr. Torrey, "let me ask you a question. Are you a Christian?" "Of course I am," the young man answered, "I was brought up a Christian and I am not going back on the training of my parents." Dr. Torrey went to the 3rd chapter of John's Gospel for his response to this, as he said, "Have you been born again?" The young man answered "What?" Dr. Torrey repeated, "I said, Have you been born again? God says, Except a man be born again, he cannot see the kingdom of God. Have you ever been born again?" The young man said, "I do not know what you are talking about. I have never heard of that in all my life." To which Dr. Torrey answered, "My friend, see here, do you know that you have committed the greatest sin a man can commit?" The young fellow answered, "I never did in my life. You do not understand me. I have been very carefully reared. My life has been a most exemplary one. I never committed the greatest sin a man can commit, never." Dr. Torrey asked him, "What do you think is the greatest sin a man can commit?" The young fellow replied, "Why, murder of course." To this Dr. Torrey answered, "You are greatly mistaken." Then he took the young man to the fountain source of truth, our Lord Jesus Christ. He opened his Bible to the 22nd chapter of St. Matthew's Gospel and asked him to read the 37th and 38th verses. He read aloud, "Jesus said unto him, Thou shalt love the Lord thy God with all thy heart, and with all thy soul, and with all thy mind. This is the first and great commandment." Dr. Torrey asked, "Which commandment is that?" The young man responded, "The first and great commandment." Dr. Torrey asked, "If this is the first and great commandment, what is the first and great sin?" The young man immediately answered, "Not to keep this commandment." Of course the question followed, "Have you kept it? Have you put God first in everything?" He answered, "No." Then said Dr. Torrey, "On the words of our Lord Jesus Christ, you have broken the first and greatest commandment and you have been guilty of the greatest sin." The young man saw and acknowledged it and submitted to the statement of God, and said "I never saw that before in all my life." Neither did Nicodemus. He was a great character. He was a Pharisee; he was taught in the Word of God, or he thought he was, and yet he did not know the first principles of the Scripture. Our Lord said to him, "Art thou a master of Israel, and knowest not these things?" What things? The fact that a man must be born again if he is to see or enter the kingdom of God.

Who Need New Birth?

Some people assume that the place to preach this type of message is in a mission, where men are dirty and unclean and unkempt and are wallowing in the mire of sin. Oh, yes, such a man needs to be born again, but our Lord never told a person of that type "Ye must be born again" because that kind of man would not need to be told it, he knows it already. But our Lord told it to a man who *did not know* it; if you please, He told it to a Fifth Avenue churchman. He told it to one of the finest members of the most religious group of His day. He told it to that man because he needed to be told. It is imperative that a man be born again. ". . . flesh and blood cannot inherit the kingdom of God." "That which is born of the flesh is flesh; and that which is born of the Spirit is spirit."

We have all been born of the flesh. Some men claim to have blue blood in their veins, most of us have red blood in our veins, but even if one had all the colors of the rainbow, the blood would still be sinful blood. ". . . all have sinned, and come short of the glory of God." Not a single, solitary person is exempt from the judgment of God. What then? "Ye must be born again." Someone once approached Spurgeon and said to him, "Mr. Spurgeon, why do you so frequently preach on the subject, Ye must be born again?" And the great English preacher responded, "Because, 'Ye *must* be born again.'" Our Lord said it. When you hear the Son of God give expression to an imperative, then it is imperative that you be born again.

How is a man born again? In the 1st chapter of this Gospel we read, "He (Jesus Christ) came unto his own, and his own (according to the flesh, that is Israel) received him not. But as many as received him, to them gave he the authority to become the children of God, even to them that believe on his name: Which were born, not of blood, nor of the will of the flesh, nor of the will of man, but of God." A man is born of God when he hears and believes the Word of God. Thus it is written, "Being born again, not of corruptible seed, but of incorruptible, by the word of God, which liveth and abideth for ever."

Walk Twelve

SELF-MADE, UN-MADE, NEW-MADE

WE have now walked with our Lord to Jerusalem, and there "listened in" on an interview which He extended to Nicodemus, who was a Pharisee and a ruler of the Jews. We noticed the alertness of our Lord in using illustrative material to bring home a spiritual truth. We learned that Nicodemus was a moral character; even a religious man. He had carefully weighed the ministry of Christ up to that hour and concluded that He was a teacher sent from God. He acknowledged that our Lord was a worker of miracles. He inferred, if he did not definitely state, that these views were representative of the entire body of men who composed the Sanhedrin, for he used the plural pronoun, "*we* know," rather than "*I* know."

To this compliment our Lord answered, "Verily, verily, I say unto thee, Except a man be born again, he cannot see the kingdom of God." That completely bewildered Nicodemus so that he replied, "How can a man be born when he is old? can he enter the second time into his mother's womb, and be born?" To this our Lord responded, "Verily, verily, I say unto thee, Except a man be born of water and of the Spirit, he *cannot* enter into the kingdom of God. That which is born of the flesh is flesh; and that which is born of the Spirit is spirit." But our Lord continued without interruption, "Marvel not that I said unto thee, Ye must be born again. The wind bloweth where it listeth . . ." and here our Lord made use of a gentle breeze to illustrate a deep spiritual truth. "The wind bloweth where it *listeth*, and thou *hearest* the *sound* thereof, but canst not tell whence it cometh, and whither it goeth: *so* is every one that is born of the Spirit."

The words of our Lord are magnificent! They could only have been uttered by one who is the Son of God. His choice of language and the care He exercised in speech beget a real thrill in a believing heart. Notice an example of this in the 8th verse of this 3rd chapter. "The wind *bloweth* where it *listeth,* and thou *hearest* the *sound* thereof, but canst not *tell whence* it cometh, and *whither* it goeth . . ." This was not a rushing mighty wind that a man felt. Nicodemus did not feel it. He was only conscious of it, probably from the rustling of the leaves. He heard it—that's all, ". . . thou *hearest* the *sound* thereof, but canst not tell whence it cometh, and whither it goeth." And our Lord added significantly, *"so is every one* that is *born* of the *Spirit."*

If we would only recognize this truth, we would save ourselves many heartaches and misunderstandings; neither would we become involved with that which is contrary to the truth of God. As one examines the New Testament, he appreciates the unique ministry of the Holy Spirit. It is no surprise to such a one that all kinds of false "isms" have developed around the Holy Spirit. There are those so-called "Second Blessing" people and "Holy Rollers" and "Four-Square Gospel" preachers and what not, all claiming to have a "corner" on the ministry of the Holy Spirit. But, alas, they have entirely lost sight of the significance and character of His ministry. I would like to emphasize, that our Lord said "thou *hearest* the *sound* thereof." There is no feeling here. I repeat, it is not a rushing mighty wind as, for example, that which was experienced on the day of Pentecost, but which has never been repeated nor experienced since Pentecost. Men are not *born* again in any other manner than that which our Lord outlined in this 3rd chapter of John's Gospel. He said "so is *every one* that is born of the Spirit." Men to be saved must hear the *voice* of the Son of God. The Spirit speaks through the Word of God. We hear; it is not a question of feeling; we hear, and as a result of the hearing, we are born by the Spirit of God.

The Kingdom

But let us examine this interview more closely. Previously we considered the *why*, or the *reason* for the new birth. I shall have one or two more things to say on that score, but in this message I want specifically to consider the *how*, or the *means* of the new birth.

Dr. A. C. Gaebelein, whose ministry has been greatly blessed of the Lord for more than half a century, has written an excellent expository volume on this Gospel. In his comments on this 3rd chapter he draws attention to a most interesting fact which many Gospel preachers have overlooked. He raised the question, To what kingdom was the Lord referring when He said to Nicodemus, "Except a man be born again, he cannot see the *kingdom* of God"? Most of us assume that the "kingdom" is a synonymous term for the church of Jesus Christ, but it ought to be self-evident that it could not be, for the church had not yet been formed, indeed our Lord had not mentioned the subject up to this time.

Nicodemus raised no question regarding *the kingdom* of God. He raised a question as to how one could *enter* the kingdom of God. Nicodemus knew of only one kingdom, the kingdom of which the Old Testament Scriptures foretold, the kingdom which the God of heaven should establish on the earth. Nicodemus was bewildered when our Lord said that entrance into that kingdom could be gained only by new birth. Of course it is true also in respect to the church and to what is taking place today. It is likewise true regarding that day when the kingdom shall actually be established on the earth.

But let me make more clear the meaning of the "new birth." When our Lord said, "Except a man be born again, he cannot see the kingdom of God" the word *again* which He used might better have been translated *above*. Thus what our Lord actually said was, "Except a man be born *from above*, he cannot see the kingdom of God." Nicodemus correctly assumed that this was a second birth but he was bewildered as to the manner in which it would find its genesis. So he asked, ". . . can a man be born when he is old? can he enter the second time into his mother's womb, and be born?"

But if that were so, the man would be no different. He might be a little wiser, he might also benefit morally, but he would not be any different spiritually, for he would still be born after the flesh, and the Scripture is clear that ". . they that are in the flesh cannot please God."

A man may be the most respected citizen of the village, or town, or city in which he lives, he may even have his name on the church roll, he may subscribe to every worthwhile effort that seeks to alleviate the sufferings of mankind, he may have a good disposition, he may be a splendid man to live with, his wife and children may reverence the very thought of him, but unless he has been born from above, all his culture and character is of no value when it comes to spiritual matters, for, said our Lord, "That which is born of the flesh is flesh; and that which is born of the Spirit is spirit." A man must be born from above through the instrumentality of the Spirit of God.

Entrance into the kingdom of which Nicodemus knew is also to be gained only on this basis. Israel is to enter into the kingdom not primarily by virtue of the first birth, nor altogether because they are the children of Abraham according to the flesh, but because they have been born from above. In other words, Israel is yet to experience the new birth before she enters into the kingdom. She will experience exactly that which Saul of Tarsus experienced on the road to Damascus. She will be born in a day, but she will be born from above, by the revelation of the risen Lord as He returns in His glory.

Nicodemus was a self-made man, a cultured, moral, self-righteous man. But there are no self-made men in heaven, neither are there any re-made men in heaven. It will do no good to *re-form* or *re-patch* a life. God is not in the business of *re-making* lives. He does not take an old garment and seek to make it over again. Only *new-made* men are in heaven. But before a man can be new-made he must be *un-made*. That is exactly what our Lord did to Nicodemus. He un-made him, He stripped him, morally and spiritually, and only then did Nicodemus see his helplessness even to understand the simplest things of God. Before a man is alive unto righteousness he must be dead to sin, as the Apostle Peter put it in 1st Peter 2:24: "Who his own self bare our sins in his own body on the tree, that we, being dead to sins, should live unto righteousness . . ."

WATER AND SPIRIT

Now let us look at the *means* which our Lord employs to bring about this second or new birth. Our Lord said, "Except a man be born of water and of the Spirit, he cannot enter into the kingdom of God." Here again men have stumbled over the words of our Lord and read into them what cannot be found there. Men have assumed that this is a religious rite, that it refers to baptism, or christening, or some other religious ceremony, whether in childhood, adolescence, or maturity. But we would be spared much if we would allow the Word of God to be its own commentary.

The Word of God never contradicts itself: man's theology frequently does. There can be no question as to what our Lord meant by the use of the word *Spirit* for He immediately added ". . . that which is born of the *Spirit* is spirit." There can be no question that the Spirit is the Holy Spirit. That is amply attested through the length and breadth of Scripture. What could He have meant by the use of the word *water*? Did He mean baptismal *waters*? Well, let's look at what the Bible says! First, let us listen to St. Peter. He is a good man to consult, particularly as many believe that he was the leader among the twelve. At least he occupied a unique position in that company. He was a member of the inner circle. Peter, James and John composed that group. Whether he was ever exalted over the others is a serious question. But let's listen to what the Apostle Peter had to say in his first letter, Chapter 1, verse 23, "Being born again, not of corruptible seed . . ." What's that? "not of corruptible seed," that means the flesh. No, Nicodemus, this new birth is not brought about through the natural method, it is not after the flesh, it is not of corruptible seed. St. Peter said it is "of incorruptible." Then he explained, "by the word of God, which liveth and abideth for ever." The two instrumentalities therefore are the Word of God and the Spirit of God. But our Lord said *water*! Did He mean the Word of God? St. Peter said He meant the Word of God.

Now look at another passage of Scripture. Let us look at what the Apostle Paul had to say. St. Paul was the Apostle to the Gentiles and probably did the most effective piece of Christian work that has ever been done in this world. Listen to his word from the 5th chapter of Ephesians, verses 25 and 26: ". . . Christ also loved the church, and gave himself for it; That he might sanctify and cleanse it with the washing of water . . ." There we have water, and we are told that the cleansing is through the water. But let's not stop there—Paul did not, nor did he even use a comma, but continued and said "with the washing of water *by the word*." There we learn that *water* symbolizes the Word of God. We thus have the testimony of St. Peter that a man is born again of the incorruptible Word of God and we have the testimony of St. Paul that water is one of the symbols of the Word of God, and so used because of its cleansing power. There is nothing in the world except the precious blood of Jesus Christ that can cleanse like the Word of God.

"As Moses . . . Even So Must"

But let us look a little further. Nicodemus was still bewildered. One can almost see him throwing up his hands and in despair saying, "How can these things be?" Our Lord rebuked him and said, "Art thou a master of Israel, and knowest not these things?" It is shocking to see a man who is a leader in the religious world who does not know the first principles of Scripture. Nicodemus may have been the first of such, but he certainly was not the last. Our Lord continued and said, "We speak that we do know, and testify that we have seen; and ye receive not our witness. If I have told you earthly things, and ye believe not, how shall ye believe, if I tell you of heavenly things?" The new birth is therefore one of the simplest things, comparatively speaking. It is just the first thing, the elementary thing. But our Lord continued and said, "And no man hath ascended up to heaven, but he that came down from heaven, even the Son of man which is in heaven." There is not a person in the world who can understand that statement unless he believes on the Lord Jesus Christ. It is seemingly the worst contradiction that could be imagined, but it is a beautiful harmony when we recognize that the speaker is God the Son, as well as the Son of God. It was here that our Lord answered Nicodemus' question, "How?" ". . . as Moses lifted up the serpent in the wilderness, even so must the Son of man be lifted up: That whosoever believeth in him should not perish, but have eternal life."

The instruments that are used in bringing about this new birth from above are the Word of God and the Spirit of God. They are the *instruments,* the *how* of it. But the basis of it all, said our Lord, was something that would occur in His life. Our Lord could not have better expressed this than in the language He chose and in the illustration He used. He went deep into the Old Testament, to a portion of Scripture that is absolutely impossible to understand apart from this reference to it by our Lord. If the 14th verse of the 3rd chapter of the Gospel of John were eliminated from the Bible, we would have one unanswerable difficulty that no man could satisfactorily explain, a difficulty that would be extremely perplexing; but it is now beautifully solved.

In the Old Testament we learn of a strange commandment of God. The children of Israel had rebelled against Him. He sent judgment amongst them; poisonous, fiery serpents had bitten many of them. Many had died and others were desperately ill. The people, finally repentant, begged Moses to intercede for them. Moses went into the presence of God and from Him received the panacea for the serpent bites. God said to Moses, Put up a pole in the wilderness, then get someone who is an artificer in brass and have him make the figure of a serpent out of brass. Have him hang this serpent around about the pole. Then tell the children of Israel, that if they will simply look at the brazen serpent hanging on the pole, they will be immediately healed of their disease and the judgment of God will be removed. There was life for a look at that brazen serpent. It is not to be wondered at that later the pole and the brazen serpent became a stumbling-block. Men love to hold on to something tangible. They are not satisfied with spiritual things. They want to touch and feel something. They even want to *"act"* religious. That brazen serpent became a source of difficulty to the children of Israel. They idolized it. Thus the instrument that had at one time brought healing, now was a curse to them and brought judgment. Nicodemus never understood that portion of the Old Testament; neither did any other ruler of Israel. No one knew the significance of it until our Lord, addressing Nicodemus, seemed to say, Do you remember that incident? Moses lifted up the serpent in the wilderness not only for the purpose of healing, but in order to illustrate exactly what would happen to Me, the Son of man; and it will happen to the Son of man "that whosoever believeth in him should not perish, but have eternal life."

Even today, this same tendency upon the part of man to want something tangible is evident. The cross which was the instrument upon which our Lord Jesus Christ made atonement for sin and stayed the judgment of God, today is also a stumbling-block to thousands who *idolize* a cross but lose sight of the Christ of the cross. Even a cross, sir, may bar one from heaven. It is not the cross that saves, it is the Christ of the cross.

Notice that the molten brass was made in the form of a serpent. Christ said that what happened to that serpent would happen to Him. He predicted therefore that He would die on a tree; that He would hang between heaven and earth; and that He would be identified with a serpent. Sin entered the world through a serpent. Christ was made sin in order to take sin out of the world. He became sin for us, that we in Him might be made the righteousness of God. Calvary was a real transaction. The new birth could only be experienced on the foundational transaction of Calvary. It is the only basis on which any one will ever enter into the kingdom of God. Is it any wonder that Jesus Christ said, "Ye must be born again"?

WALK THIRTEEN

THE GREATEST VERSE IN THE BIBLE
JOHN 3:16—PART ONE

ONE feels justified in stating that without controversy John 3:16 is the greatest verse in the Bible; certainly it is the best known. It contains twenty-five words, each of which is a gem. While I do not believe that the words of our Lord are to be considered more inspired than the writings of the Apostles in the canon of Scripture (they are equally inspired) nevertheless I disagree with those who suggest that the words of the 16th verse of this 3rd chapter are not the words of our Lord but rather the words of John the evangelist. Some people have sought to get from under the overpowering logic of this verse, by suggesting that Christ did not utter it. But such great scholars as Meyer, Lange, Henry Alford and Godet, emphatically deny this. It is an integral part of the interview which our Lord had with Nicodemus.

Again and again I am impressed with the words of my friend, Mr. Tharp, who suggested that I take a walk with our Lord through this Gospel, to observe that our Lord did His most effective work with individuals. Jesus Christ preached to crowds. Men hung on every word He spoke; but Mr. Tharp was correct, He did His most effective work with individuals. He made this magnificent statement to one man. It is arresting when we consider that this conversation has been broadcast wherever the name of Jesus Christ has been made known. Since it is true that "The wind bloweth where it listeth, and thou hearest the sound thereof, but canst not tell whence it cometh, and whither it goeth. . ." so no one can measure the influence of this conversation or the power of this word as it has gone forth throughout these almost twenty centuries of Christian evangelism. What a word! *"For God so loved the world, that he gave his only begotten Son, that whosoever believeth in him should not perish, but have everlasting life."*

Every babe in Christ has been cradled in John 3:16. If he has had a normal growth, he has gone on to enjoy the further revelation of truth found in the New Testament Epistles. But no Christian, be he ever so strong, has ever fathomed the depths of John 3:16 nor has he grown too big to return again and again to this verse, with the faith of a child, but with far greater appreciation of the cradle in which God loved him into new birth.

The Case of D. L. Moody

I never read this verse without thinking of the effect it had on the life and ministry of D. L. Moody, which took him out of the ordinary run of evangelists and made him one of the greatest this world has ever seen. We often say "God moves in mysterious ways His wonders to perform." It is also true that frequently God uses most unexpected means to bring about His purposes. Let me tell you about Henry Moorehouse, whom God used to influence Moody's life. I shall quote the words of Richard Ellsworth Day, the author of "Bush Aglow."

"Henry Moorehouse must be credited, under God, for thrusting Moody toward Bible greatness. This puny Lancashire lad lived less than forty years; burned himself to a cinder. Born in Ardwich, in 1840, he was hell-bent-on-high by the time he was twenty;

a cocky little bantam-weight prizefighter, battling equally against men and alcohol. At nineteen he was done for. One night, in an excess of remorse, he stood in a dark hall toying with a loaded pistol. Someone was holding a little meeting overhead, door open; he heard a voice reading the Prodigal Son, and the mystery of conviction covered his poor soul. *Just the Word!* And a few weeks later, a faithful fireman in a Manchester warehouse basement brought him to light with Romans 10:9, 10. *Just the Word!* He at once began to witness with *just the Word* in the mission rooms. No one 'cared enough about the little runt' to suggest a course of study. So he kept to *just the Word*; soaked it up; flavored himself therewith to the fingertips. Within four years, he was a bright and shining light. Men from every strata, burly colliers or brainy courtiers, sat spellbound before him."

Moorehouse got himself an invitation to go to Chicago. It was not a particularly fervent invitation judging from the following comments from the pen of D. L. Moody. "After I arrived at Chicago, I got a letter saying he had just arrived in New York and would come to preach. I wrote him a cold letter asking him to call on me if he came West. A few days after I got a letter stating he would be in Chicago the following Thursday. I did not know what to do with him. I said to the officers of the Church, 'There is a man coming from England, and he wants to preach. I am going to be absent Thursday and Friday. If you will let him preach on those days, I will be back on Saturday and take him off your hands.' They did not care about having him, but at my request they let him preach. On my return on Saturday, I was anxious to hear how the young people liked him, and I asked my wife how the young Englishman got along. 'How did they like him?' She said, 'They liked him very much. He preaches a little different from what you do. He tells the people *God loves them!* I think you will like him.' I said she was wrong. I thought I could not like a man who preached contrary to what I was preaching. I went down on Saturday night to hear him, but I had made up my mind not to like him because he preached different from me."

Moorehouse preached for seven consecutive nights on John 3:16 and in closing the series of seven messages, he said: "For seven nights I have been trying to tell you *how much God loves you,* but this poor stammering tongue of mine will not let me. If I could ask Gabriel how much love God has for this poor lost world, all that mighty angel could say would be that *God so loved the world, that he gave his only begotten Son, that whosoever believeth in him should not perish, but have everlasting life."*

Moody stated, "I have never forgotten those nights. I have preached a different gospel from that time, and I have had more power with God and man since."

Would God that every evangelist would have that experience. They would cease to live in the past. They would find the Bible to be their eternal source of freshness so that their ministry at all times would have upon it the kiss of God's benediction.

It is said that Henry Moorehouse was "the man who moved the man who moved millions." He did it by a series of seven messages on John 3:16.

We shall not give seven addresses on this passage, but try to pack into three short messages what Henry Moorehouse probably packed into a single message.

We have directed attention to the fact that our Lord spoke this message to one man, though the verse has been used to bring millions to a knowledge of His saving grace. It is possible to speak to a large audience and yet have the message directed to one soul.

Salvation is not by crowds. Salvation is an individual matter. You cannot get into heaven through your mother's Christianity, or your father's faith. There is only one way to get into heaven—"Ye must be born again." This message bewildered Nicodemus, but he listened to every word that fell from the lips of the Master as He said: *"For* God so loved the world. . ." Let's stop there. Note that this passage begins with the preposition *for*, which many people overlook. But it is *the* important connecting link without which it would be difficult to understand the message of this Scripture. That's how important it is. Our Lord said, "For God *so loved the world.*" He told the provincial Nicodemus who believed in a limited atonement embodying Israel only, that God's love extended to the world.

In D. L. Moody's notebook on John's Gospel, chapter three, were found these words: "God's first covenant had been

1. With a person in Abraham;
2. With a family in Jacob;
3. With a nation in the people of Israel at Sinai;
4. Finally with the world, (embracing all the other three) in Christ."

But our Lord also told Nicodemus of the character of God's love and the manner in which that love would be demonstrated. That little word *for* tells the story. It links up that which follows with that which preceded the statement. Our Lord had said ". . . as Moses lifted up the serpent in the wilderness, even so must the Son of man be lifted up: That whosoever believeth in him should not perish, but have eternal life. *For* God so loved the world . . ." Here's the answer to the problem of Calvary. Here's the answer to what some people have called "the slaughterhouse religion." Let me illustrate what I mean.

The Unattractiveness of the Cross

One bitterly cold morning after our broadcast, I drove home, picked up my wife and little girl, then stopped for two other children and drove off to Sunday School. While the church proper is a beautiful structure, the room where the little children meet is not particularly attractive. That morning the room was cold. I felt sorry for the youngsters, most of whom kept their sweaters or coats on. I sat in the back of the room putting the finishing touches on the broadcast of a previous Sunday in preparation for its printing. I became so cold that I decided to take a walk. The sun was shining beautifully but it was cold. I took a quick, snappy walk in order to work up some circulation. Not far away, I passed by a beautiful church building. As I did I thought of some pictures I had seen of the attractive rooms that this church has for its Sunday School, particularly for the little tots, and the provision that has been made for the care of the children during the church service that followed, so that the mothers could attend church. I could not avoid contrasting the two meeting places! Why did I choose to take my child to the first church and not the second? The second had all the things that would attract the eye *but* it did not have that which would attract faith. In that place they do not preach the Gospel of the grace of God. It is a citadel of liberalism. I chose the Sunday School where my child attends because I knew that there she would get the Gospel of the grace of God. Infinitely better that my child attend Sunday School in a barn if need be, than in the most beautiful place, if in that place the seeds of unbelief would be planted in her little heart. So grave an offense is it, that our Lord with a little child in their midst said to the disciples ". . . whoso shall offend one of these little ones which believe in me, it were better for him that a millstone were hanged about his neck, and that he were drowned in the depth of the sea." You Sunday School teachers have a grave responsibility. God help you to mold those children's lives in faith in Jesus Christ.

As I thought on these things, I also recalled that wonderful building, the Tabernacle. From the outside it was the most unattractive place anyone could ever imagine. It was covered with badger skins. It was drab, very drab. There was nothing to attract the eye of the natural man. But inside! What glory! There was the golden lamp stand, there was the shewbread, there was the ark of the covenant, there was the Holy of Holies, where the High Priest entered and communed with God. What a difference between the outside and the inside.

Now I want to use the same principle and suggest that we consider Calvary. We concede that it is a most unattractive place. It is a sight that will ever live in the memory. It is a little knoll outside the gates of Jerusalem. The song writer has described it as "A green hill far away; without a city wall, Where the dear Lord was crucified, Who died to save us all." But as the late Dr. Machen used to say "I do not know whether it was a green hill, or whether it was a hill at all, but I do know it was *the* place where the dear Lord was crucified."

Calvary does not appeal to the natural eye. Oh yes, some have polished and decorated it, as a place where a man died as a martyr for his ideals, but you cannot decorate an "electric chair." The "electric chair" was made for criminals and it is a horrible instrument. The cross was made for criminals and it too was a horrible instrument. But our Lord gave glory to the cross. He flashed the glory of God upon the cross and gave believing eyes to see that it was not the place of a human tragedy alone, but the place of divine reconciliation.

The World God Loves

Jesus said ". . . as Moses lifted up the serpent in the wilderness, even so must the Son of man be lifted up. . ." It was no accident that our Lord hung on a cross. He repeatedly predicted it. He knew that He would be lifted up on a cross. He knew that the spikes would be driven through His hands and the spear through His side. He knew that the crown of thorns would be placed on His brow. He knew that His blood would pour forth from every vein and that His visage would be marred so that one could hardly distinguish the face of a man. But why was all this necessary? Our Lord answered by saying, *"For God so loved the world, that he gave his only begotten Son, that whosoever believeth in him should not perish, but have everlasting life."* There was absolutely no other means whereby God in righteousness could deal with sin. Sin is high treason against God. It strikes at the very throne of God. It mutilates man and condemns him before the judgment seat of God. It is unthinkable that God could forgive sin when one understands its true character and the tragedy that it has wrought.

There is only one way for a sinner to escape his sin and that is to have a substitute pay his debt and make the matter right before God. That is what the cross means. That is why our Lord said "For God so loved the world." It was a Roman cross to be true and it was erected on Jewish soil, but you and I were responsible for it. In a true sense, it was also God who erected the cross, for it was in the determinate counsel and foreknowledge of God that Jesus was taken by wicked hands and crucified. It all took place because God *so* loved the world.

There is no limited atonement in the 16th verse of the 3rd chapter of this Gospel. "God so loved the *world*." The word that is used is *kosmos*. He loved the *world*. He prepared everything that would cater to the needs of man and that would enable him to appreciate His gracious provisions. When man sinned, the whole of creation was involved. So in Christ's death **on the cross, not** only was man's sin taken care of, but all creation was benefited. We will never be able to measure the extent of the influence of the cross. It can only be measured by the love of God.

One of the choicest bits of verse that I have ever read is entitled "The Atonement," by William Blane. Here are a few lines which I love:

> What means a universal call
> If there be not enough for all?
> As if the Saviour passed some by
> While He for others' sins did die,
> And that, though all are told to come,
> *There's but provision made for some;*
> Or that, in some mysterious way,
> The Scriptures mean not what they say.
> The mighty work of Jesus scan—
> He "tasted death for every man."
> He "died for all" that they who live
> Back to Himself that life should give.
> He has for "all" Atonement made—
> For all mankind the ransom paid.
> God loved the world; and when He gave
> His Son, it was the world to save.
> And though He knew some would not take
> Of the provision He would make,
> The foreseen choice of self-willed man
> Changed not Heav'n's universal plan,
> As in the love that moved His heart,
> All in the Atonement had a part.
>
> If not, He only mocks their fate
> Who presses *all,* "ere 'tis too late,"
> To trust a work not for them done,
> To take a pardon while there's none,
> To fly from hell without a way,
> Or perish if they disobey,
> They never can the sinner reach
> Who thus a crippled Gospel preach.
> 'Tis He who knows of food for all
> That only can afford to call
> A hungry world to come and feed—
> All others would but mock their need.
> O tell the tidings all around,
> That every soul may hear the sound—
> Th' Atoning work embraces all
> Who were enveloped in the Fall.
> To earth's remotest regions go,
> And preach to every child of woe,
> Impartial who or what they be—
> The rich, the poor, the bond, the free,
> That Christ on their behalf has died,
> That God with Him is satisfied,
> And now is ready to forgive—
> The simple terms, "Believe and live."

Walk Fourteen

THE GIFT OF GOD

JOHN 3:16—PART TWO

JUST about one hundred years ago there died in Cambridge a saintly vicar who ministered in one parish for more than fifty-four years and who carved his name deep in the walls of Kings College, Cambridge. He was Charles Simeon, one of England's great clergymen of the past century. Every Friday afternoon the upper classmen, particularly those who contemplated entering the ministry, would gather at his home. He invariably began by entertaining them at tea, and before long a most delightful and instructive period of conversation would take place. These Friday afternoon meetings soon got to be known as "Simeon's Conversational Parties."

We have lost the art of conversation, mostly because we have so little to talk about of a worthwhile character. At one of these Friday afternoon Conversational Parties Mr. Simeon gave the young men of Kings College some excellent suggestions when he said, "A minister is not the *father* of his flock; his *wife* is the mother, but he is the *pastor*, a far higher and more important office. He has more to do in the closet and the study than even in the cottage." How much our ministry today could profit by that exhortation. On that same occasion he said, "I never like to write a letter upon a delicate or much controverted point, for," he said, "if I write, the reader must take the whole and it must produce its effect upon him. But if I *speak* with a man, I can stop when I see it is doing harm." He went on to say, "You cannot *hesitate* upon paper; you cannot *weep* upon paper; you cannot give upon paper the *tone* of love; you cannot look *kindness* upon paper." That is true as far as human writings are concerned, but when it comes to divine Writ, especially such passages as John 3:16, it literally pours out love upon the page. It has *not* been our privilege to listen to the *tone* in which our Lord spoke these words; that His voice was captivating is all too evident, but we do hear "the voice of *Jesus*" in this written word.

CHRIST, THE KEY TO THE BIBLE

Our Lord was a master at holding conversations with men and women. We shall see Him frequently in this role throughout John's Gospel. Let us observe a few further things about Him in this conversation with Nicodemus. It began with a dialogue. Niceties of approach were soon over. Quietly but sternly our Lord brushed them aside and went to the heart and root of the problem. "Nicodemus (He said) Except a man be born again, he cannot see the kingdom of God." This gave Nicodemus an opportunity to express his thoughts. He came to Christ with his questions, but when he left every question was answered. He came with his doubts; he was not sure who Jesus was; he was not able to clearly appreciate His ministry; he was groping; but he knew that our Lord had light. He came in the darkness; whether he "abode with Him that night" we are not certain, but he went away with the light of God on his countenance. The dialogue soon gave way to a monologue as the inquirer listened with rapt attention to the words that fell from the lips of our Lord. It is true, never man spake as this man! As our Lord continued, He removed the clouds and the shadows as Nicodemus heard these matchless words, *"For God so loved the world, that he gave his only begotten Son, that whosoever believeth in him should not perish, but have everlasting life."*

Professor Lightfoot has said, "The Holy Ghost penned the Old Testament, and who can be so good a commentator as Himself?" He gives us His commentary in the New Testament. The Apostle Paul wrote that "even unto this day, when Moses is read, the vail is upon their heart. Nevertheless when it (that is, the heart) shall turn to the Lord, the vail shall be taken away." Nicodemus was unable to understand the Old Testament. There is no one in this world who could answer the questions which the Old Testament raises if our Lord Jesus Christ had not come. There was a vail over Nicodemus' heart as he read "the Book" but in one night's interview our Lord rent the vail and gave him to understand that He Himself was the key to the Old Testament. He had already told Nicodemus that He (Jesus) was the antitype of the brazen serpent which Moses lifted up in the wilderness, and now in these matchless words, *"For God so loved the world, that he gave his only begotten Son . . ."* He again explained a familiar portion of Scripture which was utterly inexplicable until our Lord flashed His light upon it.

There must have immediately leaped into the mind of Nicodemus that picture, found in the Old Testament, of a father who gave up his only begotten son, which until then Nicodemus and every other individual, be he scribe, publican, or sinner, had been unable to comprehend. It is the scene in which God appeared unto and called to Abraham in order to test him. With a heart of faith, Abraham immediately replied, "Behold, here I am." Whereupon the father of Isaac had to listen to strange words from the lips of the Almighty God. No man before or since has listened to such words. The words are found in Genesis 22:2: "Take now thy son, thine only son Isaac, whom thou lovest, and get thee into the land of Moriah; and offer him there for a burnt-offering upon one of the mountains which I will tell thee of." The Scripture tells us that Abraham did not quake before that startling command, but "rose up early in the morning, and saddled his ass, and took two of his young men with him, and Isaac his son, and clave the wood for the burnt-offering, and rose up, and went unto the place of which God had told him."

God's Great Love

Now let's go back to the 16th verse of the 3rd chapter of John's Gospel, to this wonderful night scene with Christ, when He said, *"God so loved the world . . ."* That could never have been said of Abraham. Of him and others of the same character, the Bible says, ". . . if they had been mindful of that country from whence they came out, they might have had opportunity to have returned. But now they desire a better country, that is, an *heavenly*: wherefore God is not ashamed to be called their God: for he hath prepared for them a city." No, Abraham did not love the *world*; he wanted to get out of it. In that he was not a type of God. But Abraham *loved God* and "is the father of the faithful." He immediately and blindly obeyed the command of God. Abraham *loved* his son. The Almighty God took recognition of that when He said, "Take now thy son, thine only son Isaac, whom *thou lovest* . . ." Jesus Christ claimed to be the only begotten Son of God. That He was the Son of God's love is too apparent to need comment. It may be too much to suggest that God had an even deeper love for the world than for His own Son, even as Abraham must have had a deeper love for God than for his only son whom he loved; but at least we can say that He has loved us as He has loved His Son. Would Abraham have been willing to give up his only begotten son if he cherished that son above all else? God gave His best in the gift of His Son. Abraham gave his best when he offered up his only son, Isaac.

Now Nicodemus began to understand the Old Testament. Now his heart was unveiled and he saw that not only was Christ the antitype of the serpent, but this Jesus who was speaking with him was the antitype of Isaac also. He saw that the experience in the Old Testament was *a pageant*, to use an expression of a friend of mine, in order that a preview of the cross might be seen in the Old Testament. Unless a man sees Jesus Christ in the Old Testament it is to him a closed book. There are question marks on every page of the Old Testament unless Jesus Christ is read into the page. For instance, no man has been able to understand the 22nd Psalm, or the 53rd chapter of Isaiah, or the 11th chapter of Zechariah, or the entire book of Jonah, or the experiences of Joseph, or those of Moses, or of Abraham, unless he sees Jesus Christ on every page of Scripture. We might well raise the same question which the Ethiopian eunuch asked Philip, while reading the 53rd chapter of Isaiah, when he said, "I pray thee, of whom speaketh the prophet this? of himself, or of some other man?" The Bible tells us that Philip "opened his mouth, and began at the same scripture, and *preached unto him Jesus*." Our Lord was preaching *Himself*, that night, to Nicodemus. He was calling Nicodemus' attention to a number of things. He was enlightening the eyes of his understanding so that he might understand the Scriptures. First, He directed attention to God's love; second, He directed attention to God's gift; and third, He directed attention to God's purpose in the giving of His gift.

If our Lord accomplished one thing that night He certainly gave to Nicodemus, and through him to the world, an overwhelming revelation of God's love, something the world never had previously. Charles Simeon said, "I love to make Christianity appear lovely and to show the world that it is not that gloomy, misanthropic thing which they fancy as commanding gloom and forbidding a smile."

Someone has said that "God's love must have an object outside the divine Being." That object He found in the world, the world of men. In Jesus Christ, God laid bare His heart; He came down to man. It is true that the sinner comes to Christ, but only because Christ came to the sinner. There could be no salvation if Jesus Christ had not come to die on a cross. Christianity is the antithesis of everything that is advocated by the religions of this world. Man labors under the impression that he must adopt a policy of appeasement in dealing with God. Man may not say so in as many words, but there seems latent in the human breast the idea that God is a dictator who needs to be appeased and that if He does not receive an offering from the hand of man He is about to smite man in judgment.

Our Lord came to manifest the Father, to reveal the Father's heart. Observe that He did not say one word to Nicodemus of what was expected of man or what God wanted from man. God does *not* want a thing: He came to *give* something. When He sought to present a gift to man He looked through the heavens; He passed by every angel and archangel, every seraphim and cherubim, every expression of His wisdom and wealth, until He came to His own Son who is the express image of His person and who upholds all things by the word of His power. He literally robbed heaven of its glory when He sent His Son into this world as the gift of God to guilty sinners.

The Son of God

What does one do with a gift? One cannot earn a gift. If a gift be offered it is to be received, and the recipient invariably returns a word of thanks to the giver. The same is true of the Gospel. God gave His only begotten Son. He does not ask nor expect a thing of man except to receive His Christ and say, "Thank you Lord for the gift of Thy Son Jesus Christ." The Father loved the world. Our Lord is the gift of the Father to this world. Christ loved the church and gave Himself for it. God has never given a gift to this world comparable to His Son, though He has bestowed many gifts on the world of men.

But just one further word regarding God's gift. Our Lord said "God so loved the world, that he gave his only begotten Son . . ." I am aware that some have suggested that as John's Gospel was written almost sixty years after our Lord Jesus Christ had ascended, it was an afterthought of John's, possibly in collusion with the other Apostles and disciples, to present a Gospel that would deify Jesus Christ. These critics boastfully point to the synoptic Gospels, Matthew, Mark, and Luke, and insist that nowhere in these Gospels is Jesus Christ called the Son of God, nor does He take unto Himself the title of the Son of God.

That claim seems too absurd to answer, but because it has received general acceptance by men who do not believe the Bible, I want to direct your attention to just one reference in the Gospel according to St. Luke. It is found in the 10th chapter. The seventy unnamed disciples had returned from a most successful tour during which they preached the kingdom of God. They acquainted the Lord with the marvelous time they had enjoyed. They were full of joy, but our Lord observed that their joy was centered in the fact that even the demons were subject unto their word (of course, when they used the name of the Lord). So our Lord as a skillful physician used the surgeon's lancet as He severed their joy from their "service" and rooted it in their relationship to Himself, by directing their thoughts to the source of true joy when He said to them, "Notwithstanding in this rejoice not, that the spirits are subject unto you; but rather *rejoice,* because your names are written in heaven." The Bible goes on to tell us that in that hour "Jesus rejoiced in spirit," and approached His Father in prayer, after which He said, "All things are delivered to me of my Father: and no man knoweth who the *Son is,* but the *Father;* and *who the Father is,* but the *Son,* and he to whom the Son will reveal him." If that is not a declaration of the deity of Jesus Christ, then words are meaningless. The gift of God is *His only begotten Son.*

In bringing this message to a close let me direct your attention to the little word *gave,* which is the pivot upon which the whole passage revolves. The *force* behind the passage is the love of God, His love for the world. The central *person* in the passage is Jesus Christ, His only begotten Son. The chief *purpose* in the passage is that men by believing may escape eternal condemnation and possess eternal life. If you please, here is an eternal triangle that has been solved. God the Father is seen at one end, our Lord Jesus Christ at the other, and the world at the third. The Father gave; the Son came; and man believes.

Walk Fifteen

THE OPEN DOOR IN JOHN 3:16

PART THREE

EXAMINING a book published in 1884, the work of Dr. Howe, the Lord Bishop of Bedford, I noted an excellent paragraph on John 3:16. The Bishop said, "These are not words to comment upon, but to feel. In this glorious verse, every word is a sermon. Mark the *greatness* of the Father's love—God *so* loved. Mark the *breadth* of that love—God so loved *the world*. Mark the *pricelessness* of the sacrifice—His *only begotten Son*. Mark the *freedom* of the offer of salvation—*whosoever*. Mark the *condition* of salvation—*believeth*. Mark the *peril* of unbelief—*perish*. Mark the *greatness* of the salvation—*everlasting life*." I do not believe that I have read anything which more clearly expresses the message of John 3:16.

While having luncheon with that fine missionary to China, James R. Graham, he called my attention to a statement which he heard two well-known Bible teachers give. I do not know which one was the author or whether either one was the author of it. But both summed up the whole of the religious question by saying that there are only two kinds of religion in the world, one which says, "*something* in my hand I bring" and the other which confesses, "*nothing* in my hand I bring." The words are choice. They distinguish the message of Christ from every other message and from every other religious system.

It is a pity that even we who live in a supposedly Christian country, and who have been raised in Christian churches and in Christian homes, seem to have had drilled into us from our earliest childhood that something must be done to merit our salvation or to make it *continuously assured*. But the whole of the Bible from the beginning of Genesis to the end of Revelation teaches one outstanding dogma—that a man is justified by faith apart from the works of the law.

The Heart of the Gospel

We do not intend to comment further upon the love of God, wonderful though that subject may be. We need only repeat that "God so loved the world." Neither do we plan to discuss the gift of His love, but simply reiterate that "God so loved the world, that he gave his only begotten Son." We desire to consider the why of it. Why was it necessary for God to do this? The answer is clear "that whosoever believeth in him (that is in Jesus Christ) should not perish, but have everlasting life." God the Father is in this verse; God the Son is also in this verse; and every man is in the verse.

There are two kinds of people in this verse as there are two kinds of people in the world; there are those who will perish and those who will have everlasting life. It is apparent from a close examination of the passage that not every man will perish, for the verse declares that whosoever believeth in Him should not perish. Thus, all perish except those who believe in Him. Here we come to the heart of the Christian message which must be given clearly but with all kindliness. We are living in a day when much is made of tolerance. Some people believe that it is a sign of bigness, of greatness, of breadth of vision, if one possesses a faith that is so tolerant that it will embrace every type of religious devotion. But Christianity is an intolerant message, though the Bible is careful to caution us who believe that we should be tolerant in our presentation of the message and in our walk and conduct in this world. Jesus Christ said, "I am the way, the truth, and the life: no man cometh unto the Father, but by me." Either He told the truth, or He gave expression to a lie. If He told the truth, it is an intolerant message that no man can come unto the Father except through the Lord Jesus Christ. That's Godly intolerance.

Now then, if Jesus Christ did not tell the truth when He said that no man cometh unto the Father but by Himself, then He was an imposter, a law-breaker, a sinner, a deceiver, a blasphemer, and unworthy to be called even a teacher. There can only be two viewpoints when considering Christ's claims.

Now notice that our passage teaches that whosoever *believeth* in Him (that is in the Lord Jesus) shall not perish. An examination of the Bible's use of the word *believeth* reveals that to believe is synonymous with *receiving* the testimony of God concerning His Son Jesus Christ. *No man* is entitled to be called a Christian unless he has definitely received Jesus Christ as his Savior and bowed to His Lordship of life.

Recently, I had a conversation with a man who sought to justify the actions of the German government in world affairs today and particularly in their persecution of the Jew. When I first met this man he suffered a bad case of mistaken identity so that I listened to a number of things that I'm certain he never would have expressed had he known my real identity. When he realized his mistake he was more than a little concerned. I observed that he continuously spoke of the German people as *Christians* and of himself as a *Christian*, and yet, a more inhuman attitude against fellow humans I have never heard. It was quite evident that he assumed that a man who was not a Jew by birth was a Christian. When I reminded him what the Bible teaches about Israel as the "chosen people" and of her future and that it is inevitable that "Gott will straf Germany" for her wicked, Satanic attack upon the Jews, he answered, "Who said so? Who wrote the Old Testament. The Jews! It is they themselves who have called themselves the chosen people." Poor man! It probably never occurred to him that our Lord was a Jew according to the flesh and that the Apostles were Jews and that almost every writer of the New Testament was a Jew and that everything a Christian holds dear has come down to him *through* the Jewish race. No, a man is not a Christian by birth; a man is a Christian by new birth. Dr. Samuel Zwemer, the great missionary to the Moslems, said, "The brightest sunlight will not turn a lump of coal into a sparkling diamond" and Billy Sunday said, "Going to church does not make anybody a Christian any more than taking a wheelbarrow into a garage will turn it into an automobile."

The Open Door

There is a wideness about the invitation of John 3:16 that thrills the heart of every believer. It is not a question of some people being predestinated to be saved and some being predestinated to be lost. The good Book says, Jesus Christ Himself being the speaker, that "God so loved the *world* that he gave his only begotten Son," God put Him on a cross and extracted from His Son the penalty due sin, in order that "whosoever will" may benefit therefrom. There is not a man on this earth excluded from that "whosoever." *Whosoever* means, as a little lad expressed it, "you, me, or anybody else." The open door in John 3:16 is wide enough for every man to participate in the benefits that flow from the matchless work which our Lord accomplished on the cross.

But we should also observe that while the door is wide-open, the word which follows *whosoever* narrows the group that *will* participate in the fruits of the redemptive work of Christ. It is whosoever *believeth*. It could not be otherwise. If it were, every man would be spared the penalty of sin, simply because the Lord Jesus Christ bore that penalty on the cross. Then a man could sin all he pleased; he could live as debauched a life as he chose. "Let us eat, drink, and be merry, for we know that on the morrow we will enjoy everlasting life —it is ours because Christ died for us." What a "tale" that would be! That would not be a gospel. That would be the worst type of iniquity. Jesus Christ died not only to remove the penalty of sin but to save us from the power and dominion of sin. The door is open wide, the invitation is given to whosoever will, but when one comes to the door, he can only go through it by believing. One cannot merit salvation; but to enjoy it, to participate in the thrill of it, one must believe God's Word.

Now notice what the individual receives by believing. First, there is a negative side; he shall not perish. Second, there is also a positive one, he will have everlasting life. The Bible nowhere teaches that if a man dies in his sin, he dies like a dog and that's the end of all things. The human soul is eternal. *Eternal existence* and *everlasting life* however are two different things.

Dr. A. C. Gaebelein has written these excellent words: "No man knows what it means to 'perish,' that awful destiny which is ours by nature, and endless, conscious existence in the outer darkness, with the load of sin unlifted, *perishing*, and no end to this perishing. Nor do we know the fullest meaning of what the glory is for which God has saved us and the joy He brings His own. Only when we shall know as we are known, when we no longer look into a glass darkly, shall we measure the heights and depths of John 3:16."

There is one further matter which should be mentioned. The man who believes does not have a hope held out that some day he *will* have everlasting life, but he finds in this verse the assurance that he has that life now! In the 36th verse of this same chapter, we read "He that believeth on the Son *hath* everlasting life . . ." He *has* it now. It is the same thought that our Lord expressed when He spoke to Martha, whose brother Lazarus had died, when He said, "I am the resurrection, and the life: he that believeth in me, *though he were dead, yet shall he live*: And whosoever liveth and believeth in me *shall never die.*" The man who believes John 3:16, really believes it, who not only gives a mental assent to it, but from his very heart believes the word spoken by the Lord, he knows that he *now,* this moment, *possesses* eternal life. He will never lose it. He has begun to participate in that life already: within him is the very life of the Lord. And some day he will have an environment—if you please a climate—in which that life can express itself in all its fullness.

It is impossible to expound this great passage. The Bishop of Bedford was right. "These are not words to comment upon, but to feel." When they get into our innermost being, a well of joy springs up in the breast, which together with the witness of the Spirit of God with our spirits, assures us that we are the children of God by faith in Jesus Christ.

Walk Sixteen

WILL GOD CONDEMN A MAN WHO HAS NEVER HEARD ABOUT CHRIST?

WE have already devoted several studies to the interview which our Lord extended to Nicodemus, a ruler of the Jews, who came to Him by night. The last thing Nicodemus said that night was "How can these things be?" Then followed a rebuke by our Lord after which He gave a revelation of God's purpose in the gift of His Son and finally Nicodemus listened to these words:

> "For God sent not his Son into the world to condemn the world; but that the world through him might be saved.
> "He that believeth on him is not condemned: but he that believeth not is condemned already, because he hath not believed in the name of the only begotten Son of God.
> "And this is the condemnation, that light is come into the world, and men loved darkness rather than light, because their deeds were evil.
> "For every one that doeth evil hateth the light, neither cometh to the light, lest his deeds should be reproved.
> "But he that doeth truth cometh to the light, that his deeds may be made manifest, that they are wrought in God."

The Gospel of John — Chapter III, Verses 17-21

There is a striking study in contrasts in this portion of Scripture when we consider that Nicodemus came to our Lord by night, while the final word our Lord spoke to him was, "he that doeth truth cometh to the light . . ." Nicodemus came to the Light. He came to One who alone could answer his questions and who could give him light. No man has light in himself; therefore before Nicodemus could enjoy light, the light had to be flashed into his darkened conscience, revealing his true state in the presence of a holy God. It is noteworthy that Nicodemus did not interrupt during the latter part of the conversation, for the words which our Lord spoke were so captivating that he was left speechless.

The Life of Christ vs. His Death

After our Lord had revealed His relationship with the Father, and the positive reason for His coming, He further enlightened the heart and mind of Nicodemus by adding, "For God sent not his Son into the world to condemn the world; but that the world through him might be saved." This passage has been badly misapplied, particularly by those of a liberal tinge. They have taken the verse entirely out of its context and have sought to make it teach something it does not teach. They insist that it was never our Lord's purpose to condemn a soul and neither did God have any such intention. But this passage does not teach anything of the kind. Before our Lord came into the world the world was in a state of condemnation. God did not need to send His Son into the world to condemn the world; the world was condemned already. That condemnation is clearly revealed in the opening chapters of Paul's letter to the Romans, that legal masterpiece of Divine writ, where the indictment is reported that "all have sinned, and come short of the glory of God . . ." and that man is "sold under sin" whereupon the verdict is given that all the world is "guilty before God." Thus every mouth is stopped and every man condemned. It would have been brutal for God to have sent His Son into this world only to add to the condemnation that had already been passed upon men because of their deeds. But, God sent His Son into the world "that the world through him might be saved." Here again we have the all *in*clusiveness of the Gospel and yet its astounding *ex*clusiveness.

The Justice of God

Recently there came to my desk a book containing the Hulsean lectures for 1938, which were delivered by Dr. John Burnaby, a Fellow of Trinity College of Cambridge, England. In it I found this sentence: "Because it is impossible for us to love a God who condemns to eternal fire all those of His children who have never heard the gospel message, it is impossible for us to believe that such a God exists." If that learned gentleman drew his "inference" from the statement of our Lord which we are considering in this study when He said "he that believeth not is condemned already, because he hath not believed in the name of the only begotten Son of God" then a serious charge has been laid at the throne of God. Then it could be said that man is more righteous than God. That, of course, is unthinkable.

This verse, however, teaches nothing of the kind. There is not the remotest suggestion made in the Scripture that God condemns to eternal fire all those of His children who have never heard the Gospel message. The fact is, not one single child of God ever will suffer the pangs of eternal fire, for every child of God has been redeemed by the precious blood of Jesus Christ and therefore is exempt from judgment. The erroneous premise in this statement is the inference that all men are the children of God, but the Bible is clear that we are the children of God by faith in Jesus Christ. Our Lord was not referring to men who had never heard of "the only begotten Son of God" for of such a one it could not be said—He hath not believed. Our Lord spoke of men who heard about Jesus Christ. Men who have never heard the Gospel, will not be judged by the Gospel. It would be preposterous to suggest such a thought. Men who have never heard the Gospel will be judged by their own works and the revelation which God has given in creation, and the conscience that He placed in the breast of every man. The Bible is clear to state, however, on the basis of that premise, and that revelation, that "all have sinned, and come short of the glory of God." It declares that the individual who lives in the darkest heathenism is without excuse, because the invisible things of God, such as His personality, His character, His righteousness, are clearly revealed by the things which God has made in this world, so that all men are without excuse.

It is interesting to note what the Lord had to say about the *world* and what the Lord had to say about the *individual* in the world. There is something about the coming of the Lord that has a message to this world, but there is also in the coming of Christ that which affects every single individual. If our Lord Jesus Christ had simply come to show us a pattern of life well pleasing to God, He would have added to our condemnation; but God sent His Son into this world not only to live a life that would doubly condemn those who are already condemned and who refuse the light, but to die a death whereby He would redeem those who were already under condemnation, but who receive the light.

A blind man cannot see nor follow light, therefore it is extreme folly, to say nothing of nauseating pride, to presume that any man can follow in the steps of our Lord. He is so far above us that none of us can approach Him. It is for that reason that the Apostle Paul never so much as once mentioned anything touching upon the life which our Lord lived prior to His death on the cross. The Gospel does not begin at Bethlehem; the Gospel begins at the cross. Thus Paul said—This is the Gospel which I have preached to you and which I desire to reiterate—"Christ died for our sins according to the scriptures . . ." Not a word is given about the beautiful life He lived, nor His exquisite teachings, nor His moral commands to men. Not a single reference is made to anything He ever did, until He hung as a victim on the accursed tree—"For God sent not his Son into the world to condemn the world; but that the world through him might be saved."

I have previously touched on the *in*clusiveness of the Lord's ministry which involves the whole world. It is a wonderful subject. It thrills the heart of a believer to appreciate and enter into the extensiveness of the benefits which accrue to God by virtue of the death of His Son Jesus Christ.

But this book not only has a message to the world. This book has a message for each individual heart, so that in the next verse our Lord said, "He that believeth on him (that is on Christ) is not condemned: but he that believeth not is condemned already, because he hath not believed in the name of the only begotten Son of God." Now what does this mean?

Jesus Christ did not come into the world to condemn the world; the world was condemned already. The Gospel is preached to men who are condemned because of their sin. Therefore the Gospel is offered to the sinner as the satisfaction for his sins. We can leave the heathen who have never heard about Christ with utmost confidence in the hands of the God of the universe who doeth all things well. But this portion of Scripture teaches that irrespective of the character or lack of character an individual possesses, if he has heard of the name of the only begotten Son of God but refuses to believe on Him, that one is doubly condemned in the sight of God for he has charged God with being a liar.

It would be sheer presumption on our part to suggest to any man that he is a sinner and that he is going to hell. Well might such a person say to us, Who made thee a judge? But our Lord said, of the man who *does not believe* in the name of the only begotten Son of God, that he "is condemned (or judged) already." If language means anything, that means that any man who does not believe in the only begotten Son of God is already judged, and that judgment is condemnation. Some have an idea that men are on parole and that God is taking a record of men's lives and some day before a great judgment throne He will examine our lives and there determine whether we are to be condemned or commended. But no such idea entered any man's mind as a result of reading the Bible. There is not even a suggestion of the kind in the Book.

Our Lord said that a man is condemned already "because he hath not believed in the name of the only begotten Son of God." But He also said that "He that believeth on him is not condemned . . ." Both statements are remarkable for their absolute assurance. Let me illustrate by a personal reference. I believe on the name of the Son of God. I believe that Jesus Christ was born of a virgin; that He suffered under Pontius Pilate; that He was crucified; that He was buried; and that He arose from the dead on the third day. I believe He died for my sin and put that sin away by His death. I believe God when His Word declares that "He that hath the Son hath life . . ." thus, I have eternal life. I am not condemned. That fact, however, is not the result of anything I have done except that I have believed God. It has not the slightest bearing upon anything I have ever done or ever shall do. It is a question of faith in the Son of God. It could not be otherwise, for every man in his natural state is condemned already. Man is a sinner; man is lost in his sin; man is absolutely condemned in the sight of God. His lips are sealed, his head is bowed, and his conscience has added its voice to his conviction. How then can a man save himself?

Light and Darkness

Note verse 19. Again our Lord was referring to the world-wide aspect of His ministry. ". . . this is the condemnation (judgment), that light is come into the world, and men loved darkness . . ." Notice the past tense, "men *loved* darkness rather than light." Why? "because their deeds were evil." Then our Lord continued and said, "For every one that doeth evil hateth the light, neither cometh to the light, lest his deeds should be reproved." That light *came* into the world is so evident as to need no comment. Jesus Christ *was* the light of this world. Despite the fact that it is approximately two thousand years since our Lord was in this world, the light that He brought still glows in this world. The world has had the benefit of light. This, therefore, is the added condemnation of the world —light came into it, but men loved darkness rather than light because their deeds were evil. Only one who knows the human heart could make a statement of that kind.

Notice our Lord said that "every one that doeth evil hateth the light . . ." *Hate* is a strong word. Dr. A. T. Robertson has given a thought-provoking comment on this subject of a man hating the light. He said: "The light hurts his eyes, reveals his own wickedness and makes him thoroughly uncomfortable. Hence, he does not read his Bible—he does not go to church—he does not pray, but goes on in deeper darkness."

There can be only two attitudes toward the Person of Jesus Christ. A man either loves Him or hates Him. The Apostle Paul by the Holy Spirit said, "If any man love not the Lord Jesus Christ, let him be Anathema Maran-atha" which means "let him be accursed at the coming of the Lord." There is no such thing as passive indifference to the Person of Jesus Christ. If a man does not love our Lord Jesus Christ, it is because that man has not come to Him. If a man has no *desire* to come to Him it is because that man fears that his deeds will be reproved. That is what the Lord told a ruler of the Jews. But He also added, "he that doeth truth cometh to the light . . ." Nicodemus came to the light though he came in the night—and "he that doeth truth cometh to the light, that his deeds may be made manifest, that they are wrought in God."

Suppose we contrast two striking personalities who came in contact with Jesus Christ—Nicodemus and Judas. One man *came* to our Lord by night and the other *left* our Lord in the night, to go out into further blackness and to commit suicide. When a man goes out from the presence of Jesus Christ, he must go out into the night. Apart from Jesus Christ, there is despair. That was never more apparent than at this very moment in history. Everywhere men are perplexed. The world seems to have gone mad and about to commit mass suicide. Vileness runs rampant. There is no light in this world! There is only one Person who has light and He is the One who is the light of the world.

It is becoming increasingly apparent to thinking men that the only hope of this present world is Jesus Christ. He is the only hope of the individual. Some day He will rectify the world's inequalities and rule as the absolute monarch of the world. Now He is saving individuals who will believe Him and receive Him. He not only imparts to lost individuals the joy of His salvation and the assurance of sins forgiven, but He floods such lives with light. This world is in darkness. The man who has received Christ into his life is able to tread through the dark world and to see his way clearly and to observe exactly what is happening here below. No one else knows. Our Lord said, "he that walketh in darkness knoweth not whither he goeth." But when "we walk in the light, as he is in the light, we have fellowship one with another, and the blood of Jesus Christ his (God's) Son cleanseth us from all sin." It is a message not alone for the world of tomorrow, but for the world of today.

Walk Seventeen

JOHN THE BAPTIST'S SWAN SONG

THIS walk with our Lord brings us to the closing section of the 3rd chapter where we read, commencing with verse 22:

> "After these things came Jesus and his disciples into the land of Judæa; and there he tarried with them, and baptized.

SEPTEMBER 10 TUESDAY

As every man hath received the gift, even so minister the same.
1 Peter 4:10

Unto every one which hath shall be given.
Luke 19:26

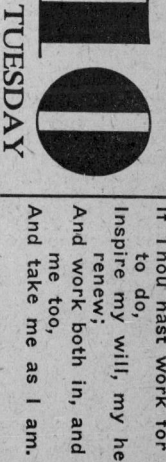

If Thou hast work for me to do,
Inspire my will, my heart renew;
And work both in, and by me too,
And take me as I am.

I am firmly convinced that if any Christian will take up the first case of spiritual need which presents itself, and endeavour to meet it, and continue so doing, it will not be long before he will find that he has some kind of gift for some kind of spiritual work. But let him not quarrel with his gift, and wish it were something else. God knew what He was doing when He conferred it, and if one will exercise his gift vigorously and cheerfully, he will find that there is untold joy and blessing to be found therein. Unless we employ our gifts, they will be taken from us, for the law which governs all our faculties is this—use them or lose them.
—H. W. P.

Daily Reading — Ez. 13; Psa. 52-54; Alt. Reading — 2 Sam. 4, 5; 1 C

The Gospel of John — Chapter III, Verses 22-36

> "And John also was baptizing in Ænon near to Salim, because there was much water there: and they came, and were baptized.
>
> "For John was not yet cast into prison.
>
> "Then there arose a question between some of John's disciples and the Jews about purifying.
>
> "And they came unto John, and said unto him, Rabbi, he that was with thee beyond Jordan, to whom thou barest witness, behold, the same baptizeth, and all men come to him.
>
> "John answered and said, A man can receive nothing, except it be given him from heaven.
>
> "Ye yourselves bear me witness, that I said, I am not the Christ, but that I am sent before him.
>
> "He that hath the bride is the bridegroom: but the friend of the bridegroom, which standeth and heareth him, rejoiceth greatly because of the bridegroom's voice: this my joy therefore is fulfilled.
>
> "He must increase, but I must decrease.
>
> "He that cometh from above is above all: he that is of the earth is earthly, and speaketh of the earth: he that cometh from heaven is above all.
>
> "And what he hath seen and heard, that he testifieth; and no man receiveth his testimony.
>
> "He that hath received his testimony hath set to his seal that God is true.
>
> "For he whom God hath sent speaketh the words of God: for God giveth not the Spirit by measure unto him.
>
> "The Father loveth the Son, and hath given all things into his hand.
>
> "He that believeth on the Son hath everlasting life: and he that believeth not the Son shall not see life; but the wrath of God abideth on him."

Among the things for which our Lord prayed at the close of His public ministry was the unity of all believers. Here are His exact words as recorded in the 17th chapter of St. John's Gospel: "Neither pray I for these alone, but for them also which shall believe on me through their word; That they all may be one; as thou, Father, art in me, and I in thee, that they also may be one in us: that the world may believe that thou hast sent me." It would appear that the visible church has striven with all its power to pile up obstacles in the pathway of the fulfillment of that prayer. And yet, the prayer *has been* and *shall be* answered.

The Subject of Baptism

If there is one thing that has caused division among professing Christians, true and spurious, it is the subject of baptism. In the passage we have just read, we have the record of the first known controversy on the subject. It began in the days of our Lord's ministry on earth; indeed, it took place very early in His ministry. It was shortly after our Lord's first public visit to Jerusalem when He granted an interview to Nicodemus. It was before John was cast into prison, in fact, John was still baptizing. The disciples of Jesus were in the same vicinity and it is evident that they were performing the same rite. We learn from the 4th chapter and the 2nd verse that our Lord himself baptized not, but His disciples. Immediately a question arose between some of John's disciples and the Jews. Though the details are not revealed, sufficient is given to clearly indicate that an attempt was made to develop a spirit of jealousy, for John's disciples came to him and said, "Rabbi, he that was with thee beyond Jordan, to whom thou barest witness, behold, the same baptizeth, and all men come to him." They were so evidently "wrought up" over the multitude that were following the Lord and His disciples, thus gradually leaving John with but a few disciples, that they refrained from mentioning the name of Jesus, being content to refer to Him as "he." There is nothing that can destroy fellowship between men as effectively as the cancer of jealousy. It has been well said that "of all the passions in the human breast, there is none more hateful than envy." It ought never to be once mentioned among Christians, but it is apparent that even the world has taken recognition of this condition. We shall observe how magnificently John answered this question and how graciously our Lord responded to the situation also. For the moment, let's look at the subject of baptism.

We meet with it on the pages of the New Testament Scriptures. Every believer at some time or another is obliged to face the question. The pathetic part of it is, that as a result of the many and varied interpretations as to the meaning as well as the mode of baptism, Christian bodies have been separated into seemingly hopeless divisions, and yet all will concede that the vital thing is a man's relationship to Christ.

In the closing verse in this 3rd chapter we read, "He that believeth on the Son hath everlasting life . . ." Not one word is suggested relative to the mode of baptism which the individual might have experienced or "suffered." The statement is without qualification—"He that *believeth* on the Son hath everlasting life." This is followed by a statement equally clear and unqualified—"and he that *believeth not* the Son shall not see life; but the wrath of God abideth on him." It must be evident to every clear thinking Christian, especially when he lays his heart bare before the Lord, that Satan has been busy and that we have been his willing tools in dividing the "body" of Christ into separate little cliques, on the basis of one's attitude in respect to the ceremony or rite of baptism. However, one is increasingly appreciative of the trend which has recently characterized those who have spiritual discernment, that the unity of believers is not based on any rite or ceremony but on the solid fact that they are one because they have believed on the Lord Jesus Christ. I am not talking of organic union. No enlightened or intelligent believer can be interested in the organic union of professing Christian bodies. The Bible is as clear as crystal that Christendom is made up of the true and the false, of wheat and tares; therefore it is utterly impossible to have an organic union between professing Christians where there is no spiritual union between people of varying beliefs.

If there is one thing in the experience of this man for which I praise God, it is the fact that though I have consistently avoided taking any denominational stand, I have been privileged to minister the Word of God in various denominational churches, irrespective of ceremonial barriers. Such great institutions as the Moody Bible Institute of Chicago, the Dallas Theological Seminary of Dallas, Texas, and other Bible Schools throughout this country have done yeoman service in bringing believers into a true union with kindred hearts and kindred spirits about the glorious Person of our risen Lord and Savior Jesus Christ, irrespective of denominational differences. By the grace of God I should like to do everything in my power to further that kind of union.

It is thought-provoking to observe that it was not a believer who raised the question about baptism, it was an unbeliever. But believers lent a listening ear to the questions that were raised, with the result that they allowed themselves to be instruments to sow seeds of discontent and division among brethren.

Incidentally, while we may not be able to locate exactly on the map where our Lord's disciples were baptizing and where John was baptizing, it is quite evident that they were near at hand, yet no attempt was made at proselyting or seeking to make the matter a competitive proposition.

His Increase—John's Decrease

Now notice how beautifully John the Baptist handled these disciples who came to him with their questions. John said, ". . . A man can receive nothing, except it be given him from heaven." That is a wonderful declaration because it is true; but alas, we have lost sight of the fact, or at least we act as if it were not true. Then John called attention to his own testimony. He said, I call you to witness that I frequently said, I am not the Christ, but am sent before Him. John knew his calling. Happy is the man who does. I believe that every Christian has a calling and that the Lord will reveal it to him if that man will tarry long enough in the Lord's presence to know the Lord's mind. Furthermore, I believe that no Christian experiences the fulness of joy that is available to him unless he learns his calling and his place in life and thereupon yields himself to the Lord to be faithful in that calling.

John used some interesting words to describe his relationship to Christ. He said, "He that hath the bride is the bridegroom: but the friend of the bridegroom, which standeth and heareth him, rejoiceth greatly because of the bridegroom's voice: this my joy therefore is fulfilled." The picture is an Eastern one, an Eastern wedding scene. The friend of the bridegroom had the task of bringing the bride and groom together, and the friend's joy was full when "he heard the music of the bridegroom's voice." That ought to be true of every man who is called to minister the Word of God. His joy should be found in leading men and women to Christ—who thus become members of the church of Christ, which is the bride of Christ.

But John continued, and speaking of the Lord Jesus said, "He must increase . . ." and speaking of himself he said, "I must decrease." As a result of these studies in this Gospel I have come to greatly admire John the Baptist. While he was an extremely young man he had a marvelously developed spiritual life. It is interesting to observe the language which the Baptist used in this connection. There is the thought of continuity in the verbs so that, literally translated, John said concerning Christ, "He must go on *increasing*, but I must go on *decreasing*."

If one were to diligently search for the motivating power behind the remarkable ministry of this young man who faded out of the scene almost as quickly as he entered upon it, I believe it would be found in the words that the angel Gabriel spoke to the father of this young man even before the boy was born. In Luke's Gospel, Chapter 1, verse 15, the angel said: "he shall be great in the sight of the Lord . . ." By the way, if a man is great in the sight of the Lord, invariably he exercises a tremendous influence over the lives of men. That was true in John's case for his ministry was so powerful that even kings quaked before his message. The trouble with many of us is that we seek to be great in the sight of men. But Gabriel said concerning John that he would be great in the sight of the Lord. But hear these words, ". . . and (he) shall drink neither wine nor strong drink; and he shall be filled with the Holy Spirit, even from his mother's womb." That was the secret of the power of this astounding Baptist.

It is a striking thing that there is only one other passage in the New Testament where the injunction against wine and the reference to the filling of the Holy Spirit are found in a single verse. This other reference is an exhortation to every believer. It is found in the 5th chapter of Ephesians, verse 18, where the Apostle Paul exhorted Christians as follows: "And be not drunk with wine, wherein is excess; but be filled with the Spirit . . ." Scholars have called attention to that word translated *filled*. It is not in the past tense in the Greek, it is in the present tense. It means to be continuously filled with the Spirit. That was what John experienced and it can be experienced by every Christian.

Moral Rearmament vs. New Birth

In the latter part of this 3rd chapter we have what I believe to be the "Swan Song of John the Baptist." Here is his final word concerning the Christ. "He that hath received his testimony (that is, the testimony of Christ) hath set to his seal that God is true." The inference of course is strong that if a man does not receive the testimony of Christ, he has refused to believe that God is true. John continued and said: "The Father loveth the Son, and hath given all things into his hand." Then this final word, "He that believeth on the Son hath everlasting life . . ." This is an unqualified statement and it is in the present tense. It is not "He that believeth on the Son, at some future time shall have everlasting life." A man who has faith in Christ possesses eternal life this very moment. Contrariwise, "he that believeth not the Son shall not see life; but the wrath of God abideth on him." Again, this is in the present tense. It does not say that if a man does not believe on the Son of God, he will one day experience the wrath of God, but rather "the wrath of God *abideth on him.*" He is still under condemnation. The wrath of God must express itself against sin. It must strike somewhere. It is inevitable that it be so. The wrath of God will either strike the sinner or the sinner's substitute. Christ is the sinner's substitute. The wrath of God was borne by the Son of God in order that he "that believeth on the Son" might have "everlasting life." This is not "Moral Rearmament" about which we have been hearing lately.

One may dress up a corpse with finery and even preach a sermon over it, but alas, it is still a dead corpse. To morally rearm a sinner may outfit him with a new and modern suit of clothes, but he is still a sinner upon whom the wrath of God abideth. Clothes never make a man! If a sinner is to experience life he must place his faith and confidence in Christ. Men do not need to rearm—men need new life, a new birth—and that can only be accomplished by faith in the Gospel of Jesus Christ and His love. The Gospel could not be put in clearer language than when it was expressed in the "Swan Song of John the Baptist."

Walk Eighteen

A TREK THROUGH SAMARIA

OUR Lord was the master soul winner. He had just dealt with one who was an aristocrat, a ruler, a Pharisee, a wealthy gentleman. Few of us could move in such circles. Few of us could hold the attention of such a man, especially during the night hours. Our Lord's personality was captivating. He drew all men to Himself. Since His crucifixion His magnetism in this respect has been greatly increased and enlarged. Men and women from all walks of life have bowed before the Christ of God.

In the 4th chapter of this Gospel, we see Him dealing with a character diametrically opposite to that of Nicodemus, the Pharisee and ruler. First of all, let us examine the incidents which led up to this interview. The interview was not sought *of* our Lord but *by* our Lord. It was not a case of the Samaritan woman seeking Christ, but of Christ seeking the woman. Our Lord knew all about Nicodemus; He did not have to consult a "Who's Who in Judea" to get the Pharisee's background. He knew him. Nor did He have to visit the slums to learn the "case history" of this unnamed woman of Samaria. The One with whom we have to deal in the pages of John's Gospel is the One before whom our lives are as an open book. The opening verses of this wonderful chapter read:

> "When therefore the Lord knew how the Pharisees had heard that Jesus made and baptized more disciples than John,
> "(Though Jesus himself baptized not, but his disciples,)
> "He left Judæa, and departed again into Galilee.
> "And he must needs go through Samaria.
> "Then cometh he to a city of Samaria, which is called Sychar, near to the parcel of ground that Jacob gave to his son Joseph.
> "Now Jacob's well was there. Jesus therefore, being wearied with his journey, sat thus on the well: and it was about the sixth hour."

We shall consider the woman of Samaria in our next study, contenting ourselves now with an examination of the events which led up to the interview. We have already dealt with the controversy which arose on the subject of baptism. We noted how John magnificently answered the veiled suggestion of jealousy raised by his disciples. At that time we said that we would also consider how graciously our Lord conducted Himself under the same circumstances. First we observe that when Jesus knew that the Pharisees had heard that Jesus made and baptized more disciples than John, He left Judea and departed again into Galilee. Oh yes, there were additional reasons for His leaving Judea besides the fact that one Pharisee entered into a discussion with a group of John's disciples on the subject of baptism. Our Lord also knew that the Pharisees, through their network of espionage, had learned that He made and baptized more disciples than John.

The Power of the Preached Word

We are prone to minimize the extensiveness of the ministry of our Lord. We assume too readily that He only appealed to a small company of people. But that is not true. When we considered John the Baptist we learned that his congregation consisted of all Judea, and Jerusalem, and all the region round about Jordan. The crowds went out to a wilderness to hear him preach. John had a great following and men from all walks of life came to his baptism. John, however, did no miracle. That also is interesting. We labor under the illusion that the church today needs something besides a pulpit on which an open Bible rests and behind which a man of God speaks. We think if the church would give a display of the miraculous, men would give attention. Yes, crowds come when someone arises to suggest that he or she has the power to do miracles. But John did *no* miracle. However, he had the power of the Holy Spirit. And that which broke the hearts of men was the power of the Word of God as spoken through his lips. And the same is true today. The church is impotent today because it has discarded the Bible from the pulpit and substituted a pleasing, suave personality for a man of God.

Our Lord accomplished miracles, but never with the idea of enticing the crowds or to get an audience. His miracles were signs, at least those recorded in John's Gospel. They were performed that men might know that He was anointed of the Lord, that He was *the* Christ. Imagine therefore the crowds that must have followed our Lord when we consider the size of the audience that John had, for we learn from the 1st verse of this 4th chapter, "the Pharisees had heard that Jesus made and baptized more disciples than John . . ." The Pharisees could tolerate John, though with much difficulty, but they despised the Son of God in order that the prophecy might be fulfilled which Isaiah wrote, "He is despised and rejected of men . . ."

Now notice the movements of our Lord. "He left Judæa, and departed again into Galilee." He quietly but decisively withdrew Himself. He said nothing, but His actions spoke volumes. "He left Judæa, and departed again into Galilee" first, to stop the gossip regarding any possible suggestion that there was not the utmost harmony between Himself and His forerunner; and, second, as a definite testimony against a provincial people who had lost sight of God's purpose in His dealings with them. The verb *left* in the 3rd verse "He left Judæa" is particularly interesting. It has in it the idea of leaving it alone or letting it go. This particular verb does not appear anywhere else in the New Testament. It suggests that our Lord abandoned Judæa, though of course He went back to it occasionally.

There may come a time in the life of a people and in the life of an individual when the opportunity for salvation is past. God has said: "My spirit shall not always strive with man . . ." I do not believe that any of us possess such discernment that we can definitely state that God has entirely left this man or that man. It is a good thing that we do not know. But it is a solemn thought, for when Christ leaves a nation or a man, that nation or that man is left alone to grope in the dark. An illustration of this is found in the 36th verse of the 12th chapter of this Gospel where we read, "These things spake Jesus, and departed, and did hide himself from them."

Going Through Samaria

When our Lord *abandoned* Judea to go into Galilee, John tells us "he must needs go through Samaria." Now it is of interest when the Bible tells us our Lord *must* do certain things. There are several occasions in the Gospels where the imperative is used in respect to our Lord. Here it is said that Jesus *"must . . . go through Samaria."* When we look at a map we discover that one country lies in the north and the other in the south and that Samaria lies between them. So the shortest distance between the two places would be a straight line through Samaria. But that was not the usual way a ritualistic Jew would travel from Judea into Galilee. The Jews had no dealings with the Samaritans. "They were a mongrel race and practiced a religion that was partly Jewish and partly heathen." They were despised by the Jews. A devout Jew would not defile himself by going through Samaria to get to Judea. He would take a roundabout journey to avoid coming into contact with the Samaritans. But here was a Jew, an Israelite of the Israelites, who did not avoid going through Samaria, but it is written "he *must needs* go through Samaria."

There were no accidents in our Lord's life. I whole-heartedly believe in a planned economy and a planned life, but *only* under the direction of the eternal God. He is the only Planner who can properly plan a life or an economy. Our Lord's life was planned to the minutest details. He had an appointment with this woman, though the woman of Samaria knew nothing about the appointment.

It is a question what time of the day He arrived at Sychar, for while the time is given as being the sixth hour, it cannot be definitely stated whether the reckoning was Roman time or Hebrew time. If it was Roman time, it would be the evening hour, but if it was Hebrew time, it would be the noon hour.

The history of Sychar is enhanced by the fact that it was near to a parcel of ground that Jacob gave to his son Joseph and we are told that Jacob's well was there. Some bigoted Gentiles do not like to concede much to our Jewish friends, but even such individuals must acknowledge that wherever the Israelites have gone, they have always left their mark. It was more than 1700 years since Jacob purchased this parcel of ground and digged a well and yet his name was stamped indelibly into it.

And now let's look at the weary traveller who approached the well and in His tiredness sat at the well. In theology we speak of Jesus Christ being very God of very God, yet very man of very man. It is a perplexing contradiction to man, at least the natural man, but to the man who has been *born again* by the Spirit of God, it is one of his chief delights to behold the *man* Christ Jesus, the Lord of Glory. While He was not born as other men, nevertheless, He was of the seed of Abraham. While He was tempted in all points like as we, yet He was apart from sin. He never knew what it was to be tainted with a sinful desire. The sorrows that entered His life, which caused the tears to trickle down His cheeks, the weariness of mind, and heart, and body were never the results of sin; they were the fruits of His service for man. This man who could walk on the water, and still the storm and bid the waves to calm down at His word; this man who gave sight to the blind by merely touching their eyes, this man who could walk through a crowd intent upon murdering Him and yet go untouched and unrecognized—this man knew what it was to be wearied in body. He, therefore, could extend the invitation "Come unto me, all ye that labour and are heavy laden, and I will give you rest." In the breast of this woman of Samaria, whom we will consider in our next study, was a cancer that gnawed at the very vitals of her being and which made her continuously wearied and tired. But there was no cancer in Christ. Yet He was weary. Traveling through that hot oriental country, He chose an oasis at which He could recline and rest. We shall observe that He experienced the refreshment of body not by drinking from Jacob's spring, but rather through ministering to another. Our Lord during His ministry was weary, but He was never overtaxed and no one was ever turned away from Him.

We leave Him here, sitting at the well. He is the Star of Jacob. He is the one with whom Jacob wrestled. He is the one who sustained Jacob through all his trials and disappointments and his rebellions. How wonderful that in the economy of God the well that Jacob digged was to be the place where the Son of man would go to rest from the heat and burdens of the day. It is an inspiring thought to consider that the children of God can bring comfort and joy to the heart of the Son of man. It is impossible to minimize the joy that a believer gives to Christ. We are even told that there is joy in the presence of the angels of God when a sinner repents. What a man is this Man of Galilee! But the marvel of marvels is that we may know Him now and touch Him by faith, and thus experience His love and His salvation.

My friend Dr. Wilbur M. Smith of the Moody Bible Institute drew my attention to a quotation* which I believe is fitting right here: "A company of English literary men, including Charles Lamb, Hazlitt, Leigh Hunt, and others, one day fell to discussing persons they would like to have met, and after naming every possible name in the gallery of fame, whether worthy or unworthy, Charles Lamb said in his stuttering way to the company: 'There is only one person I can ever think of after this . . . If Shakespeare was to come into this room, we should all rise up to meet him; but if that person was to come into it we should all fall down and try to kiss the hem of His garment.'"

---

* Charles Lamb (1775-1834) from Hazlitt's Sketches, Anthology of Jesus, by Sir James Marchant.

Walk Nineteen

AN ENTICER BECOMES AN EVANGELIST

WE come now to the heart of the conversation which our Lord had with the woman of Samaria. The Holy Spirit has painted a masterpiece of the Man of Galilee on the trek from Judea to Galilee in the course of which He must needs pass through Samaria. And now we read in verse 7, "There cometh a woman of Samaria to draw water . . ." That of course was a familiar sight, but it is noteworthy that she was alone and likewise our Lord, for His disciples "were gone away unto the city to buy meat."

Our Lord broke a long established precedent by beginning a conversation with this woman, saying "Give me to drink." Jesus was never circumvented by religious and racial barriers, neither can He be molded into any man's prejudices. He is the Savior of the world, the universal Christ. The startled Samaritan woman immediately remonstrated, saying, "How is it that thou, being a Jew, asketh drink of me, which am a woman of Samaria? for the Jews have no dealings with the Samaritans." To this question Jesus answered, "If thou knewest the gift of God, and who it is that saith to thee, Give me to drink; thou wouldest have asked of him, and he would have given thee living water."

Ignorance No Longer An Excuse

There were two things of which the woman was in complete ignorance. First, she did not know the gift of God; and second, she did not know who He was. Our Lord not only pointed out her ignorance of these two facts but suggested that if she were not ignorant and blind, she would have immediately responded by asking of Him, and He would assuredly have given her what she asked for. The Bible declares, ". . . if our gospel be hid, it is hid to them that are lost: In whom the god of this age (a title given to Satan) hath blinded the minds of them which *believe* not, lest the light of the glorious gospel of Christ, who is the image of God, should shine unto them."

Ignorance frequently causes a man as well as a nation to violate every law of reason. It was ignorance that caused the princes of this world to crucify the Lord of glory. The whole Gentile world at one time was actuated by ignorance of God with the result that they thought the Godhead was "like unto gold, or silver, or stone, graven by art and man's device." And this ignorance reached its greatest depths in the era of the philosophers, when human wisdom was at its zenith. Because Jesus Christ had not lived and died God "overlooked" ignorance of Himself in that period. But there is no longer any excuse for ignorance. *"Now* (God) commandeth all men everywhere to repent: Because he hath appointed a day, in the which he will judge the world in righteousness by that man (Jesus Christ) whom he hath ordained; whereof he hath given assurance unto all men, in that he hath raised him from the dead."

In this 4th chapter of John's Gospel salvation is expressed by our Lord under the symbolism of living water. The only way one can receive it is by asking for it; not by paying for it or earning it. We cannot pay God. God is a benefactor, not a recipient. All that is required of us is to ask in faith, believing, and we shall receive.

Our Lord's answer aroused the curiosity of the woman, and incidentally her unbelief also, which was one more evidence of her blindness. She said, "Sir . . ." and by the way, here is another matter worthy of note. First she saw only "a man," a Jew if you please, one who despised and was despised by the Samaritans. What a potent force this incident exerts against the Satanic anti-Semitism of the day. First she only saw in Him "a Jew," but as she listened her appreciation of Him grew, so she addressed Him, "Sir." Before the interview ended she confessed Him to be a prophet and finally worshipped Him as the Christ of God. However, before she exercised faith she indulged in "rationalistic sophistry." Our unbelieving friends love to gloat over their self-admitted superior ability to see clearly and to rationalize every spiritual proposition presented to them. This woman said, "thou hast nothing to draw with . . ." And she was right. He had not a thing with Him, not a pail, or a waterpot, or a rope to let down the waterpot, not a thing to draw with. And then as if to clinch her scientific observations, she reminded Him that the well was deep. It has been suggested that it was at least 75 feet deep. So the woman added, "from whence then hast thou that living water?"

Having rationalized her unbelief, she began to match wits with our Lord, who still was a stranger to her, by asking, "Art thou greater than our father Jacob, which gave us the well, and drank thereof himself, and his children, and his cattle?" To this our Lord answered (pointing to Jacob's well), "Whosoever drinketh of this water shall thirst again: But whosoever drinketh of the water that I shall give him shall never thirst; but the water that I shall give him shall be in him a well of water springing up into everlasting life." Our Lord thus proved Himself to be a "spiritual naturalist." He used the natural to compare and to contrast with the spiritual.

Realism—What and Where Is It?

Ponce de Leon vainly sought for the fountain of youth in the bogs of Florida, but the fountain of eternal youth is a well, bubbling within a man's being, which springs up into everlasting life. A man receives it by asking, and gets it because God gives it to him.

The woman was a realist also, so she answered our Lord's comment by saying, "Sir, give me this water, that I thirst not, neither come hither to draw." She saw a way out of her dilemma, a way out of her drudgery, so she took Him at His word and asked for it. She craved it for two reasons. One, so that she would never thirst again, and second (probably primarily) so that she would not have to go to Jacob's well again to draw water. It was an embarrassing place for her to come. It was not surprising that she was alone on this occasion. The women of the town undoubtedly refused to associate with her. They knew her "case history." They knew her reputation (or lack of reputation) and she wanted to avoid the condemning glances of her sisters, the daughters of Eve.

I am sure her facial expressions must have been a remarkable study in contrasts. First, she registered disgust and contempt. Then a gleam of interest was evident, and finally a note of expectancy was clearly revealed. But suddenly our Lord said something which changed her outward expression as if a flash of lightning had paralyzed her. Jesus said, "Go, call thy husband, and come hither." Her face fell and a guilty look began to emerge. The woman answered, "I have no husband." To this our Lord responded, "Thou hast well said, I have no husband: For thou hast had five husbands; and he whom thou now hast is not thy husband: in that saidst thou truly." She was a Hollywood model though living almost two millenniums ago. Thank God, salvation is available to all. We make a grave mistake in assuming that our Lord is interested in church people only He loves sinners and it was for sinners He died. This Samaritan woman was to learn that "Christianity is the only realism on earth." Everything else is a sham.

She must have been ill at ease when our Lord flashed the X-ray of His irresistible righteousness into her darkened conscience. So would we all be under the same circumstances. While He did not say much, what He did say clearly indicated that there was not a thing hid from His eyes.

Salvation is from sin. Before there can be any appreciation of the gift of God there must be a consciousness of the need of cleansing from sin. This woman first sought refuge behind "religion," as so many people do when the Holy Spirit begins to convince them of sin. She said, "Sir, I perceive that thou art a prophet." She lost no time but immediately launched into a "discussion of religion." She said, "Our fathers worshipped in this mountain; and ye say, that in Jerusalem is the place where men ought to worship." In effect she said, we Samaritans have our own religion—you Jews have another—ours is as good as yours! We are all seeking the same God so what difference does it make? Let's talk religion—that was the substance of her reply.

But our Lord was not to be side-tracked. And wise is that soul winner who follows the Lord in his dealing with souls. He said to her, "Woman, believe me, the hour cometh, when ye shall neither in this mountain, nor yet at Jerusalem, worship the Father. Ye (Samaritans) worship ye know not what: we know what we worship: for salvation is of the Jews." The Jews alone, of all the races in the world, worshipped the one true and holy God. But our Lord continued and said, "But the hour cometh, and now is, when the true worshippers shall worship the Father in spirit and in truth: for the Father seeketh such to worship him. God is a Spirit: and they that worship him must worship him in spirit and in truth."

When our Lord dealt with Nicodemus, who incidentally was a deeply religious man, He told him that it was imperative that he be born again. He did not need to preach new birth to the woman of Samaria. She knew that she needed regeneration.

On first impression it is arresting that the Lord should have talked with a guilty, sinful woman about the truth of worshipping God. But it becomes crystal clear when we consider that men and women are sinners, and God is anxious that sinful men and women become worshippers of His holiness. Yet it was nothing short of revolutionary then, and it still is, to announce that it is no longer a *place* of worship, no longer an *institution* of worship, no longer a *ritualism* that matters, but it is the *attitude of the heart* that counts. "God is a Spirit: and they that worship him must worship him in spirit and in truth." In *spirit,* of course, is in the Holy Spirit, and in *truth* is the truth and righteousness as it is in Jesus Christ.

The Unveiled Christ

The woman said unto Him, "I know that Messias cometh, which is called Christ: when he is come, he will tell us all things." Up to this moment our Lord had unveiled to the woman her own heart, and as a result she saw her nakedness, her sinfulness, indeed her whole life passed before her in panoramic view. As it did, she sought for covering by hiding behind a religious system; but religion will never hide a man's sin from the eyes of God. It may shield us from the eyes of man, but never from the eyes of God. The atoning blood of Jesus Christ alone can cover a man's sins.

Only after our Lord had uncovered this Samaritan did He take the veil off His own face and give her to see Himself in all His glory. To her question regarding the Christ He said, *"I that speak unto thee am he."* The power of that answer can never be measured. It is devastating but it is also assuring.

Upon this, His disciples came and marveled that He talked with the woman. As they looked on in silence they observed that the woman left her waterpot and went her way into the city. There she indicated that she had lost the art of enticing—as she began to evangelize. To the men of the city she said, "Come, see a man, which told me all things that ever I did: is not this the Christ?" This woman immediately upon conversion became a missionary. She had a past to be true, but she met the Savior and now she had a message. She did not believe she had "a monopoly" on Christ. She understood that the knowledge of Christ and His forgiving grace made her a debtor to all to tell them of Christ.

But did you notice that the woman left her waterpot at the well? How unbecoming it would have been if she had taken it with her. She had asked for living water—she had received Christ, who is the living water. She now had eternal life. How absurd to carry around a waterpot or to go back to the wells of this world for temporary satisfaction. No man or woman can bear an effective testimony to the world while carrying around "a waterpot" on his or her head.

This Samaritan woman told the men first about Christ then about herself. That's the order of true testimony. We ought never to reverse it. We ought not to talk about ourselves first. Let us talk about Christ first, then if advisable tell of our own experience. "Come, see a man, (that's an invitation) which told me all things that ever I did: (that's a confession) is not this the Christ? (that is an affirmation)." Her testimony was effective. The men of course knew of her past life, but now her face was aglow with the smile of God's grace and evidenced the possession of a peace that "passeth all understanding."

The men left the city to go out to the well side to see and hear the Christ and when they came, the woman did not have another word to say. She had borne her testimony, she had given her witness and now, seeing they had come into direct contact with Christ, she left them with Him. Would that our testimony might be as effective, so that men will come to Him! If they do, the result will be identically the same as it was in their case.

But I must not leave this incident in the ministry of our Lord without proclaiming the fact that this interview between Christ and the Samaritan woman declares with dynamic power that a broken, sin-bound life has unlimited possibilities when Christ touches that life. How appropriate are the words of William Blane:

> She left her waterpot, and ran
>   The wonderful tale to tell
> Of living water, and the Man
>   Whom she met at Jacob's well.
>
> "I found Him wearied," she said, "and lone,
>   Beneath the shadowing tree,
> And in a sweet, heart-thrilling tone
>   He craved a drink from me.
>
> "Then He spake of water to quench the thirst
>   From a living well unseen;
> But when I sought it, He showed me first
>   What a sinner I had been.
>
> "He told me all that ever I did—
>   Each act of my life lay bare—
> O! nought from His searching gaze was hid
>   As I stood before Him there.

"I owned Him a prophet, and asked Him where
   True worship could be giv'n;
But my life and my worship, He show'd me, were
   Alike unfit for Heav'n.

" 'Messiah's coming,' I said, 'is nigh,
   And then we shall all agree';
And with heavenly sweetness He answered, 'I
   That speak unto thee am He.'

"And I know it is true, for a power divine
   That moment my spirit freed.
I believe what He said and I claim Him mine,
   For He meets my deepest need.

"Come, see! in my bosom cannot be hid
   A blessing so unpric'd;
He told me all that ever I did—
   Oh, say, is He not the Christ?"

WALK TWENTY

THE POWER OF A TESTIMONY

WE have been considering the setting as well as the substance of the remarkable conversation which our Lord had with the unnamed Samaritan woman. Many lessons may be learned from an examination of the interview, not least among which is the power of a living witness. Christ said to His disciples, just before His ascension, "ye shall be witnesses unto me . . ." Every Christian ought to be a witness for Christ. The world has a right to an examination of our lives, for alas, far too few people take time to even open the Bible, much less read it to determine what the Gospel really is.

It is thrilling to observe the influence this questionable character exercised over the men of the Samaritan city when she said, "Come, see a man . . ." There was such sincerity in her tone, such evident possession of a peace in her heart, such apparent transformation of life that they were *compelled* to leave the city and go directly to the One of whom the woman witnessed.

Nathanael said, "Can there any good thing come out of Nazareth?" Philip said, "Come and see." Many of us *argue* the Gospel because our walk is inconsistent with our profession. Arguments generate strife. A Christian's business is not to argue but to present Christ.

When a man's life is consistent with his testimony, when there is evident transformation of character, it is inevitable that the testimony will carry weight.

"Come, see a man, which told me all things that ever I did: is not this the Christ?" said the Samaritan woman. Reading from verse 30 of the 4th chapter of John's Gospel, we learn:

> "Then they went out of the city, and came unto him.
> "In the mean while his disciples prayed him, saying, Master, eat.
> "But he said unto them, I have meat to eat that ye know not of.
> "Therefore said the disciples one to another, Hath any man brought him ought to eat?
> "Jesus saith unto them, My meat is to do the will of him that sent me, and to finish his work.
> "Say not ye, There are yet four months, and then cometh harvest? behold, I say unto you, Lift up your eyes, and look on the fields; for they are white already to harvest.
> "And he that reapeth receiveth wages, and gathereth fruit unto life eternal: that both he that soweth and he that reapeth may rejoice together.
> "And herein is that saying true, One soweth, and another reapeth.
> "I sent you to reap that whereon ye bestowed no labour: other men laboured, and ye are entered into their labours.
> "And many of the Samaritans of that city believed on him for the saying of the woman, which testified, He told me all that ever I did.
> "So when the Samaritans were come unto him, they besought him that he would tarry with them: and he abode there two days.
> "And many more believed because of his own word;
> "And said unto the woman, Now we believe, not because of thy saying: for we have heard him ourselves, and know that this is indeed the Christ, the Saviour of the world."

It is interesting to compare the reactions men experienced as a result of coming in contact with Jesus of Nazareth. There were those who constantly and persistently cried out, "Show us a sign." The same "Missourian" word is heard today from the lips of multitudes. They say, "We want to *see* before *believing*—show us a miracle, then we will believe!" But the reaction is still the same as at the time when our Lord Jesus said that He did not commit Himself unto such men, who believe merely because they see. Miracles do not beget faith. ". . . faith cometh by hearing, and hearing by the word of God." Our Lord did not perform a single miracle while He was in

Samaria. It was the power of His word that convinced the Samaritan woman and that also convinced the men of the city. "The entrance of thy words giveth light . . ." said the Scriptures.

Abraham answered the rich man accordingly when he suggested that someone from the dead be sent back to warn his brethren so that they would not come into the same predicament in which he was found. Abraham rightly said, "They have Moses and the prophets; let them hear them . . . If they hear not Moses and the prophets, neither will they be persuaded, though one rose from the dead."

The Lone Master and His Disciples

The shifting scenes which the Holy Spirit has drawn for us in the 4th chapter of this Gospel are all thought-provoking. For instance, we can clearly observe the disciples and see the expression upon their faces as they returned from the city where they had purchased some food. They were speechless as they saw the Lord talking to a Samaritan woman. Then they noticed that the woman left her waterpot at the well and proceeded to go to the city. Finally they got up sufficient courage to speak two words to the silent Man who sat by the well side. They prayed Him, saying, "Master, eat." To this our Lord gave a simple reply, "I have meat to eat that ye know not of." That they did not understand Him was evident by their immediate discussions one with the other as they whispered, "Hath any man brought him ought to eat?" Even a whisper is heard by the Lord, so He responded, "My meat is to do the will of him that sent me, and to finish his work."

No man has ever been able to honestly make such an assertion. None of us can say that our meat is to do the will of God or, for that matter, to finish the work that God may have given us to do, but our Lord could say it because it was true. "My meat is to do the will of him that sent me, and to finish *his* work." Back in the 40th Psalm it is written:

> "Sacrifice and offering thou didst not desire; mine ears hast thou opened: burnt-offering and sin-offering hast thou not required.
> "Then said I, Lo, I come: in the volume of the book it is written of me,
> "I delight to do thy will, O my God: yea, thy law is within my heart."

The Holy Spirit has been pleased to tell us in the Epistle to the Hebrews that it was the Lord Jesus who was speaking in the 40th Psalm, where in the volume of the book it was written of Him that He was to come to do God's will. That *will* involved the offering up of His body, once for all, by which *will* we are sanctified who believe in Him.

Our Lord did not say, "My meat is to do the will of him that sent me, and finish the work *that God has given me to do.*" Oh no! He said, ". . . and to finish *his* work." Salvation is of the Lord. Redemption is God's work. God was in Christ reconciling the world unto Himself. When did Christ finish the work? On the cross, where He cried out, "It is finished." In fact, He used one word only—"Finished." Jesus Christ came to do God's will and to complete God's work. He is the only *man* ever born into this world with the express purpose of dying on a cross to put away sin by the sacrifice of Himself.

Of course the words were an enigma to the disciples, but they listened further as He said, "Say not ye, There are yet four months, and then cometh harvest? behold, I say unto you, Lift up your eyes, and look on the fields; for they are white already to harvest." Someone has suggested that as the men left the city, clothed in their white garments and white hoods, they looked like a field, white already to harvest. They were ready to be harvested because one woman bore an effective testimony concerning Christ. No man can measure the influence of a sincere testimony. Neither can any man tell how long it will take between the time the seed is sown and the harvest reaped.

A Commission—A Witness

I am very strong in the belief that men are called for a specific ministry and that this is done exclusively by the Holy Spirit. A ministry, if it is to be effective and honoring to God, must be under the direction of the Viceroy of Christ, who is the Holy Spirit. For example, our Lord commissioned twelve disciples and gave them a special ministry. He also called seventy unnamed men and gave each a specific task to perform. He sent them out, two by two, and told them how they were to conduct themselves and what they were to preach. Not a single detail was left to their imagination. A supervised ministry is the only ministry that is effective. I do not mean supervised by men—that's tyranny; but supervised by the Holy Spirit—that's power!

But here is an interesting thing. This woman was never commissioned by the Lord. He did not command her as He did the man out of whom He drove the legion of demons. That man delighted to sit in His presence and prayed the Lord that he might remain with Him. Yet our Lord answered, "No," and then commissioned him to go home and tell his friends what great things the Lord had done for him. Incidentally that man, previously demon-possessed and bound, became the first home missionary. But this woman received no such commission. She was urged to go out and witness for Christ solely by an overwhelming sense of relief from sin and bondage, and the conscious peace of God which was abiding in her heart.

Every Christian is a witness. Any Christian who fails to witness for Christ is untrue to his Lord and unfaithful to himself and to the world about him.

It is impossible to measure the influence which followed this woman's testimony. It thrills one to the depths of his being to realize that a woman upon whom a cloud previously rested, a despised person, a woman sunk in sin, could be redeemed and lifted up, so that she could go out to bear a witness so effective that the men of the city had to take cognizance of it. They came to the Lord and heard Him themselves. It is astounding what can be accomplished through a life devoted to Christ. It is equally startling to observe the effects of the aftermath of a life of sin.

In a recent issue of "Christian Life and Faith," there appears an interesting article along this line, giving details of a research that had been made. It told about "a very licentious man who married a licentious woman in 1677. From that union there were 1,900 descendants. Of these, 771 were criminals, 250 were arrested and tried for various crimes; 60 were thieves and 60 spent 120 years in prison; 39 were convicted of murder, 40 of the women were known to have a social disease; only 10 of the great number ever learned trades and they learned them in prison. The entire descendants spent 1,300 years in prison, costing the State of New York $2,700,000 to prosecute them, maintain them in prison and in the poorhouse. That is what two people in marriage did for the United States.

"Now for the contrast let us refer to the Edwards' family. Mr. Edwards, a godly man, married a beautiful godly woman; a son was born who turned out to be a godly man. That son came to America and later became a lawyer and his son became a minister upon whom Harvard conferred two degrees in one day. This last mentioned was Jonathan Edwards who was president of Princeton University. When the Edwards' investigation stopped, the number of descendants totalled 1,344. Of this number, 295 were college graduates, 13 college professors, 65 college presidents, 186 ministers of the Gospel, 101 were lawyers, 86 were State Senators and three were Congressmen, 30 Judges, and one Vice-President of the United States; there were 75 laymen and Sunday School officers. In the entire record of the Edwards' family, none were ever arrested or tried for crime. That is what two godly people can do for the world."

Speaking of Jonathan Edwards, who had "a delicate and nervous constitution and who was an habitual invalid," I like the comments of Oliver Wendell Holmes, who certainly could not be classed as a "fundamentalist." He rebelled against Jonathan Edwards' theology, but he readily acknowledged the power of his intellect, the purity of his heart and life, and the tremendous influence he exercised not only in New England, but all over this country and the British Isles. Seeking to account for what Edwards was and did, Holmes took a look at his ancestry and environment, and this is what he wrote: "His (Jonathan Edwards') ancestors had fed on sermons so long that he must have been born with scriptural texts lying latent in his embryonic thinking-marrow, like the undeveloped picture in a film of collodion . . ." To put it in other words, Jonathan Edwards was brought up on the Bible. You mothers and fathers can do nothing more necessary for your children than to bring them up on the bottle of the sincere milk of the Word of God.

Every Christian has read or heard about Andrew Murray, that saintly man "who had 11 children, all of whom grew to adult life. Five of the six sons became ministers of the Gospel, and four of the daughters became ministers' wives. The next generation had a still more striking record in that ten grandsons became ministers and thirteen became missionaries." Measure the influence of a godly life? Impossible!

But let me take you down to the present day. I think of my friend, the late Mr. Peter Stam whom I greatly admired. He was raised in a saloon, at least, his father had a saloon in the Netherlands and this young man entertained the customers with his antics. He came to America from Holland about 1890 and shortly thereafter met a godly young lady who led him to Christ. Now that couple, in the autumn of their lives, had seven children living and twenty-two grandchildren. One child died in infancy and one son, John, gave his life as a missionary in China. Another son is a missionary in Africa, another is a pastor. Still another is in Christian educational work. Two daughters are in volunteer Christian work. The other two sons are actively engaged in business but equally alert in bearing testimony for Christ. Several of the grandchildren have already borne effective witness for Christ. The power of a testimony—who can measure it? One of the sons who is now the father of four children, is a contractor by trade, and interested in Building and Loan Association work. Some time ago he was made President of the New Jersey State organization and a dinner was given in his honor. As he walked into the room filled with friends and business associates, the band struck up, "Hail, hail, the gang's all here" and all sang until they came to the second line "what the . . . ." Then everyone stopped. The orchestra leader wondered what was wrong till somebody told him. "This man is a Stam and the Stams, you know, are Christians." It was a striking testimony to the effectiveness of a Christian life.

The Savior of the World

But again it is arresting to observe how quickly reaping may follow the sowing of seed. The woman had sown the seed through her testimony. The men came out from the city to hear Christ. Many believed as a result of the witness of the woman. But after listening to the Lord, many more believed because of His own word, and they said to the woman, "Now we believe, not because of thy saying: for we have heard him ourselves, and know that this is indeed the Christ, the Savior of the world." And they besought Him that He would tarry with them: and He abode there two days.

Here also is a noteworthy thing—It was these Samaritan men who first gave to our Lord that magnificent title, "The Savior of the world." It did not take them long to discover that racial and religious barriers were of no concern to the Christ.

Our Lord said, "God so loved the *world*" and that He sent His Son into the *world*, not to condemn it, "but that the *world* through him might be saved." The Samaritan men said, He is "the Savior of the *world*." The Apostle Paul said that He "is the Savior of all men, especially of those that believe." The unsaved man never takes cognizance of the fact that if it were not for the grace of our Lord Jesus Christ he would be immediately condemned to eternal banishment from God. It is only the grace of God that prevents immediate judgment from being expressed against sin. The goodness of God is available in order that men may repent and turn to the Lord Jesus Christ. For my eternal welfare, the fact that Jesus Christ is the Savior of the *world* will not be of great importance, but that He is *my* Savior, because I have personally appropriated Him and have believed the record that God has given concerning His Son, means that I am eternally sheltered under His blood and that some day I shall eternally enjoy His presence. It is for that reason the Apostle Paul said, He (Christ) "loved me, and gave himself for me." Can you say the same? If you can, your destiny is settled.

Walk Twenty-One

SICKNESS—A TRAGEDY OR A BLESSING

IN the 3rd verse of the 4th chapter we learned that our Lord left Judea and departed to go into Galilee. On His journey He stopped at a Samaritan city for two days and after that He went into Galilee. What happened upon His arrival we learn from verse 44 to the end of the chapter, where we read:

> "For Jesus himself testified, that a prophet hath no honour in his own country.
> "Then when he was come into Galilee, the Galilæans received him, having seen all the things that he did at Jerusalem at the feast: for they also went unto the feast.
> "So Jesus came again into Cana of Galilee, where he made the water wine. And there was a certain nobleman, whose son was sick at Capernaum.
> "When he heard that Jesus was come out of Judæa

> into Galilee, he went unto him, and besought him that he would come down, and heal his son: for he was at the point of death.
>
> "Then said Jesus unto him, Except ye see signs and wonders, ye will not believe.
>
> "The nobleman saith unto him, Sir, come down ere my child die.
>
> "Jesus saith unto him, Go thy way; thy son liveth. And the man believed the word that Jesus had spoken unto him, and he went his way.
>
> "And as he was now going down, his servants met him, and told him, saying, Thy son liveth.
>
> "Then enquired he of them the hour when he began to amend. And they said unto him, Yesterday at the seventh hour the fever left him.
>
> "So the father knew that it was at the same hour, in the which Jesus said unto him, Thy son liveth: and himself believed, and his whole house.
>
> "This is again the second miracle that Jesus did, when he was come out of Judæa into Galilee."

It is quite evident that John was not quoting our Lord as insisting that He had no honor in Galilee, but rather that He had no honor in Judea, for when He was come into Galilee, "the Galilæans received him, having seen all the things that he did at Jerusalem at the feast: for they also went unto the feast."

The Second Miracle

The remainder of this chapter is devoted to the second miracle which our Lord performed while in Cana of Galilee. Previously He had changed water into wine. Now He was met by a man whom the Scripture calls a nobleman. He probably was a member of the court of Herod. This nobleman's son was sick. That of course was nothing unusual. Sickness is no respecter of persons. It enters the hovels of the poor as well as the palaces of the rich. Wherever sickness enters, it strikes horror into the hearts of the loved ones who watch over their sick. This man evidently was in a position to engage the best of physicians; but alas, the boy was at the point of death.

When the young man's father heard that our Lord had left Judea to go into Galilee, he immediately proceeded to contact our Lord. When he met Him, he besought Him that He would come down and heal his son. One can readily appreciate the state of mind of this father. There was nothing more important in his mind than the well-being of his son. He had correctly concluded that only one could help him and that was our Lord Jesus Christ. He requested our Lord to do two things: first, to come down to where the boy was; and second, to heal him. He evidently had some confidence in Christ, yet there was something lacking, for our Lord's answer was in the form of a rebuke "Except ye see signs and wonders, ye will not believe." But this did not deter the father, for he knew that every moment's delay made the condition of the boy that much worse, and so he said, "Sir, come down ere my child die." Our Lord did not answer his request. He did not go down, He did not visit the boy, but He said to the father, "Go thy way; thy son liveth." Do not mistake this for "absent treatment," whatever that may be. There was no treatment in this case—absent or otherwise. The response of the father to the word of our Lord is best expressed in the language of the writer of this chapter when he wrote, "And the man believed the word that Jesus had spoken unto him, and he went his way."

It is striking that the father did not immediately return home. The journey was no more than twenty miles and certainly could have been made in four or five hours; and yet the father tarried. He evidently placed confidence in the words of our Lord. He stayed somewhere overnight for some purpose and the next day proceeded home. As he was going down the servants met him and they told him, "Thy son liveth." They used the very words which our Lord used. But the father's faith was a bit shaky, for he enquired of them the hour when the boy *began* to amend, but the servants said, "Yesterday at the seventh hour the fever *left* him." The father knew that the seventh hour was the very hour that Jesus said unto him, "Go thy way; thy son liveth." As a result the man believed; that is, he believed on the Lord Jesus Christ; and not only did the father believe, but his whole house.

In our last study I suggested that miracles do not beget faith; but that ". . . faith cometh by hearing, and hearing by the word of God." And yet there is a place for miracles. In this Gospel, our Lord's miracles were *signs* to attest the fact that He was the anointed of God. Signs and wonders accompanied His ministry for that purpose exclusively. In this particular case, it was the word of our Lord which the man believed. He heard the word of our Lord, faith was begotten, and his faith was confirmed afterward by the miracle that had taken place.

The Lessons This Miracle Teaches

Now let us look at the lessons which may be learned from this portion of Scripture. Sickness has been in this world since sin entered into it. The very blood flowing through our veins carries the germs that will bring about our death. Sickness is a common experience of man. The most important possession that a man has is his life. Satan properly analyzed man's philosophy of life when he said, ". . . all that a man hath will he give for his life." We fight against death—and well might we do so. Multitudes are willing to give everything in exchange for physical well-being. So I want to discuss the subject of sickness and what the Christian's attitude should be in respect to it.

Recently one of the most saintly women of this generation died and her body was buried in the dust of the earth. For quite an extended period she lay on a sick bed and during the last few days of her life was entirely unconscious. Her name is almost as well known as that of Fanny Crosby, and if our Lord's coming does not take place shortly, her name will become increasingly better known because of the remarkable work which she did. I refer to Mrs. Abigail Luff, better known by the name "Sister Abigail," who wrote the tract "I am not going to a Christless grave, are you?" and concerning whom "Little is Much when God is in It" was written. For years she conducted in her own home a hospital for incurable invalids. To many people her experiences were remarkable. They were remarkable because most of us walk so far off from the Lord that we miss His guidance in our lives. Mrs. Luff was the kind of woman who believed God and walked with Him. For example, being assured that the Lord wanted her to go to New York City for a specific task, yet living in Buffalo and without money in her pocketbook, she would proceed to the railroad station and approach the ticket agent's booth for a ticket, knowing full well that her God would supply the money before the ticket passed the hand of the ticket agent. And the God of all grace never once disappointed His trusting child. Yet He allowed her to be sick; He permitted her to suffer excruciating pain and finally took her to Himself.

Did not our Lord say to this nobleman, "Except ye see signs and wonders, ye will not believe"? A strong faith has confidence in God, signs or no signs, and expresses itself in the language of the patriarch, "Though he slay me, yet will I trust in him . . ." I am not minimizing the discomfiture nor the heartaches that come as a result of a loved one being sick, nor am I unmindful of the aching void that comes when death stalks into the sick chamber. How true are the lines of Horatius Bonar:

> "Few understand deep sorrow; fewer care to be beside it;
> For the world loves not sackcloth, hides its eyes
> From dust and ashes, fears the name of death,
> Shuns the mute mourner in his day of tears,
> Thrusts away all that mars its festive mirth,
> Or mocks the music of its reckless song.
>
> "Ere man can comfort man, he first must suffer,—
> The tearless dry no tears; the whole in heart
> Bind up no broken spirits; 'tis not theirs
> To mix and minister the balm that heals.
> It is by sorrow that God trains His own,
> And moulds them for the highest service here,
> Like His who, as the Man of sorrows, knew
> To soothe the sad, to speak the words that cheer."

But there is another lesson to be learned from this incident. In this case the Lord did not use means to bring about the healing of the boy's body, He simply told the father, "Go thy way; thy son liveth." On other occasions our Lord did use means. Once he took some dust of the earth and mixed it with spittle and from it made clay and put it on a blind man's eyes and then told the blind man to go to the pool of Siloam and wash, and assured him that he would come seeing. On other occasions He would touch the person's eyes, or lift up the sick. It is a mistake therefore to insist that God does not permit the use of means for the bodily healing of His saints.

But again, it is noteworthy to observe that in this case our Lord healed the sick boy though He did not do it in the manner which the father asked and supposed He would. It is inadvisable to dictate to God the method or the means which He should employ, but we have a right to pray. It is better to put our problem before Him and allow the Lord to use His own wisdom. Again, it is a mistake to assume that because God healed in this particular case He must heal in every case. One need only refer to two or three notable names to refute the notion. The Apostle Paul had a thorn in the flesh, which was undoubtedly a physical ailment. He pled three times that the Lord would remove it, but the Lord refused, but added, "My grace is sufficient for thee . . ." The Apostle Paul, mighty man that he was, went so far as to say, "Most gladly therefore will I rather glory in my infirmities, that the power of Christ may rest upon me." Timothy was an invalid. So likewise have been many of God's choicest saints.

Let us never assume that a weak body is necessarily a detriment to Christian service. But whether God heals or not, and whether He uses means or not, we can all say from the bottom of our hearts:

> "Bless the LORD, O my soul: and all that is within me, bless his holy name.
> "Bless the LORD, O my soul, and forget not all his benefits:
> "Who forgiveth all thine iniquities; who healeth all thy diseases . . . "

There is no physician so irrational as to suppose that he has brought about the healing of any human being. He has simply studied God's other book, the book of Nature, and learned God's laws of remedy and applied those laws to the body of the sick man or sick woman. It is always God that healeth.

WORTHY TO BE BELIEVED

There are other lessons in this portion of Scripture, not least of which is this: our Lord is worthy to be believed. When He speaks there is no higher service we can render to Him than to believe His word. His promises have never failed. I am glad that though this man's faith *began* to waver, the promise of God was yea and amen in Christ. Most of us will have to confess that we have very little faith. Our Lord said that if we had faith like a grain of mustard seed, we could remove mountains. Despite the fact that the disciples were constantly with our Lord for three years and saw how He made provision for every need, nevertheless they were weak in faith. But did you notice this: the disciples never questioned the power of God. Neither do we. The disciples questioned the love of God and we are equally guilty. When the storm broke on the lake of Gennesaret, the Son of God was asleep in the hinder part of the ship, unconscious of the storm. The disciples, struggling against the forces of nature, were terrified and finally rebuked the Lord by saying, "Master, *carest* thou not that we perish?" There was no question about His *power,* but a definite question about His *care* for them. You will recall that our Lord stilled the wind and the sea, and then rebuked the disciples saying, "Why are ye so fearful? how is it that ye have no faith?"

Now for one final word. Did you observe what happened as a result of the miracle? The boy was healed; he was again vibrant with life. The father had his prayer answered and the home was filled with joy, and now the center of joy was the Person of Christ. It is written, "So the father knew that it was at the same hour, in the which Jesus said unto him, Thy son liveth: and himself believed, and his whole house."

Oliver Wendell Holmes delivered a lecture before the medical class of Harvard University on November 6, 1867, which he entitled "Scholastic and Bedside Teaching." Not a bad title! There are many things in the address which are thought-provoking. He said that the most essential part of the student's instruction is obtained not in the lecture room, but at the bedside, and that the bedside is always the true center of medical teaching. He drew attention to the old-fashioned method of instruction, which consisted of a student accompanying his master. Holmes pictured a worthy master, Firman by name, making his round of visits accompanied by a student to whom he gave the Scriptural name of Luke. The first dwelling they entered, they found a stout fellow bellowing with colic. The doctor diagnosed the ailment and prescribed a remedy. Then the conversation that took place between the doctor and the youth is reported. The youth in a whisper said, "He will die, master, of a surety methinks." But the wise doctor said, "This fellow is at his prayers today, but I warrant thee he will be swearing with the best of them tomorrow." I am inclined to think we have little difficulty in recognizing ourselves in the picture. How many of us in our extremity, in an hour of need and in a time of sickness, prayed earnestly for God's healing and blessing; we vowed that if God answered our prayer we would yield our lives to Him and serve Him faithfully and honestly; but the extremity was met, the need past, the healing was extended, but we forgot about our promise and continued our lives in the very same manner as heretofore. Not so with this nobleman nor his family. They believed on the Lord Jesus Christ, the whole household was saved. As far as I know, this is the first case in the New Testament where a whole household believed.

God has a way of making the wrath of man to praise Him. He can take unpleasant experiences and make them to be stepping stones to a deeper and more personal relationship with Himself. Were we to ask this nobleman and his wife and family if the experiences of anguish and disappointment were worthwhile, they would immediately have responded, "By all means." It was the sickness of this child that led the father to Christ and opened the way for Christ to enter that home. As far as Christians are concerned, ". . . we know that all things work together for good to them that love God, to them who are the called according to his purpose." But on the basis of this experience we can say that God may also use the disappointments in the life of an unsaved person to bring that individual to a knowledge of Himself.

Walk Twenty-Two

THE CLINIC AND THE ANGEL OF BETHESDA

IN the library of the American Antiquarian Society there is a curious document entitled "The Angel of Bethesda" with a sub-title describing the contents as "An essay upon the *Common Maladies of Mankind*, offering, first, the sentiment of Piety; etc., etc., and a collection of plain but potent and Approved Remedies for the Maladies." There are 36 chapters in this interesting work. It was written by Cotton Mather, one of the earliest of the Puritans, who himself was a godly man. It is quite evident that Mather took his thought-provoking title from the 5th chapter of St. John's Gospel.

There is an old medieval saying that "where there are three physicians, there are two atheists," and, it is probably true. Yet some of the most notable physicians have been devout Christians. In our own day, scores upon scores could be named but we shall mention only one, the eminent Dr. Howard Atwood Kelly of Johns Hopkins in Baltimore, Md. The immortal words of Ambrose Pare, who a few generations ago occupied the Professor's chair in the French School of Medicine—"I dressed his wound and God healed it"—epitomizes the Christian physician's viewpoint of the medical profession.

Hospitals are a by-product of the Gospel of Jesus Christ. The earliest American physicians were mostly ministers. I personally do not believe that a physician's education is complete without a definite knowledge of the Word of God; for the Bible is not only occupied with the souls of men but with their bodies as well. Much of the ministry of our Lord was devoted to the healing of bodily ills. In fact, a large part of His ministry was of the clinic variety.

The first anesthetic that was ever given was administered by our Lord when He put Adam into a deep sleep, and the first operation was performed by the same Physician, even without the aid of a nurse, when He took a rib from the side of Adam and from it formed a woman to be a helpmeet to the man. There are a number of suggested medical helps in the Bible, none of which can be improved upon by the most modern medical science.

But let's read the divine record as to what our Lord did when He entered The Clinic Of Bethesda:

> "After this there was a feast of the Jews; and Jesus went up to Jerusalem.
> "Now there is at Jerusalem by the sheep market a pool, which is called in the Hebrew tongue Bethesda, having five porches.
> "In these lay a great multitude of impotent folk, of blind, halt, withered, waiting for the moving of the water.
> "For an angel went down at a certain season into the pool, and troubled the water: whosoever then first after the troubling of the water stepped in was made whole of whatsoever disease he had.
> "And a certain man was there, which had an infirmity thirty and eight years.
> "When Jesus saw him lie, and knew that he had been now a long time in that case, he saith unto him, Wilt thou be made whole?
> "The impotent man answered him, Sir, I have no man, when the water is troubled, to put me into the pool: but while I am coming, another steppeth down before me.
> "Jesus saith unto him, Rise, take up thy bed, and walk.
> "And immediately the man was made whole, and took up his bed, and walked: and on the same day was the sabbath.
> "The Jews therefore said unto him that was cured, It is the sabbath day: it is not lawful for thee to carry thy bed.
> "He answered them, He that made me whole, the same said unto me, Take up thy bed, and walk.
> "Then asked they him, What man is that which said unto thee, Take up thy bed, and walk?
> "And he that was healed wist not who it was: for Jesus had conveyed himself away, a multitude being in that place.
> "Afterward Jesus findeth him in the temple, and said unto him, Behold, thou art made whole: sin no more, lest a worse thing come unto thee.
> "The man departed, and told the Jews that it was Jesus, which had made him whole."

Some men have used a lot of paper and ink in a futile attempt to determine the exact feast to which John referred. When the Bible is silent, it is the part of wisdom to forget about the matter, for no amount of speculation will ever answer the question. For some good reason, known only to Himself, the Holy Spirit has chosen not to reveal the time of the year when this event took place. All we know is that it was at one of the feasts of the Jews, and that our Lord went up to Jerusalem. We do not know whether He was accompanied by His disciples or whether He was alone. If alone, then He later rehearsed the incident to John and possibly some of the other disciples.

Was It An Angel?

Again, some learned and godly men have questioned whether the last part of verse 3 and all of verse 4 belong to the divine record, where we are informed that this great multitude of impotent folk, blind, halt, and withered, were "waiting for the moving of the waters. For an angel came down at a certain season into the pool, and troubled the water: whosoever then first after the troubling of the water stepped in was made whole of whatsoever disease he had." There are a number of ancient manuscripts, including the Sinai, in which these words are not to be found. In other manuscripts the statement appears to have been added as an interpolation, possibly with the idea of conveying the popular understanding of what took place. That the water was troubled no one denies, for the diseased man said to our Lord, "Sir, I have no man, when the water is troubled, to put me into the pool. . . ." But whether the water was actually troubled by an angel or the idea was only the common superstition, is a matter for conjecture. I personally find no difficulty in believing that an angel did go down into the pool at a certain season of the year, for in the history of Israel, the ministration of angels was not an uncommon thing. Of this we can be sure, however, the people believed there were healing qualities in the water, but beneficial only to the one who first entered after the water was stirred or troubled. Again, this too may have been a common superstition. If it was, it certainly is in harmony with everything we know about the condition of the people in the land at the time mentioned.

The pool which in the Hebrew tongue was called "Bethesda" which means "house of mercy," was located by the sheep gate where the lambs were kept for temple sacrifices. This pool had five porches, and in those porches lay a great multitude of impotent folk, blind, halt and withered. There was much sickness at the time of our Lord's ministry and *here* was a tremendous multitude suffering from various ailments. It was a Sabbath day. It appears that each man or woman had a bed and lay on it waiting until the water was stirred.

Our Lord walked unrecognized into this clinic. He went to what was probably the most desperate case. Here was an instance of our Lord seeking a sick man, not the sick man seeking Christ. We are told that this man had had an infirmity thirty-eight years. It does not say that he was at the pool thirty-eight years but that he was incapacitated for that long period. If you please, he was a confirmed invalid. It appears that he had no friends.

There is a suggestion in the words of our Lord that would justify the comment of Marcus Dods, "not always are the miserable willing to be relieved." In our Authorized Version the words of our Lord are translated, "Wilt thou be made whole?" But our Lord never talked like that. Frequently He used the vernacular of the day. What He did say was this: "Do you want to be made whole?" or "Are you willing to be made whole?" There are some people who are perfectly content to remain invalids just as there are many people who are satisfied to live in their sins. They do not want to be saved. No man will ever be saved unless he wants to be saved.

Our Lord never performed a miracle or a healing ministration just for the sake of healing the sick. There was always a lesson in spiritual truth connected with it.

In this case, the man did not honestly answer our Lord's question, "Are you willing to be made whole?" He evaded by saying, "Sir, I have no man, when the water is troubled, to put me into the pool: but while I am coming, another steppeth down before me." To this our Lord responded, "Rise, take up thy bed, and walk." The Bible record is clear, and thoroughly attested by witnesses, that immediately the man was made whole. He took up his bed and walked and caused a great stir among the religious leaders of the day.

The Healing

Now let's look more closely at the command of our Lord and the response on the part of this man. It is nothing short of a miracle that a man who was infirm for thirty-eight years could arise in the flash of a moment, and have sufficient strength in his legs and arms, not only to walk with a snap, but to carry a bed with him. That a notable miracle was performed that Sabbath day is beyond contradiction. But here is an interesting thing: the man did not know the name of his benefactor nor who He was; nevertheless there is one thing for which he should be highly commended: he blindly obeyed the Lord. His was a case, not so much of faith, but of obedience.

But notice our Lord. He was unrecognized and that certainly is startling. When we think of the reception that was given to their Majesties, the King and Queen of England on their visit to the United States, to say nothing of the multitude who strained their necks and sweltered in a hot sun to get a look at them, it is nothing short of amazing that the Son of God and God the Son, Who upholds all things by the word of His power, the King of kings and the Lord of lords, should have come to a Spa and been unrecognized by the multitude. There was no reception committee awaiting Him. He was not even formally introduced to anybody. How true it is that only God could act like Jesus Christ. He went directly to this man. He saw him lying and knew that he had been there a long time. He did not have to refer to a chart or ask the man any question except "Are you willing to be made whole?"

Our Lord used no means on this occasion. He simply spoke the word of power, "Rise, take up thy bed, and walk." This man was told to do three things: stand up—pick up—and walk. He did exactly as he was told and immediately he was made whole. He never asked the name of our Lord nor inquired any details concerning Him, but proceeded on his way in blind obedience to the commands of the "unrecognized" Christ.

Then our Lord conveyed Himself away unbeknown to the multitude. But our Lord did not lose sight of His "patient." He later found him in the temple and there said to him, "Behold, thou art made whole: sin no more, lest a worse thing come unto thee."

Sickness and Sin

From the words of our Lord we learn that this man's infirmity was due to his own sin. This has led some people to the erroneous conclusion that all sickness is due to sin in the individual's life. Nothing can be more far-fetched. In the 9th chapter is the record of a man who was born blind. As the Lord passed by and saw him, the disciples noted that our Lord's eyes were fixed on the young man; therefore they raised the question, "Master, who did sin, this man, or his parents, that he was born blind?" To this our

Lord answered, "Neither hath this man sinned, nor his parents: but that the works of God should be made manifest in him." But in the case of the man at the Bethesda pool, we do know that the moral malady led to the physical ailment. Our Lord reached the moral through the physical as He often did.

But there are also a few other things we ought to notice about the man himself. There was no period of convalescence; he was immediately made whole. I like the comment of Dr. Marcus Dods, to whom we have already referred, who said, "the Lord did not make a provision for a relapse." He told the man to *pick up* his bed. That illustrates a beautiful spiritual truth. When our Lord saves a man, He saves him whole. He does not make provision for a relapse. Some religious systems have devised a theory that a man may be saved today but lost tomorrow and saved the following day but lost the next, and so on, ad infinitum. The Bible knows only of *eternal* salvation which is ours immediately upon receiving the Lord Jesus Christ as our Savior and obeying His commands.

"The National Sabbath Relations Board"

There was one untoward situation which developed as a result of this miracle. The "delegates" from the Sanhedrin who watched the behavior of the people on the Sabbath day as closely as any "Union delegate" does today in his respective field, caught this man doing something which they decreed unlawful on the Sabbath. They found that he was exerting himself by carrying his bed. What a calamity! That was "anathema" to a "Religious Unionist Delegate." So they said to him, "See here! It is not lawful for you to carry your bed. Don't you know today is the Sabbath day?" Regimentation of the lives of human beings is nothing new. These religious leaders thought they could do it but their efforts ended in disaster. All similar efforts at regimentation have failed in the past and always will fail. The man simply answered, "He that made me whole, the same said unto me, Take up thy bed, and walk."

It is inconceivable that these "Pharisees" were unaware of the man, nor the circumstances surrounding his illness. He probably was the "talk of the town" for having been ill so long. Instead of showing a spirit of wonder and amazement for his complete healing, (they raised no question about that) with all the self-imposed dignity of their position as members of the cloth, commissioned by the Sanhedrin which was the "National Sabbath Relations Board" of the day, they reminded him that he was doing something that was not lawful on the Sabbath. When the man answered "He that made me *whole,* the same said unto me, Take up thy bed, and walk" they asked no questions concerning the *physician* who had *healed* him; they asked "What *man* is that which *said unto thee,* Take up thy bed, and walk?" Oh the blindness of those who pretend to see, especially in the spiritual realm. Just as some politicians have overlooked that government was made for man, not man for government, so these leaders erred in assuming that the Sabbath was made for man and not man for the Sabbath. It never occurred to them, as was expressed by our Lord later, that even the Father Himself works on the Sabbath day.

There is a vast difference between "religion" and the "salvation" of the Lord. Religion invariably is a series of "do's and don'ts" which most of us have had drilled into our minds since we were children, hardly able to talk. Salvation is of the Lord.

We have already noted that our Lord later found this man in the temple. At least the man went into the temple, probably to express a word of thanks to God for the healing of his body. When our Lord approached him He said, "Sin no more, lest a worse thing come unto thee." It was only then that the man knew that it was Jesus who had made him whole. "The Angel of Bethesda" was none other than the Lord Jesus Christ.

Walk Twenty-Three

WHAT JESUS CLAIMED FOR HIMSELF

AMONG the books reviewed in a recent issue of the "London Times" Book Review, devoted to foreign publications, was one by Jules Supervielle, the French poet. It has been four years since M. Supervielle offered a book of poems. The reviewer observed a change in the poet's philosophy of religion. In his previous works, his journey was toward the stars and the sky, but he found that there was no response from the silent though brilliant heavens. But in his latest book, "The Story of the World," he sought to "disentangle himself from the stars" to seek and address a God of whose existence he has no knowledge. In one of his poems, entitled "Prayer to the Unknown" (which reminds one of the inscription the Apostle Paul observed on one of the altars in Athens) Supervielle not only expresses his own desperate fears and those of his contemporaries, but he also laments that there are some things where "God himself can do nothing in spite of his good will." He concludes that "God knows no more how to talk to man than a potter knows how to talk to his pots." This silent God the poet accepts, as the reviewer suggests "with a kind of reverent pity, searching always for a deeper understanding and the explanation of the fact of God's impregnable isolation."

I have no doubt that Supervielle is sincere. But he is like a blind man, handicapped further by deafness, groping in the sunlight. He concludes, that there is something wrong with the heavens and that God is unable to reveal himself, whereas that which is wrong is the blindness of the poet's own eyes and the deafness of his ears.

There is plenty of light in this world. It is not more light that a blind man needs; he requires sight. The scales must drop from his eyes. Man's blindness, not God's "impregnable isolation" is the problem. God has spoken. He came down and clothed Himself not with "impregnable isolation" but with a garment of flesh. In the person of His Son He spake as never man spake.

We shall listen to "the voice of God" recorded in this chapter as He spoke to "the clay" that His hands had formed and into which He breathed the breath of life, and to whom He gave the prerogative of will and reason. We read in verses 15 and 16 of this 5th chapter that the man who experienced the healing, departed from the temple and told the leaders of the people that it was Jesus who had made him whole. Therefore the Sanhedrin persecuted Jesus and sought to slay Him because He had violated their picayune understanding of the Sabbath.

The Charge and the Defense

As they approached Him, our Lord disarmed them by saying, "My Father worketh hitherto, and I work." It was the only occasion that any man ever confessed that God was his own father. The members of the Sanhedrin were well aware of the implication of that claim, for the 18th verse of this chapter reads, "Therefore the Jews sought the more to kill him, because he not only had broken the sabbath, but said also that God was his Father, making himself equal with God."

Had our Lord referred to the Father in language which would have embraced all other men, the Sanhedrin would not have had cause to complain, but our Lord made it as clear as language possibly can express that He had a unique relationship to God which only He possessed and none other ever did or could possess. At another time He put it in the following language, "Ye are from beneath; I am from above: ye are of this world; I am not of this world." On this occasion He stated clearly and unequivocally that there was such unity and equality between Himself and God the Father that they worked together in unity. "My Father worketh hitherto, and I work." If Jesus Christ were only a man, then He was a blasphemer, and, they of the Sanhedrin were justified in their efforts to kill Him. They should have stoned Him to death as the law of Moses commanded them to do.

Now let us read a few verses forming part of the defense our Lord presented to answer the accusation of blasphemy and in which He gave the "First public explanation of His claims" to deity. Dr. Marcus Dods observed a great fact when he wrote of this part of the 5th chapter, "This five minutes' talk . . . contains probably the most important truth ever uttered on earth." We all talk too much and when finished, have said little or nothing. But our Lord only took five minutes to tell about Himself and to completely disarm a company of people intent on killing Him.

Here's an interesting thing: the first recorded words of our Lord Jesus, were in the form of a question which as a boy of twelve, He addressed to His mother when He said "How is it that ye sought me? wist ye not that I must be about *my Father's business?*" The first word that proceeded from his lips in his first public explanation of His claims to deity—was this: *"My Father worketh hitherto, and I work."* As a boy of twelve our Lord was fully conscious of His deity. He knew even then that His task was to be about His Father's business. As a mature man He acknowledged that He and His Father always worked together. Let's listen to Him as He utters His defense.

> "Then answered Jesus and said unto them, Verily, verily, I say unto you, The Son can do nothing of himself, but what he seeth the Father do: for what things soever he doeth, these also doeth the Son likewise.

> "For the Father loveth the Son, and sheweth him all things that himself doeth: and he will shew him greater works than these, that ye may marvel.
>
> "For as the Father raiseth up the dead, and quickeneth them; even so the Son quickeneth whom he will.
>
> "For the Father judgeth no man, but hath committed all judgment unto the Son:
>
> "That all men should honour the Son, even as they honour the Father. He that honoureth not the Son honoureth not the Father which hath sent him.
>
> "Verily, verily, I say unto you, He that heareth my word, and believeth on him that sent me, hath everlasting life, and shall not come into condemnation; but is passed from death unto life.
>
> "Verily, verily, I say unto you, The hour is coming, and now is, when the dead shall hear the voice of the Son of God: and they that hear shall live.
>
> "For as the Father hath life in himself; so hath he given to the Son to have life in himself;
>
> "And hath given him authority to execute judgment also, because he is the Son of man."

It is quite apparent that in these words, and, as we shall observe later, in the remainder of the chapter, we do not find revealed that spineless effusion which the modern religious world calls *Jesus*. These are not the vaporous words of a non-resisting pacifist. Every word that He used was sharper than any two-edged sword. They were biting and cutting. They were so devastating that His critics were left limp before He finished. His only weapon was the power of His own word, in which, in masterly fashion, He presented a clear declaration of His glorious Person, as the Son of God and yet, the Son of Man.

The Deity of Christ

In this part of the defense our Lord thrice prefaced His argument with the emphatic phrase, "Verily, verily, I say unto you." In the first of these, He elaborated on His original declaration "My Father worketh hitherto, and I work" which so antagonized the Sanhedrin. Here is what He affirmed: that "The Son can do nothing of himself, but what he seeth the Father do: for what things soever he doeth, these also doeth the Son likewise." How thoroughly these words dynamite the foundations of the superstructure of modern Christendom which has been built by an unbelieving group of "Doctors of Divinity," and supposed religious leaders. Here our Lord called Himself "the Son." In the very same breath He acknowledged His dependence upon His Father and yet His ability to do everything the Father does. But more than that, we are told that the Father loveth the Son, and because of that love He revealed to Him all the things that He would do and even greater works than these; not that the Son may marvel, but that His critics may marvel.

Again, as the Father has the "right" to raise the dead, so the Son has the same prerogative coupled with the exercise of His own will, for even "the Son quickeneth whom He will." But as the Son was willing to subordinate Himself in His devotion to the Father, so the Father divested Himself of the right to judge and committed all judgment unto the Son so that all men should honor the Son even as they honor the Father. Our Lord climaxed the statement, saying, "He that honoureth not the Son, honoureth not the Father which hath sent him." In these verses we are confronted with the heart of Christianity.

If Jesus Christ is not God, then He was a blasphemer, every apostle was a deceiver, every Christian is deceived, and every church is a mockery. But if Jesus Christ is the Son of God, then no man can honor the Father except he honor the Son. God will never tolerate an infraction of His revealed truth. On the authority of our Lord Jesus Christ, no prayer ever uttered by any man in any place, if not offered in the name of the Lord Jesus Christ, ever rises above the ceiling. God refuses to accept honor from any man who does not honor the Son. He that does not honor the Son cannot honor God. No wonder the Apostle Paul said, "Woe is me if I preach not the gospel."

We have men today in Protestant pulpits and in seminaries who compromise on every hand in order to maintain their popularity with the crowd, but they do it at the expense of our Lord Jesus Christ, and to the detriment of their own souls. They go so far in public prayer that they avoid the name of Jesus Christ so as not to offend any man, but alas they thereby give offense to God. Oh for a ministry that stands foursquare upon the written Word, refusing to compromise but presenting the truth in all kindliness. Our Lord said, "He that honoureth not the Son honoureth not the Father which hath sent him." Notice, our Lord declared that He was *sent* into this world by the Father. Since He claimed that, every man, woman, and child is under obligation to examine His claims. Our eternal destiny depends upon our attitude toward Jesus Christ.

Now let us look at the second statement preceded by the phrase, "Verily, verily, I say unto you." In the first, our Lord uttered a devastating word which crushes to dust every religious system and every other attempt to worship God apart from Jesus Christ. The second is a comforting word. Jesus Christ tore down before He built up. There must always be a tearing down before *He* can build. If we build on any foundation other than Jesus Christ, on the authority of the Word of God we are building on a false foundation. Our foundation must be blasted first. When it has been crushed; when we have seen ourselves as we truly are in the presence of God, then we will find Jesus Christ to be the Savior.

But He is the *judge* as well as the Savior. The Father committed all judgment unto the Son. He not only committed all judgment unto the Son, but the Son was willing to take the expression of that judgment, suffering the violence of it in order that He might have salvation to offer men who are willing to receive it. So the next statement begins "Verily, verily, I say unto you, He that heareth my word, and believeth on him that sent me, hath everlasting life, and shall not come into condemnation; but is passed from death unto life." Here is a word of salvation. Our Lord had already declared His equality, His pre-existence, and His relationship to God. Now He revealed His present ministry to the sons of men. "He that heareth my word . . ." It is quite evident that we do not now hear the physical voice of Jesus but we hear His word in the written Word, the Word of God. We hear His word just as definitely and with equal clarity as when He spoke the words audibly.

The Way of Salvation

We have given expression in this study not to our words, but to His. We are hearing the words of Christ. "He that heareth my word"—that's the first proposition, "and believeth on him that sent me." A Christian is not guilty of substituting a man in the place of God. It is not a case of believing Christ and rejecting God. Our Lord came to manifest the Father. Thus He said on another occasion, "I and my Father are one." We hear Christ's words and we believe on Him, that is, on God who sent Him. When we do, our Lord assures us we have everlasting life; not will have in some future day, but have it now.

But that is not all one receives. The Lord continued, and said, "and shall not come into condemnation (judgment); but is passed from death unto life." A man or woman who has heard the words of Christ and believed on God who sent Him, will never come into judgment for his sin. That is the statement of Christ. Not only will he never come into judgment for his sin, but he has already passed from the state of death unto life. Previously we were dead in trespasses and in sins; now we have life, eternal life by faith in Jesus Christ. We have a clear understanding why the evangel is called the Gospel. It is good news to guilty men that they will never be brought into judgment for their sin because another bore the judgment of their sin.

And now a final word regarding the last of the three statements prefaced by the emphatic "Verily, verily, I say unto you." Our Lord said, "The hour is coming, and now is, when the dead shall hear the voice of the Son of God: and they that hear shall live." The "dead" in this passage does not refer to men who are in the "graves." We learn what will happen to them in the verses which follow, and which we shall consider in our next study. The *dead* to whom our Lord referred are those who are *dead in* trespasses and sins. They are alive physically but dead spiritually.

Men are raised from spiritual death by hearing the voice of the Son of God as definitely as Lazarus was raised from the dead by hearing the words of Christ as He addressed them unto him when He said, "Lazarus, come forth." It is only they that *hear* who live. Our Lord was driving home the point that faith cometh by hearing and hearing by the word of God. This prerogative of raising spiritually dead people into spiritual life, has been given to our Lord. That is not all. He has been given authority to execute judgment also because He is the Son of man.

Walk Twenty-Four

THE TWO RESURRECTIONS

WE have already given two addresses on the 5th chapter of St. John's Gospel. The first was devoted to the miracle, performed on the Sabbath day, when our Lord at the pool of Bethesda, healed the impotent man who had been an invalid for thirty-eight years. The second consisted of an examination of a part of our Lord's response to the accusation that He had broken the Sabbath and to the further charge of blasphemy, seeing that He had made Himself "equal with God."

There are a number of people, in the pulpit and out of the pulpit, who make the unfounded statement that "Jesus Christ never claimed to be God." Such a statement is made through sheer ignorance or it is a deliberate attempt to express a falsehood. He not only claimed to be God, but He accepted worship as God and exercised all the prerogatives of God.

The last statement we considered in our previous study, was the claim of our Lord in which He said, "As the Father hath life in himself; so hath he given to the Son to have life in himself; And hath given him authority to execute judgment also, because he is the Son of man." One could gather a wealth of material from the last phrase of that statement ". . . because he is the Son of man." We desist, however, in order to consider the remaining part of our Lord's claims. Commencing at verse 28, we read:

> "Marvel not at this: for the hour is coming, in the which all that are in the graves shall hear his voice,
> "And shall come forth; they that have done good, unto the resurrection of life; and they that have done evil, unto the resurrection of damnation.
> "I can of mine own self do nothing: as I hear, I judge: and my judgment is just; because I seek not mine own will, but the will of the Father which hath sent me."

Practically every non-Christian who believes in immortality or a life beyond the grave, believes that there will be a general judgment at the last day, sometimes called "the end of the world." In that day it is claimed that God will sit upon a throne and before Him every life will be examined. At that tribunal the good deeds which a man has accomplished during his life, will be placed on one side of a scale; his evil deeds on the other side. If the scales balance or the good deeds outweigh the evil, the man will enter into eternal life or Heaven. But if the side of the scales containing the evil deeds is weighted down, then the individual will be cast into eternal death, or he will have another chance to expiate his sins, etc., etc., etc.

I dare say that probably nine professing Christians out of ten entertain the idea of a general judgment. Yet there is not a line in all the Bible to support such a view. On the contrary, our Lord insisted that there would be *two* resurrections. He said ". . . the hour is coming, in the which all that are in the graves shall hear his voice, And shall come forth. . . ." If that were all He had said, then we could conclude there would be a general judgment day, but He went on to say that since there are two classes of people in the world, therefore there will be two resurrections. The one class is described as "they that have done good." They participate in what He called "the resurrection of life." The other class is designated as "they that have done evil" and their resurrection He termed "the resurrection of damnation." From other passages we learn that the one is called "the first resurrection." Of those who participate in "the first resurrection," in the 20th chapter of the Book of Revelation, verse 6, it is written, "Blessed and holy is he that hath part in the *first* resurrection: on such the *second* death hath no power, but they shall be priests of God and of Christ, and shall reign with him a thousand years." After that thousand year reign has ended, then the second resurrection will take place, not before. Only one class of people will participate in the second resurrection—"they that have done evil."

Heaven's Recording Studio

Let us read what the Bible has to say about them. We read from Revelation 20: commencing with verse 11. The same writer who wrote the Gospel according to St. John, is the author. He said, "I saw a great white throne, and him that sat on it, from whose face the earth and the heaven fled away; and there was found no place for them. And I saw the dead, small and great, stand before God. . . ." Let us stop there. That's a terrifying statement, "and I saw the dead." All throughout the 20th chapter of the Revelation we have the expression "the dead; the dead; the dead." The phrase peals forth like the toll of a death bell, or the theme in a funeral dirge—"the dead." Observe that "the dead" are both small and great, and that they stand before God.

There we find the Hitlers, and the Dillingers, the Neros, etc. Our Lord Jesus Christ affirmed that His Father had given to him authority to execute judgment—because He is the Son of man. In the book of the Revelation, the dead are seen standing before God. They stand before Jesus Christ, for Jesus Christ is God.

But observe further, as we continue reading from the Revelation, chapter 20: ". . . and the books were opened. . . ." The context is clear that these books contain the record of the individual's life. ". . . the books were opened: and another book was opened, which is the book of life: and the dead were judged out of those things which were written in the books, according to their works." Therefore those who will participate in the second resurrection will be *judged according to their works*. We will come back to that subject in a moment. Let us read further, "And death and hell (hades) were cast into the lake of fire. This is the second death. And whosoever was not found written in the book of life was cast into the lake of fire." It is clear that there will be two resurrections, separated from each other by a thousand years. During that interval the Bible declares that our Lord will reign as the King of kings and Lord of lords. That period is called "The Millennium."

Let us look at the second resurrection before we look at the first one. I have already called attention to the fact that each of the dead who appear before the great white throne will stand before our Lord Jesus Christ. Each will be judged out of those things which are written in the books, according to his own works. That which will send a man to the lake of fire, which, incidentally, is what the Bible calls hell, is the man's own works.

Some years ago men ridiculed the idea of the existence of a set of books in the glory in which a complete record of every man's life was kept. Sneeringly some suggested that heaven would have to be a sort of glorified "bookkeeping department." Imagine the task for the millions upon millions of angels *to write* in a record, everything that every man had ever done! But we have learned some things from the inventions of our day. Science is a great help in the understanding of the Scriptures. Yes, strange as that may seem, it is true. For instance, when I speak over a microphone, my words enter into thousands of homes. Is it fantastic to believe that these words are also heard in heaven by short wave, if you please, and that a recording of them is being made for permanent reference? Absolutely not. Everything a man does, or says, or thinks, is recorded somewhere. It is not said that an angel writes the record. It's quite possible that we make our own recordings. It has been said of men who were on the verge of drowning that in the flash of a moment their memories became vivid and the whole panorama of their life passed before them instantly. We cannot destroy memory. We can attempt to dull it, but there it is—memory has safely stored in our mind the record of our life. Some scientists believe that the day may be near when out of the very walls of a building men may extract the voices of persons who have spoken in the room.

If it should be your ill fortune to participate in "the second resurrection" you will then discover that everything you have ever said or done has been recorded in those books. Talk about phonographic records! Don't you think God has a better recording machine in heaven than men have on earth? Don't you think God knows more about the laws of nature which incidentally He made than any human mind? If we know how to make recordings, does not God?

Some of you will remember Bishop J. Taylor Smith whose short friendship was a great benediction to my life. He participated in one of our Forum programs. Fortunately, I had a recording made of that program. It is now one of my precious possessions. I delight to put that record on a machine, turn on the switch and then listen to the voice of a dead man. But here is an interesting thing about recordings: In the course of broadcasting, sometimes I speak quite rapidly and occasionally but inexcusably, mispronounce a word. That word goes out; I cannot call it back. Oh yes, I can say pardon me, and then correctly pronounce it, but as it has already gone out, I cannot call it back. So in the Bishop's record, every little grunt, every poorly composed question which I addressed to him is there—I cannot erase it. Sir, it will be a fearful thing to stand in the presence of God and hear the record that *we have made* by our own works. If I were to appear before that judgment seat and my record was examined, I would want to run away, to hide myself, not only from the face of God but from my own conscience.

The Lamb's Book

The *unbelieving* dead we are told are judged out of those things which were written in the books according to *their works*. Escape can only be found by recourse to an examination of another book which is called the book of life. It is the Lamb's book of life. In it are written *only* the names of every man, woman and child who has trusted the Lord Jesus Christ as his or her Savior, every patriarch and every individual in the Old Testament who placed his confidence in the Lord and who looked forward to Him as the Redeemer. As all whose names are in the Lamb's Book of life participated in the first resurrection, it is evident that all who participate in the second resurrection and who stand before the Great White Throne, are not found in the Lamb's Book of Life.

In the 16th chapter of St. John's Gospel, the Lord announced to His disciples, the ministry of the Holy Spirit which He would exercise on the earth after our Lord had returned to glory. Let us note what He said: "Nevertheless, I tell you the truth; it is expedient for you that I go away: for if I go not away, the Comforter will not come unto you; but if I depart, I will send him unto you." Talk about a claim to deity! Do you know of a man who can command the Holy Spirit—"I will send him unto you?" Either Jesus Christ was God when He spoke that statement, or he was the most vicious liar that ever lived. Of the Holy Spirit our Lord said,

> "When he is come, he will reprove the world of sin, and of righteousness, and of judgment:
> "Of sin, because they believe not on me;
> "Of righteousness, because I go to my Father, and ye see me no more;
> "Of judgment, because the prince of this world is judged."

Here is the introduction of a new sin. The Holy Spirit does not need to reprove a man of the sins of his flesh. That's the function of a normal conscience, though I well know almost anything can be excused by a distorted conscience. The Holy Spirit convinces a man of *sin* because he does not believe on Jesus Christ. It is only the Holy Spirit who reproves men of that sin. That is *His* business.

The First Resurrection

Now let's look at this first resurrection. The only reason men participate in the "first resurrection" is because they have believed on the Lord Jesus Christ and so their names were written in the Lamb's book of life. Our Lord spoke of those participants as "they that have done good." Now some will say this is a question of *doing good*, not a question of faith; it is a question of works. The Bible is its own best commentary. If we could get to the place where we would accept the Bible's own explanation of its message, our problems would all be solved. For instance, we get the answer to this problem by merely turning one page in our Bible to the 6th chapter of John's Gospel. In the middle of that chapter we have an interesting scene.

It was the day after our Lord had fed the multitude with five loaves and two small fishes. The crowd followed Him to the other side of the sea. Our Lord never mistook the adulation of the mob. Politicians do. They forget that the mob that one day cries shouts of praise, the next day will call for their heads. So our Lord said, "Verily, verily, I say unto you, Ye seek me, not because ye saw the miracles, but because ye did eat of the loaves, and were filled. Labour not for the meat which perisheth, but for that meat which endureth unto everlasting life, which the Son of man shall give unto you: for him hath God the Father sealed." So they said unto Him, "What we *do*, that we might work the works of God?" Listen to the response of our Lord Jesus. "This is the work of God, that ye believe on him whom he hath sent."

The highest work a man can render to God is to believe the record that God has given concerning His Son. And God constitutes good (I use that expression advisedly—I will explain it in a moment), those who trust in Him. When the Bible uses the term *good*, it uses it in the superlative degree; it is equivalent to God's goodness, which is perfection. The sinner convicted of his sins, convinced, reproved by the Holy Spirit because of his rejection of Christ which doubly condemned him, but who cries out to the Lord and receives God's testimony concerning His Son, that individual is *declared* righteous. He has *imputed* unto him a righteousness which he never earned, and, his name has been written in the Lamb's book of life. He will participate, if he dies, in the first resurrection. You notice I qualified that by saying "if he dies," for there will be one generation of believers who will never die because the first resurrection will take place when the Lord comes, as we learn from the 4th chapter of 1st Thessalonians.

Walk Twenty-Five

THE WITNESSES AND THE SUMMATION

WE have been looking into the claims of our Lord presented in the 5th chapter. In previous messages on this chapter, we mentioned that our Lord handled His defense as a lawyer argues a case. First, He presented His claims, then He supported His claims by calling upon several witnesses, and finally, He gave His conclusion or summation.

We therefore begin at verse 30 and continue to the end of the chapter.

"I can of mine own self do nothing: as I hear, I judge: and my judgment is just; because I seek not mine own will, but the will of the Father which hath sent me.
"If I bear witness of myself, my witness is not true.
"There is another that beareth witness of me; and I know that the witness which he witnesseth of me is true.
"Ye sent unto John, and he bare witness unto the truth.
"But I receive not testimony from man: but these things I say, that ye might be saved.
"He was a burning and a shining light: and ye were willing for a season to rejoice in his light.
"But I have greater witness than that of John: for the works which the Father hath given me to finish, the same works that I do, bear witness of me, that the Father hath sent me.
"And the Father himself, which hath sent me, hath borne witness of me. Ye have neither heard his voice at any time, nor seen his shape.
"And ye have not his word abiding in you: for whom he hath sent, him ye believe not.
"Search the scriptures; for in them ye think ye have eternal life: and they are they which testify of me.
"And ye will not come to me, that ye might have life.
"I receive not honour from men.
"But I know you, that ye have not the love of God in you.
"I am come in my Father's name, and ye receive me not: if another shall come in his own name, him ye will receive.
"How can ye believe, which receive honour one of another, and seek not the honour that cometh from God only?
"Do not think that I will accuse you to the Father: there is one that accuseth you, even Moses, in whom ye trust.
"For had ye believed Moses, ye would have believed me: for he wrote of me.
"But if ye believe not his writings, how shall ye believe my words?"

When our Lord said, "I can of mine own self do nothing . . ." He did not infer any impotency or weakness in His being. To the contrary, it was an assertion that His holiness prevented Him from doing anything that was contrary to the will of His Father. He is the only man who could honestly say ". . . I seek not mine own will, but the will of the Father which hath sent me."

Having accepted the charge of equality with God, He called His witnesses, for He rightly acknowledged that if He bore witness of Himself, His witness would not be true, seeing that the Old Testament had decreed that in the mouth of two witnesses a matter shall be established. It is well known that ". . . in Jewish, Greek and Roman jurisprudence, the testimony of a witness is not received in his own case."

Before considering the testimony, it is a point of interest to observe that from verses 19 to 29 inclusive, our Lord did not use the pronoun I, but He employed the expression *The Son,* saying for instance in the 19th verse, ". . . The Son can do nothing of himself, but what he seeth the Father do . . ." But, commencing with verse 30, He returned to the use of the personal pronoun.

As we examine the balance of the chapter not only do we observe the frequent use of the first person, but we are also impressed with the sharpness of the rebuke He administered. In His own name, He judged those to whom He gave His defense. Every time He brought an indictment, His accusers must have wilted as with biting satire He smote them with telling effect when He said unto them:

> "*Ye* sent unto John . . . "
> "*Ye* were willing for a season to rejoice in his light."
> "*Ye* have neither heard his (God's) voice at any time, nor seen his shape."
> "*Ye* have not his word abiding in you . . . "
> "*Ye* believe not."
> "*Ye* will not come unto me . . . "
> "*Ye* have not the love of God in you."

Our Lord, therefore, reversed the proceedings; it ceased to be a case of the Jews judging and examining Him before their court, but to the contrary, He as the judge brought His scathing indictment against them. Finally, He closed His summation with a scorpion-like word saying, ". . . if ye believe not his (Moses') writings, how shall ye believe my words?"

The Testimony of the Witnesses

Now let's look at the testimony of these witnesses.

In the 32nd verse, our Lord spoke of "another" who bore witness of Him, and He added this comment, "I *know* that the witness which he witnesseth of me is true." He was not referring to John. He referred to the Father since the one to whom He referred bore a continuous witness. John's testimony was already silenced at that time. John was in prison.

This continuous witness of the Father to His Son is to be observed in two places. First, in the Scriptures; and secondly, in the heart of a man who is willing to receive God's testimony concerning His Son.

For a moment our Lord dropped the witness of His Father although He came back to it later. Meanwhile, He referred to John and with an emphatic use of the pronoun *ye,* He said, "Ye sent unto John, and he bare witness unto the truth. But I receive not testimony from man: but these things I say, that ye might be saved." Referring to John's witness, He spoke of it in the past tense "He was a burning and a shining light: and ye *were* willing for a season to rejoice in his *torch*."

In this chapter, there are two things which our Lord said He refused. They are worthy of our consideration. First, in verse 34, He said, ". . . I receive not testimony from man . . ." and second, in verse 41, "I receive not honour from men."

While our Lord was not willing to receive a man's testimony, He permitted the witness to be used in order that men might be saved. But there was a testimony that He was willing to receive. The force of its presentation is somewhat lost in our translation of verse 36, where we read "But I have a greater witness than that of John . . ." Literally, our Lord said, "I have the witness greater than John's; that witness is the works which I have done which the Father hath given me to do and which works bear witness of me."

Finally, He again referred to the testimony of His Father. Observe that it is in the past tense in contrast to verse 32 where He spoke of the continuous witness of His Father. In verse 37, He said, ". . . the Father himself, which hath sent me, hath borne witness of me." The very next verse indicates where and when that witness was borne. It is in the Word of God, for He said, ". . . ye have not his *word* abiding in you: for whom he hath sent, him ye believe not."

By the way, there is another interesting thing that we ought not to pass by. Of the Father, our Lord said, ". . . Ye have neither heard his voice at any time, nor seen his shape." While it is true that God is a spirit, and as such, is without flesh and bone, our Lord clearly evidenced that the Father has a voice and a form; while the Son has a voice and likewise a form. Each is a separate and distinct member of the Godhead. There is the Father, and the Son, and the Holy Spirit.

Our Responsibility

But someone may raise the question, What has all this to do with me? It has much to do with you and with me. We are confronted with the same three testimonies today. There is first of all, the testimony of men. Literally thousands upon thousands of men and women have borne testimony that Jesus Christ is the Son of God and that they have come to know Him as their Lord and Savior. If we have heard the testimony of even a single man concerning his faith in Christ, we have become responsible to act upon that testimony. Secondly, we have the witness of the works of Jesus. The life and ministry of our Lord makes every man doubly responsible before God. Jesus of Nazareth cannot be accounted for on any other basis, but that He is God manifest in flesh. His works bear testimony to His character and His being. If a man rejects Christ, he does so, not because of lack of evidence, but the refusal to receive the overwhelming evidence that the life and ministry of Christ presents. It is for that reason that those of us who have come to know Christ, delight to present Him, and in the language of the Apostle Paul, ". . . we preach not ourselves, but Christ Jesus the Lord; and ourselves your servants for Jesus' sake." You cannot ignore Jesus. To ignore Him is to reject Him. You become morally responsible persons before God as a result of our Lord's life and ministry on earth.

Finally, there is the testimony of the Father concerning His Son, which is chiefly to be found in the Bible. Refusal to read the Bible, refusal to consider God's testimony, will never excuse any man before the judgment seat of God.

Our Lord also revealed how we should use the Bible, and that is a most important subject. In the case of Israel, He cited proof that the book "which had been given to guide them to Christ they used as a veil to blind themselves to His presence." Dr. Dods has well said, "The Scriptures do not give life, they lead to the Life-giver. . . . To worship the Bible as if it were Christ is to mistake a finger-post for a house of shelter. . . To set it on a level with Christ is to do both it, Him, and ourselves the gravest injustice. . . . God speaks in Scripture for a definite purpose, to reveal Christ: and this fact is the key to all difficulties about the Bible and inspiration."

In conclusion, look at the 40th verse of this chapter, where our Lord said (literally) *"And yet* ye will not come unto me, that ye might have life." The evidence is overwhelming. The responsibility is ours to act upon the evidence. To receive it is to acknowledge the Lordship of Christ. To reject it, is to seal our damnation.

WALK TWENTY-SIX
CHRIST AND THE ANTI-CHRIST

WE are now to consider an interesting and timely passage of Scripture. It forms a part of the summation of our Lord's response to the charge of blasphemy. It is found in the 43rd verse of the 5th chapter of St. John's Gospel. This is what our Lord said: "I am come in my Father's name, and ye receive me not: if another shall come in his own name, him ye will receive."

I am aware that the language which our Lord employed was not completely positive. He did not say "Another *shall* come in his own name . . ." He said *"If* another shall come in his own name . . ." But we have two pertinent words of instruction in the Bible which must always be observed in examining anything of a prophetic character if one is to maintain a sane interpretation. The words came from the pen of the Apostle Peter as he was moved along by the Holy Spirit. Peter said, "Knowing this first, that no prophecy of the scripture is of (its own) any private interpretation." That means that no word is to be taken without due consideration being given to everything that has been written on that subject in the Bible. And, second, that "prophecy came not in old time by the will of man: but holy men of God spake as they were moved by the Holy Ghost." These holy men of God never *ventured* into the sea of prophecy. They did not give their suggestions, or guesses, or speculations. They were *carried* along by the Holy Spirit. It was the Spirit of God who *guided* their pens as they described events which were to take place in the future.

The Bible was written over a period of 1600 years. It was written by some 30-odd men from varied circumstances of life. No one prophet, or no one man said all that there was to be said on any given subject. There was growth and development and progress in the revelation of God's truth; here a little, there a little; here a line and there a line. The only logical method to approach anything of a prophetic character is to assemble all that the Word of God has to say on that given subject and focus every passage on that event. That method will enable one to see clearly not only the full picture, but the proper place where each detail appears in the plan of God.

Would Be Prophets

We have already noted that our Lord did not use positive language but said, *"If* another shall come . . . ," but we learn from other passages of Scripture that that other to whom our Lord referred, shall come, and when he does come, as our Lord said, he will be almost universally received.

There are no prophets at the present time. Any man or woman who claims that God has called him or her to be a prophet simply is not telling the truth. The last word of inspired prophecy was written almost nineteen hundred years ago. But there are men who have the *gift of prophecy,* which is quite another matter. Such men are not prophets, but they know what the prophets have written. When the New Testament speaks of a man as having the gift of prophecy, it does not mean that he is able to *foretell* future events, but rather that he is able to *forthtell* what the Word of God has already written on the subject.

Whenever anyone, whether in the pulpit or out of the pulpit, ventures into the field of speculation, irrespective of what the subject might be, he usually invites upon himself the scorn and laughter of men, since the possibilities of being right are slim while the chances of being wrong are overwhelming.

A glaring instance of this may be gathered from a current book, published in *1939,* written by a scholar and one of the most loved professors in America. His name is well known. It is William Lyon Phelps. His book is an autobiography, which I have read with interest and some pleasure. As I came toward the close of the book, I read this paragraph in a chapter devoted to a trip the professor made to Munich in 1932 (not very long ago) which contained what the Professor said was his "contributory thought to disarmament and world peace." This is what he wrote:

> "It seemed to me that it would be a good idea to abandon Geneva as a meeting place and have all sessions of international delegates in the Hofbrau Haus at Munich."

To indicate that he was a good prophet, he added in parentheses, (Munich was chosen in 1938) and then continued,

> "Frenchmen, Germans, Italians, British, Russians, Japanese, Chinese, Americans, all would lose their animosities after associating two or three evenings in this genial atmosphere."

But 1939 has already written the dismal failure of Munich as a place where "disarmament and world peace" would possibly blossom. No, let's not be prophets. The only person in all the world who knows the end from the beginning, is God. And, the only book in all the world that tells us anything authoritatively about future events, is the Word of God.

The Christ

Now then, part of our Lord's statement is history, and part of it is prophecy. The historical part is contained in the first half of the statement, "I am come in my Father's name, and ye receive me not." There are two facts of history stated therein. First, our Lord did not come in His own name. The implication is clear; He elaborated upon it frequently. He emphasized that nothing He *said* was of Himself—nothing He *did* was thought up by Himself. His was a *planned economy* of life. Every detail of it was arranged by God the Father. He did not come in His own name; He came in His Father's name. He had the credentials, which should have been clearly appreciated by those to whom He came. Certainly the people were anticipating Him. They never were in a more expectant mood. When anyone arose who had a unique ministry, immediately they were interrogated as reporters do when a distinguished guest arrives at our shores. For example, these leaders approached John the Baptist and asked, Who are you? Are you Elias? Are you that prophet? Are you the one that we are expecting? If not, are you by any chance his forerunner of whom the prophets have written? On a later occasion they asked our Lord, "Who art thou?" And Jesus answered, "Even the same that I have said unto you from the beginning." Our Lord continued and said, "When ye have lifted up the Son of man, then shall ye know that *I am he,* and that I do nothing of myself; but as my Father hath taught me, I speak these things."

Notice He said, *"I am he."* Who? "The Christ." "I am come in my Father's name," and He added, "and ye receive me not." It is a fact of history that He was rejected by the elders of Israel and the sad part of it is, He is still being rejected by the masses of the world. But another shall come in his own name. That one is called the Antichrist, and when he comes, he will be received.

The Antichrist and His Ministry

It is of course apparent that in this study we cannot look at every passage of Scripture referring to the Antichrist nor even do more than briefly outline his character and ministry. We shall merely look at the subject seeking the answer to the questions, What do we mean by the term Antichrist? What will be his peculiar ministry?—When will he appear?—What will be his reception?

The First Epistle of John is a most intimate letter to Christians. In it the aged Apostle said, "Little children, it is the last time (days): and as ye have heard that antichrist shall come, even now are there many antichrists; whereby we know that it is the last time (days) ... Who is a liar but he that denieth that Jesus is the Christ? He is antichrist, that denieth the Father and the Son."

Laying aside the divine record for the moment, let's look at the dictionary definition of the Antichrist. There we find that he is "Any opponent or enemy of Christ, whether a person or a power; a false Christ, specifically, a great enthroned antagonist, foretold in the Scriptures, who, as some have understood, is to precede the second coming of Christ."

John said there were many antichrists in his day, and he added that one could tell an antichrist by observing that He denies both the Father and the Son. There have been men who have been energized by the spirit of Antichrist. Dr. A. C. Gaebelein correctly points out that "After the death and resurrection of our Lord, during the first century of our era, over three score Messiahs appeared. They all came in their own names and were miserable deceivers; yet no matter how brazen they were, each of them had a vast following and each led them to disaster." But there is one whom the Bible specifically labels the Antichrist who will appear in the future, opposing and exalting himself against the Lord. The saintly scholar, Archbishop Trench, has an interesting comment on the Antichrist. He said, "He will not call himself Christ. For he will be filled with direst hate against the name and the office, against the Holy Spirit and temper of Jesus of Nazareth, now the exalted king up in glory. He will not assume the name of Christ and so will not to the letter, be a false Christ. And yet assuming to himself Christ's office, presenting himself to the world as the true center of its hopes, as the satisfaction of its ends, the healer of its hurts, he will in fact, take upon himself all names and forms of blasphemy: will be a false Christ and the Antichrist both at once."

In the 13th chapter of the Revelation, we have a description of two beasts who are to make their appearance in the future. They are not actually beasts, for the book of the Revelation employs a sign language. It is the characters of these men that are beastial. One is seen rising out of the sea, the other out of the earth. The first beast has seven heads and ten crowns and upon his head the name of blasphemy. The second beast out of the earth has two horns like a lamb, but he spake like a dragon. Any man acquainted with the terminology of the Scripture, knows that the sea represents the Gentile nations and the earth represents the Israelites. One man rises out of the Gentiles and the other rises out of Israel. One is a political leader and the other is the Antichrist. One will head up civil authority while the other is a false prophet who heads up an apostate ecclesiastical system. The one will head up the Empire while the other will mislead and deceive them that dwell on the earth by a display of miraculous power. He will cause all, both small and great, rich and poor, free or bond, to receive a mark in their right hand or in their foreheads, so that no man might buy or sell save he that had the mark of the beast or the number of his name.

So much for what we mean by the term "Antichrist" and what will be the ministry of the "Antichrist." Now let's look at the time of his appearance and also his end. There have been many men energized by the Antichrist during the history of the Church since the first century. But the Antichrist, the one who is given that specific title, will not appear while the Church is on this earth. When I use the term *Church*, I do not mean the organized Church: I mean the invisible body of Christ; I refer to the men and women who have been born again by the Spirit of God and who comprise the body of Christ. They are the bride of Christ. As long as the Holy Spirit is here on earth embodied in the Church, just so long will He prevent the manifestation of the man of sin and the Antichrist. The Antichrist's ministry will not be revealed until after the Church has been taken out of this world. His reign will be of short duration.

The Future

The Bible speaks of a series of events that will take place after the Church has been taken out of this world. Some day, there will be a large number of people missing in this world. They will suddenly disappear in the flash of a moment. Every Christian who has been born again by the Spirit of God will be taken out of this world and caught up to meet the Lord in the air. It will probably take the world a little time to get over the shock, but the true Christian's absence will soon be forgotten, as the Man of Sin, the beastial dictator, arranges a beautiful set-up in Europe to assure peace and tranquility. The Jews will then return to Palestine in great droves and the Dictator of the Empire will enter into a covenant with them, permitting their re-establishment in Palestine and the restoration of their Temple worship. This treaty will be for a period of seven years. For three and a half years everything will be tranquil and quiet so that men will really believe that the millennium has arrived. The nations of the world will appear to have beaten their swords into plowshares and their spears into pruning-hooks. But suddenly the head of the Empire will become Satanically energized and vent his wrath against the people of Israel. He will break off his agreement with them and subject Israel to a terrific persecution. His triumph will be complete when he will seat himself in the holy place at Jerusalem and demand that he be worshipped as God. When that hour comes there will take place what Daniel the prophet called, "the abomination of desolation." Israel will cry out to God in desperation. God will answer their prayer by the return of His Christ, who will slay the false prophet, and the beast and all who are their followers. He will then restore Israel to her place of fellowship with God and take His place as King of kings, and Lord of lords—breaking down every power that is opposed to Him and reign in peace.

But before this takes place, Satan will be cast into the bottomless pit. Not a thing that I have said is an expression of my opinion—it is emphatically stated in the Bible. This Antichrist, as our Lord said, will come in his own name. He will be the world's worst egotist. He will make the present egotistical dictators in Europe look like kindergarten children. He will be a suave gentleman. He will appear like a lamb but he will speak like a dragon. He will be the incarnation of Satan as Jesus was the incarnation of God. He will be received by the mass of mankind. Alas, alas, that men should reject the true Christ and receive the false Christ.

One must acknowledge as he looks at the present unrest in the world through the Bible, that the immediate days ahead of us are dark, that is, if we are now living in that period which the Bible speaks of as the close of this dispensation, which many Bible teachers believe is certainly upon us. But the future is bright for the child of God who will be spared the horrors of an enraged God-defying beastial man.

I bring this message to a close by asking a pointed question. In your case, who will it be, the Christ of God, or the Antichrist of Satan? The choice is either one or the other.

WALK TWENTY-SEVEN

THE ECONOMIC PROBLEM IN THE HANDS OF THE LORD JESUS

WE often think of our Lord Jesus as belonging only to the spiritual realm, forgetting that He is to be Lord over every part of man's tripartite being. Man has a spirit, a soul, and a body. His spirit was given so that he could have a consciousness of God, to understand that God is a Being to whom he is accountable, and yet, with whom it is possible to have communion. He has a soul whereby he can have intimate relationship with men; understanding their motives and their desires. He has a body which enables him to have direct physical relationship with the world. Most men assume that the body is supreme; therefore they devote all or a major part of their waking and sleeping hours to the encouragement, the support, and sustenance of the body. Consequently, the spirit is given minor consideration. The best among such men usually set aside an hour to an hour and fifteen minutes on a Sunday morning for the spirit's development and sustenance. They may not express themselves in so many words, but their actions reveal that in their thinking, the body is of foremost importance and under man's own sway and domination; while the spirit is a minor matter which involves or contemplates God. Having that type of a philosophy of life, it is to be expected that men relegate the Lord to the spiritual realm and give Him only one hour out of a total of 168 hours a week.

But the Lord Jesus Christ is not only the Savior of the souls and spirits of men; He has also very much to say about the bodies of men.

THE PROBLEM

The world has one supreme problem in the present hour: it is the economic problem. It is the cause of all the strife in this world, both in Europe and in our own land. We have men who devote their whole life time to a study of the subject. We speak of them as economists, and professors of economics. But alas, with all the economists et al, the problem is still acute and unsolved. Probably it has never occurred to the leaders of this world that Jesus Christ has something to say about the economic side of life and that He *is* also the answer to the economic problem. He alone can unravel the mess we are in. We get an insight regarding His ability in this sphere from this 6th chapter. Let us note carefully as we read the divine record of it, found in the first 14 verses of this chapter.

> "After these things Jesus went over the sea of Galilee, which is the sea of Tiberias.
> "And a great multitude followed him, because they saw his miracles which he did on them that were diseased.
> "And Jesus went up into a mountain, and there he sat with his disciples.
> "And the passover, a feast of the Jews, was nigh.
> "When Jesus then lifted up his eyes, and saw a great company come unto him, he saith unto Philip, Whence shall we buy bread, that these may eat?
> "And this he said to prove him: for he himself knew what he would do.
> "Philip answered him, Two hundred pennyworth of bread is not sufficient for them, that every one of them may take a little.
> "One of his disciples, Andrew, Simon Peter's brother, saith unto him,
> "There is a lad here, which hath five barley loaves, and two small fishes: but what are they among so many?
> "And Jesus said, Make the men sit down. Now there was much grass in the place. So the men sat down, in number about five thousand.
> "And Jesus took the loaves; and when he had given thanks, he distributed to the disciples, and the disciples to them that were set down; and likewise of the fishes as much as they would.
> "When they were filled, he said unto his disciples, Gather up the fragments that remain, that nothing be lost.
> "Therefore they gathered them together, and filled twelve baskets with the fragments of the five barley loaves, which remained over and above unto them that had eaten.
> "Then those men, when they had seen the miracle that Jesus did, said, This is of a truth that prophet that should come into the world."

That this is an important event in the life and ministry of our Lord is evident from the fact it is the only miracle recorded by each of the writers of the four Gospels. It is true "Man shall not live by bread alone, but by every word that proceedeth out of the mouth of God." But he *must* have bread. Our Lord did not say that man did not need bread; He said he must have something *more* than bread. God has so constituted these bodies of ours that they need bread for their support and sustenance. But we need the Word of God equally as much, yea more than we need bread. Our Lord Jesus Christ is supreme in both realms. He makes every economist of this world look like an infant. He demonstrates through this miracle that He not only can, but has met the need of the hour.

THE SETTING

Now let's look at the circumstances. Some of the other Gospel writers give certain details that John does not carry. It is not necessary for every writer to record every fact concerning an interview, ministry, or act of our Lord Jesus. But when we put all four together, or all two or three together, whichever the case may be, we find that they dove-tail, and are in perfect harmony. Each will supply a detail lacking from the other, but when pieced together, present a complete picture of the circumstances. John simply tells us that this event took place when Jesus went over the sea of Galilee which is the sea of Tiberias. In the second verse we are told that a great multitude followed Him because they saw His miracles which He did on them which were diseased.

Dr. G. Campbell Morgan has pointed out that this translation misses the point slightly. He reminds us that the tenses of the verbs used by John are suggestive, and that the passage should read, "And a great multitude were following him because they were beholding the signs which were being done." In other words, the tenses indicate continuous activity.

From Matthew's account we learn that the event occurred shortly after the death of John the Baptist, and that the thinking of King Herod, who had heard of the fame of Jesus, also had something to do with our Lord's desire to cross the sea and enter into a desert place.

Herod's conscience was troubling him. He had heard previously of Jesus of Nazareth but paid no attention to Him. The fame of our Lord, however, was increasing; the multitudes were following Him; His miracles were so numerous and so awe-inspiring that even the king could not overlook them or Him. At one time Herod was moved by the ministry of John and gladly heard him, but in a moment of debauchery he succumbed to the wiles of a designing woman and gave the decree that the head of John was to be brought into the dance hall on a charger. Herod feared that Jesus was John the Baptist raised again from the dead. Our Lord knew that what had happened to His forerunner was an omen of His own crucifixion. He probably wanted to go into a desert place to be alone with His Father in contemplation of Calvary.

Mark tells us another detail which is also interesting. He gives a further point of time, saying that it was after the disciples had returned from their first preaching tour. Our Lord noticed the lines in their faces and the lack of sparkle in their eyes. He knew they needed rest. So, He said to them, "Come ye yourselves apart into a desert place, and rest awhile: for there were many coming and going, and they had no leisure so much as to eat."

We also are told that our Lord departed into this desert place by a ship privately with His disciples. But the people saw Him depart and many knew Him and ran afoot thither out of all cities, and outwent them and came together to the place where our Lord took His disciples. Furthermore, we learn that our Lord ministered the Word throughout the entire day, healing the sick as well, for our Lord was moved with compassion toward the multitude because they were as sheep not having a shepherd.

Mark also tells us that when the day was far spent His disciples came to the Lord and said, "This is a desert place, and now the time is far passed: Send them away, that they may go into the country round about, and into the villages, and buy themselves bread: for they have nothing to eat." This was the setting for the miracle.

The Provision

Let's look at some of these details. We have already intimated that there was a divine reason that drove our Lord into the wilderness. There was also a human reason—the tiredness of the disciples. It is well to bear this in mind for the Bible was written for our instruction. We may not always be permitted to see the divine reason behind the actions and the experiences of our lives, but we do see the human, yet every Christian can say with absolute assurance ". . . we *know* that all things work together for good to them that love God. . ." Another thing, when our Lord observed that His disciples needed physical relaxation, He bade them go into a desert place. We make the mistake of going to a resort.

It is also interesting to observe how the disciples tried to help get our Lord out of a tight place. We are often guilty of the same thing. It is preposterous, but it is so! Note the words of the disciples: "This is a *desert* place . . ." as if our Lord did not know it was a *desert* place. Had he not said, "Come ye yourselves apart into a *desert* place, and rest awhile?" They also said ". . . the time is far passed." I feel certain our Lord never carried a watch with Him, but He did not need anyone to tell Him the time of the day.

But here's a point of great interest. John tells us that when our Lord "lifted up His eyes, and saw a great company come unto him, he saith to Philip, Whence shall we buy bread, that these may eat?" John also added the following comment, "And this he said to prove him: for he himself knew what he would do." It is the *only* time in all the ministry of Christ where our Lord asked for advice from any man or from His disciples. Notice carefully what He asked: ". . . Philip, *Whence* shall we buy bread, that these may eat? Philip answered him, Two hundred pennyworth of bread is not sufficient for them, that every one of them may take a little." He had not answered our Lord's question! Our Lord did not ask Philip *How* shall we feed the multitude, He asked *where* shall we buy bread? Philip's answer may be paraphrased in this fashion: "Lord, what's the use of asking *where* shall we *buy* bread; we do not have the money to *buy* bread; between the whole crowd of us, we could not raise $30.00." By the way, that was long before the church became rich and increased in goods, which has proved one of her greatest deterrents to effective spiritual ministry. But our Lord *knew* what He Himself would do. He simply asked the question to prove Philip.

I again refer to Dr. G. Campbell Morgan. More than sixty years ago, in the city of Bristol, England, he was taken by his father to hear George Mueller preach, that wonderful man who was a giant of faith. George Mueller preached on the text, "He himself knew what he would do." Said Dr. Morgan, "Mueller could not pronounce it in good English. He had a quaint and picturesque German accent. More than sixty years have gone by, but I have never lost the effect of that sermon for it helped me to understand the *ways* of my Lord." Oh to trust Christ, and to understand His *ways*.

Remember it is written: "He made known his *ways* unto Moses, his acts unto the children of Israel."

John tells us that Andrew, Simon Peter's brother, was also around. Andrew had a *little* faith. Possibly that is why so many Scotch lads are called Andrew! We might paraphrase what Andrew said by using a good Scotch word, "Lord, there's a wee bit of a laddie here who has five barley loaves and two wee fishes, but what are these among so many?" A *little* lad with five *little* barley loaves and two *little* fishes! Not a sumptuous provision, but quite all right for a little fellow's luncheon. But in the hands of the Lord, the Creator of the universe, a little lad and five little cakes and two little fishes can be used to feed a multitude! Matthew tells us there were "about five thousand men, beside women and children." There must have been twenty thousand mouths fed that day, and still there were twelve baskets full of fragments left over after everybody had well eaten. Talk about our Lord's principles of economics! Talk about meeting the economic problem of the hour! Talk about the ability to feed the physical man as well as the spiritual man! Talk about Christ being interested in every phase of our being! Every question is overwhelmingly answered in this incident.

But here's an additional point of interest. It was the passover season. It was the *springtime* of the year. Yet, as in the case of changing the water into wine, our Lord did not need to wait until the fall season to reap a harvest. He is the only one that can meet every emergency without regard to time, space, or need!

What Our Lord Did

We are told that the Lord took the barley loaves and two small fishes and instructed His disciples to make the men sit down. There was much grass in the place. It was an oasis in the desert. Mark tells us that ". . . they sat down in ranks, by hundreds, and by fifties." Whenever the Lord has anything to do with a situation, orderliness is always observed. No wonder the Apostle Paul urged in the matter of a church service, "Let all things be done decently and in order." That's exactly the way the Creator works.

Now note what our Lord did with the loaves. He took them: that's the first thing. He was willing to accept the little lad's luncheon. Then He gave thanks. It did not make any difference to him that five thousand men besides women and children were watching Him. He returned thanks for the bread. Some of us are such cowards that if even one person is watching us in a restaurant we hesitate to bow our heads and return thanks to God for the food we are about to partake. Then He broke the bread; after which He gave the broken bread to the disciples, and the disciples in turn gave it to the people. In the same manner they handled the fishes.

Our Lord did not feed the multitude directly. He fed the multitude *through* the disciples. He did not give the disciples a whole loaf. It was broken bread that the people ate.

From the balance of the 6th chapter we learn that the next day our Lord used this miracle of the bread as a symbol of Himself as the bread of God. He could never be eaten or assimilated by the sons of men as a *whole* loaf. Before we can assimilate Him, He must become the broken bread in the hands of His Father. Jesus Christ before the cross has no message to a guilty sinner! His life spells condemnation to every man, woman, and child under the sun. But He came not to condemn the world, but that the world through Him might be saved. And so He was broken at the cross. We now eat of His broken body. It is the broken body, the death of our Lord Jesus that enables us to enjoy salvation and feast upon Him as the bread of God.

Since the ascension of our Lord, there is only one case on record, that of Saul of Tarsus, where a man was brought to a knowledge of Christ directly by a revelation from the Risen Lord. Every other person, man, woman, and child, has been given the bread of God through the hands of a disciple. Someone spoke a word; somebody put a tract into the hand; someone quoted a portion of Scripture; some mother or father brought up their children in the nurture and admonition of the Lord; some Sunday School teacher gave a word of testimony; some minister preached the Gospel; but in every case, the bread of God was given through the hands of disciples. That is a solemn thought! It means that if any man, woman, or child has never had the bread of the Gospel presented to them it is our fault. We have kept it from them. God has been pleased to limit His Gospel ministry to men, through men who have been born again by His Spirit. Therefore, there rests upon the conscience and heart of born again people, a tremendous oblion to give the bread to those who have never yet tasted that ... Lord is good.

Finally, observe that our Lord was not a profiteer. He did not take advantage of the dire circumstances of the people to boost the price of food. Only sinful men do that! The bread was given without money or price. Spiritual bread is priceless, it cannot be bought. Do not let anyone tell you, you must pay a price. Salvation is free. It is yours and mine by appropriating by faith which Jesus Christ has Himself *purchased* for us by His own precious blood.

WALK TWENTY-EIGHT

WHY DO CHRISTIAN PEOPLE HAVE TROUBLE?

IN our preceding study we considered the miracle of the feeding of five thousand men besides women and children through our Lord's use of five barley loaves and two small fishes. It is interesting to note that the word used by John translated *small fishes*, occurs in this Book only; nowhere else in the New Testament. Literally it means a *little relish*. They were probably no larger than our canned sardines. At any rate, it is thought provoking to consider the meagre provision in the hands of a beneficent Creator-Redeemer and then to observe how our Lord fully met the need of a crowd that doubtless totalled twenty thousand. That it was a notable miracle was evidenced by the reaction of the multitude who participated in the simple feast. When they had seen the miracle which Jesus did, the men said, "This is of a truth that prophet that should come into the world."

And now reading from verse 15 to and including verse 21 of this chapter, we note:

> "When Jesus therefore perceived that they would come and take him by force, to make him a king, he departed again into a mountain himself alone.
> "And when even was now come, his disciples went down unto the sea,
> "And entered into a ship, and went over the sea toward Capernaum. And it was now dark, and Jesus was not come to them.
> "And the sea arose by reason of a great wind that blew.

> "So when they had rowed about five and twenty or thirty furlongs, they see Jesus walking on the sea, and drawing nigh unto the ship: and they were afraid.
> "But he saith unto them, It is I; be not afraid.
> "Then they willingly received him into the ship: and immediately the ship was at the land whither they went."

There are many timely lessons that we can learn from this portion of Scripture. We call attention to only a few. Note the reaction of the mob: they were literally swept off their feet. They looked upon Jesus as a hero. They were about to rush Him and by force make Him a king. Rest assured that the disciples were all for it and would have been happy to lead the multitude in a coronation of Jesus of Nazareth as King of the Jews. But, both the mob and the disciples mistook the whole point of the proceedings, failing to recognize the significance of what was done when our Lord broke the bread. Our Lord never committed Himself to a mob. He knew more about the motives that govern the conduct of men than all the psychologists put together. He psychoanalyzed, if you please, the motives behind the onrush of the crowd and observed that insatiable desire of the mob to get something for nothing! The very next day many followed Him and when they found Him, He said, ". . . Ye seek me, not because ye saw the miracles, but because ye did eat of the loaves, and were filled." He knew that if another came along and offered them "two chickens in a pot" the mob would be all for the next leader. One can always get a crowd, as our politicians know, by offering more for nothing than the next fellow. The thing that the politicians so often fail to sense however, is the ficklemindedness of the crowd.

The Social Message vs. The Gospel

Then, too, the disciples missed the point of the miracle. So also has the professing church in the world of today. They think as the disciples thought at that moment, that Jesus Christ was a social reformer and had come to aleviate the needs of the poor; to give men better and more food; better homes, and a better environment; to make this world a better world for men to live in. It is a futile, hopeless task as long as there are sinful men in this world! Our Lord never entertained the idea for a single moment. The Christian church of today in its social service program, is blind to its chief function in this world.

There were only two Persons that day who understood the miracle: our Lord, and His Father, unto Whom He withdrew when He departed again into a mountain Himself alone.

The next day, our Lord explained, both to his disciples and to the multitude, the significance of the miracle. He did not come to feed men's bodies, but to save their souls. The bread made of barley, merely symbolized His own body which would be given on the cross in order that men might eat of His flesh and drink of His blood, so that they might have His life in them. To the modern churchman and modern Christendom, the message of a crucified Christ and a blood sacrifice is anathema. "Away with it," they suggest; "let's preach a social gospel." But unless a man is born from above, unless a man has personally appropriated the flesh and blood of our Lord Jesus Christ, not only has he no life in him, but he is a doomed sinner, without God and without hope in this world.

Again we have a striking lesson when we observe that on the same day the disciples whom the Lord used to feed the multitude, actually interfered with His purposes, so that He got rid of the disciples first before He dispersed the mob. In Matthew's account of the event, we read, "And straightway Jesus constrained his disciples to get into a ship, and to go before him unto the other side, while he sent the multitudes away." The word translated *constrained* is a strong word. It literally means He *compelled* His disciples to get into a ship. It was quite evident why! There could be no kingship of Christ apart from His Saviorhood. Sin must be dealt with, before God in grace can come down to men and raise them to a place of fellowship and communion with Himself. It is a solemn thought that it is possible for a Christian at one moment to be used as an instrument in the hands of the Lord to bring blessing to others, and before the day is done, he may become a hindrance to His Lord.

Matthew tells us that after our Lord compelled His disciples to get into a ship, instructing them to go before Him *unto* the other side, that He sent the multitude away and then He went up into a mountain apart to pray. When evening was come He was there alone. In this record, the Holy Spirit has given us one of the world's masterpieces in word paintings. If we were to see that scene on a canvas, it would captivate our attention for hours. There were twelve men in a boat; every one with a disgusted expression on his face, obeying a command with dejected hearts and distraught minds; then the crowd dispersed by the Lord with a spoken word. What a picture! If you have ever been in a mob scene, you will appreciate the power of our Lord in dispersing a crowd of twenty thousand people. There is only one person in all the world capable of handling a mob! We know that today better than ever. The problems of Europe are traceable to the fact that the mob have given their consent to one man, but a man incapable of handling the mob. From whatever angle we examine our Lord Jesus Christ, He is everything that He ought to be. None but God could fill the scene that our Lord fills; He is God!

By the way, here is something interesting. It impressed itself on my mind as the result of a conversation that took place when a group of us sat down to luncheon. We talked about the conditions in Europe and the possibility of Hitler resigning so that another and more acceptable man might take up the reigns of government in Germany and so permit a peaceful solution of the present problems in Europe. One of the gentlemen present at that luncheon who formerly was an officer on the General Staff of the German army during the World War, made this comment: "There has been only one Person in history who withdrew Himself at the hour of His supreme triumph, and that was Jesus Christ."

The Unseen But Not Unmindful Savior

This picture of our Lord alone in the mountain at eventide in prayer, is another fine touch in this masterpiece. *Unseen* by the disciples, He was not *unmindful* of their struggles. He knew about the twelve men in the ship. He knew that the boat was tossed with waves. He knew that the wind was contrary. He knew that those husky fishermen faced a storm which was too much for them. Yet He waited until the fourth watch of the night before going to their rescue. We are not told what conversations took place that night on board the ship, but they most certainly did not sing hymns!

The disciples had a similar experience on a prior occasion, but then, the Lord was a fellow passenger on the ship. Now they faced the onslaught of the elements stirred up by an angry antagonist, alone. They were to have many similar experiences later which they would be able to endure as a result of what they experienced that night. Notice the mob escaped the storm. They went home by foot. It was the disciples alone who suffered the terrors of a distraught mind, battling against overwhelming odds.

They had forgotten one thing however, which, if they had remembered, would have encouraged them to face the storm with the assurance that they would conquer it rather than it envelop them. Our Lord had said that they were to go before Him *unto* the other side of the sea. He did not command them to get into the ship in order to drown in the midst of the lake. He said they were to go *unto* the other side and when He gives such orders, all the demons in the world; all the forces of evil combined cannot prevent the fulfillment of His command. Our Lord never promised His disciples a bed of roses. He said, "In the world ye shall have tribulation . . ." But He did not stop there, He added ". . . be of good cheer; I have overcome the world."

Back in the Old Testament, through the prophet Isaiah, God said to His ancient people ". . . Fear not: for I have redeemed thee, I have called thee by thy name; thou art mine. When thou passest through the waters, I will be with thee; and through the rivers, they shall not overflow thee: when thou walkest through the fire, thou shalt not be burned; neither shall the flame kindle upon thee. For I am the Lord thy God, the Holy One of Israel, thy Saviour . . ." He did not say that they would be spared the deep rivers nor the fire. But neither did He say they would be left in the waters. But He said, "When thou *passest* through the waters, I will be with thee." The disciples were unaware of their *praying Lord*. We too have been unaware of the intercession by our Lord on our behalf when we have gone through deep waters. He will never permit a child of His to fail to complete the journey. And, what's more, He will never allow one of His own to go through the water or to suffer through fire without His company. "I will be with thee." It is for that reason that saints have gone triumphantly to the stake and into the dens of lions rejoicing in the companionship of the Lord Jesus Christ.

Troubled Christians

Christians are not spared trouble. Almost without exception they suffer more trouble than do the worldlings. Dr. William Lyon Phelps in his Autobiography, has given two excellent illustrations of the faithfulness of Christians under trial. He mentions the names of two New Haven women who were living examples of the triumph of Christian faith. One lady lost her husband early in life. She had two sons in his class in college. Tom was the valedictorian and John the fourth in rank. Only a few years after graduation Tom died of a fever; and John, who was at a distant sanatorium after a nervous breakdown, committed suicide. This lady, Dr. Phelps said, was informed of this tragedy by a newspaper reporter who woke her at two o'clock in the morning. She lost the major part of her fortune by a frost in Florida that destroyed her property. A highly educated woman, she went to bed one night without any premonition of evil and woke up in the morning incurably and totally blind. Dr. Phelps said, "I often talked with her after these shattering disasters, and never heard her utter one word of complaint. She was always calm . . . she was a devout Christian."

The other lady was the wife of the Dean of Yale College. She also had two brilliant sons who were in the highest group of scholars. One son died of tuberculosis shortly after graduation and the other became a Professor at Yale and exerted a widespread and inspiring influence on both his colleagues and students, but he died suddenly in early middle age. Her husband died before the death of this son and before the death of her daughter. Then this lady too became totally blind. While the one, Dr. Phelps said, was serene and composed like a Stoic, the other was cheerful and *radiantly happy*. She told the Professor on one occasion that she was so grateful for life. Said the first of these two women, "If religion were not true, life would be meaningless, a tragic farce."

But we must not leave this message without noticing one or two more things. When the disciples first saw the Lord walking on the sea and drawing nigh unto the ship, they were afraid. They thought they saw a spirit and cried out for fear. Strange that we do not recognize Him at times. No, our Lord did not walk *by* the sea, as some critics would have us believe. He did not walk along the shore. He walked *on* the sea. Oh the inconsistencies of the critics! I read one this week who said that our Lord walked alongside of the sea. He admitted that our English Bible correctly translates the word which John used when we read ". . . Jesus walking *on* the sea . . ." yet he insists it does not mean that! It means *by* the sea. Let's see how consistent that is! When our Lord gave His comforting word to those distraught disciples, Peter responded ". . . Lord, if it be thou, bid me come unto thee on the water." Jesus answered "Come." Peter came down out of the ship and walked *on* the water to go to Jesus; but when he saw the wind boisterous, became afraid and beginning to sink, cried out ". . . Lord, save me." Immediately Jesus stretched forth his hand, and caught him, and said unto him, "O thou of little faith, wherefore didst thou doubt?" Our Lord must have had an *awfully long* arm if He were on the shore to have reached Peter and taken him by the hand; to say nothing of the silly suggestion that this group of fishermen could have been so ignorant as to fail to appreciate that they were right at the shore! No, there can be no compromising the Word of God. Either it is true, or it is false. I believe it is true. I have no difficulty in accepting the statement of Scripture that Jesus walked on the water. If you knew who Jesus is, neither would you have any difficulty with the proposition!

Finally, the bitter disappointing experiences of the disciples that night were amply repaid by the knowledge that their Lord knew all about it and by what they witnessed when our Lord entered into the ship, stilled the waves and quieted the winds so that a perfect calm was experienced. Is it any wonder that Matthew says "Then they that were in the ship came and worshipped him, saying, Of a truth thou art the Son of God." That revelation of Christ was not given to the mob, it was reserved for the disciples. The troubled disciples received a glorious revelation of the Person of their Lord.

Walk Twenty-Nine

SEEKING FOR JESUS

I HAVE entitled this study, "Seeking for Jesus." The words are found in that portion of Scripture which we are now to consider. Commencing with verse 22 of the 6th chapter, to and including verse 29, we read:

> "The day following, when the people which stood on the other side of the sea saw that there was none other boat there, save that one whereinto his disciples were entered, and that Jesus went not with his disciples into the boat, but *that* his disciples were gone away alone;

> "(Howbeit there came other boats from Tiberias nigh unto the place where they did eat bread, after that the Lord had given thanks:)
> "When the people therefore saw that Jesus was not there, neither his disciples, they also took shipping, and came to Capernaum, seeking for Jesus.
> "And when they had found him on the other side of the sea, they said unto him, Rabbi, when camest thou hither?
> "Jesus answered them and said, Verily, verily, I say unto you, Ye seek me, not because ye saw the miracles, but because ye did eat of the loaves, and were filled.
> "Labour not for the meat which perisheth, but for that meat which endureth unto everlasting life, which the Son of man shall give unto you: for him hath God the Father sealed.
> "Then said they unto him, What shall we do, that we might work the works of God?
> "Jesus answered and said unto them, This is the work of God, that ye believe on him whom he hath sent."

It is difficult to realize that a worthy act might be the result of an unworthy motive. Most of us are thrilled when we hear of an individual or group of people *seeking for Jesus*. Here was a crowd that sought Him. It was part of the same group who had previously participated in the supper which our Lord had provided. The next morning they observed that He was not on the other side of the sea. They knew there was only one boat there and that our Lord had sent the disciples away in that boat. It was not even curiosity which motivated their actions, when they went so far as to take shipping and came to Capernaum, *seeking for Jesus*. When they found Him on the other side of the sea, they said to Him, "...Rabbi, when camest thou hither?" As Dr. G. Campell Morgan has noted, "He did not answer their question. They asked Him *when He* came there. He told them *why they* had come."

There were some Greeks who came up to the feast near the close of our Lord's ministry. They also came *seeking for Jesus*. They sought an interview out of curiosity, but these people sought Him only because they did eat of the loaves and were filled. They were not interested *in* Him, but rather in what they could get *from* Him. The world has not changed since that day. Every Christian worker knows there are multitudes who are interested in the loaves and the fishes, the by-product of Christianity, but reject the Person of our Lord Jesus Christ.

Wasted Labor

Now let's notice how our Lord handled these seekers. In the first place, He stripped them of their veil of hypocrisy. There can never be an unveiling of Christ before the unveiling of the individual has taken place. In other words, no man will ever come to know Christ until he comes to know himself. What's the use of talking about salvation until we know that we are lost and in need of a Savior? Our Lord never permitted a prolonged interview before He made that issue clear. He never committed Himself to any man until that man recognized his need of a Savior. Our Lord came not to call the righteous, but sinners to repentance. He came to seek and to save that which was lost. After stripping these people, then He began to unfold the purpose of His ministry. Notice what He said. "Labour not for the meat which perisheth, but for that meat which endureth unto everlasting life, which the Son of man shall give unto you: for him hath God the Father sealed." The phrase *labour not* means *"be not busy about."* These people were occupied with the loaves and the fishes. They were concerned with that which perisheth. It is amazing how much time we spend on ourselves, on that which will perish.

We eat bread to sustain our bodies, but it does not stay with us very long. Most of us require three meals a day. But there is a meat which if a man eat, he will never hunger again. It is that meat which endures unto everlasting life. Our Lord said this meat ". . . the Son of man shall give unto you: for him hath God the Father sealed." Later He made clear that the meat was his own body, His flesh, which He would give for the life of the world.

The simplicity and clarity of our Lord's words is arresting. Archbishop D'Arcy put it succinctly when he said, "The words of Jesus shine by their own light, they carry with them their own credentials. There are no other words like them anywhere. Like the Person who uttered them, they are unique. They are simple, yet profound; calm, yet intense; 'mild yet terrible.' They have a peculiar force which expresses authority. They do not persuade or intreat or reason with the hearer: they penetrate, they convict, they reveal. The charm and the wonder of them are as fresh today, for the unlearned as well as the learned, as when the people were astonished at His doctrine."

Bishop J. C. Ryle has ably summarized the 27th verse of this chapter when he suggested that there are four things in it. First, there is something forbidden: Labor not for the meat which perisheth. There is also something commanded: Labor for the meat which endureth unto everlasting life. Then there is something promised: The Son of man shall give unto you. And finally, there is something declared: "For him hath God the Father sealed." We all know what a seal does to a document. It authenticates it. When our Lord said of himself that God the Father had put his seal upon Him, He declared God had authenticated Him. Such being the case, is there a more imperative matter for us to consider than the Person of Jesus Christ?

Christ Our Passover

Note the care which our Lord exercised in the choice of words when He said "Be concerned about the meat which endureth unto everlasting life, which the Son of man *shall give,* or *will give* unto you . . ." He was talking about something in the future. He was not ready to give it *then.* He knew that His life and ministry were not the means of salvation for a sinner; it was the death that He would die that would provide the basis of a sinful man's approach unto God.

It was the Passover season when our Lord gave this discourse. It was the springtime of the year. The message which He spoke therefore comes with peculiar force when we consider that fact. You will recall what took place on the Passover night. A lamb had to be chosen for each household in Israel. It had to be kept four days to assure that it was without blemish or without spot. Then it was slain and the blood poured into a basin and applied with hyssop to the door posts and lintel. The promise of God was emphatic. He said, ". . . and when I see the blood, I will pass over you. . ." The blood in the basin would not have availed, it was the blood on the door posts that protected the first-born. Then the slain lamb was taken inside the house. The door was shut and the lamb was roasted with fire. Israel was told to eat *none* of it raw. The lamb roasted with fire was eaten and enjoyed by the family inside the house who were filled with peace, unmolested by any fear that the first-born would be smitten.

The Scripture says, "Christ our passover is sacrificed for us." He was the lamb of God without blemish or without spot. He was examined minutely by friend and foe who alike confessed that He was without blemish and without spot. But as there was no salvation for Israel in a live lamb, so there is no salvation in an uncrucified Christ. Apart from the cross, our Lord Jesus has no word of salvation to offer to the sons of men. While the life of our Lord Jesus is intensely interesting to observe, and we are observing it as we walk with our Lord through this Gospel, it is the death of our Lord Jesus Christ that gives a sinner the right of approach unto a holy God. We cannot feast upon an uncrucified Christ. We cannot eat of His flesh raw. We must eat of the flesh that has been roasted by the fire of God's judgment. I realize that I am using material terms in presenting spiritual truth, but that principle is exactly the method which our Lord employed. Is it any wonder therefore, that in the writings of the Apostle Paul, he brushes aside the earthly ministry of Jesus, hardly making any reference to it, but when he enumerated the facts of the Gospel, he began with this majestic statement: ". . . Christ died for our sins according to the Scriptures." But mark this closely. As it was the blood on the door posts that protected the first-born in Israel from being slain with all the first-born in Egypt, so it is the blood on the heart that saves, not the blood on the cross. There must be personal appropriation before there can be salvation from judgment due sin.

The Gospel: A Feast

We do well also to ponder the background which our Lord Himself provided at this time in order to set forth the message of the Gospel. Professor Stalker caught the scene when he wrote, "It was indeed, but the common fare He gave them; the table was the ground, the tablecloth was the green grass, and the banqueting hall was the open air; but never did His guests enjoy a better meal, for love presided at the table and it is love that makes an entertainment fine. As we see Him there, beaming with genial delight over the vast company, it is impossible not to think of such words of His as these: 'I am the bread of life; the bread which I shall give is my flesh which I will give for the life of the world.' In His teaching He delighted to represent the gospel as a feast, to which He invited all the sons of men in the beautiful spirit of a Royal Host."

Our Lord had said, "Labour not for the meat which perisheth, but for that meat which endureth unto everlasting life." Immediately the people asked, "What shall we do, that we might work the works of God?" To this our Lord gave the answer, "This is the work of God, that ye believe on him whom he hath sent." What must we do? Jesus answered: just one thing; believe. Is there nothing else? Oh yes, but that something else was done by God in the Person of His Son. It is the work of God, not yours, nor mine. Both David and Jonah stated ". . . salvation belongeth unto the Lord." That principle is carried straight through the Bible from Genesis to Revelation. Salvation is the work of God. He planned it; He executed it; He accepted it. The only thing that is left for us to do is to believe on Him whom He hath sent. Simple? No, it is simple only to the minds that do not understand it. But it is clear. There is no necessity for stumbling. Salvation was planned by the might of God and the wisdom of God. It is so wonderful that both "the learned and the unlearned" have never been able to comprehend its profundity, but both have been able to enjoy its clarity.

Walk Thirty
TRUE BREAD

OUR Lord had answered the question which was addressed to Him by the people when He said, "This is the work of God, that ye believe on him whom he hath sent." Nevertheless they immediately said, "What sign shewest thou then, that we may see, and believe thee? what dost thou work? Our fathers did eat manna in the desert; as it is written, He gave them bread from heaven to eat." The question was presented subtly, but the sting of it was quite apparent.

The day before, these same people had seen Jesus take five barley loaves and two fishes (about the size of sardines) and with these, feed five thousand men besides women and children. It was a notable miracle. The people were not only impressed, but they were swept off their feet and wanted to make Him king. Yet the very next day, they asked, "What sign shewest thou then, that we may see, and believe thee? what dost thou work?"

We have all met men and women who have insisted that they could not believe until they *saw.* "Seeing is believing" they said. Well, now is it? These people *saw.* They *saw* a notable miracle that could only be accomplished by a Creator. Forty thousand eyes at least *saw* the performance of this miracle. What did they want to *see* in order to believe? Seeing is not believing! Certainly not in the spiritual realm. Men do not receive the testimony of Christ through having their eyes thrilled. Faith does not come that way. "Faith cometh by hearing, and hearing by the word of God." Irrespective of what sign the Lord may have accomplished, it would never have satisfied the unregenerate heart or mind.

Our Lord had said, "This is the *work* of God, that ye believe on him whom he hath sent." But they said, "What dost thou work?" And to put our Lord in His place, they reminded Him, "Our fathers did eat manna in the desert; as it is written, He gave them bread from heaven." In other words, "we concede it was impressive when you fed five thousand men besides women and children with five small barley loaves and two fishes, but you have a long way to travel to compare with Moses! Moses fed a whole nation for forty years without sowing a seed or reaping a harvest. Moses is *our* man—he who fed a whole nation without visible means for forty years! But you, you have only given us one meal and it was limited to five thousand men besides women and children."

Observe our Lord's answer. "Verily, verily, I say unto you . . ." (whenever our Lord used that introduction, it was intended to add force to what He was about to say) ". . . Moses gave you not that bread from heaven; but my Father giveth you the true bread from heaven. For the bread of God is he which cometh down from heaven, and giveth life unto the world." Notice, He was talking about a Person, Himself. *He* is the bread of God. Moses did not give them *that* bread. It is the *Father* who giveth the true bread from heaven. Notice our Lord had said, ". . . the Father *giveth* the true bread." In verse 27 of the same chapter, our Lord said, . . . the Son of man shall *give* unto you the meat which endureth unto everlasting life. In both cases He used the word *give.* Salvation is a gift. Eternal life is a gift. We do not earn it, we do not work for it. A gift is received and the recipient offers a word of thanksgiving. That is all. That is the Gospel!

As the people did not object to being given bread, they still mistook His message and said, ". . . evermore give us this bread." But they murmured when they heard from the lips of our Lord these wonderful words: "I am the bread of life: he that cometh to me shall never hunger; and he that believeth on me shall never thirst." By the way, here is irony in all of its effectiveness. They had called attention to Moses. They mentioned the manna that fell from heaven. Our Lord reminded them inferentially at least— "You have always been a stiff-necked people. You have always rebelled against God. Yes, Moses gave you manna in the wilderness. Your fathers ate the manna. They didn't work for it. They picked it up from off the ground every day as God gave it. But the manna did not satisfy your fathers. They complained because they did not have any water to drink." So our Lord said, ". . . he that cometh to me shall never *hunger;* and he that believeth on me shall never *thirst.*"

THE INCOMPREHENSIBLE CHRIST

Now notice one or two other things from this part of the 6th chapter before we sum them up. Continuing His conversation, our Lord said:

> ". . . ye also have seen me, and believe not.
> "All that the Father giveth me shall come to me; and him that cometh to me I will in no wise cast out.
> "For I came down from heaven, not to do mine own will, but the will of him that sent me.
> "And this is the Father's will which hath sent me, that of all which he hath given me I should lose nothing, but should raise it up again at the last day.
> "And this is the will of him that sent me, that every one which seeth the Son, and believeth on him, may have everlasting life: and I will raise him up at the last day."

Now notice the reaction to this message of our Lord. We read from verse 41:

> "The Jews then murmured at him, because he said, I am the bread which came down from heaven.
> "And they said, Is not this Jesus, the son of Joseph, whose father and mother we know? How is it then that he saith, I came down from heaven?
> "Jesus therefore answered and said unto them, Murmur not among yourselves.
> "No man can come to me, except the Father which hath sent me draw him: and I will raise him up at the last day."

There was no question in the minds of these people that the manna had come down from heaven. Their fathers saw it come. It did not grow, it fell from heaven. But our Lord said, the manna was not the true bread. He said, He, Himself was the true bread and He came down from heaven.

The people were unable to comprehend Him or His sayings. From that hour to this, our Lord and His sayings have never been understood or comprehended. He remains today as great an enigma if not greater than at the time He walked the hills of Judea. He is the only Person that men have been unable to comprehend. We can comprehend and understand Washington or Lincoln or Gladstone or Shakespeare or Plato or Socrates. We have no difficulty in mastering their writings, but when it comes to the Person of Jesus Christ and His words, He and they are utterly incomprehensible.

We have witnessed in our generation, a debunking of some of the great heroes of the past, but not so with our Lord. All that men can do is to murmur against Him and to go away with a million questions in their minds unanswered. There is only one way to comprehend the Person of Christ and to understand His ministry. Only as we receive His own testimony can we do that. He is not like us, He is not of this earth, but is from above. He came down from heaven to do His Father's will. When that is understood and received, then the Person of Christ becomes glorious and His ministry becomes clear. The people said to Jesus, "Lord, evermore give us this bread." The woman of Samaria, when He told her about the well of water springing up into everlasting life, said, "Sir, give me this water, that I thirst not, neither come hither to draw."

What It Means To Trust

How can we get this bread or receive this water? What are we to do? If we read carefully through this chapter, we will discover three things are given to illuminate the answers to this question. First, in verse 35, "he that believeth on me." Again in the same verse, ". . . he that cometh to me." And in verse 54 "Whoso *eateth* my flesh, and *drinketh* my blood, hath eternal life . . ." Dr. Marcus Dods has called specific attention to these three things, declaring that each of these expressions has its own significance. He said that "Belief must come first—belief that Christ is sent to give us life; belief that it depends upon our connection with that one Person whether we shall or shall not have life eternal. We must also come to Him. The people He was addressing had followed Him for miles, and had found Him and were speaking to Him, but they had not *come* to Him. To come to Him is to approach Him in spirit and with submissive trust; it is to commit ourselves to Him as our Lord; it is to rest in Him as our all; it is to come to Him with open heart, accepting Him as all He claims to be; it is to meet the eye of a present, living Christ, who knows what is in man, and to say to Him, 'I am Thine, Thine most gladly, Thine for evermore.'

"But most emphatically of all does our Lord say that we must 'eat His flesh and drink His blood' if we are to partake of His life. That is to say, the connection between Christ and us must be of the closest possible kind; so close that the assimilation of the food we eat is not too strong a figure to express it. The food we eat becomes our blood and flesh; it becomes our life, our self. And it does so by our eating it, not by our talking about it, not by our looking at it, and admiring its nutritive properties, but only by eating it."

Let me place alongside of these words of Dr. Marcus Dods, the words of another. This past week I was glancing through a book by Winston Churchhill, one he wrote just before the first World War. It is a well known work, entitled "The Inside of the Cup." I got it some time ago while in Boston rummaging through one of the famous second hand book stores of that city. The copy I have came out of the library of Dr. A. Z. Conrad, the late pastor of the historic Park Street Congregational Church of Boston, Mass., which pulpit is now occupied by one of the ablest young men in America, Dr. Harold Ockenga. Dr. Conrad must have read "The Inside of the Cup" carefully, for there are many notations on the side of the pages. One particularly impressed me. Winston Churchill had put into the lips of the rector of St. John's these words, "True faith was simply trusting." The rector had preached a sensational sermon on the text, "Except a man be born again, he cannot see the kingdom of God." Dr. Conrad had written on the side of the page in pencil, this comment: "Trust is loving belief in a person."

To trust Christ is not only to believe in His Person, but it is the expression of a loving belief in His Person.

Walk Thirty-One
THE HARD SAYINGS OF JESUS

WE have already given four addresses from the 6th chapter of St. John's Gospel. Yet we have only skimmed the surface. We shall give two more before leaving this important part of the Scripture: this one, which we have entitled "The Hard Sayings of Jesus," and another on "The Sovereign Grace of God and the Free Will of Man" which subject is presented to us in this 6th chapter by the repeated declaration of our Lord that before a man can come to Him, the Father must draw him.

It is no exaggeration to suggest that one cannot over-emphasize the importance of this part of the Scripture, at least it is *one* of the great chapters in the Bible. It is not surprising to find therefore that it has developed to be the battleground of Christendom. Here is the chapter which has caused the various branches of the professing Church in the world to separate into their own little nooks and corners and by-paths. It is conceded that it is a hard chapter. The people who heard our Lord speak these words for the first time said, "This is an hard saying; who can hear it?" But when they said it, they expressed the thought of revulsion. It was so degrading to them that they literally said, "Who can listen to it?" If they did not actually put their hands to their ears, at least they figuratively did so. Even some of His disciples felt the same way. Our Lord sensed it and said, "Doth this offend you?"

What was it that offended some of the disciples? What was it that caused the people to rebel against Him? What are the hard sayings of Jesus? Here they are:

> "I am the living bread which came down from heaven: if any man eat of this bread, he shall live for ever: and the bread that I will give is my flesh, which I will give for the life of the world.
> "The Jews therefore strove among themselves, saying, How can this man give us his flesh to eat?
> "Then Jesus said unto them, Verily, verily, I say unto you, Except ye eat the flesh of the Son of man, and drink his blood, ye have no life in you.
> "Whoso eateth my flesh, and drinketh my blood, hath eternal life; and I will raise him up at the last day.
> "For my flesh is meat indeed, and my blood is drink indeed.

> "He that eateth my flesh, and drinketh my blood, dwelleth in me, and I in him.
> "As the living Father hath sent me, and I live by the Father: so he that eateth me, even he shall live by me.
> "This is that bread which came down from heaven: not as your fathers did eat manna, and are dead: he that eateth of this bread shall live for ever."

For us to appreciate how these words shocked and offended the people who listened, it is necessary to note one or two passages from the Old Testament. For instance there is the 17th chapter of Leviticus, commencing with the 10th verse, where we read:

> "And whatsoever man there be of the house of Israel, or of the strangers that sojourn among you, that eateth any manner of blood; I will even set my face against that soul that eateth blood, and will cut him off from among his people.
> "For the life of the flesh is in the blood: and I have given it to you upon the altar to make an atonement for your souls: for it is the blood that maketh an atonement for the soul.
> "Therefore I said unto the children of Israel, No soul of you shall eat blood, neither shall any stranger that sojourneth among you eat blood."

This same injunction is repeated several times in that chapter, and likewise in the book of Deuteronomy, the book of the "twice told law." And yet, here is Jesus of Nazareth, claiming to be the Son of God and declaring that He had the seal of God upon Him, making the astounding statement, "Except ye eat the flesh of the Son of Man and drink his blood, ye have no life in you. . . For my flesh is meat indeed, and my blood is drink indeed." A hard saying? Indeed it is. So hard, or, as the word also means, so *rough* and *rash,* that even in this generation which has had the benefit of nineteen centuries of Christian advocates and expositors, there are yet numerous so-called "disciples" who revolt and rebel against what they term, "the gospel of the slaughter house and the shambles."

"Doth this offend you?" said our Lord Jesus! If you please, it *is* offensive to every natural man, be he cultured or uncultured. But to the man who has obeyed the Lord Jesus, this word of our Lord is the most precious thing in his life.

What It Means To Eat His Flesh

I do not intend to evade the clear, unequivocal statement found in the book of Moses. I believe it to be the Word of God as I do every other part of the Bible. But we should observe something of extreme importance. There is *no* injunction in the Old Testament against drinking blood. There *is* an injunction against eating flesh that has the blood in it. As long ago as in Noah's day, the Lord had commanded that the "flesh with the life thereof, which is the blood thereof, shall ye not eat." The blood had a vital ministry in the Old Testament economy. To begin with, it was the life of the flesh. But God had a special interest in it, for He had said, "I have *given* it to you upon the altar to make an atonement for your souls." Just as there was an injunction against eating flesh with the life thereof, which is the blood thereof, even so it is impossible to have life with God or in Christ by feasting on the man Christ Jesus after the flesh.

In other words, the Gospel of Christ centers in His death, not in His life. We may admire His life; we may seek to emulate His walk; we may extol His virtues; we may speak glowingly of His ministry, His principles, and His benefactions; but unless we eat of His flesh and drink of His blood, we have no life in us.

We have already observed that there is no injunction in the Scripture against drinking blood, but there is an injunction against eating flesh with the blood in it. Our Lord made the distinction clear in His words also. He never once suggested that His flesh was to be eaten while the life was still in it. He said the flesh was to be eaten, but it was evident that the life had already gone out of it, for He spoke also of drinking His blood.

There are two positive things that our Lord said a man possesses when he eats His flesh and drinks His blood. One is in verse 54 of this chapter. "Whoso eateth my flesh, and drinketh my blood, *hath eternal life.*" The other is in verse 56, "He that eateth my flesh, and drinketh my blood, *dwelleth in me, and I in him.*"

He also made one negative declaration which is found in verse 53. "Except ye eat the flesh of the Son of man, and drink his blood, *ye have no life in you.*" We need not spend time on that negative statement. It requires neither explanation nor elaboration. It is too clear to be misunderstood. One may disagree with it, or ignore it, but the declaration of Christ is that we have no life in us. Of course He did not refer to physical life. We all have that. Every man has that by birth. The life He was speaking of was the life which He characterized as eternal life. That's spiritual life. That's

THE GOSPEL OF JOHN — CHAPTER VI, VERSES 51-58

the gift of God. That enables one to have relationship with God, to know Him, to walk in His ways, and to have fellowship with Him. That's exactly what our Lord expressed in the two positive statements. By eating His flesh and drinking His blood, He said we would first of all, have eternal life; and secondly, we would dwell in Him and He would dwell in us. There is no more magnificent statement in all literature than these words of our Lord that we would dwell in Him and He in us. In the 17th chapter of John where He addressed His Father in prayer, He put it in this language: "The glory which thou gavest me I have given them; that they may be one, even as we are one: *I in them, and thou in me, that they may be made perfect in one.*"

I once heard Dr. Lewis Sperry Chafer, President of the Dallas Theological Seminary, give one of the most thrilling addresses it has ever been my privilege to listen to on this very subject. He gave it its theological term. I shall not confuse you by repeating it. The men of this world think it is a sign of the possession of a superior intellect to be able to express a thought in choice verbosity, but our Lord used the simplest words. As I listened to that man of God expound the glorious truth of the incarnation, God in Christ, and then follow it with an unveiling of the glorious fact of the indwelling Christ, "I in them," I experienced one of the greatest blessings that I have ever enjoyed. I repeat, there is no more magnificent statement than the word of our Lord that if we eat His flesh and drink His blood, He will dwell in us and we in Him.

I listened to Gypsy Smith recently. He touched upon this same subject in the course of his address when he referred to an interesting time he had had with his father. They were walking along the sands by the sea shore while discussing this wonderful truth. Suddenly his father picked up a bottle, then walked to the water, dipped the bottle into the water, filled it up to the brim, then pressed a cork into the bottle so that the salt water splashed over it. Then he took the bottle, swung it around with his powerful arm and threw it out into the ocean, and turned to his son and said, "There, the ocean is in the bottle and the bottle is in the ocean."

We may have a small capacity for entertaining the risen Lord by His Spirit in our being, but what might be said of the glorious ocean of His Own Being into which we have been implanted.

That's the Gospel. It is a magnificent message. It is the only message in all the world that can take a man out of his sin, deliver him from its power and crown his life with godliness.

The Communion Table

Now then, what did our Lord mean when He said, it was necessary for us to eat His flesh and drink His blood? Again theology, the queen of the sciences, is apt to be bewildering rather than enlightening. In theology men have grappled with this subject and made it a problem. Some schools have coined the word *transubstantiation*. Others, *consubstantiation*. It has been suggested by these schools that our Lord was referring to the Communion table or the Lord's Supper. Some have suggested that when we eat the bread and drink the wine, that by a priestly act, the bread and the wine become in substance the very flesh and blood of our Lord; and we thereby eat His flesh and drink His blood in the Communion. There is another school who say this portion of Scripture has nothing to do with the Communion table, though the Communion table enables us to better appreciate and understand its message. That school looks upon the bread and the wine as memorials of a finished sacrifice. They see nothing potent in the bread or in the wine. They do not refer to it as a sacrament, but only as a memorial. A simple feast to be true, but a most amazing provision to warm the heart of a believer and to express his remembrance of the Lord.

It is to be sincerely regretted that the feast that our Lord instituted to be a remembrance of Himself, should have become the arena of the theologians. But these words of our Lord Jesus Christ are to be understood in the very same way that all similar statements of our Lord are to be received. For example, when He said, "I am the vine, ye are the branches," it is self evident that He did not mean He was a piece of wood. It is impossible, literally, for us to eat His flesh and to drink His blood, but we can do that which is symbolized by bread and wine. We do eat of His flesh and drink of His blood when we personally appropriate His death on the cross as the atonement for our sin, when we bathe under His blood and receive cleansing from sin. Our Lord said, "It is the spirit that quickeneth; the flesh profiteth nothing: the words that I speak unto you, they are spirit, and they are life." Therefore He said, "He that believeth on me hath everlasting life."

We already have intimated the result of this kind of preaching by our Lord; but we learn from the 66th verse of this 6th chapter that from that time, some disciples went back and walked no more with Him. Then our Lord said to the twelve, "Will ye also go away?" What a wonderful scene is presented here. The day before our Lord had fed five thousand men besides women and children. The crowd surged about Him. Now the crowd left Him. Even those who professed to have some measure of faith in Him found it impossible to continue. So here He was, *alone* with His little group of twelve. He asks, "Will ye also go away?" Simon Peter answered, ". . . Lord, to whom shall we go? thou hast the words of eternal life. And we believe and are sure that thou art that Christ, the Son of the living God."

What a magnificent confession! It is an acknowledgment that although we may not be able to understand the full import of our Lord's words, we believe and are sure that He is the Christ. There are those who cannot understand such a confession. They believe it is a sign of weakness in a Christian's position, whereas in fact, it is a Gibralter of his faith. We have only a puny, finite mind. At best it has been stimulated by the presence of the Spirit of God within us, for ". . . now I know in part; but then shall I know even as also I am known." To whom shall we go for an answer to the many questions that press themselves upon our hearts and minds? To whom can we go so that these consciences of ours may be at peace and our sin that gnaws at the very vitals of our being be dealt with? The Apostle Peter gave the only answer: "Lord, to whom shall we go? thou hast the words of eternal life." No one else possesses them, and we believe and are sure that He is that Christ, the Son of the living God.

Walk Thirty-Two

THE SOVEREIGN WILL AND GRACE OF GOD AND THE FREE WILL OF MAN

FOR our final study in this 6th chapter we shall consider the perplexing problem of the Sovereign grace of God and the free will of man. The subject has disturbed many men. In fact, multitudes have used it as an excuse for a do-nothing attitude in respect to the Person and work of our Lord Jesus Christ. They conclude, "If I am to be saved, I will be saved. If I am one of the elect, then I am certain to be saved. If not, what's the use? I am lost anyway." That of course, is fatalism, but nevertheless it is a view held by a multitude of people. It is a problem that is constantly being presented to one who preaches the Gospel.

Before we go further, we do well to consider a few passages from this chapter. In each case, our Lord Himself is the speaker.

In verse 37, He said, "All that the Father giveth me shall come to me; and him that cometh to me I will in no wise cast out." It is inadvisable to quote that passage out of its context. In order to get the full import of what our Lord declared, it is necessary to read the preceding verse where our Lord said to the people ". . . ye also have seen me, and believe not." Their unbelief was the expression of their own will. Then the Lord followed it with the statement, "All that the Father giveth me shall come to me; and him that cometh to me I will in no wise cast out."

Again, in verse 39: "And this is the Father's will which hath sent me, that of *all* which he hath given me I should lose nothing, but should raise it up again at the last day."

Again, verses 42-44. The people said ". . . Is not this Jesus, the son of Joseph, whose father and mother we know? how is it then that he saith, I came down from heaven?" Jesus therefore answered and said unto them, "Murmur not among yourselves. No man can come to me, except the Father which hath sent me draw him: and I will raise him up at the last day. It is written in the prophets, And they shall be all taught of God. Every man therefore that hath heard, and hath learned of the Father, cometh unto me."

When our Lord observed that these sayings were offensive to some He said, (verses 62-65) ". . . Doth this offend you? *What* and if y shall see the Son of man ascend up where he was before? It is the spirit that quickeneth; the flesh profiteth nothing: the words that I speak unto you, *they* are spirit, and *they* are life. But there are some of you that believe not. For Jesus knew from the beginning who they were that believed not, and who should betray him. Therefore said I unto you, that no man can come unto me, except it were given unto him of my Father."

The Will of Man

It is clear from these passages that our Lord believed and preached the Sovereign will and grace of God. It is our task if possible to reconcile that principle with the theory that man is a free moral agent and that he has been given a will to exercise in all matters pertaining to life, and thus, he is an inexcusable character.

Whether or not we can reconcile these two apparent contradictory principles, no sane person questions the power, the right, and the prerogative of God to exercise His own will: nor will any rational thinking person question that God has created man with a will of his own. Every father and mother will acknowledge, that it is surprising how quickly this *will* asserts or manifests itself in a little babe. It is there! It is inborn! It is inbred! Even before a child can speak, it expresses its own will.

We observed in our studies in the 5th chapter of this Gospel that our Lord presented an unanswerable charge to those who questioned His claims to deity, when He said, "Ye search the Scriptures; for in them ye *think* ye have eternal life." Incidently, here is evidence that human wisdom is faulty. But our Lord continued and said, that ". . . they, (the Scriptures) are they which testify of men. And ye *will* not come to me, that ye might have life." Our Lord declared the one thing that prevented those Pharisees from coming to him that they might have life, was their own free, stubborn, determined will. He had presented His claims in a logical and reasonable manner. The evidence itself was irrefutable. But their prejudice and their will prevented or beclouded their thinking so that they refused to come unto Him.

The problem (in my judgment) is wholly solved by a verse or two that appears in the 7th chapter of this Gospel. Our Lord was in Jerusalem at the time. It was during the feast of tabernacles. About the midst of that festive period He taught in the temple. The people marveled, saying, "How knoweth this man letters, having never learned?" Our Lord answered, "My doctrine is not mine, but his that sent me." Then follows this clear statement, "If any man *will do his will,* he shall *know* of the doctrine, whether it be of God, or whether I speak of myself." What a passage, and how it illumines our subject! Here is a threefold acknowledgment of our Lord. First, that there is such a thing as a human will. Second, that there is such a thing as a divine will. Finally that there is such a thing as a divine revelation. Furthermore, one only gets to know divine revelation when the human will is made subservient to the divine will. "If *any man will do his will,* (God's) he shall *know* of the doctrine . . ."

Our Lord did not exclude a single person. If *any man will* do God's will, he shall know. Obedience comes before knowledge, and there is no truer scientific statement in this world than that. No scientist ever learned the secrets of creation's powers until he first bowed before creation's laws. He had to become obedient to the principles of creation before he could understand the operation of those forces and harness them to do his bidding. Let me illustrate by a plain, simple, everyday occurrence. Let's enter a room. It is at the midnight hour. There is electric current available throughout the entire house, including the room which we enter. There are the proper switches in every room to turn the current into the lamps so that the lamps can give their light. But we will never enjoy the light until we turn on the switch. It is simple, it is almost childish, we do it so frequently, every day of our lives. We do not hesitate to do so. We do not argue about it. We know it is so! We know that the first thing to do is to *obey* the laws of electricity, by turning on the switch. Then only will we enjoy the light. Our Lord said, "If any man will do his (God's) will, he shall know of the doctrine . . ." He will never know it any other way.

God's Will

What is God's will? Jesus said this is the will of God ". . . that every one which seeth the Son, and believeth on him, may have everlasting life." When we are willing to do God's will, then we will know. Knowledge always follows obedience. That is true in every realm as well as in the spiritual.

Now then, where does God's will come in? It is Sovereign—so too is His grace. He has declared emphatically, without qualification that every man that will do His will, i.e., will believe His Son, and receive Him as his Savior and bow to His Lordship, He will give to him everlasting life, and will raise him up at the last day.

Our Lord had said "No man can come to me, except the Father which hath sent me draw him." A quick reading of that statement might lead some to conclude that since it is the Father's business to draw a man to Christ, man is relieved of all responsibility. But before arriving at such a conclusion, it seems advisable for us to compare spiritual things with spiritual! If we do, we only have to turn over a few pages to the 12th chapter of John's Gospel where we read these words: "And I, if I be lifted up from the earth, will draw *all* men unto me." Not a single man is excluded, but we must take the first step in blind obedience to the will of God. We must do His will. Only then shall we know of the doctrine, whether it is of God, or whether our Lord Jesus Christ as a man spake of himself.

We shall look at one more verse of Scripture before bringing our message to a close. In Paul's letter to the Ephesians, chapter 2 verse 8, he wrote: "For by grace are ye saved through faith; and that not of yourselves: it is the gift of God." From that passage it is evident that even the faith we possess is a gift of God. It is not our own. It was given to us. Does this present another insurmountable obstacle?

Listen to the words of Bishop Moule on this subject. He said: "For whether or no faith is the gift of God, it is most certainly the act of man; none should assert this more decidedly than those who hold (as we do) that Eph. 2:8 does teach that where saving faith is, it is there because God has 'given' it. But how does He 'give' it? Not, surely, by implanting a new faculty, but by so opening the soul to God in Christ that the divine magnet effectually draws the man to a willing repose upon such a God. But the man *does* this, as an act, himself. He trusts God as genuinely, as personally, as much with his own faculty of trust, as he trusts a man whom he sees to be quite trustworthy and precisely fit to meet an imperative need."

God has given us faith. We exercise it every day of our lives. Let's put it to work in believing God. He has made provision for every man in Christ. Our Lord's death is sufficient to atone for the sins of the world. God has made the way of salvation so clear that it cannot be misunderstood unless a man deliberately seeks to do so. Words could not be clearer than those our Lord used when He said,

"He that believeth on me hath everlasting life." We have nothing to do to merit it for we are already "inexcusable sinners." Our sin has barred us from the presence of God. Our sin has condemned us; our sin has played havoc with our lives. We cannot do anything about it, but we can trust God if we are willing to do so. And if we are, it is the Sovereign will of God that He will save us for all time and eternity on the basis of what He did in Christ on the cross two thousand years ago.

Walk Thirty-Three

THE CHRIST MEN THOUGHT THEY KNEW

IN chapter 6 we found a Passover setting; in chapter 7, we have a fall festival, which Dr. Dods has referred to as "a kind of national harvest home gathering." It was the Feast of Tabernacles which lasted eight days. "It was a feast, therefore, full of rejoicing. Every Israelite appeared in holiday attire, bearing in his hands a palm-branch, or wearing some significant emblem of earth's fruitfulness. At night the city was brilliantly illuminated, especially round the Temple, in which great lamps, used only on these occasions, were lit, and which possibly occasioned our Lord's remark at this time, as reported in the following chapter, 'I am the Light of the world.' "

We should not forget the purpose of the writing of this book as we examine the introductory part of this chapter. John said that he wrote these things in order that we might believe that Jesus is the Christ, the Son of God, and that believing we might have life through His name. Our Lord Jesus Christ is today as much of an enigma to most people as He was on this occasion. Here we learn that even His brethren did not believe on Him. But they kept a close, scrutinizing and skeptical watch over Him.

Our Lord avoided Jerusalem at the time, preferring to stay in Galilee because the elders of the people sought to kill Him. When the Feast of Tabernacles was at hand, His brethren, never missing an opportunity to show their contemptuous unbelief, said unto Him, "Depart hence, and go into Judea, that thy disciples also may see the works that thou doest. For there is no man that doeth anything in secret, and he himself seeketh to be known openly. *If* thou do these things, shew thyself to the world."

Notice the little word *if*. "If thou do these things, shew thyself to the world." To this our Lord responded, "My time is not yet come: but your time is alway ready. The world cannot hate you; but me it hateth, because I testify of it, that the works thereof are evil. Go ye up unto this feast: I go not up yet unto this feast; for my time is not yet full come."

However when His brethren had gone up, then He went up also unto the feast; not openly, but as it were, in secret. He was the talk of the town. The people sought Him and said one to the other, "Where is He?" There was also much murmuring among the people concerning Him, for some said, "He is a good man: others said, Nay; but he deceiveth the people. Howbeit no man spake openly of him for fear of the Jews."

The Unlearned But Lettered Man

Literally tens of thousands of books have been written on the Person of Jesus Christ. Some have been true to the Word as recorded in the Gospels. Others have sought to set Jesus right before the world. Recently, another such book has been added to the list. It has been suggested by one reviewer that the author has made it possible for countless thousands to read for the first time, a most human and most unmistakable answer to the great lie of the Christian era. Of course the author has attempted to strip our Lord Jesus Christ of His supernatural glory. Of all the trash that has ever come from the pen of a man, I think the following takes the prize: "Jesus was a social protest against the burdens of living in that day. . . But Jesus was not the Messiah, and so when a sign was demanded of Him, He failed to give it." I suppose it is not surprising therefore, to find that this same writer attempts to prove that "Judas simply could not accept anything but the Messiah in Jesus and for that reason he betrayed him, so that the promise of death and resurrection could be kept by a Jesus who seemed on the wrong Messianic path."

It is not any wonder that men of today are unable to understand our Lord Jesus; they were unable to "assimilate" Him when He was here. Wherever He went, He caused a division. He did on this occasion at Jerusalem, for some said, "He is a good man: others said, Nay; but he deceiveth the people."

In the very midst of the Feast, Jesus went up into the Temple and taught. The people marvelled saying, "How knoweth this man letters, having never learned?" Not only were the people wondering at the scholarly demonstration of the Lord's learning, but they were astounded at the lashing that He poured out on the rulers of the Temple, so that the people said, "Is not this he, whom they

THE GOSPEL OF JOHN — CHAPTER VII, VERSES 1-30   213

seek to kill? But, lo, he speaketh boldly, and they say nothing unto him. Do the rulers know indeed that this is the very Christ?"

Now let's try to picture this scene. Here are large groups milling around in every street in Jerusalem. Upon the roof tops can be found booths and tents under which the people slept at night to commemorate the wilderness journey of their forefathers. Here also is the magnificent Temple of Herod. When the sun shone on its golden roof, there was a halo of light that almost dazzled the eye. The crowd pressed in the Temple. Everybody was talking about one man, an unschooled carpenter's son; a laborer, if you please, who had suddenly emerged, making astounding claims. Is this the prophet, or is he a deceiver? Wherever people gathered they were discussing Him. Invariably the mere mention of His name brought a sword into the discussion groups. During the early days of the feast, they sought for Him in vain, as they asked each other, "Where is he?" Suddenly He appeared in the Temple and began to speak. Despite all the antagonism of the rulers against Him, He taught without interruption from any of them. Why did the people marvel at Him? "They marveled that Jesus showed himself familiar with the literary methods of his time which were supposed to be confined to the scholars of the popular teachers. He had not attended either of the two Rabbinical theological schools in Jerusalem, and while men sometimes called him rabbi, technically speaking he was only a carpenter." And yet without schooling, He surpassed the wisdom of the Pharisees and of the rabbis, for He spake, not as the scribes, but as one having authority.

But the people were more amazed when they observed His bold speech and the impotency of the rulers to lay hold upon Him. They naturally asked the question, "Do the rulers know indeed that this is the very Christ?" And they added, "Howbeit we know this man whence he is: but when Christ cometh, no man knoweth whence he is." This of course was the popular notion of the day. They knew all about Jesus. They knew He was raised in Nazareth, they knew many details about His youthful days. That in itself was contrary to their popular belief concerning the Messiah. Their masters had said, "There are three things which come along unexpectedly, Messiah, a God-send, and a scorpion." There were some who entertained the idea that the Messiah would suddenly fall down from the pinnacle of the Temple, a suggestion that incidentally was advanced to our Lord by Satan, for Satan undoubtedly had attended both theological seminaries of that day. But notice the answer of our Lord. "Then cried Jesus in the temple as he taught, saying, Ye both know me, and ye know whence I am: and I am not come of myself, but he that sent me is true, whom ye know not. But I know him: for I am from him, and he hath sent me." The message of our Lord so antagonized the leaders that the Scripture says, "they sought to take him: but no man laid hands on him, because his hour was not yet come."

We are living in a day when a man is highly regarded if he straddles the fence and is all things to all men everywhere. It is supposed to be a sign of a gentleman, a scholar and a broadminded individual if a member of the cloth preaches in a manner that will not stir up any antagonism in any individual. Let's talk platitudes. Let's preach the principles of Jesus. Let's say nice, lovely things. Do not antagonize, do not stir up the emotions of the people. Is it any wonder that the vast majority are lulled to sleep? But no man can preach Christ and Him crucified without antagonizing people. No man can present Christ to an audience, whether numbering two or a multitude, without having the same reaction as our Lord experienced in His day. If the reaction is otherwise, then we are not true in our presentation of Christ. Wherever He is presented, He causes a division among people. Some say, "He is a good man: others said Nay; but he deceiveth the people." In fact, that very word *division* is used in this 7th chapter of this Gospel: "So there was a division among the people because of him."

The Cause

We might profitably raise the question, "What was it in the teaching or ministry or Person of Jesus that caused such antagonism against Him?" I have referred already to a contemporary author who suggested that "Jesus was a social protest against the burdens of living in that day." But there is not a line in the New Testament to justify that conclusion. Remember, there is not a single person in this world who knows anything about Jesus of Nazareth of an authoritative source apart from what we find in the four Gospels. If any man suggests that he knows anything about the Person and ministry of Jesus of Nazareth that is contrary to or in addition to that which is written in these four Gospels, we can be assured that that man is a deceiver. There is nothing in profane literature or history of an authoritative character that has anything to say about Jesus of Nazareth. All we know about Him is from the testimony of the writers of the four Gospels. If we bear that clearly in mind, we will know what to do with any comment concerning Jesus which is not in accordance with these records.

By the way, let no one suppose that these records are untrustworthy. They have been subject to every conceivable literary test, so that no man who has any respect for his intellect will raise any question regarding their authenticity. One may disagree with them, one may be set against them, or he may refuse to accept them, but the fact remains, the four Gospel records are the most authenticated writings that we have in our possession. We know therefore with what we are faced when we raise the problem, "Why did the people rebel against Him? Why were they so intent in their hatred of Him? What was it that caused the antagonism against Him?" In the first place, note the incident that led to this exhibition. Listen to the words of our Lord Jesus found in the 21st verse of this chapter. "I have done one work, and ye all marvel." What was that one work which led to this expression of amazement, and which also was the very thing that caused their antagonism? Listen to verse 23. ". . . because I have made a man every whit whole on the Sabbath day." Of all the narrow-minded bigoted viewpoints, this is the climax, that a people should proceed to kill one who had made a man whole who had previously lived in a state of infirmity for thirty-eight years—all because He did it on the Sabbath day? I repeat, this was the incident. It was not the motivating factor. It was the excuse for exhibiting the antagonism against him.

Some who were present could not understand the impotency of the rulers who were in the Temple when He spoke those words and yet no man laid hands on him. The people said, We know this man. We know where he was born, where He comes from. But when they considered their viewpoint of the Messiah, they were bewildered. Their attitude caused our Lord to cry in the Temple. It was an emotional outbreak and carried with it a terrific charge. He said, "Ye both know me, and ye know whence I am: and I am not come of myself, but he that sent me is true, whom ye know not. But I know him: for I am from him, and he hath sent me." Our Lord in effect said, You say you know me? You know whence I am? Isn't it strange therefore that you do not know the One who sent me?

The act of healing the impotent man was the incident used to exhibit their antagonism. But that which filled the rulers with a vituperous spirit was our Lord's insistence that He was sent of His Father; that His doctrine was not His own and that He sought His Father's glory. Furthermore, He said of Himself that He was true and that there was no unrighteousness in Him. That meant our Lord declared His sinless perfection. He insisted that He came down from heaven to do His Father's will. That means one of two things. Either it was true, or it was blasphemous. The rulers concluded that it was blasphemy, but their conclusion was the result of their sin. Despite the biting sting of the words of our Lord which must have flamed the antagonism of the rulers, to such an extent that they sought to take Him, yet no man laid hands on Him. The Scripture says that their impotency to do so was because His hour was not yet come.

Now it is one matter to escape death because a time bomb did not go off until ten minutes after one left the platform, but that was not the situation in the case of the Lord Jesus. He never traveled in a bullet-proof car; He did not have gathered about Him a secret service bodyguard; He stood upright in the midst of His enemies and spoke the words that condemned them. It was the authority of His Person and the power of His words that made them impotent. They could never take Him until His hour was come, that hour for which He came into the world; that hour when He would lay down His life as a ransom for many. No man could take His life from Him, but He had power to lay it down and to take it again.

Any fair consideration of Jesus of Nazareth must lead the individual to a place where he will acknowledge His deity and fall down before Him and worship Him as Thomas of old did, and acknowledge Him, "my Lord and my God."

Walk Thirty-Four

NEVER MAN SPAKE LIKE THIS MAN

WE brought our initial consideration of this 7th chapter to a close by referring to the fact that though our Lord at this festive time spoke boldly in the temple ". . . no man laid hands on him, because his hour was not yet come."

The Feast of Tabernacles lasted eight days. Our Lord did not get to Jerusalem until the midst of the period but, before it was over, He caused everything but a riot. We are told many of the people believed on him. Some had only a vague conception of what it was all about, for they said, "When Christ cometh, will he do more miracles than these which this man hath done?"

No one in Jerusalem had any question regarding the reality of the miracles of Christ. They saw the evidence. The case at issue was so irrefutable, no one dared suggest that it was an illusion of the mind, a sort of "heathen science." That kind of an idea has been the brain-child of unbelievers in subsequent ages—not one of whom knew anything about the facts. No one in our Lord's day denied His miracles. But there were some, particularly among the Pharisees and rulers of the people, who refused to receive the *testimony* of the miracles. They claimed that they were accomplished by the power of Beelzebub, the prince of demons. Even these could not deny His miracles.

At any rate, the Pharisees were unable to stand the whispering of the people. So, together with the chief priests, they sent officers unto the Temple to take Him. The officers entered, saw the mob gathered there, listened to the words which our Lord spake. Ere long they stood spell-bound. In fact, they became absolutely impotent and failed to carry through the command that was given to them. When the officers returned to the chief priests and Pharisees without their prisoner they were asked "Why have ye not brought him?" The only answer the officers gave was, "Never man spake like this man."

The Ritualism

We learn from verses 43 and 44 that there was a division among the people because of our Lord. Some would have taken Him, but no man laid hands on Him. Let's see what it was that caused the trouble and which also brought about that confession from the lips of the officers. This thing took place at the close of the Feast. It was the last day, that great day of the Feast, when Jesus stood and cried, saying, "If any man thirst, let him come unto me, and drink. He that believeth on me, as the scripture hath said, out of his belly (innermost being) shall flow rivers of living water."

In order to appreciate that statement of our Lord, it is necessary to know something of the ritualism that was practiced during the Feast of Tabernacles. "For seven days the people dwelt in booths; on the eighth day, they celebrated their entrance into the Promised Land, forsaking their booths and went every man to his own house. On each of the first seven days a golden pitcher was in use and the procession that followed the priests who carried it from the pool of Siloam to the Temple praised God who had brought water out of the rock in the desert: but on the eighth day, the commemoration of their entrance into 'the land of springs of water', this rite of drawing the water ceased." It is singular that on *that* day our Lord should have stood up and cried, "If any man thirst, let him come unto me, and drink. He that believeth on me, as the scriptures hath said, out of his belly (innermost being) shall flow rivers of living water."

The ceremony of pouring out water seven days during the Feast was to symbolize the miraculous provision that God had made for the children of Israel during their wilderness journey, when they went through a desert. There was no water there. The people were faint and were about to perish. They cried out to Moses, who in turn interceded with God. The Lord instructed Moses to smite a rock and forthwith would come water. This Moses did and the water gushed forth. On a later occasion, the people again complained because of lack of water. Again Moses interceded for them. But on this occasion the Lord said unto Moses that he was only to speak to the rock and forthwith would come water. Moses, however, though he was the meekest man on the earth, lost his temper over a rebellious people, and instead of speaking to the rock, he smote it twice. The water gushed forth, but Moses paid an awful penalty for failing to sanctify the Lord in the eyes of the children of Israel. For that infraction both Moses and Aaron were forbidden to enter into the Promised Land. Moses merely saw it from the top of Mt. Nebo.

We learn from the New Testament that the rock was Christ. In smiting the rock a second time, Moses not only failed to sanctify

God before the people of Israel, indeed, he also spoiled the picture. The rock, Christ, was to be smitten once, not twice. He died once; He will never die again.

Our Lord said to the woman of Samaria, "If thou knewest the gift of God, and who it is that saith to thee, Give me to drink; thou wouldst have asked of him, and he would have given thee living water." But here our Lord said, "If any man thirst, let him come unto me, and drink. He that believeth on me, as the scripture hath said, out of his belly (innermost being) shall flow rivers of living water."

Notice the contrast between the 4th chapter of John and the 7th chapter. In the 4th our Lord said to the woman, that if she knew who He was and the gift of God, she would have asked of Him, and He would have given her living waters. Later He said that that water would be in her a well of water springing up unto everlasting life. But here, the Lord is talking about something that not only satisfies the individual, but which pours out of the individual in streams of blessing to others. To understand the significance of our Lord's statement, the Spirit of God added ("But this spake he of the Spirit, which they that believe on him should receive: for the Holy Ghost was not yet given; because that Jesus was not yet glorified.") Our Lord Jesus Christ came into the world, not only to put away sin by the sacrifice of Himself. The cross was not an end in itself. The cross was a means to an end. Salvation is a two-fold matter. We are saved from something to something. We are given a new life upon receiving Christ. But we may enjoy a more abundant life as we continuously drink from the fountain of life. Therefore, our Lord said on another occasion, "I am come that they might have life, and that they might have it more abundantly."

THE MATCHLESS SPEAKER

Even on the part of those who reject the testimony of Jesus there is almost unanimity in regard to two facts. First, that Jesus of Nazareth is the greatest character that ever lived. Second, that He has exercised the greatest influence over men. He was born in the poorest of circumstances; He was brought up in a town that had a reputation for filth. He came out of obscurity and only ministered within the confines of a very limited territory. He never wrote anything, He was not a man of many words. Yet, "never man spake like this man."

I have been carrying in my pocket for some time a choice little booklet that has been a great blessing to my heart. In fact, even the booklet itself, touching it, handling it, and contemplating it has brought a blessing. The booklet contains all the words of Jesus as recorded in the New Testament chronologically arranged with dates and places inserted. It is a pocket-size booklet of approximately 100 pages. It startles one to consider that this is all that we have of the recorded words of Jesus. Can anyone measure the influence and power of the words that He uttered? Step aside a moment; divorce yourself from your prejudices, and consider the power of His word; the influence of His life; the millions of people who have gladly given their lives for their faith in Christ. Is it possible that the One who uttered these words was a deceiver? He is either one or the other. He is either the Son of God as He claimed to be, or He is a deceiver. Of course, I believe Him to be the Son of God. Therefore, every movement that He made is filled with significance. For example, notice Him in the 13th chapter of Matthew's Gospel, which incidentally is one of the great chapters of the New Testament. We read, "The same day went Jesus out of the house, and sat by the sea side." As every Bible student knows, the sea is symbolic of the Gentiles. His movement indicated a change in His ministry. Great multitudes were gathered together unto Him and the Scriptures say that He went into a ship and sat down, and the whole multitude stood on the shore, and then He gave expression to those remarkable parables of the Kingdom of Heaven. But He sat down and the people stood. By their posture they unconsciously gave Him a tribute both as to His deity and to the fact that He was a teacher sent from God. In our churches, the minister stands, while the people sit down, but in the 13th of Matthew, the Bible tells us that Christ sat down and the people stood. But here in the 7th chapter of John our Lord rises. That in itself is significant. Dr. G. Campbell Morgan has referred to that posture as being that of a Herald, about to make a great proclamation.

Now notice what He said. Every word is significant. "If any man thirst. . . ." I love the all-inclusiveness of our Lord's words.

His ministry is not limited to a few, though the benefits of that ministry in this age has been limited to an increasing minority, but the invitation is as wide as the world, "If any man thirst." What is one to do. "Let him come unto me, and drink." It is not only necessary for a man to come to Jesus. He must go a step further. He must drink of the water of life which our Lord will give unto him.

On another occasion He said, "Come unto me, all ye that labour and are heavy laden, and I will give you rest." The natural attitude of a sinful man is to flee from a holy God. That is what Adam and Eve did; and every sinner since has done the same. But what a revelation our Lord Jesus Christ is of the heart of God. It seems as if He bares His breast and invites the sinner to come, not to flee from Him, but to come unto him and drink. Have you a thirst for God? Has this world lost its attraction for you? Have you drunk at its wells and found them unsatisfying? Our Lord said, "Come unto me, and drink." When you do, that means you will have life. Ponce de Leon sought for the Fountain of Youth, but with our Lord Jesus is the Fountain of Life.

Now notice this more abundant life: "He that believeth on me, as the scripture hath said, out of his belly (innermost being) shall flow rivers of living water." He, of course, was speaking of the Holy Spirit who comes in to dwell in the body of all who believe on the Lord Jesus Christ. He comes in, not only to live but to be a vital, throbbing force and power in our lives, so that we may live above ourselves, above the domination of our flesh and become a blessing to others with whom we may come in contact.

THE EFFECT OF HIS WORDS

In the remainder of the chapter we have the reaction on the part of the several groups of people to this ministry and message of Christ. In verse 40 we read, "Many of the people therefore, when they heard this saying, said, Of a truth this is the Prophet." The next verse tells of another group who said, "This is the Christ." But still another is heard to say, "Shall Christ come out of Galilee? Hath not the scripture said, That Christ cometh of the seed of David, and out of the town of Bethlehem, where David was?" These people evidently were ignorant of, or they entirely overlooked the fact, that our Lord was born in Bethlehem of Judea, though He was brought up in Galilee. Then we have the reaction of the officers of the chief priests and Pharisees to which we have already alluded several times.

Picture the scene if you will. Here is an august assembly of long-bearded and long-robed men, with long, solemn faces; men who love the uppermost seats in the synagogue and who delight to have the people honor them with titles. Into this assembled group of seventy men came the officers without *their* man. The chief priests and Pharisees said unto them, "Why have ye not brought him?" All that the officers could say was, "Never man spake like this man."

There was consternation in that assembled group. The Pharisees said to the officers, "Are ye also deceived? Have any of the rulers or the Pharisees believed on him? But this people (the people on the outside of whom they were supposed to be the leaders) who knoweth not the law are cursed." Suddenly one man rises to his feet, one of the few honorable men in that particular company. Nicodemus says, "Doth our law judge any man, before it hear him, and know what he doeth?" Nicodemus was a master in Israel; He objected to a mob scene. In effect he said, "We have a system of jurisprudence, the cornerstone of which requires that a man be not pre-judged. Our law requires that before a man be judged, he must be heard and we must know what he does.

They could not answer his logic, therefore they made a personal attack on him. "Art thou also of Galilee? Search, and look: for out of Galilee ariseth no prophet." Dr. Gaebelein has pointed out that these men quite forgot that Elijah, Elisha, Jonah and probably Nahum were Galilean prophets. That ended the day. Verse 53 tells us, "And every man went unto his own house."

Walk Thirty-Five

SNOOPING RELIGIONISTS

SINCE our Bible is broken up into chapters and verses, frequently we lose the continuity of thought which would be perfectly obvious if we read the record without a break. We have such a case in the opening of the 8th chapter. There actually is no break between the 7th and 8th chapters. At the close of the 7th chapter we read, "And every man went unto his own house." The meeting of the Sanhedrin broke up in utter confusion "and every man went unto his own house." The next thing we read is this: "Jesus went unto the mount of Olives." On another occasion our Lord said, "The foxes have holes, and the birds of the air have nests, but the Son of man hath not where to lay his head."

It seems that the mount of Olives was one of our Lord's favorite resorts. He spent many nights there. The chief priests and Pharisees composing the Sanhedrin went away with distorted minds and certainly with angry spirits. They probably were so angry that they did not speak to one another. Every man went to his own house! But Jesus went to the mount of Olives. It is singular that the Son of God should not have a "house" that He could call His own, and to which He could go.

And now we come to a scene that has been the subject of much controversy. It seems that there are a few ancient manuscripts in which the first 11 verses of this chapter are not found, while others have it as a part of Luke's Gospel. Yet most all are agreed that these verses belong somewhere in the divine record. I am absolutely ignorant about ancient manuscripts, but I do know that the spirit in my own heart is perfectly satisfied that these verses belong exactly where they are found. They would not fit anywhere else, but when read in connection with what precedes and what follows, there is perfect harmony, whereas if these verses were left out, there would be a decided break. Some have assumed that the record gives license to sin. But no man or woman who knows experimentally the saving grace of God, finds anything in the record that in the remotest degree lowers the bars of Christian conduct. In fact, they find it a source of great encouragement for it accurately illustrates the grace of God to guilty sinners. Now let's look at the record itself.

> "And every man went unto his own house.
> "Jesus went unto the mount of Olives.
> "And early in the morning he came again into the temple, and all the people came unto him; and he sat down, and taught them.
> "And the scribes and Pharisees brought unto him a woman taken in adultery; and when they had set her in the midst,
> "They say unto him, Master, this woman was taken in adultery, in the very act.
> "Now Moses in the law commanded us, that such should be stoned: but what sayest thou?
> "This they said, tempting him, that they might have to accuse him. But Jesus stooped down, and with his finger wrote on the ground, as though he heard them not.
> "So when they continued asking him, he lifted up himself, and said unto them, He that is without sin among you, let him first cast a stone at her.
> "And again he stooped down, and wrote on the ground.
> "And they which heard it, being convicted by their own conscience, went out one by one, beginning at the eldest, even unto the last: and Jesus was left alone, and the woman standing in the midst.
> "When Jesus had lifted up himself, and saw none but the woman, he said unto her, Woman, where are those thine accusers? hath no man condemned thee?
> "She said, No man, Lord. And Jesus said unto her, Neither do I condemn thee: go, and sin no more."

The day before was the great day of the Feast of Tabernacles. It ended with some people receiving Christ and some rejecting Him. The Pharisees and the rulers were in disagreement regarding Him, but the overwhelming majority of its members were intent on expressing their disgust with Him in some tangible way. It is evident that they did not hesitate to go to any extent to ruin or to hinder His ministry or to lay hands upon Him. We do know from the record that no man laid hands on Him for His hour was not yet come. But here they thought a perfect trap had been laid. It was early in the morning. The Scripture tells us that our Lord came again into the Temple and all the people came unto Him and He sat down and taught them. That, incidentally, is a beautiful touch also.

But immediately a discordant note enters into the record. We read that the Scribes and Pharisees brought unto Him a woman taken in adultery, and when they had set her in the midst, they said unto Him, "Master, this woman was taken in adultery, in the very act." That was not all that they said, but before we examine their further comments, let's look at the circumstances already related. We can be assured that there was not a spirit of sympathetic regret expressed on the faces of those Pharisees. To the contrary, they gave clear evidence that they were not nearly so much occupied with the sin that the woman had committed, as the fact that they had laid an inescapable trap to catch our Lord Jesus. In the first place, their own demeanor in connection with the woman calls for considerable denunciation and reveals the true state of their hearts and minds. They must have been out sleuthing during the night hours.

Snooping Religionists

There are some members of "the cloth" who believe that a part of their duty and ministry is to go "sleuthing" in order to crusade for righteousness in this world. I am thinking of a young man whom I knew some years ago. At the time, his name was in the metropolitan newspapers in glaring headlines. One day I accidentally met him. The first words out of his lips were these, "Have you been reading about my crusades to clean up ——— City?" In order to get evidence, he had gone into night clubs, unholy dens of iniquity and vice; and now from the public platform he was naming individuals and discussing specific sins. Undoubtedly he thought that I would have a word of commendation to give, for he looked shocked and chagrinned when I suggested that he had lowered the standard, that he had lost sight of the purpose of his ministry, and that he was on a rampage that would lead to disappointment. I suggested that he was not the first who had tried to clean up a city. Lot tried it in Sodom, but without success. It is not the business of the Christian minister to clean up any city, or to go sleuthing or slumming in order to get evidence of vice and wickedness. A member of the cloth should be a minister of the Gospel. What is the Gospel? It is good news. A man of God therefore, should be one who proclaims good news. He does not need to go into dens and caves and places where those who indulge in fleshly activities run wild. It would be highly desirable if he went in with the idea of snatching some from the burning as did the Apostle Paul when he went to Corinth. We can be assured that Paul went there with the Gospel. He told those people of a Savior who loved them, who died for their sins, who was willing to redeem them, to cleanse them and impart to them His own life. So much for the "snooping religionists."

"Moses in the Law"

The accusation they brought against this woman was evidently based on the testimony of eye witnesses; it was not hearsay. So these Pharisees, with that spirit of self-righteousness which so characterizes men of their type, said, "Now Moses in the law commanded *us,* that such should be stoned: but what sayest *thou?*" In the first place, Moses had never commanded them to spend their night hours seeking those who inhabit dens of vice. Secondly, they are condemned by their own words. Since Moses commanded that such should be stoned, *they* were disobedient to the law of Moses. *They* should have stoned the woman. Finally with biting suaveness, they added these words *". . . but what sayest thou?"*

It would be interesting to know why they only brought the woman with them. If, as they said, she was caught in the very act, why did they not also bring the man? It is evident that they were unconcerned about the sin of this man and this woman, or their duty as members of the priestly caste. They merely brought her in order that they might have an occasion to accuse Him. Incidentally their attitude gives some justification for the suggestion which has often been advanced that there is one law for men and another for women, but in the eyes of God, there is only one law for both and one Savior for both.

Here was a perfect trap. If He should absolve the woman, they could say He was not a friend of Moses. He could not therefore be the Messiah. He could not be the Christ if He disregarded the law and flagrantly threw it aside. And yet, if He should command that the woman be stoned, where was His mercy of which the prophets had also witnessed? But these poor people did not know Christ. Now notice the picture the Holy Spirit has painted for us. "Jesus stooped down." Up to that time He was seated in the posture of a teacher. The multiudes were standing about Him.

This group of would-be religious leaders pushed their way through the crowd like vultures with their victim and subjected her to the gaze of every eye. When our Lord heard their words, He simply stooped down and with His finger wrote on the ground "as though He heard them not."

The Christ — and the Sinner

I mentioned in our last study that every movement of our Lord was significant. This one was also. The "stooping down" seems to indicate in a graphic manner that the burden of sin would be carried by Him and that He would be bowed down under the load of it in order to pay sin's penalty. But He also wrote something in the dust of the ground with His finger. That act illustrates in an equally graphic manner, the words of the 22nd Psalm ". . . thou hast brought me into the dust of death." We can be sure there was a terrifying silence that early morning hour! Everyone was almost breathless. What would He say? What would He do? But He continued to write with His finger as though He heard them not. We do not know what He wrote. It is the only time we have any record that He wrote. I like the words of Dr. Robertson: "Certainly Jesus knew how to write—yet more books have been written about this One who wrote nothing that is preserved than any other person or subject in human history." We are sure that the wind soon erased the characters or words Jesus wrote in the sand.

Those Pharisees and scribes were not to be disposed of so readily, for they continued pressing Him. And now notice verse 7. ". . . he lifted up himself." On another occasion He said, "No man taketh it (my life) from me . . . I have power to lay it down, and I have power to take it again. This commandment have I received of my Father." As He stooped down, it symbolized that He was bearing our sins, yours and mine, and this woman's, and when He wrote in the dust of the earth, it was an indication that He would die. When He lifted up Himself it was a perfect portrayal that He would be resurrected from the dead. We can be sure He looked those men squarely in the eye, and without any vindictiveness in His voice, He said, "He that is without sin among you, let him first cast a stone at her."

"He that is without sin *among you* . . ." How penetrating! Our Lord thus did not abrogate the law of Moses. He gave those leaders authority to execute the judgment, but He added one stipulation, "He that is without sin among you, let *him first* cast a stone at her."

To give an opportunity for His words to sink in, Jesus again stooped down and wrote on the ground. And now notice an arresting detail. The Scripture says they were convicted by their own consciences and one by one they began to walk out, beginning at the eldest and even unto the last, every one of them, all the Scribes, all the Pharisees, and also all the people. Their own consciences convicted each. They saw their nakedness in the eyes of a Holy God. They were stripped in His Presence. His holy eyes had penetrated into their innermost being while His light gave them to see their own darkness so that their consciences began to prick and convict them, making them so uncomfortable that one by one they "slunk" out like beaten dogs. When the last one had gone, Jesus was left alone with the woman standing in the midst. When our Lord had lifted up Himself and saw none but the woman, He asked, "Woman, where are those thine accusers? hath no man condemned thee?" She answered, "No man," but she added the word *Lord*. Thus she confessed His lordship, silently acknowledged her sin before Him, made no defense of it, sought no evasion of it, but stood in His presence and simply said that no man had condemned her.

The Gospel

Then our Lord uttered the most remarkable words that ever fell upon the ear of a sinner; words that could not come from the lips of only a man. No man has the authority to speak the words that our Lord spoke. Only God can forgive sin! So He said to her, "Neither do I condemn thee: go, and sin no more." That is the setting! It is a beautiful gospel scene. It was a sordid scene in the beginning. If we had been present in that audience, every one of us would have gone out with the rest, our consciences pricking us and making us uncomfortable. But the record ends with a heavenly scene and a glorious sight: a redeemed woman in the presence of a Holy God who justified her because He would bear her sin and would go into the dust of death to atone for it.

But when He let that soul go, He did not allow her to go in her own strength. He would not command, "Go, and sin no more," without giving the woman the power to do that very thing. That's the Gospel. It is two-fold. The Gospel is by blood and by power. There is the blood of the Lord Jesus to cleanse from sin. There is the power of the Holy Spirit to cause one to live above sin. Our Lord Jesus Christ does not invite us to receive His death as the atonement for our sins and then leave us in our sins. The Gospel is not a message exclusively devoted to one's past life. God is not saying, "I will give you another chance; I will wipe out the record of your past life and you can start all over again." No, that's not a Gospel. Certainly God does not need to be convinced that man is absolutely impotent to do any right act. Man is a sinner, and everything He does is tainted with sin. What God offers to sinful men is this: complete atonement through the blood of His own Son from every sin that has ever been committed by man. But more than that. In the Person of His Son, He put sin to death, so He gives the pardoned sinner a new life in Christ. With that new life, comes the indwelling of the Holy Spirit to give power to that new life so that He can dominate and be supreme in the life. But more than that, through the intercessory work of our Lord at the right hand of God the Father, He also has made provision for any infraction by any believer through confession of his sins before the Lord.

Walk Thirty-Six

THE LIGHT OF THE WORLD

WE found a Passover setting in the 6th chapter, and a Feast of Tabernacles setting in the 7th chapter, while in the 8th chapter in which this study is centered, it appears that our Lord remained in Jerusalem after the last and great day of the Feast of Tabernacles. It is interesting to observe the manner in which our Lord made use of the ritualism associated with the feast in order to set forth the reality of which the ritualism was only a symbol. The human heart seems to have a craving for something tangible, something it can grasp hold of and embrace. Sometimes there is divine authority for the symbol when God intended through it to teach men a vital truth. But more frequently ritualism is a man-made substitute for reality.

During the Feast of Tabernacles, there were two rituals symbolizing the provision that God had made for Israel during the journey from Egypt to the Promised Land. In our previous study, we commented on one of these, that of pouring out water in the Temple which commemorated the fact that God provided the Israelites with water in the desert. But there was a second and most interesting ritual. During the evenings of the festive period, the two huge golden candelabras which hung in the women's court were lighted. Their light radiated for long distances, caused by the reflection from the golden roof of the Temple. This ritual symbolized another provision which God had made for the nation during the wilderness trek. Israel had a pillar of cloud to guide them during the day and a pillar of fire during the night. The candelabras to which we have referred were used only during the celebration of the Feast of Tabernacles.

We observed that our Lord remained in Jerusalem the day following the last day of the Feast. In the early morning the Pharisees had left our Lord alone when the penetrating power of His words convicted them of their sin. At night we see Him back in the Temple. Again the multitude have crowded around Him listening intently to His words. The Pharisees are also present. We learn from the 20th verse of this chapter that the words we are about to consider were spoken by Jesus in the Treasury, as He taught in the Temple. He therefore was in the very place in which the candelabras hung, but they were not used that night. He took advantage of the darkness and the ritual in order to reveal the truth of God when He said, "I am the light of the world: he that followeth me shall not walk in darkness, but shall have the light of life." What He meant was apparent to all. He said in effect, "The light that your fathers had in the wilderness came from me. I am that light."

I Am

It will help if we try to visualize the scene. Here was the group about Him. The Pharisees were still as much His enemies as ever. They wanted to lay hands on Him; yet they were impotent in His Presence. He was bewildering to them. They could not understand Him. They hated Him for He testified against them. It was to that crowd, while everybody was silent, straining to grasp every word, that He said, "I am the light of the world: he that followeth me shall not walk in darkness, but shall have the light of life."

The Gospel of John — Chapter VIII, Verses 12-28

It is essential to note not only what our Lord said, but also what He did not say. For example, He did not say that He came to bring light. He did not put Himself on a level with other teachers whose ministry and message enlighten the heart and mind. But what He did say was this, "I (personally) am the light of the world." In that same connection, it is well to bear in mind that our Lord did not say, I am the way to God. He did not say that He came to show the people a way to God, but He said, "I, (personally) am the way, the truth, and the life: no man cometh to the father but by me."

At the time He uttered the words, He was only a little more than thirty years of age. He had no cultural background (I use that expression advisedly), He was brought up in a despised village, His father (they said) was only a carpenter. No man ever taught Him letters. He never travelled more than one hundred miles from Nazareth at any time. Someone has made a search of the Gospel records and observed that He visited no more than eighteen villages and cities. Yet He said, "I am the light of the world."

Now then, we ought to examine that claim and ask some questions, especially in the light of the day in which we live. If ever there was a dark hour, it is this day. The world is in deep darkness. The wicked prosper; the smaller nations are ground under the power of larger and more wicked neighbors. Some people have been so bewildered by what has happened in Finland this past week that they are asking, "What has happened to God? Where is God? Is God concerned about what is happening in this world? What did our Lord mean when He said, 'I am the light of the world'? Certainly if He is the light of this world, His ministry is decidedly limited." Let's face the facts frankly, and when we do, we will receive a great blessing, to say nothing of some needed enlightenment.

If we are to get any illumination on the perplexing problems of this hour, we are limited as to whom we can go. There is no light in this world! There is no one in this world who possesses any light at all. There is no man who dares to venture a prediction of what will happen. Men are groping in darkness, deep darkness. In fact, they are groping in as deep a darkness as did the Pharisees on this occasion when though right in the presence of the One who at that very time said, "I am the light of the world"; were bewildered, were perplexed, were angry, were hateful, were rebellious and finally asked, "Who art thou?" At least it should be clear that our Lord never entertained the notion that because He was *the light* of the world that He *lights* the world.

Light and Darkness

We should also bear in mind the ritualism during this feast to which our Lord undoubtedly alluded. Let's go back and notice what happened when the Israelites were experiencing the reality of which this ritualism was but the symbol. God delivered the nation out of the Egyptian bondage by an outstretched arm. The people left Egypt and proceeded on their journey. As they went, they were led by the Lord. We read in Exodus 13:21, 22: "And the Lord went before them by day in a pillar of a cloud, to lead them the way; and by night in a pillar of fire, to give them light; to go by day and night: He took not away the pillar of the cloud by day, nor the pillar of fire by night, from before the people." Thus did the children of Israel have light in their camp. Notice that the Lord Himself was in the pillar of cloud and the pillar of fire.

Shortly after Israel left Egypt, Pharaoh rose up with an army of chosen men to pursue them. They came to the brink of the sea where the poor Israelites were shaken like reeds until they observed the provision of God. That night when under ordinary circumstances they would have been greatly disturbed, something happened. From Exodus 14:19, we learn, "And the angel of God, which went before the camp of Israel, removed and went behind them; and the pillar of the cloud went from before their face, and stood behind them: And it came between the camp of the Egyptians and the camp of Israel; and it was a cloud and darkness to them, but it gave light by night to the *children of Israel:* so that the one came not near the other all the night." The cloud which was a pillar of fire giving light to the camp of Israel, was a pillar of darkness to confuse the enemies of Israel.

Our Lord Jesus Christ is the light of this world, the only light in this world, but that light is limited. For He immediately added, "he that followeth me shall not walk in darkness, but shall have the light of life." It is only the man who follows the Lord, that basks in the sunshine of His light. To the man who does not, our Lord is still an enigma, even as He was to the Pharisees. And the world still gropes in darkness because they persist in their refusal to receive Him as the light of this world.

It is also interesting to observe that our Lord promised to the man who followed Him that he would have the light of life. On a previous occasion He referred to Himself as the *bread of life,* and at still another time, He spoke of Himself as the *water of life;* but here He speaks of Himself as *"the light of life."* We need all three elements. We need bread and water and light. Our Lord not only supplies all of these three elements, but is Himself these three elements.

I have already suggested that we attempt to picture this scene—the crowded court of the temple, the reflected light on the faces of some and the deep darkness on the faces of others. And there were the Pharisees. They missed no opportunity to attack Him. They said, "Thou bearest record of thyself; thy record is not true." What they did was to throw back into the face of our Lord His own words! For in the 5th chapter of this Gospel, He said, "If I bear witness of myself, my witness is not true." Now they thought they had Him, they had trapped Him in His own words! His record was not true on His own premise, for He was simply bearing record of Himself. Our Lord accepted the challenge and said, "Though I bear record of myself, yet my record is true: for I know whence I came, and whither I go; but ye cannot tell whence I come, and whither I go. Ye judge after the flesh; I judge no man. And yet if I judge, my judgment is true: for I am not alone, but I and the Father that sent me. It is also written in your law, that the testimony of two men is true. I am one that bear witness of myself, and the Father that sent me beareth witness of me."

It is noteworthy to observe the retort of the Pharisees. They did not say "Who is thy Father?" They asked, "Where is thy Father?" To this our Lord responded, "Ye neither know me, nor my Father: if ye had known me, ye should have known my father also."

And that touches the heart of the Christian message. It is impossible to know one member of the Godhead apart from the other. It is not possible to know God the Father apart from God the Son, nor God the Son apart from God the Father, nor to experience the joy or the communion of the Holy Spirit apart from the knowledge of God the Son and God the Father.

But our Lord continued. He said, "I go my way, and ye shall seek me, and shall die in your sins: whither I go, ye cannot come." Then they said to each other, "Will he kill himself? because he saith, Whither I go, ye cannot come." But our Lord answered them, "Ye are from beneath; I am from above: ye are of this world; I am not of this world." Notice the cleavage that our Lord made between Himself and all other men. He immediately added, "I said therefore unto you, that ye shall die in your sins: for if ye believe not that I am he, ye shall die in your sins."

"Ye Cannot Come—Ye Shall Die"

These comments of our Lord should be considered with care. He said, "Whither I go, ye cannot come." And secondly, unless ye believe that I am the light of the world, unless you believe that I am what I say I am, "ye shall die in your sins. Here is a negative and a positive statement. "Ye cannot come whither I go." And, "Ye shall die in your sins." It is the testimony of our Lord Jesus Christ, that no man can come unto the Father except by Him; which means that none of us will ever get to heaven apart from the Lord Jesus Christ. Secondly, He said unless a man believes in Christ, he will die in his sins. Therefore, a man cannot get rid of his sins apart from believing in the Lord Jesus Christ. In desperation, the Pharisees said to Him, "Who art thou?" Our Lord answered, "Even the same that I said unto you from the beginning." But He added, "When ye have lifted up the Son of man, then shall ye know that I am he . . ." In other words, the cross would demonstrate that He is the One that He claimed Himself to be, even the Eternal Son of the Father.

It is evident that our Lord knew that He would die. He also knew the manner of that death. He knew who would be responsible for it, and He also knew the powerful demonstration that that death and the manner of it would attest the veracity of His words and claims.

Neither the cross, nor His death on the cross, was an accident. It was in the determinate counsel and foreknowledge of God. It threw light on the Old Testament. It explained and made clear all the ritualism of the Law. It illuminated the 22nd Psalm, the 53rd chapter of Isaiah, and revealed the typology of all the sacrifices of the old covenant.

Our Lord Jesus Christ is the light of the world to the man or woman who will follow Him. He is the light of the world. There is no salvation in any other. The nations of the world have rejected Him and therefore walk in darkness, and do not the truth.

When He left this world, rejected of men, the Light of this world went out. The world has groped in darkness ever since. What we see today in Europe, Asia, and all other parts of the world is a result of man's rejection of Christ as the Light of this world.

This world will never receive Christ voluntarily but this world will be made subject to Christ. In the 2nd Psalm, we also learn that He "shall break them (the nations) with a rod of iron; and shall dash them in pieces like a potter's vessel."

God speed the day when the heavens will be rent, and the nations of the world made to bow in obedience before the Lord's Christ. But how much better for us individually to receive Christ now as our Savior than to have Him as our Judge in that day.

Walk Thirty-Seven
THE TRAGEDY OF MISTAKEN PARENTAGE

THERE are important questions that occupy the mind of man in this day. We have several pressing problems which confront us. A few personal, some regarding our own nation, and others confronting the world. These perplexities seem to defy solution, and yet, who will question the fact that the greatest problem centers around the question, "Who is Jesus of Nazareth?" The welfare of nations may be determined by the action that we take in respect to the problems confronting the nations; but as we well know, such results may last for only a short period; but a man's destiny for time and eternity is determined solely and forever by his attitude toward Jesus of Nazareth. Let's bear that in mind as we continue our Walks with our Lord through his wonderful Gospel according to St. John.

In this 8th chapter we found our Lord in Jerusalem, in the Temple, in fact, in the women's court, seated by the Treasury. He had just borne testimony to Himself. He said, "I am the light of the world: he that followeth me shall not walk in darkness, but shall have the light of life." A vast crowd was listening to Him, including the Pharisees, who asked Him, "Who art thou?" To that question He answered, "Even the same that I said unto you from the beginning." And then He revealed that when they had lifted up the Son of man, then they would know that He was Jehovah. From the 30th verse of this chapter we learn, "As he spake these words, many believed on him." To *those who believed* He said, "If *ye* continue in my word, then are *ye* my disciples indeed; And *ye* shall know the truth, and the truth shall make *you* free."

From the record, it is apparent that they who received His words appreciated the message. A spiritual man understands the words of our Lord. He knows that as one *grows* in grace and in the knowledge of the Lord Jesus, there is a greater appreciation of the Person of Christ and a commensurate increase in the liberty that one enjoys by virtue of this growth. It is only *the truth* that makes one free. Our Lord had said, "Ye shall know the truth, and the truth shall make you free." The Pharisees thought it was about time for them to break in, and so they said, "We be Abraham's seed, and were never in bondage to any man: how sayest thou, *Ye* shall be made free?" That they were never in bondage was a lie, amply refuted by their history beginning with the Egyptian bondage. Notice that they did not say, "How sayest thou that *we* shall be made free?" It appears they recognized that the message was not for them, but was intended for those who believed on His words.

Our Lord answered, "Verily, verily, I say unto you, Whosoever committeth sin is the servant of sin. And the servant abideth not in the house for ever: but the Son abideth ever. If the Son therefore shall make *you* free, *ye* shall be free indeed." He continued: "I know that ye are Abraham's seed; but ye seek to kill me, because my word hath no place in you. I speak that which I have seen with my Father: and ye do that which ye have seen with your father."

The Pharisees

Here is a powerful statement. We need to examine it carefully. The Pharisees had said that they were Abraham's seed and were never in bondage to any man. Now let's look at these Pharisees. Who were they? What position did they occupy? They were the best people of their day. They were the most cultured, the most educated, the most religious people. They were the elders who had spent their lifetime in a study of the traditions of their fathers. They sat in Moses' seat and urged the people to observe the law—but they themselves did not attempt to keep it. They made broad their phylacteries, and enlarged the borders of their garments. They claimed to be the upper strata of the nation. They were religious to the core. What a surprise to be told that they were "bond slaves to sin." A comment of Dr. Samuel Zwemer is particularly pertinent. He said, "The Pharisees were scrupulous but not conscientious. They would not have the trial and death of Jesus take place on the Sabbath lest they should be defiled, and yet they spat on His face on Friday."

"Whosoever committeth sin is the servant or slave of sin." The word that our Lord used translated *committeth* is in the active tense and means a continuous practice of sin. The man who continues in sin is a slave to sin. Can any of us deny that we have continuously sinned? "The slave," our Lord said, "abideth not in the house for ever: but the Son abideth ever."

Yes, said our Lord, "I know that ye are Abraham's *seed*"; but you forget, so was Ishmael, Hagar's son. Ishmael was called the son of the bond woman in contrast to Isaac, who was called the son of the free woman. The Lord specifically commanded Abraham that he was to cast out the bondwoman and the son of the bondwoman, for that son was not to be heir with the son of Promise. We shall seek to make clear that allegory in a moment; but let us continue to quote the Scripture:

> "I speak that which I have seen with my Father: and ye do that which ye have seen with your father.
> "They answered and said unto him, Abraham is our father. Jesus said unto them, If ye were Abraham's children, ye would do the works of Abraham.
> "But now ye seek to kill me, a man that hath told you the truth, which I have heard of God: this did not Abraham.
> "Ye do the deeds of your father. Then said they to him, We be not born of fornication; we have one Father, even God.
> "Jesus said unto them, If God were your Father, ye would love me: for I proceeded forth and came from God; neither came I of myself, but he sent me.
> "Why do ye not understand my speech? even because ye cannot hear my word.
> "Ye are of your father the devil, and the lusts of your father ye will do. He was a murderer from the beginning, and abode not in the truth, because there is no truth in him. When he speaketh a lie, he speaketh of his own: for he is a liar, and the father of it.
> "And because I tell you the truth, ye believe me not."

Our Lord never gave a stronger message nor used more cutting words than on this occasion. Here was this group of Pharisees. They were all well on in years. They boasted of the fact that they were Abraham's children. They were Abraham's *seed;* but they were not

Abraham's *children*. What a tragedy, to reach an age such as these men reached, only to be told that they were mistaken in their parentage.

This world has many heartaches and disappointments and into many lives there has come that which is tragic; but it is questionable whether anything is quite so tragic as the tragedy of mistaken parentage. Some will remember from their school days the story of Oedipus, who unwittingly killed his father and married his own mother. From that union he had four children. When the mother learned the secret, she committed suicide while Oedipus put out both his eyes. That was a tragedy. It is a shock to learn late in life that those whom you have been addressing as father and mother, are not in reality your father or your mother. Adopted children often experience it and sometimes it takes them a long period to become adjusted to their new knowledge. I've often thought of a person who came into my office some years ago. She was well along in life, at least fifty years of age. She had spent the last ten years in a fruitless search to determine who she was. It was a tragedy, but there is nothing in the world so tragic as to labor under the impression that you are a child of God when in reality you are a child of the devil. Orphans can adjust themselves to loving foster parents, though the shock of learning that these foster parents are really not their own parents, is terrific. But can we imagine the shock that one will receive as he departs this world assuming that he is a child of God, only to discover that he has been mistaken. Do you wonder why we said at the beginning of this message that the greatest question that can be put to a man is this, "What think ye of Christ?" If He is what He claims Himself to be, the Son of God and God the Son, then your destiny and mine is determined by our attitude toward Him and His message. No excuses to the contrary will be received. You will not find a haven by hiding behind your background, or your bringing up, or your religion. The stark reality of your rejection of Christ will then be tragically revealed.

Abraham's Seed—Abraham's Children

These men were Israelites. They traced their ancestry back to Abraham. There was nothing wrong with their family tree. They were of the seed of Abraham. They came out of the loins of Abraham, but as the Apostle Paul declared in the closing verses of the 2nd chapter of his letter to the Romans, "For he is not a Jew, which is one outwardly. . . But he is a Jew, which is one inwardly . . . whose praise is not of men, but of God." Ishmael, the son of Hagar, could insist that he was of the *seed* of Abraham, but even those Pharisees would not admit an Ishmaelite into the congregation. And the Edomites could maintain that they were of the seed of Isaac, and therefore of the seed of Abraham; for their father Isaac came out of the loins of Abraham. But would any Israelite suggest that the Edomites are the children of Abraham? Thus it is not a question of a man's bringing up, nor a man's birth, nor a man's ancestry. It is a question of a man's relationship to God.

Now notice further. Our Lord had said that if they were of the children of Abraham, they would do certain things. First: His word would find a place in their hearts; second: they would do the works of Abraham; and third: they would love our Lord. Who was this one Who made such statements? In this apology He called God His Father; declared that He was the Son of the Father; said He proceeded forth and came from God the Father; and declared that every word that He spoke was the truth. Was a greater apology ever made?

We have referred to happenings in Abraham's household as an allegory. From the New Testament we learn that God used the domestic affairs of that household to illustrate an important spiritual truth. Hagar was Sarah's handmaiden. God had promised Sarah and Abraham that they would have a son who would be called the son of promise. God delayed, or at least they thought so, and to help Him out, Sarah suggested that there were other means at Abraham's disposal. Abraham obeyed Sarah. Ishmael was born, but he was not the promised son. At the set time, God visited Sarah and she gave birth to a son and called his name Isaac. The Jewish nation has come out of the loins of Isaac. The descendants of Isaac and the descendants of Ishmael have been enemies all through the years, even to this very day.

From the 4th chapter of Galatians we learn that the story of two women and their sons is an allegory, that is, an illustration of a spiritual fact. The one, the bond woman and her son, answers to Mt. Sinai and to Jerusalem that is in bondage with her children. The other, Sarah and her son, answers to the Jerusalem which is above, which is free, and represents the children of faith. The fact that your mother or father are or were Christians is no assurance that you will get by on their faith. Salvation is not one of the gifts of heritage. Salvation is a personal, individual matter. You as a man or a woman will come face to face with Jesus Christ as either your Savior or your Judge.

There are some people who assume from the statement our Lord made to the Pharisees, "Ye are of your father the devil, and the lusts of your father ye will do," that He therefore insisted that a man was either a child of God, or a child of Satan, whereas in fact, He said nothing of the kind. He said so, to those self-righteous Pharisees who had rejected His word, refused to believe Him, sold themselves to sin and to Satan, and who became His bitterest enemies. Men become the children of the devil exactly as they become the children of God. We become a child of God by faith in the Lord Jesus and by believing *His* word. Men become the children of Satan by *refusing* to receive Christ and His word and thus believe Satan's lie. Let's not forget that Satan has a counterfeit Jesus; Satan has a gospel; and Satan has a spirit that energizes his gospel. Satan is the most religious character in this world. His ministers are ministers of righteousness, and the shocking part of it is that they are to be found in the places where God's people meet. They *were* found in the temple on this occasion. They were the very leaders of the people, whereas in fact, they were the emissaries of Satan.

The Three Families

There are three families of people in the world. There are those who are the children of God by faith in the Lord Jesus Christ. There are those who are the children of Satan by virtue of their refusal to receive God's Christ and by believing Satan's lie. And there is a vast company of people whom the Apostle Paul called "the children of disobedience" who are by nature "children of wrath." Now let me become personal to illustrate the point I am making. I received Jesus Christ as my Savior when I was a young man in my teens. I believed His Word and received Him. On the authority of His Word I became a child of God. Prior to that time I was not a child of Satan. The devil was not my father. I had never received his message nor believed his lie. I had never rejected the claims of Christ nor His Word. I had neglected them

—that's quite another matter. But sin made me a *child of disobedience* and the Scripture says, "The soul that sinneth it shall die." The wrath of God was upon my soul because I had sinned against God. That is the condition of the vast majority of people. They have sinned. They are children of disobedience. But let us not forget that the Apostle Paul stated, "But if our gospel be hid, it is hid to them that are lost: In whom the god of this world hath blinded the minds of them which *believe not,* lest the light of the glorious gospel of Christ, who is the image of God, should shine unto them." If a man has the claims of Christ and the Word of Christ presented to him and then refuses to believe, and rejects the Word, it is then that Satan blinds him to the glories of Christ and His Gospel.

It's tragic to consider that these men who had gotten along in years, who had spent their lives in religious devotion, had to be told late in life, "Ye are of your father the devil, and the lusts of your father ye will do. He was a murderer from the beginning, and abode not in the truth, because there is no truth in him. When he speaketh a lie, he speaketh of his own: for he is a liar, and the father of it." What a tragedy! May you never experience it.

Walk Thirty-Eight

THE UNANSWERABLE CHALLENGE

EXCEPT for the chapters devoted to the crucifixion scene, there is none in all of the four Gospels which more graphically presents a turbulent scene or a series of contrasts between the participants than the 8th chapter of St. John's Gospel.

When one carefully examines this chapter he can readily picture the expressions upon the faces of the people, on the brow of our Lord, on His antagonists and those whom He befriended. The chapter opens with the introduction of a *sinful woman,* but it closes with an unanswerable challenge that fell from the lips of a *sinless Man.* In between, we have a multitude of people, some perplexed at our Lord's words, while others understand Him. We find the leaders opposed to Him and openly flaunting their venomous hatred of Him. And yet, in every encounter with Him, these critics felt the cutting lash of a two-edged sword.

They assumed that Abraham was their father. Christ said the devil was their father. He said the devil was both a murderer and a liar. Those two words fully describe Satan's character. He said when the devil speaketh a lie, he speaketh of his own, for He is a liar and the father of it. Satan is not only the father of the lie, but the father of the liar. His lie of course is related to the spiritual realm and concerns the *Person* of our Lord Jesus Christ.

Now notice our Lord's denunciation of the Pharisees. We should remind ourselves once again that the Pharisees were the best people in their day. They occupied the chief places in the synagogues. They dressed in long robes. They were the religious leaders. They thought themselves the cream of society. They were given titles and greetings in the market places and wherever they went. Yet our Lord scourges that group in the presence of the people.

The Rejection of His Person

The words of our Lord are incomparable. The rarest, the most beautiful, the most comforting words fell from His lips. He reserved His verbal thrashings to one class of people only—the religious racketeers of His day. That's noteworthy. We seem to think that racketeering is a modern persuasion, limited only to social, business and political fields. But alas, the most sinister racketeers have always functioned in religious circles. They flourished in the days of our Lord's humiliation. It was to this group our Lord addressed the words, "because I tell you the truth, ye believe me not." Thus we have revealed the motivating force behind the rejection of Christ by the religious leaders of His day.

In another passage of Scripture, we learn that men love darkness rather than light because their deeds are evil. These people refused and rejected Christ because He told them the truth. There is nothing that will produce venomous hatred in the hearts of individuals as that which is revealed when one rejects the truth. There are even some men in the ministry today, leaders of religion, who almost froth at the mouth when someone witnesses to them concerning the Person and work of our Lord Jesus Christ on the cross. They hate the Gospel and the Person of Jesus Christ. The Pharisees were their forerunners. Oh yes, they had all the dress and the paraphernalia that went with religious observances; they could put on the finest sanctimonious faces on high religious feast days; but the Person of Jesus Christ as He is presented in the Scriptures was anathema to them.

Our Lord not only informed those people that they "believed not" because He told them the truth, but He hurled a challenge in the presence of them all "Which of you convinceth me of sin?" I have no doubt as He threw it out that He waited a moment or two until it sank deeply into their consciences before He proceeded with His further word: "And if I say the truth, why do ye not believe me? He that is of God heareth God's words: ye therefore hear them not, because ye are not of God."

One can clearly detect from the written record the trenchant sarcasm that was expressed in the tone of their voices as those Pharisees curled their lips and said, ". . . Say we not well that thou art a Samaritan, and hast a devil?" Observe that they did not accept the challenge of Christ. Neither has any other man since the day it was given. But those unbelieving religious leaders cast inuendoes at Him regarding His Person. Every other Christ-rejector has followed in their steps. I have never met a man with any respect for his intelligence who rejects the Lord Jesus Christ, who has ever raised one word of criticism regarding the *character* and behavior of Jesus of Nazareth; but they have attacked His Person and rejected the claims that the Bible makes for Him and those that He Himself made.

Our Lord did not say that they would not reject His claims. He well knew that they would refuse Him as He knows there are those in this day who refuse Him. But He challenged that crowd of antagonists as He has challenged every other antagonist since, with this unanswerable challenge: "Which of you convinceth me of sin? And if I say the truth, why do ye not believe me?" Let me try to make this as clear as I know how. I repeat, no man has ever accepted this challenge of Christ. Modernists, Liberalists, Communists, Socialists, Fascists, and every other type one can possibly imagine, all acknowledge that no finger of accusation can be lodged against the Lord Jesus Christ for anything He ever did or said during His entire life. The record of His life has been subjected to the closest scrutiny. The motives that actuated Him, His denunciations of existing hypocrisy, whether in high or low places, is acknowledged by friend and foe to be the most perfect and without flaw. He is the *only* sinless Man that has ever walked this earth. Those Pharisees would have taken up

His challenge in a split second if they had found a flaw in His character or in His walk or in any work that He did. There was no such flaw. His candor and consistency even His enemies could not gainsay.

Remember, those to whom He extended this challenge were the very people He had whipped. I have referred to them as religious racketeers. They had even gone so far as to besmirch the priesthood, by offering priestly rights to the highest bidders. They were not priests of God, they were political priests. Do you think those men would have hesitated to accept His challenge if there was anything in our Lord's life inconsistent with His position? Never!

The Consistent Christ

Our Lord was a friend of publicans and sinners. He was constantly in their presence, ministering to them. If you please, He was and has always been the poor man's friend. He spoke words of comfort to all except hypocrites and destructive liberalists who undermined the faith of the people in the integrity and inspiration of the Scriptures. He became poor, that we through His poverty might become rich. He never used or abused the poor to enrich His position or purse. He lived as a simple laboring man. He was born in a stable. He was called "the carpenter's son." He had no degrees nor an education worthy of the name. The people said "He had not learned." His hands ministered to His needs. He had no place He could call His own, or lay His head. Frequently He spent whole nights in the mountains. He always ministered unto others. Of course those Pharisees would not have hesitated to accept His challenge if they could have found one thing inconsistent in His life.

The candid, consistent, plain life of our Lord impressed me afresh as a result of something I recently witnessed. I had an appointment to meet someone outside of one of the finest of New York City hotels. As I stood there, a taxicab drew up; the door opened, out came a man with a small traveling bag. I immediately recognized his face and black bushy hair. It was not a case of mistaken identity for the doorman greeted this man by name, and I judged from his familiar greeting that he frequently or always stays at that hotel when in New York. I since verified that. I recalled, I had read in a recent magazine article that this labor leader receives a salary of $25,000 a year. Not a bad stipend for one who pretends to be a friend of the laboring man! And of course, I recalled the dilapidated "shacks" that I had seen as I had driven my car in the vicinity of the country where the members of his particular union live. The contrast was startling to say the least. If our Lord's life and conduct were as inconsistent as this man's, don't you think the Pharisees would have justly attacked Him as an exploiter and racketeer of the poor especially considering the fact that it was exactly the charge He had made against them? No, our Lord never stopped at the finest hotels of His day. His life was consistent throughout. His life was stainless and sinless. He alone could stand before a crowd of biting antagonists and challenge them "Which of you convinceth me of sin?"

The early morning of that same day, these men had brought before Him a woman, who, they said, was taken in adultery. They hypocritically wanted Him to decide what was to be done about her. But he clearly and calmly with all the dignity of the Godhead, suggested that "He that is without sin among you, let him first cast a stone at her."

It is a great joy to present One in whom no man can find a flaw. He is the answer to every man's sin. He is the answer to the problems of this world, He is the answer to every "ism" of this age, to all the new-fangled ideas that men have thought up. He is the only One who speaks *the* truth. He had just said that God was His Father, that He came from God and that He was sent by God. He said that those Pharisees had the devil as their father. Our Lord said, "If I say the truth, why do you not believe me?"

They could not attack His character, so they attacked His Person. To arrive at the conclusion that Jesus Christ was a sinless man does not require any revelation from God. It is a fact of history, absolutely indisputable and unchallenged. But to recognize in Jesus of Nazareth the Christ of God, the Son of God, the Lamb of God, the light of the world, the bread of God, the way to God, the truth and the life, does not come by the exercise of the human intellect, but by the revelation of God. Therefore, our Lord said, "He that is of God heareth God's words."

The Inconsistency of Unbelief

The Pharisees answered, "Say we not well that thou art a Samaritan, and hast a devil?" Frankly, one could hardly come to any other conclusion if he rejects the claims of our Lord Jesus Christ. Our Lord is either what He claimed to be and what the Word of God declares Him to be, or He was a diabolically insane man. For one to claim logic in a reasoning which concludes that Jesus Christ was a sinless, perfect Man and that His principles and teaching are superior to anything that has ever been expressed by any man, and yet conclude that He was either insane or demon possessed, requires some explanation. How could He be such a deceiver or be so deceived and yet possess a character that no other person ever possessed or manifested in this world? If some think this is an extreme picture, I confess that it is a clear presentation of the matter, but it is exactly word for word as we find it in this 8th chapter of St. John's Gospel.

How could a sinless, perfect character say that He had seen God; that He possessed equal powers with God; that unless one believed on Him, he would die in his sins; that there is no possible access to God apart from Him; that He is the light of the world; that He is the resurrection and the life; that he that believeth on Him should never die, if His claims were baseless? If they were, He would cease to be a sinless man. Men do not gather good fruit from a corrupt tree. These statements are utterly incomprehensible apart from the revelation of the Scripture that Jesus of Nazareth is God manifest in the flesh, the Son of God, the Christ of God, the anointed of God.

To the charge that our Lord was a Samaritan and possessed of a demon, our Lord answered, "I have not a demon; but I honour my Father, and ye do dishonour me. And I seek not mine own glory: there is one that seeketh and judgeth." To this He added, "Verily, verily, I say unto you, If a man keep my saying, he shall never see death."

It is not my intention at this time to consider that startling statement of our Lord, "If a man keep my saying, he shall never see death." We intend starting with that promise in our next study. We close this meditation with the rejection by Christ of the suggestion that He was a demon possessed man, and that most unusual assurance, "I seek not mine own glory." I say unusual because no man has ever been able to make that statement honestly. It was quite evident that those to whom He addressed His message sought their own glory. Should one desire an evidence of that, it is found in the 14th chapter of St. Luke's Gospel in which we have the record of our Lord's presence in the house of one of the chief Pharisees where He was being entertained on a Sabbath Day. There were many doctors of the law and Pharisees present at that feast. As our Lord looked on, He observed how they chose out the chief rooms and the chief places at the table. They were most ambitious for their own glory. Do we know of a single leader in public life in the world today who is not seeking his own glory? But our Lord said, "I seek not mine own glory" and that He honored His Father. If there is one characteristic about the ministry and Person of Christ, it is the fact that all through His life He honored His Father. How wonderful that it is a sinless One Who is the sinners' Friend and Savior!

WALK THIRTY-NINE

THE INCOMPARABLE I AM

THE suggestion has frequently been advanced that the Apostles, particularly Paul, succeeded in clothing the historic Jesus with a web of religious doctrine, and that it was they who built up the system of dogma, called Christianity. Therefore, those who reject the supernatural in Christ have proposed that the Church go back to Jesus. The proposal sounds logical and ideal, for in the final analysis, our Lord Jesus Christ is the fountain head of truth. Is it not better to go back to Him rather than to one of the Apostles?

If we grant the premise that it was the Apostles through their writings who built up the system of dogma called Christianity, let's see if getting back to Jesus in any way reveals that His zealous disciples wrapped about Him the grave clothes of deification in order to hide the stark fact of their disillusionment of Messianic hopes. Who is this Jesus of Nazareth? Well, let's see what He has to say about Himself. Let's go back to Jesus.

Remember the setting of this 8th chapter of John. It was at the Feast of Tabernacles. It was the day following the great day of the Feast. The crowds were still at Jerusalem. It may be suggested that our Lord was matching wits with His chiefest antagonists, the Pharisees. I prefer to think that He entered into a combat, He using the sword of the Spirit, which is the Word of God, and they, their own manufactured bitter darts of hatred.

He had just said that the devil was their father, and had challenged them to find anything in Him that remotely resembled sin. They answered by attacking His person. They suggested that He was a Samaritan and possessed by a demon. This He answered effectively. We have considered the initial section of His answer. We shall now examine the final phase of it, beginning at verse 51.

> "Verily, verily, I say unto you, If a man keep my saying, he shall never see death.
> "Then said the Jews unto him, Now we know that thou hast a devil. Abraham is dead, and the prophets; and thou sayest, If a man keep my saying, he shall never taste of death.
> "Art thou greater than our father Abraham, which is dead? and the prophets are dead: whom makest thou thyself?
> "Jesus answered, If I honour myself, my honour is nothing: it is my Father that honoureth me; of whom ye say, that he is your God:
> "Yet ye have not known him; but I know him: and if I should say, I know him not, I shall be a liar like unto you: but I know him, and keep his saying.
> "Your father Abraham rejoiced to see my day: and he saw it, and was glad.
> "Then said the Jews unto him, Thou art not yet fifty years old, and hast thou seen Abraham?
> "Jesus said unto them, Verily, verily, I say unto you, Before Abraham was, I am.
> "Then took they up stones to cast at him: but Jesus hid himself, and went out of the temple, going through the midst of them, and so passed by."

Scholars are agreed that a more accurate translation of the statement in verse 51 would be: "If a man keep my *word* he shall never see death." On the face of the record, it is evident that our Lord Jesus Christ could not have meant physical death, for every one of the Apostles and every believer in Christ subsequent to that day (except those who live in this generation) have died. But not one of them saw or tasted death! What did our Lord mean by that statement? Just this: death is the wages of sin. Death is eternal separation from God. Death is the judgment due every sinner. Death is the bitter cup which every one who is not "in Christ" must drink. No believer in Christ has ever seen it or tasted it, for Christ bore the judgment of their sin in His own body on the tree. When a believer dies physically, it merely means the transfer of dwelling from earth to heaven. Immediately he goes home to be with the Lord, to rejoice in His presence.

The Pharisees assumed that our Lord meant physical death. Therefore, they said unto Him, "Now we *know* that thou hast a devil (demon). Abraham is dead, and the prophets; and thou sayest, If a man keep my saying, he shall never taste of death. Art thou greater than our father Abraham, which is dead? and the prophets are dead: Whom makest thou thyself?"

Yes, Let's Go Back To Jesus

That put the question bluntly. That was going directly to the fountain source of all life and truth. That was going right back to Jesus! The Pharisees thought He was dangerously close to committing blasphemy; and indeed in the manner in which they couched their question, they were laying the basis for the charge of blasphemy against Him. Let's see what He had to say about Himself in answering their question. He repeated that He had honored His Father; that He had not sought His own glory, and that His Father was honoring Him. He went a step further and declared that those Pharisees had not known God, but that He knew Him, and that if He should make the negative statement that He did not know God, He would be a liar like unto them. These were sharp words. They cut into the heart of the Pharisees. Now notice something most interesting. The Pharisees asked, "Art thou greater than *our* father Abraham, which is dead?" Listen to the answer of our Lord. *"Your* father Abraham rejoiced to see *my* day: and he saw it, and was glad."

A hurried reading of that passage is apt to rob one of a blessing which he is justly entitled to receive from it. Our Lord did not say, *"Our* father Abraham rejoiced to see my day," but, *"Your* father Abraham rejoiced to see my day." Jesus did not put Himself on the level with those Pharisees nor with any other man; nor did He put Himself in a position whereby He acknowledged that He came from Abraham. Another fact needs also to be noted. While those Pharisees had Abraham as their father, they were not Abraham's children. They did not partake of the blessings of Abraham nor the joy of Abraham. Our Lord said, "Abraham rejoiced to see my day," but more than that, he saw it, and as a result he was glad.

Our Lord was the first to use the phrase "My day!" What thoughts excite the mind as one meditates upon that phrase, especially when one places alongside of it the further word of our Lord on the night of His betrayal when He addressed the chief priests and the captains of the temple and the elders who were come out to Him with the soldiers, "This is *your hour,* and the power of darkness." A volume could be written on those two illuminating phrases of Christ, *"My day"* and *"your hour."* The fact of the matter is, *every* prophet saw this day of Jesus Christ.

"Hast Thou Seen Abraham?"

Our Lord claimed that Abraham (who lived more than two thousand years prior to the day when our Lord spoke these words) looked forward to what was transpiring in the very day that those Pharisees lived. Abraham, He said, came to see that day, by faith. He rejoiced in it and was glad. But here are the Pharisees. They too see His day. They see Him however, in His humiliation, personally, visibly before their naked eyes. But they are not *rejoicing* in His day, they are thoroughly angry in His day! How effectively that answers the suggestion that faith is born by sight. Men claim that if they could only see, they would believe. Well, the Pharisees saw, yet did not believe! They were blinded by anger and by sin. Abraham, because he looked by faith, saw an event which was not to take place until more than two thousand years after he had died. The Christian now, and may I get personal and say that I, living nearly two thousand years after our Lord made this statement, look back by faith and have seen the day of Christ. I too rejoice in it and am glad. I am glad because in the death He died nearly two thousand years ago, He atoned for the very sins that I have committed twenty centuries subsequent to His death even as He atoned for Abraham's sins committed twenty centuries prior to His death. If Jesus is only a man, then I am guilty of idolatry, for I worship Him—I adore Him as my Lord and my God.

The Pharisees again attacked Him and said, "Thou art not yet fifty years old, and hast thou seen Abraham?" Of course our Lord's statement appeared preposterous. Incidentally, at this time, our Lord was only about thirty-two years of age. Now it may be that He did not look a day older than thirty-two, but it seems that there is an inference here that He looked older than His years, which would not be surprising when one bears in mind the fact that He was "a man of sorrows, and acquainted with grief." But isn't it the wild imaginations of a distorted mind for one to claim that Abraham had seen Him whereas in fact, when the statement was made, He was not fifty years old and Abraham had died two thousand years previously? Let's go back to Jesus! Is He making extraordinary claims for Himself? Did He weave the robe of glory about Himself? Did He lay claim to the supernatural? Notice His response as He begins it with the double emphatic "Verily, verily, I say unto you, before Abraham was, I Am."

I shall take liberty with this answer of our Lord Jesus, and yet remain in keeping with it. What Jesus said and what was implied by His remark, which the Pharisees understood properly was this, "Before Abraham *was born,* I am."

There is a sense in which each of us may refer to our own personality through the use of the expression "I am." For example, *I am* a man. *I am* a personality. *I am* myself. Concededly, we know very little about personality, about life, what it is, how it springs forth. Even as well known a scientist as Dr. Alexis Carrell concedes that we know so little that we do not even know how a thought is born! How then can we set ourselves up as authorities on the question of what is life? But our Lord was not using the "I Am" expression in the sense that you or I use it in speaking of our personalities.

We hear much about the *I am,* these days. Men have always loved to start new cults. So they have referred to this *little I am* in exalted terms, preaching that there is power in the recognition of personality, and that there is such a thing as imbibing the power of the personalities of the "exalted masters of the past." Yes, there is power, tremendous power in personality, both in the individual himself and from his forebears, if you please; power to sin, power to ruin life, power to throw a whole world into commotion, power to destroy, power to build. Power! What a wonderful word! The power of personality is a captivating subject, but if one follows it through logically, he will be driven into the presence of Christ crying out unto Him for salvation. The prophet put this power of the "I am" personality in these words: "The heart is deceitful above all things, and desperately (incurably) wicked: who can know it?" It is incomprehensible—it is a cesspool of iniquity—it is constantly outpouring in geyser-like eruptions its innate nature which defies human reason. Read the stories that have come out of Poland for evidence of the devastating power of the sinful human heart. You and I are sinners. Our Lord was not talking about the power of that personality, and those Pharisees knew He was not. He said, "Before Abraham was even born or saw the light of day, I am."

The Incomparable I Am

So long as our Lord Jesus Christ only made claims to Messianic ideals, the Pharisees did not throw stones at Him. But the moment in their judgment, He blasphemed by ascribing and taking unto Himself the prerogatives of Deity, they took up stones to cast at Him, which was in order if He were only a man.

Let's go back to Jesus. What does He claim for Himself? He claims that He was the one that spoke to Moses out of the burning bush; that He was the one who conversed with Abraham and called him out of his father's country to go out to a land that He would afterward show him. When our Lord Jesus Christ therefore said, "Before Abraham was, I am," He most emphatically took unto Himself not only the title of Deity, but all the claims and the prerogatives and the glory that goes with that Jehovistic name. He is the *incomparable I Am*.

Already in this Gospel we have heard our Lord Jesus Christ make the claim, "I am the bread of life," followed by that equally important assertion, "I am the light of the world." We shall observe Him using the title "I Am" more frequently in the remaining record of this Gospel, but these do not compare in glory with His simple statement, "Before Abraham was, *I am*." Note He did not say, "Before Abraham was, *I was*." That would of course indicate prior existence to Abraham, but it would not make Him more than a man, though undoubtedly a most extraordinary man. He said, "Before Abraham was born, *I am*." That declares His pre-existent glory; that declares His equality with God; that reveals that He is God manifest in flesh.

"Jesus Hid Himself"

Now we shall note the reaction of the Pharisees to this statement. They took up stones to cast at Him, but when they looked around, their target had disappeared. The Scriptures state, "Jesus hid himself, and went out of the temple, going through the midst of them, and so passed by."

There are several occasions in the Gospels where we learn that Jesus hid Himself. How thought-provoking that statement is. In the first place, it is another of those interesting evidences of His Deity. No man could lay hands on Him until His hour was come. No stone could ever strike Him until He came to that place where He was ready to lay down His life.

Again, how equally thought provoking that the Son of the eternal God should hide Himself from man, especially when we consider that the first earthly scene we find in the Bible describes a man's attempt to hide from God. Man then hid himself from a seeking Savior-God. We of course know that it was impossible for man to hide himself successfully from God. Neither can we. It has been the pastime of men from the early dawn of history to hide themselves from God, but such attempts will never be successful. But on the other side, let's consider the glorious fact that a man can have his life *hid with Christ* in God. That's quite another matter. That's a safe, comforting place. That's a place of indescribable peace and quiet. That's a place of joy. That's the place to which the Psalmist yearned when he cried out for God to hide him in the secret of His pavilion. Who will question the fact that it is infinitely better to have his life hid with Christ in God than to attempt to hide oneself from God?

But again, we should consider the fact that Jesus hid Himself from men and went out of the temple, going through the midst of them and so passed by. We raise the question, "Is it possible for that to be repeated?" We do know that He hid Himself from men during His earth ministry and as a result, they groped in the darkness, not knowing whither they went. "Is it possible that today God hides Himself from some men?" We will not attempt to answer the question but we will say this, that if one is unable to recognize upon the face of Jesus Christ the abiding glory of God, it is due to one or two things. Either refusal to believe has enabled Satan, the God of this age, to blind the heart and mind, or it is because our Lord has hid Himself from such a one. We ask, Is God just in hiding Himself from men? Yes, but we should be reminded that He hid himself from those who persistently and consistently rejected His claims. *Only* from such men did He hide Himself. Those were the men who said He was a Samaritan and **possessed of a demon.**

Walk Forty

THE SEEING EYE—THE BLIND MAN'S FRIEND

WHILE sitting at luncheon with three friends, one gentleman asked if I had read Sholem Asch's book, "The Nazarene," which opened the way for some interesting conversation. This same gentleman, a keen lawyer, past sixty years of age, addressed a remark to another gentleman at the table whom we both respect but who has not yet *bowed* the knee to Jesus Christ. He said, "The longer I live, the more amazed I am at that life which was lived within limited confines, by this Jesus, a young man who came from a small village and humble surroundings. What an influence He has exercised in this world for two thousand years since He lived that short life!"

I am aware that our Lord never accepted a compliment. Our Lord demands worship, not admiration. We shall be assured of that as we enter into a study of this 9th chapter of St. John's Gospel. But we introduce our comments on this chapter with the above incident because of the amount of space in the divine record devoted to the healing of one man, born blind. I do not have the figures available, but I remember hearing an address some years ago by that eminent physician, Dr. Howard A. Kelly of Baltimore, Md., wherein he quoted the results of his own investigation into the facts regarding the space devoted in the four Gospels to the birth, life, and oral ministry of Christ, compared with the space given in those Gospels to the events which happened during the last week of His life. The figures were startling. The overwhelming proportion of the four Gospels is occupied with what took place during that final week which led up to His crucifixion, followed by His resurrection. That clearly indicates that it is the death of Christ which is supreme and not His life. It is noteworthy therefore that within the small space devoted to His life, a full chapter should be given to our Lord's dealings with one man. We shall soon discover why so much prominence is given to it. Before going further let's read the record.

The Gospel of John — Chapter IX, Verses 1-7

> "And as Jesus passed by, he saw a man which was blind from his birth.
> "And his disciples asked him, saying, Master, who did sin, this man, or his parents, that he was born blind?
> "Jesus answered, Neither hath this man sinned, nor his parents: but that the works of God should be manifest in him.
> "I must work the works of him that sent me, while it is day: the night cometh, when no man can work.
> "As long as I am in the world, I am the light of the world.
> "When he had thus spoken, he spat on the ground, and made clay of the spittle, and he anointed the eyes of the blind man with the clay,
> "And said unto him, Go, wash in the pool of Siloam, (which is by interpretation, Sent.) He went his way therefore, and washed, and came seeing."

He Saw a Man

We have observed previously that while chapters and verses are a great help for reference purposes, nevertheless, they sometimes spoil the sense and continuity of the Scriptures. Let's forget that there is such a thing in our Bibles as the phrase "chapter 9" in this part of the record of John's Gospel. If we do, we will read in the last verse of the preceding chapter, "Then took they up stones to cast at him: but Jesus hid himself, and went out of the temple, going through the midst of them, and so passed by. And as Jesus passed by, he saw a man. . . ." Let's stop there. While our Lord hid Himself from, and passed by His enemies, in doing so, He was not unmindful of the dire need of a single individual. "And as he passed by, he saw a man. . ." The statement is qualified— "he saw a man which was blind from his birth." This blind man could not see Him. This blind man needed someone to guide him, to lead him, to be his "seeing eye."

There was something unusual in the glance of our Lord that the disciples took cognizance of it and immediately used the occasion to present a perplexing problem, saying, "Master, who did sin, this man, or his parents, that he was born blind?" It is interesting to observe that our Lord saw a *man* in need, saw a *man* blind from his birth, saw an opportunity for work, while the disciples saw an occasion for a discussion, saw a problem, saw a perplexity.

Evidently this man was well known for both the disciples and our Lord knew that he was blind from his birth. It may seem a little surprising to us that the disciples should raise the question, "who did sin, this man, or his parents, that he was born blind?" How could the man have sinned himself since he was born blind? But if we understood and were acquainted with rabbinical teachings and with the philosophy of the day in which our Lord lived, we would not be surprised. Men may philosophize on the number of angels that might dance on the point of a needle, and they may spend much time in discussing who is responsible for a man's blindness, but our Lord saw the man and his need and proceeded immediately to meet the man in his need. That's the difference between our Lord Jesus and all the religiously minded leaders of this world.

It is a question whether the man was acquainted with the conversation that took place between the Lord and His disciples. Nevertheless, our Lord's answer to the disciples' question throws a flood of light on the man's dilemma. We are justified in arriving at certain deductions from it. The man had not the slightest knowledge up to this occasion why he should have been singled out to suffer the loss of sight. But our Lord said "Neither hath this man sinned, nor his parents: *but that the works of God should be made manifest in him.*" I do not believe that our Lord's answer conveys the impression that this blind man or his parents had never sinned; but that there was no specific sin in this young man's life nor in the lives of his parents that caused or was responsible for his blindness. That effectively answers the suggestion that has sometimes been made that all sicknesses and disabilities are the results of sin in individuals' lives. That answer enables us to understand some of the perplexities and inequalities of life. This man was *permitted* to be born blind and, if you please, he had been blind for a long time; for his parents said later, "he is of age; ask him: he shall speak for himself." Our Lord said his blindness was sanctioned in order that the works of God should be made manifest in him. Christian, do not jump at the conclusion that since the Lord has permitted sorrow, disappointment or the loss of limb or sight, that it is your sin which is responsible. Who knows, but it might be that the works of God should be made manifest in you? This man did not know. Neither do you. But, because our Lord told us this in respect to the blind man, we have a right to trust God; we have an obligation not to question His love. The highest honor any of us can pay to God is to be faithful unto Him in the face of trials and disappointments.

I have just finished reading a new book which has brought more pleasure to my heart and incidentally, more tears to my eyes, than any book I have read in many a year. It was written by my beloved friend, *"Mel" Trotter, and is entitled, "These Forty Years." It is a small volume devoted to the record of forty years of his ministry as Superintendent of the City Rescue Mission of Grand Rapids, Mich. Dr. Trotter has done a remarkable piece of work. As I read the book, and was reminded afresh of some of the disappointing experiences that entered into that man's life, one in particular, when even a minister suggested to him that the way out was to commit suicide—it prepared me for an understanding of the 9th chapter in St. John's Gospel. True, at times, it is our own sin that gets us into trouble, but frequently in the life of a Christian, it is the work of the enemy. Quite often it is to give you and me the privilege of being faithful to God in the face of obstacles so that we may trust God and rejoice in Him and believe Him.

Talking vs. Working

We shall not get very far in this initial study but there are still a few things that should be considered which appear right on the surface. Notice that our Lord continued and said, addressing His disciples, "We must work the works of him that sent me, while it is day: the night cometh, when no man can work." Our Lord had said that the man was born blind in order that *the works of God* might be made manifest in him, then He proceeded to tell His disciples *"We* must work *the works of him* that sent me . . ." Our King James Version carries the pronoun in the first person *"I* must work the works," but literally our Lord said to His disciples, *"We* must work the works of him that sent me . . ." The Revised Version carries it accurately.

That's startling, for we shall observe as we read further that the disciples did not do *one single thing,* but *talk.* The *work* was done by our Lord! What a lesson that teaches us. It is surprising that even those who have the high privilege of ministering the Word of God or occupying a position of service in the Church of Jesus Christ develop an exaggerated ego and become so occupied with

---

* Since gone home to be with the Lord.

the position and the work that they think it is their work and their position.

We should never get into a position where we think it is *our* work. It is *God's work*. He will give us the privilege of being co-laborers with Him. But it is not He *with us,* but we *with Him*. Effective work is not done by us, as it was not done by the disciples on this occasion. The effective work was done by the Lord.

No doubt our Lord has a keen sense of humor. He must frequently laugh at the distorted sense of our own importance. He remembers of course that we are but dust, and excuses us as we excuse a child who does not know any better. Recently, my little youngster who is not yet four, was at the office. Whenever she comes, if there is one thing she delights to do, it is to typewrite! One of the young ladies allowed her to use her machine and as was to be expected, instead of touching one key at a time, she pushed down half a dozen keys and of course jammed the entire works, as you stenographers well know. It was necessary for the young lady to pull down the keys so that the typewriter could work, and as she did, she soiled her fingers. She turned to my little girl and said, "See Clare, I have dirtied my fingers pulling down those keys." Clare immediately looked at her own fingers which were clean, and gloatingly answered, "I typewrite right— my fingers are clean." How much like children we are! How wonderful that our Lord understands and is willing that we should still work *with* Him.

Now another thing. Notice that our Lord *said,* "As long as I am in the world, I am the light of the world." When He went out, the light of this world went out. It has been dark ever since and the only light that this world has is that which is reflected by individual Christians who shine as lights in this world. They can be likened to the stars which shine in the night.

Now notice what our Lord *did*. "When he had thus spoken, he spat on the ground, and made clay of the spittle, and he anointed the eyes of the blind man with the clay." The record does not tell us that He even gave the disciples the privilege of stooping down and picking up the dirt. *He* did it Himself. *He* spat on the ground. *He* made clay of the spittle, *He* anointed the eyes of the blind man with clay. No wonder David the Psalmist and the Prophet Jonah said "Salvation is of the Lord!"

There probably was no particular virtue in the clay that was placed upon the blind man's eyes. Our Lord could have opened that fellow's eyes with the spoken word. He did not need the clay. The incident teaches us, however, that our Lord is not adverse to using means to bring about the restoration or healing of an individual.

Our Lord said only one thing to the man: "Go, wash in the pool of Siloam." The pool was near the temple. We are told that the young man went his way and washed and came seeing.

That young man would never have received his sight if he had not done what the Lord commanded him to do. It does not make any difference what the command is. In this case, it was, "Go, wash in the pool of Siloam." If he went to the Jordan, and washed, I do not think he would have come seeing. In fact, I know he would not. If he went home and took some water from a basin it would not have done one bit of good. He could have had the clay on his eyes for the rest of his days and it would not have done him any good. He had to *go*. Not only did he have to go, but he had to *wash,* and he had to wash in a specific *pool* of water.

Spiritual Eyes

The application of this incident to the spiritual realm is clear. Every man is born blind, spiritually. None of us have any sight from birth. We were born in sin and conceived in iniquity. We need to have our eyes opened. We need to be born again. There is only one person in the world who can give us spiritual sight and He is the Lord Jesus Christ. There is only one way that we can get it and that is by being obedient to His word. But has He given us a word? Yes, He has. He has given it so clearly that there is no more possibility of misunderstanding it than there was of this young man misunderstanding His command.

The words of the Lord are simple. The people asked Him on one occasion, "What shall we do, that we might work the works of God?" He answered, "This is the work of God, that ye believe on him whom he hath sent." On another occasion He said, "If ye believe not that I am he, ye shall die in your sins."

There is only one place in all the world where one can go and wash and come seeing, and that is at the foot of Calvary, where the precious blood of Jesus Christ cleanses us from all sin. Obedience, that is all which is required. We cannot go our own way, we cannot choose our own means. It will not do one bit of good to follow the suggestion of another, irrespective of who that other might be. Our soul is too valuable a thing for us to place any confidence for its salvation in any other than in Jesus Christ our Lord.

Walk Forty-One
"THE NEIGHBOURS THEREFORE"

AS I opened my Bible in preparation for this message, knowing that we had already considered the first 7 verses of the 9th chapter of St. John's Gospel where we have the record of the healing of the young man who was born blind, I was struck with the opening words of the 8th verse, "The neighbours therefore . . ." What an arresting phrase! One can almost hear their chatter and sense the stir that was aroused as a result of what took place in the life of that young man. That is as it should be. Something is wrong if a man or a woman young or old, can have an experience with God and the neighbors not know about it or talk about it. Conversion should produce such a radical change in the life of an individual that it should be utterly impossible for its influence to be unrecognized by our neighbors. I am not referring to that mistaken notion entertained by some people, that they have to impress their experience upon others by always talking favorably about themselves, and sometimes in an obnoxious manner. This young man never said a word! He did not have to say a word. It was apparent to all what had happened in his life. This does not mean that a Christian is to be a mute individual; but nothing speaks so eloquently and so affects the influence that we exercise over our neighbors, as a life revolutionized by the incoming of the Holy Spirit at conversion.

Up to this moment the young man did not have a spiritual experience with Christ. He merely had the benefit of a miracle upon his natural eyes which gave him sight. But the miracle was for a sign, since our Lord had said that the man was born blind in order "that the works of God should be made manifest in him."

But note: not only do we find the neighbors impressed with what they had seen, but we read in verse 8 about some other people who were merely onlookers who said, "Is not this he that sat and begged?" Thus the influence not only extended to the man's neighbors, but also to others who had merely seen him and knew that he sat and begged. He became the talk of the town. All of us do not have such a startling conversion that we became the talk of the town, but we ought to exercise an influence. One thing is absolutely certain—both our neighbors and our acquaintances watch every step that we take seeking to observe what changes have taken place in our lives as a result of our communion with Christ.

Not only did this miracle provide conversation on the part of the young man's neighbors and acquaintances, but it also produced a controversy among the religious leaders which finally led up to his excommunication from the Synagogue. And mind you, all because the young man had testified to what had actually taken place in his life. Our attention is arrested at this startling contradiction, that a man born blind, who had sat and begged, and now by a miraculous act of God was able to see, should have disturbed those who professed to be religious leaders to an extent where they literally frothed at the mouth. Oh what sins have been committed in the name of religion! I have little interest in religion or religious profession or religious observances. My interest lies in the fact that sinful men can be redeemed from sin through the precious blood of Christ and then be introduced into fellowship with God so that they not only possess eternal life, but know God.

A Man That is Called Jesus

The neighbors and acquaintances gossiped among themselves and as they saw the young man, some said, "this is he," others said, "he is like him." The young fellow knew who he was, and so he said, "I am he." They asked him, "How were thine eyes opened?" As a good witness, he told exactly what had happened. I particularly like that phrase, of his answer—"A man that is called Jesus." He began with that Man and then told what the Man did. He made clay. He anointed his eyes. Then he told what this Man said, "Go to the pool of Siloam, and wash." Finally he added, "I went and washed, and I received my sight."

"A man that is called Jesus." If you desire a stirring Bible study, underscore every occasion in this 9th chapter where Jesus is called a *man*. All that the young fellow knew about him was the fact that he was a *man* called Jesus. The people asked, "Where is he?" The young man answered "I do not know." When he was hailed before the Pharisees to suffer the tortures of an inquisition by a commission, the Pharisees said, "This *man* is not of God." But there were a few even in that company who were honest, so they raised the question, "How can a *man* that is a sinner do such miracles?" The one who was formerly blind listening to this discussion was asked, "What sayest thou of him, that he hath opened thine eyes?" He answered, "He is a prophet." But later on the Pharisees said, "This *man* is a sinner." And by the time they finished, they would not even call him a man, for they said, "As for this *fellow*, we know not from whence he is."

The controversy which developed was not over the fact that the young man was given his sight, but that it was accomplished by "a *man* that is called Jesus." It was Jesus who was the subject of controversy and it was the religious leaders who reviled against Him. They even adjured the blind man to "give God the praise: *we know* that *this man* is a sinner."

It is advisable to remind ourselves once again why this Gospel was written. "These are written, that ye might believe that Jesus is the Christ, the Son of God; and that believing ye might have life through his name." This book therefore, is occupied with two things; first, presenting evidence that Jesus is the Christ, the Son of God; and second, interweaving into the evidence, that all one has to do, is to believe on and in Jesus to enjoy eternal life. Isn't it interesting in a book devoted to the claims of His oneness and Sonship with God, that such stress should be laid in this 9th chapter on His manhood. But He is the *Man* Christ Jesus. Son of God to be true, but Son of man also. He is the God-man. By becoming Man and clothing Himself with garments of flesh, He was able to come down to us so that we might get an exhibit of the very heart of God.

One of the more fascinating studies to which a mind can be devoted is a study of the four Gospels to observe the manifestation, the unfolding, the revelation which Jesus Christ of Nazareth gave us concerning God the Father. For instance, in the 15th chapter of St. Luke's Gospel, particularly the 32nd verse, the father of the prodigal son is seen coming out to entreat the elder son who stubbornly refused to enter into the house and enjoy the merriment of the home. The father said to this recalcitrant son, "Son, thou art ever with me, and all that I have is thine. It was meet that we should *make merry,* and *be glad:* for this thy brother was dead, and is alive again; and was lost, and is found." Has it ever occurred to you that no person in all the world ever presented God the Father as one full of merriment and gladness? Jesus did. He was the only one who did, for He was the only one who knew Him. We are so accustomed to thinking of God as an austere Person. We think we must come into His presence with fear and trembling. We must bow down before Him. We are fearful to look up into His face. We are awe-stricken in His presence. We think He is busily running the universe. That He does; but our Lord also pictured Him as enjoying music and making merry over the return of a prodigal son.

And in this 9th chapter of St. John, our Lord presented the Father as being so vitally interested in a single human being that He sent His Son to heal that one of physical blindness in order that He might be led into the joys of spiritual sight. What a father is God the Father! He is only the Father of those who have bowed the knee to Jesus Christ and have received Him as their personal Savior.

The Trial

We shall not devote much time to the details of the *trial* before the Pharisees except to remind ourselves that the one great objection to Christ exhibited by these Pharisees was our Lord's utter disregard of their Sabbath day—blue laws! They interrogated the young man but could not move him because he testified to the truth. Then they called upon his parents to witness that he was their son. Finally they recalled the young fellow and pronounced their decision, urging him to give God the praise for they knew that this man Jesus was a sinner. The young man said, "Whether he be a sinner or no, I know not: one thing I know, that, whereas I was blind, now I see." Thus, the young fellow knew practically nothing about Christ except that He had given him sight. He could not be moved from that; he had experienced it. And he was also correct when he said, "Since the world began was it not heard that any man opened the eyes of one that was born blind." It was the first time that it had ever been done. It should have caused those Pharisees to bow before the One who had performed the miracle.

The young man said to them, "If this man were not of God, he could do nothing."

This young man's testimony concerning Christ is the limit to which the natural mind can go in comprehending Christ. Nicodemus concluded the same thing for he said, "We know that thou art a teacher come from God: for no man can do these miracles that thou doest, except God be with him." Nicodemus said to Christ, "God is *with* you." The blind man said concerning Christ, "This man is *of* God." Neither one of them could say "This man *is* God." That kind of a confession comes only as a result of a revelation from God.

When the young man closed his testimony before the tribunal, the religious leaders were so full of hatred, not having been able to successfully break his testimony that they answered, "Thou wast altogether born in sins, and dost thou teach us? And they cast him out." In other words, they excommunicated him. And his only offense was that he had testified to what he had seen and what he knew!

It might be interesting to observe that at this particular time the Sanhedrin had three different kinds of excommunication from temple worship. We learned from this chapter that the parents of the blind man feared the Sanhedrin, for they had agreed already that if any should confess that Jesus was the Christ, he should be put out of the synagogue. For a minor offense, a person was excommunicated for thirty days, during which the excommunicant might not come within four cubits of anyone. For a worse offense, a man was excommunicated from all intercourse and worship for an indefinite period. The final curse involved absolute exclusion forever and was an irrevocable sentence. The type of excommunication this fellow received we cannot definitely state. Certainly he did not confess that Jesus was the Christ. He said he did not know, though he did conclude that the man must be of God, for it had never been heard that any man had opened the eyes of one that was born blind.

The Miracle

Let's look at the subject of miracles for a moment before we bring this "walk" to a close. These religious leaders sought to break down the evidence that supported the miracle. They refused to believe the testimony of the young man. Therefore, they brought in his parents to find if he really was their son and that he was born blind. But when they asked "how then doth he now see?" the parents demurred; they could not answer. The Pharisees still refused to believe the miracle. Their passion had caused them to conclude that it was impossible for God to be with a man, to energize him or be in him who would break the Sabbath day.

We have the same type of persons today. They too are religious people, and some are religious leaders, exactly as those Pharisees. They occupy chief places. They present themselves as authorities in the field of religion. They would feel affronted if someone suggested that they were not religious, but they do not believe in the miraculous. They boast in their liberalism. They conclude, as Godet observed, "the supernatural cannot exist," therefore the miracles attributed to Jesus and others are fictions. And as that same writer pointed out, "the logic of reason had to yield to the logic of facts." It is a striking testimony to the sinful nature of a man, irrespective of what kind of a man he might be, that he refuses to accept facts because of his personal rebellion against the miraculous. Those Pharisees went so far in their deluded blindness as to place themselves on a pedestal when they said to this young fellow, "Thou wast altogether born in sins, and dost thou teach us?"

But even their excommunication of the young man could not break down the facts. He had been healed. His sight had been restored "by a man that is called Jesus."

It was blind obedience on the part of the blind man that caused him to receive his sight. That principle has always been the Divine method of Salvation. It is not that God desires that we throw our reason to the wind. Did He not say through the prophet Isaiah, "Come now, and let us *reason* together . . . though your sins be as scarlet, they shall be as white as snow . . ."? But God has a right to ask men to believe His Word. No man who has believed ever found occasion to regret his decision. Did the blind man rue the fact that he obeyed the Lord? Indeed not!

Walk Forty-Two

THE FIRST EX-COMMUNICANT

IT is undoubtedly true, as we have had occasion to mention several times before, that one of the greatest aids ever devised for reading and studying the Bible was the division into chapters and verses. Yet one must confess that frequently, at least the chapter divisions have a tendency to break the continuity of the record and to obscure the plain meaning of the Scriptures. We again have such a case in the closing verses of this 9th chapter and the opening verses of the 10th chapter of St. John's Gospel.

Personally, I am often amazed at my own ignorance and failure to observe the continuity to which I have already alluded. Take for instance this particular case. I have read John's Gospel more than a hundred times, yet only now did I discover that it was the excommunication from the synagogue of the young man who was born blind and healed by our Lord, that led up to our Lord's discourse on Himself as the Good Shepherd. The fact of the matter is, it was called to my attention by some reading I did of a work by a man, who in the early days of his ministry, was one of the greatest powers for good in evangelical Christian circles in this country. That gentleman referred to this man, born blind as "the first member of a new society," in fact, "the first Christian." He was the first man of whom we have any record who was excommunicated from the synagogue because of his testimony to our Lord Jesus. Therefore, the closing verses of this 9th chapter are filled with intensely interesting details.

The definite testimony of the young man which was impossible to break down or answer, so disturbed at least the majority of the ruling Pharisees that they excommunicated the young fellow. They cast him out. They said to him, "Thou wast altogether born in sins, and dost thou teach us?" as if they were exempt from sin or were born in righteousness, whereas, according to the Scripture, everyone of us was conceived in sin and shapen in iniquity.

Now notice what happened to the young man after they cast him out. We will begin at verse 35 of the 9th chapter and read to the end.

> "Jesus heard that they had cast him out; and when he had found him, he said unto him, Dost thou believe on the Son of God?
> "He answered and said, Who is he, Lord, that I might believe on him?
> "And Jesus said unto him, Thou hast both seen him, and it is he that talketh with thee.
> "And he said, Lord, I believe. And he worshipped him.

> "And Jesus said, For judgment I am come into this world, that they which see not might see; and that they which see might be made blind.
>
> "And some of the Pharisees which were with him heard these words, and said unto him, Are we blind also?
>
> "Jesus said unto them, If ye were blind, ye should have no sin: but now ye say, We see; therefore your sin remaineth."

The record does not tell us that the young man sought our Lord. We know he did not seek Him for healing. He could not even see the Lord Jesus in his blindness. It was our Lord who sought him and had compassion on him and gave him the word which led to his sight. And when the young fellow was cast out, it was the Lord who sought him and found him. How true that God is always seeking the sinner to bring him into relationship with Himself. When our Lord found him, He said, "Dost thou believe on the Son of God?" The young man answered, "Who is he, Lord, that I might believe on him?" To this our Lord responded, "Thou hast both seen him, and it is he that talketh with thee."

The Simplicity of Christian Worship

There are some shallow thinking people who make the statement that our Lord never claimed to be the Son of God. There is absolutely no basis in fact for such a statement. Our Lord asked, "Dost thou believe on the Son of God?" A few manuscripts read "son of man" but the context is clear that our Lord referred to His Deity. When the young man asked, "Who is he, Lord, that I might believe on him?" our Lord answered, "Thou hast both seen him, and it is he that talketh with thee." The young man said, "Lord, I believe." As an evidence of it, he worshipped Jesus.

If we are to consider this young man as "the first member of a new society" or "the first Christian," it is arresting to observe what took place in his life. Let me not be misunderstood. I believe that the church *began* at Pentecost when all believers in our Lord Jesus were baptized into one body; the body of Christ, the church of the living God. The church is a company of people who have been *called out* of this world. But here was a fellow who was *cast out*. Other men have had similar experiences. But it is interesting that when the young fellow was cast out, our Lord sought and found him. Observe that our Lord drew him unto Himself, and the young man worshipped Him.

How significant! If you please, our Lord is the central gathering point of Christian fellowship, Christian service, and Christian worship. We are not drawn out of something to *something*. We may be drawn out of something, but we are drawn unto and become linked up to a *Person*. It is the Person of our Lord Jesus Christ. Therefore, He said on another occasion, "Where two or three are gathered together in my name, there am *I* in the midst." Strictly speaking, that is what constitutes a local church. It is to be regretted that Christendom has built up a complex system of religious observances so that the simplicity of Christian worship has been almost if not entirely lost sight of in a great many cases. But here it is in all of its beauty and simplicity. It is a drawing *unto* the Person of Christ and it involves the worship of Christ.

Our Lord never sought admirers. He never looked for compliments. Like His Father, He sought worshippers, men who would bow the knee to Him and worship, adore, and yield themselves to Him. "Lord, I believe." That was all. And the young man worshipped the blessed Lord!

If our Lord Jesus Christ were not the Son of God; if He were not God manifest in the flesh, then He was guilty of taking unto Himself a divine prerogative, which is a blasphemous thing. He did not rebuke this man for worshipping Him. He did not say, "Stand up, I am only a man, worship God." He did not do what angels have done on numerous occasions when men have bowed down before them. Our Lord accepted the worship. He accepted it because He was and is God!

It is interesting that when our Lord sought this young fellow and found him and the young man received Him and worshipped Him, that there were some of the Pharisees around. They invariably are. Our Lord addressed the young man and said, "For judgment I am come into this world, that they which see not might see; and that they which see might be made blind." You ask, Is that the Gospel? Yes, it is part of it. Our Lord came into this world to save sinners; but He also came into the world for judgment. He said on another occasion that He came to bring a sword, to set fathers against sons, and children against parents. The very presence of the Person of Christ causes a division. One is either for Him or against Him. He came into the world in order that those who did not see spiritual things, but who wanted to see, might see. But to those who professed that they could see, but in reality were blind, His coming added to their blindness. Thus the Christ of God does two things. He enlightens the minds of those who receive Him and He adds to the blindness of those who reject Him. God is glorified in both cases.

BLINDNESS VS. SEEING

The religious leaders *thought* they saw but in reality they were blind. So some of the Pharisees who were present asked, "Are we blind also?" Jesus answered, "If ye were blind, ye should have no sin: but now ye say, We see; therefore your sin remaineth." Let me give this reply in the words which Godet, the theologian, gave. "It were better that you were blind and knew it—If you felt your ignorance, I could heal you, but you boast presumptuously of your knowledge: for this reason your malady is incurable." It is the man who thinks he sees, who has an incurable malady. How thought provoking, that those Pharisees could look into the face of our Lord Jesus, who was the very effulgence of God, the very visibility of God, and yet they were unable to see Him. They were unable to recognize His glory. If they had, they would have immediately done what the blind man did, they would have fallen down at His feet and worshipped Him!

This matter of *seeing* God is a tremendous fact. In the New Testament letter to the Hebrews in the 11th chapter, we have a summary of the life of Moses. We are told, "By faith Moses, when he was born, was hid three months of his parents, because they saw he was a proper child; and they were not afraid of the king's command." We are also informed that Moses, when he was come to years, refused to be called the son of Pharaoh's daughter, "Choosing rather to suffer affliction with the people of God, than to enjoy the pleasures of sin for a season." Then we read, "By faith he forsook Egypt, not fearing the wrath of the king: for he endured, as seeing him who is invisible." Moses saw the Lord Jesus in His preincarnate glory. Oh, some will suggest, is not this a contradiction of terms, *"seeing the invisible"?* No, it is an accurate Scriptural truth. As Pascal once put it, "truths may be above reason, and yet not be contrary to reason."

This young man like Moses of old, suffered the disgrace of excommunication from the synagogue because he *endured* "seeing Him who is invisible." He saw the visibility of the invisible God. He saw Christ, and when he saw Christ, he saw God. That's exactly the proposition that our Lord made to His disciples on the night of His betrayal when one of them asked Him, "Shew us the Father, and it sufficeth us." He answered, "Have I been so long time with you, and yet hast thou not known me, Philip? he that hath seen me hath seen the Father." "The first member of the new society," if we may use that expression, was not a *come-outer;* he was an *ex-communicant,* but unto the Person of the Lord Jesus Christ.

The great facts of Christianity are not the theories men have developed; the great central facts of Christianity are the Person of the Lord Jesus Christ and the testimony of the Bible concerning Him.

In this connection I quote from a newspaper report of the funeral service which was held in Ottawa, February 14th, for the late Lord Tweedsmuir, Governor General of Canada. The Reverend Mr. Alexander Ferguson, who conducted the services in St. Andrew's Church, delivered a brief memorial address in which he drew on the writings of Lord Tweedsmuir, who was born John Buchan, son of a Presbyterian minister. The clergyman quoted from the writings of Lord Tweedsmuir, "Today there is a tendency to smooth away all concepts of Christian dogmas into a vague theism or a vulgar pantheism and to flatten out the firm lines of Christian ethics with a pious sentiment. But the foundation of our faith is not only 'God is love.' It is still more the historical fact that 'God so loved the world, that he gave his only begotten son, that whosoever believeth in him should not perish, but have everlasting life.'" What a fine testimony from the pen of the late Governor General of Canada. Every Christian heartily adds his *amen* to it.

To Whom Shall We Turn

This is a day when the very foundations of civilization are being shaken. To whom shall we turn? To a mere man who is as a reed shaken by the wind, or should we turn to a decadent Christendom which has lost its power because it discarded its message and rejected its Lord? Indeed, in this 9th chapter of St. John's Gospel, we have a comparable situation. Here was a religious system to use the language of Dr. G. Campbell Morgan, ". . . the great economy of the past, a stately and wondrous economy, the Divinely arranged and appointed economy, stretching way back to Moses, and coming down through the centuries, with all the rites and ceremonials Divinely appointed. At this moment it was moribund, decadent and dead. No breath of spiritual life was in it. This moribund and decadent and dead organization of religion had excommunicated one man, a blind beggar as he was, but who was now a seeing man. Then Jesus found him. Thus I see something happening, in which there is a rupture between the Divinely arranged religion that fails, and the economy of God that never fails."

The same thought is expressed in the leading editorial of the London Times Literary Supplement, dated January 20, 1940, in which the editor succinctly summarized Christianity when he wrote, "It is incarnate in a man who is the revelation of God."

To whom shall we go? To the very One Who found the man who was excommunicated, the Lord Jesus Christ Himself, the only hope of this world. I quote from Dr. Morgan once again, since he recognized the powerful significance in this instance of the excommunication of the man. Dr. Morgan writes, "What happened that day was not, in the last analysis, that organized religion excommunicated a man. It was that a man in fellowship with Jesus excommunicated organized religion."

Walk Forty-Three

SHEEP-STEALERS IN SHEPHERDS' CLOTHES

AS we consider the parable of the Good Shepherd, we should take a discerning glance at the group who were gathered about our Lord. There was of course the young man born blind who had received his natural sight and who also had entered into the spiritual glories of fellowship with Christ. Then there were those same Pharisees, or at least some of them who had cast out the young fellow, and who raised the question, "Are we blind also?" And finally there were the disciples; while in the midst of all was our Lord Jesus Christ. He was in Judea at the time.

Every person in the group was familiar with the geography of the land; with its history; and the sacred memories of every square foot of its territory. It was in that setting that our Lord said,

> "Verily, verily, I say unto you, He that entereth not by the door into the sheepfold, but climbeth up some other way, the same is a thief and a robber.
> "But he that entereth in by the door is the shepherd of the sheep.
> "To him the porter openeth; and the sheep hear his voice: and he calleth his own sheep by name, and leadeth them out.
> "And when he putteth forth his own sheep, he goeth before them, and the sheep follow him: for they know his voice.
> "And a stranger will they not follow, but will flee from him: for they know not the voice of strangers.
> "This parable spake Jesus unto them: but they understood not what things they were which he spake unto them."

Pastoral Ministry in Palestine

It is possible that our Lord pointed to a specific sheepfold, for as every one knows who is acquainted with Judean geography and history, "the prevailing character of Judea was pastoral with husbandry only incidental to her life." Sir George Adam Smith has referred to Judea as "the land of shepherds," declaring that "It is the stateliest shepherds of all time whom the dawn of history reveals upon her fields... The founder of its one dynasty, and the first of its literary prophets, were taken from following the flocks. The king and every leader of men was called a shepherd. God was the shepherd of His people and they the sheep of His pasture."

But here is a most interesting comment from the pen of that well-informed gentleman. Said he, "Judea offers as good ground as there is in the East, for observing the grandeur of the shepherd's character." He also added that he could not remember having seen in the East a flock without a shepherd.

With that description of the land and its pastoral background, let us look carefully into this inspiring scene. I am sure I will bore none with a further quotation from Sir George Adam Smith. Describing his own and his parties' experiences on the hillsides of Judea, he said: "Sometimes we enjoyed our noonday rest beside one of those Judean wells, to which three or four shepherds come down with their flocks. The flocks mixed with each other, and we wondered how each shepherd would get his own again. But after the watering and the playing were over, the shepherds one by one went up different sides of the valley, and each called out his peculiar call; and the sheep of each drew out of the crowd to their own shepherd, and the flocks passed as orderly as they came."

We should also remember that close at hand to this hill country was the great wilderness of Judea, which in the Old Testament is called "the Yeshimon, a word meaning devastation." It was the desert place, inhabited by wild beasts and hooting owls and howling hyenas, and where vipers dwelt and into which place our Lord was led to be tested by Satan. The Shepherd's fold was in close proximity to this wilderness. It has always been so in the spiritual experience of every sheep of the fold in every age of this world's history. This wilderness "gave the ancient natives of Judea, as it gives the visitor of today, the sense of living next door to doom; the sense of how narrow is the border between life and death."

But let's look a little closer. There are really two parables in this chapter. We shall be occupied in this study with the first only, in which our Lord pictured a sheepfold and presented Himself as the Shepherd of the sheep.

It is evident that there were other sheep in the fold belonging to other flocks. It seems also clear that our Lord pictured a morning scene. There was the porter or the watchman at the door and it was to him that the shepherd first appeared.

Dr. Marcus Dods calls attention to the fact that this general description by our Lord of the relation between sheep and shepherd was drawn from what may be seen any morning in Palestine. "At night the sheep are driven into a fold, that is, a walled enclosure, such as may be seen on our own sheep farms, only with higher walls for protection. . . Here the sheep rest all night, guarded by a watchman or porter. In the morning the shepherds come, and at a recognized signal or knock, are admitted by the porter, and each man calls his own sheep. The sheep, knowing his voice, follow him, and if any are lazy, or stubborn, he goes in and drives them out, with a gentle, kindly compulsion. A stranger's voice they do not recognize, and do not heed. Besides, not only do they disregard a stranger's voice, but the porter also would do so, so that no robber thinks of appealing to the porter, but climbs the wall and lays hold of the sheep he wants."

SHEEP-STEALERS AND THE PORTER

Now we can better appreciate the setting. Remember the presence of those Pharisees who had raised the question, "Are we blind also?" and bear in mind that they took to themselves the title of the shepherds of Israel. Oh yes, they were garbed in shepherd's clothing, they had all the religious paraphernalia that any priest ever possessed. They wore long garments, and how they could pray *long* prayers! Yes, they were clothed in shepherd's clothing but our Lord called them sheep-stealers.

There is no doubt that the porter or the watchman in the parable was none other than the Holy Spirit. And there can be no doubt that the walls around the sheepfold were the predictions of the Old Testament describing the Shepherd. Those predictions formed an effective barrier against any false christ or false shepherd seeking to enter into the sheepfold. The fact of the matter is, no false shepherd ever sought to enter into the sheepfold legitimately, for he well knew that the porter would not recognize his voice. The only hope of a false shepherd was to climb the wall into the sheepfold. The Holy Spirit effectively barred the door.

But when our Lord Jesus Christ came, fulfilling in every detail the predictions made in the Old Testament concerning the Shepherd of Israel, the porter not only observed His garb, but recognized His voice. To Him he opened the door and our Lord entered into the sheepfold. But our Lord did not enter in order to remain therein. He entered to call out His own sheep. As the sheep heard His voice they followed Him and He led them out.

There are those who believe that Christianity is merely an offshoot of Judaism. One of the most pathetic sights has been the attempt of some Christian leaders to Judaize the Christian message. They erroneously assume that the writings of the Old Testament concerning Israel and the Kingdom and Palestine, refer to the Church, to Christianity, and the heavenly Zion, with the result that a little mixture of Judaism and a little mixture of Christianity has been palmed off as the Gospel. While in a measure the foundation of the Gospel is based on the writings of the Old Testament, it is only so in regard to the predictions concerning the Christ and the fact that God in justifying men has never changed His policy in any age from the principle that a man is justified by faith apart from works. Our Lord went into the sheepfold to take out of the fold His own sheep, and to make an entirely new flock.

The first parable therefore in this 10th chapter is a picture of Israel, and Judea, into which fold our Lord entered. From this fold He took His own sheep, called them by name, and led them out. As every student of Scripture knows, that actually took place. Everyone that He led out paid a terrific price, as each turned his or her back upon all the ritualism dear to a Judean's heart and embraced the rejected Nazarene, content to go outside the camp in fellowship with the true Shepherd.

I would strongly urge a careful reading of the 34th chapter of the prophecy of Ezekiel. It will aid materially in an understanding of this 10th chapter of St. John's Gospel. We will content ourselves by quoting two or three passages from that prophecy. Ezekiel said, "The word of the Lord came unto me, saying, Son of man, prophesy against the shepherds of Israel, prophesy, and say unto them, Thus saith the Lord God unto the shepherds; Woe be to the shepherds of Israel that do feed themselves! Should not the shepherds feed the flocks?" Again the Lord spake against the shepherds by saying, "The diseased (sheep) have ye not strengthened, neither have ye healed that which was sick, neither have ye bound up that which was broken . . . neither sought that which was lost."

Then follows a comment that reveals the *true* character of those *false* shepherds. The Lord said, "but with force and with cruelty have ye ruled them." Is it any wonder that Ezekiel added, "Thus saith the LORD GOD; Behold, I am against the shepherds; and I will require my flock at their hand, and cause them to cease from feeding the flock; neither shall the shepherds feed themselves any more; for I will deliver my flock from their mouth, that they may not be meat for them." We can appreciate why our Lord Jesus Christ said, "All that ever came before me are thieves and robbers." In shepherd's clothing to be true, but how far from true shepherds.

THE SHEPHERD'S VOICE

It would not be amiss to underscore in your Bible the phrase, "His voice." The Lord said the sheep, "hear *his* voice." He also said that the sheep "know *His* voice" and that they know not "the voice of strangers." Sheep are dumb animals. It is nothing particularly commendable to us to be called sheep. But in this portion of Scripture there is a characteristic of sheep revealed which is particularly marked. There is one thing they know. It is the *voice* of the shepherd. They may be dumb in other respects. They may be as Plato said, "the aptest to stray." They may give the shepherd many a heartache and much inconvenience, but they will never follow the voice of a stranger. Why do you suppose the sheep recognize the voice of their shepherd, if it were not for the fact that from the time they were little lambs the shepherd guarded them every moment of the day? The only voice they heard was the voice of the shepherd so that their shepherd's voice became so familiar that they could recognize his call from all other voices. They were not interested in the garb that the shepherd might wear. They were never deceived by outward appearances. Isaac was deceived because he wanted to *feel* as well as to *hear*. When he felt the hands of Jacob, because his eyes were dim, they felt like the hands of Esau; they even smelled like the hands of Esau, but the voice was the *voice* of Jacob. Instead of depending upon the voice, Isaac depended upon the feel of the hands and was deceived. But sheep will not depend on the garb that the shepherd wears—they listen exclusively to the *voice* that they know so well. What is more, our Lord said, "A stranger will they not follow, but will flee from him."

THE GOSPEL OF JOHN — CHAPTER X, VERSES 1-6

I had a letter recently from a lady who spoke on behalf of herself and others, saying that they were disturbed and totally confused because someone suggested to them that Jesus was really Michael the archangel. The suggestion so disturbed these ladies that they did not know how to pray and to whom to address their prayers. They asked what was the difference if any between "Jesus and God." I want to deal kindly with that situation because such a reaction reveals first of all, that the suggestion came from the voice of a stranger, it did not sound right in their ears. At the same time, it also reveals the fact that they had not stayed sufficiently long in the presence of the Lord to become thoroughly acquainted with the voice of the Shepherd.

The Lord has given us an open Bible. That book is the green pasture wherein sheep feed and rest. But pray, how can sheep become familiar with the voice of the shepherd if the sheep do not stay close to the shepherd?

Nowhere in the Scripture is it remotely suggested that Michael the archangel is any other person than himself. It is not inferred or intimated that Michael ever changed his character or his name. He was always the archangel and he will always be the archangel. He is so separate and distinct from our Lord Jesus Christ that one can only draw contrasts and not comparisons. Our Lord Jesus Christ was always the Son of His Father's love. In the very opening verses of this Gospel we learn that "In the beginning was the Word, and the Word was with God, and the Word was God. . . . And the Word was made flesh, and dwelt among us, (and we beheld his glory, the glory as of the only begotten of the Father,) full of grace and truth." Our Lord Jesus was always with God and He was God. But at the time of the incarnation, He, the Word of God, was made flesh and dwelt among us. He took possession of a body, fashioned by the Holy Spirit in the womb of a virgin. In that body, He dwelt with the sons of men. He was none the less God while dwelling in that body than when He was in the very presence of His Father. He is the same yesterday, today, and for ever. He is distinct from God the Father and God the Holy Spirit. Our Lord taught His disciples how to pray. Our Lord developed the subject of prayer. We are told in the Scriptures that we are to address the Father in the name of Lord Jesus and to pray in the Holy Spirit.

The sheep who graze in the green pastures and who are constantly by the side of the shepherd know the voice of the shepherd. They are able to distinguish that voice from the voice of all others; and all others are strangers!

When our Lord said, The sheep "know not the voice of strangers," we should not read into it that the sheep were ignorant of any stranger's voice. They heard that voice as they heard all other voices but they knew the difference between the voices of strangers and the voice of their shepherd. They knew there was only one person in the world they could trust and that was their shepherd! They would flee from any other. That's the sign of a sheep.

It is to be regretted that sometimes one meets a man who has been called to be an under-shepherd of the flock who fails to permit the sheep to become acquainted with the voice of the Shepherd. Such a man seems more concerned that the sheep hear his voice. The Lord never intended that any under-shepherd should lord it over the sheep or gather sheep about himself. The sign of a true under-shepherd is when that under-shepherd as the pastor and the minister of the Word, thoroughly instructs the sheep in the Word of God. Sheep should be taught the voice of the Shepherd, not the voice of the under-shepherd. They should not follow the under-shepherd but they should follow the Shepherd of the flock.

When our Lord went into the sheepfold of Judea, He not only called His own sheep by name, but He *led* them out. He did not push them out. I am sure He never dealt in any other way than in a kindly way, even as we learned from Dr. Dods comment, that when a sheep was lazy or stubborn, the shepherd went in and drove the sheep out "with a *gentle, kindly compulsion.*" In other words, the shepherd never carried an axe with him. It was not part of his equipment. Nor did he have a hammer. He had a staff and a rod, and when the sheep went astray, the shepherd never hesitated to spend and be spent. When he found the straying sheep, he never rebuked them, but he loved them back into the fold. And that incidentally also clearly reveals the distinction between the true shepherd and sheep-stealers in shepherds' clothes.

Walk Forty-Four

THE MORE ABUNDANT LIFE

OUR Lord first came as a minister of the circumcision. In other words, as a Jew, for the Jews and to the Jews. There was a definite provincial aspect about His early ministry. But there came a time when He changed His approach and His message. The record of that event is found in the 16th chapter of Matthew's Gospel. It took place at approximately the time when our Lord gave this presentation of Himself as the Good Shepherd. It was in Cesarea Philippi where Peter made his great confession. "Thou art the Christ, the Son of the living God." Verse 21 of Matthew 16, reads, "From that time forth began Jesus to shew unto his disciples, how that he must go unto Jerusalem, and suffer many things of the elders and chief priests and scribes, and be killed, and be raised again the third day." The culmination of that ministry broadened its influence and its sphere, so that it was not limited to a single *fold* but to the whole world.

With that in mind, let us consider what our Lord said, commencing with the 7th verse of this great chapter of Scripture. He was talking to the same group of people, as we observed in the earlier verses, though He gave them a further revelation. It is not a repetition of the former parable, although what we are about to consider is still couched in the imagery of a pastoral scene. Our Lord said, "I am the door of the sheep." In the first parable He was "The Shepherd," now He is "the door." He has already taken His sheep out of the fold and they are about to enter a new life, entrance to which is by Himself as the door. He said that all that ever came before Him were thieves and robbers, but the sheep did not hear them. Then He repeats Himself, "I am the door . . ." and then follows these significant words, "by me if any man enter in, he shall be saved, and shall go in and out, and find pasture."

The word *saved* in the 9th verse is a good "Jesus word," as "Mel" Trotter would say. It is not only a *good* word, it is a characteristic word, and one that fell from the lips of the blessed Lord. It describes an event "that cannot be rationalized, but thank God, can be experienced." It tells of a life that starts as far as human experience is concerned, from the moment the individual embraces Christ. It describes a transformation that is as vitally necessary to every individual as was the raising of Lazarus from the grave if he were to live. It is a revolutionary word. It changes the individual's whole life. From then on his walk is different, his attitude is changed, his outlook ceases to be pessimistic. The grave no longer is the end of all things to him, death is past; life begins. Life begins, not at forty, but at the hour of salvation! It makes an apostle out of a publican. It produces a flaming preacher out of a cursing fisherman. It takes degenerate men and women steeped in sin and filth, and, as Dr. Norberg of the Philosophy Department of the University of Minnesota expressed it, "It lifts them into real communion with God." It *is* a good "Jesus Word!"

The Enigmatic Christ

One cannot read this 10th chapter without being conscious of the presence of others lurking about. Sometimes our Lord called them thieves, and again, robbers and murderers, and hirelings; and yet everyone was garbed in shepherd's clothing. I wish it were possible for us to transport our thinking to the very place and hour when our Lord gave this message. He was an enigma to the best people of His day. In fact, as we look at the 24th verse of this same chapter, we find that those religious leaders who were Pharisees and members of the ruling class came and said unto him, "How long dost thou make us to doubt? If thou be the Christ, tell us plainly."

Let me draw a parallel picture which might enable us to understand this strange phenomenon. Remember, I am only *drawing a picture*. Every city has its Fifth Avenue or its Main Street, where the best people live and attend church. The religious leaders are to be found occupying those fashionable pulpits. They are gloriously robed. They even speak with a religious intonation. They are grand people. Out of the pulpit, these men are splendid mixers; everybody likes them. A summary of their sermons appear in the Monday morning papers. They see to it, by hiring publicity agents. But there is another side to this picture: it is a slum scene where the poor, the lame, the halt, and the blind, are to be found. We also find some disreputable people. There are some politicians; also some thieves. They are what some call "uncultured people." They are not nicely dressed. Their language disturbs the sensitive ears of the refined. It is a stark contrast from the scene on Fifth Avenue or Main Street. And yet here comes One not particularly impressive in appearance, certainly not garbed in the way one would expect to find Him. He has no degrees behind His name, but there is something powerful about His words and His Person. His words disturb a certain group of people while others revel in them. This One who speaks and who is so commonly garbed, claims to be the promised Messiah, the Son of God and God the Son. We find Him, not on Fifth Avenue or Main Street, but in the slums, and the people that crowd around Him are not the religious leaders, but the poor, the halt, the sinful, with the result that the religious leaders lift their eyebrows in utter horror and say, "this man receives unto himself *sinners* and *eateth* with them." It is degrading!

This scene is exactly the picture which is presented in the Gospels. The reaction depicted is that which our Lord Jesus Christ had upon the people. It is written "the publicans and sinners drew near for to hear him." In our day, the word *publican* does not convey as much as it did at that time. But as Dr. W. M. Christie notes from a Talmudic quotation, the publicans "were robbers, highwaymen, and murderers." Matthew was a publican. In his new book "Palestine Calling," Dr. Christie, the great scholar from Mt. Carmel draws a picture of what he considers "must have been" the scene during the time of our Lord's ministry. He describes Capernaum where Peter fished. He said it was here, on the harbor steps at Capernaum that Peter learned to swear. When he landed his fish, there sat Matthew the publican, demanding his tax of one from every five. History tells us that the Galileans were "disputatious," and Dr. Christie adds, "quiet work was never done, especially when both sides were out to cheat." In those days, tax *avoidance* was considered lawful. Now listen to these words of Dr. Christie, a man who has spent more than forty years in Palestine. "And if ever cursing was justifiable, it was when such as Peter the fisherman, cursed Matthew the publican. Both, however, learned their lesson in the school of Christ . . . Christ changed them both, and we can think of Peter and Matthew walking up the hill of ordination together and then descending the other side, arm in arm." Only Christ can make of a tax collector and a cursing fisherman, a communion of saints!

Our Lord said that He was a physician. He did not waste His time on the people who believed they were well and had no need of a physician. He went down to the clinic and dealt with sin-sick souls and He healed them. He enabled them to breathe, no longer the smelly air of the slums, but the pure air of heaven. He made them fit to sit in His Presence and enjoy His company.

The Shepherd Who Is Also The Door

After our Lord said that these others dressed in shepherd's garments were actually thieves and robbers and that the sheep did not hear them, He said, "I am the door: by me if any man enter in, he shall be saved, and shall go in and out, and find pasture." Notice the freedom that the Lord extends to His sheep. He gives them the privilege of going *in* and *out* and *finding* pasture. There is of course another side to this matter of freedom. We can do no better than to quote the words of Bishop Moule on this subject. Said he, "Our freedom is 'in the Lord' alone, and to be 'in the Lord' is to belong to Him, as wholly as a healthy hand belongs in its freedom, to the physical center of life and will. To be a bondslave is terrible in the abstract! To be Jesus Christ's bondslave is paradise, in the concrete. Self-surrender, taken alone, is a plunge into a cold void. When it is a surrender to the Son of God, who loved me and gave Himself for me, it is the bright homecoming of the soul to the seat and sphere of life and power."

There is nothing confining in being a Christian, for our Lord said, "I am come that they (my sheep) might have life, and that they might have it more abundantly." It is only the man who knows Christ as his Shepherd, who has received Him as his Savior, who knows anything about *"the more abundant life."*

When our Lord used that expression, He was not referring to the same thing that politicians do when they talk about "the more abundant life." There is nothing here about "two chickens in the pot or two cars in the garage." One can enjoy this abundant life promised by our Lord without a chicken in the pot and without a car in the garage, and in fact, without a garage.

Let us read a Psalm that gives a picture of this more abundant life. No, we shall not read the 23rd Psalm, though that is the most precious and best known Shepherd Psalm. We read the 100th Psalm.

"Make a joyful noise unto the LORD, all ye lands.
"Serve the LORD with gladness: come before his presence with singing.
"Know ye that the LORD he is God: it is he that hath made us, and not we ourselves; we are his people, and the sheep of his pasture.

> "Enter into his gates with thanksgiving, and into his courts with praise: be thankful unto him, and bless his name.
>
> "For the LORD is good; his mercy is everlasting; and his truth endureth to all generations."

That's life! That's the more abundant life! It is a life filled with joy, praise, thanksgiving, gladness, and singing. Only one class of people fit into that picture; it is they who know the Lord and who have a definite experience with Christ.

In this 10th chapter of John our Lord speaks of Himself not only as the door, but also as the *good shepherd*. In our last study we quoted Sir George Adam Smith rather profusely. He has written some very choice things. In this particular connection, regarding our Lord as the door as well as the shepherd, Dr. G. Campbell Morgan points out that they are interlocked in a wonderful way, in the light of eastern language. Then that eminent preacher goes on to say that it was once his privilege to cross the Atlantic with Sir George Adam Smith. Let me give you the words of Dr. Campbell Morgan as he describes that trip.

"I shall never forget the fascination of that voyage, as he talked of the Eastern lands he knew so well. One story he told me was this. He was one day traveling with a guide, and came across a shepherd and his sheep. He fell into conversation with him. The man showed him the fold into which the sheep were led at night. It consisted of four walls, with a way in. Sir George said to the shepherd, 'That is where they go at night?' 'Yes,' said the shepherd, 'and when they are in there, they are perfectly safe.' 'But there is no door,' said Sir George. 'I am the door,' said the shepherd. He was not a Christian man, he was not speaking in the language of the New Testament. He was speaking from the Arab shepherd's standpoint. Sir George looked at him and said, 'What do you mean by the door?' Said the shepherd, 'When the light has gone, and all the sheep are inside, I lie in that open space, and no sheep ever goes out but across my body, and no wolf comes in unless he crosses my body; I am the door.'"

That Arab was a *good* shepherd. He was not like the hireling to whom our Lord referred, who when he saw a wolf coming, fled, because the sheep did not belong to him. But the good shepherd to whom the sheep belong, is well able to meet the wolf and protect them and make perfectly safe, every sheep of His pasture.

Sheep vs. Goats

We close this study by pointing out another fact that our Lord related about His sheep. They entered in by Him. When they entered in they were saved, but after they were in, they went in and out and found pasture. David said, the Lord "maketh me to lie down in green pastures." The shepherd not only leads his sheep in green pastures, but he makes them to rest therein. He searches out the green spots for He knows that the sheep only want one type of food. They like green pastures. What are the green pastures? Will anyone question that they are the books of the Bible? The sheep feed on the word of God. Indeed, they feed on nothing else. Goats may be satisfied with tin cans, but sheep want green grass.

A true pastor will see to it that the sheep graze in the midst of God's Word. He will not do what a well known Fifth Avenue minister in New York City did recently, if he was correctly quoted in the newspapers. This man spoke at an Annual Bible Breakfast of a prominent association. He spoke on the subject "The Art of Succeeding in Life," a splendid subject for young people. The minister told that group, and I quote from the newspaper, " 'the reason most people fail is because they don't know where they are going and how they are going to get there. For the individual to succeed, he must be able to see his way clearly, to understand, to have some knowledge of life.' The best way to attain this insight, and strength, he said, is to 'study the works of great authors, such as Charles Dickens and Shakespeare!' He added that the greatest example of a person who had insight was Jesus Christ. And concerning Him, he said, 'He is considered by every thinker to have had the most penetrating intelligence.' " It's too bad Jesus didn't have the advantage of Dickens and Shakespeare!

I enjoy Shakespeare, and I like some of Charles Dickens' works, but sir, if we are to know where we are going and how to get there, neither Shakespeare, nor Dickens, nor for that matter Plato, nor Homer, nor any other of the great philosophers or poets can be of any help. There is only one book in the world that can tell us, and that's the Bible. And there is only one Person in the world who knows and He is the Lord Jesus. He said, "I am the way, the truth, and the life; no man cometh unto the Father, but by me." Thank God our Lord never fed sheep with rubbish. He fed them with the sincere milk of the Word; the bread of God; and, to mature Christians, "the strong meat of the Word." What a Savior is Jesus Christ our Lord!

Walk Forty-Five

ONE FLOCK AND ONE SHEPHERD

IN this 10th chapter of St. John's Gospel there is a statement by our Lord Jesus Christ which seems to be contradicted by the apparent irreconcilable differences that exist between professing Christian bodies. I refer to verse 16 where we read: "And other sheep I have, which are not of this fold: them also I must bring, and they shall hear my voice; and there shall be one fold (flock) and one shepherd." There is no *apparent* oneness in professed Christendom. Was our Lord mistaken? Have men thwarted His purposes? Just what is the situation and how can this statement by our Lord be reconciled with what we see on all sides? Before we look into this particular subject however, there is one other fact in connection with this portion of St. John's Gospel that we should handle first.

In the 11th verse, our Lord said, "I am the good shepherd: the good shepherd giveth his life for the sheep." I would like to make clear what our Lord said; not that I believe any statement which our Lord made needs to be clarified; but frequently men take a passage of Scripture out of its context and thereby becloud its simple, plain, teaching. There never has arisen a man who had the temerity to criticize or tear apart the life which our Lord Jesus Christ lived. By friend and foe alike His life is acknowledged to be absolutely unique. He demonstrated the kind of a life that is well pleasing to God. But the Gospel, while it does not ignore the life that He lived, proclaims that it is the death that He died which is the basic fact of the Christian message. The Apostle Paul put it, "Christ died for our sins according to the Scriptures." When our Lord therefore made the statement that as the good shepherd, He "giveth" his life for the sheep, it is a definite mistake to assume He inferred that this "giving up" of His life meant a life of devotion rather than an act of atonement. For instance, we sometimes refer to a member of a family devoted to a sick father or mother or brother, and we say concerning their labor that they have "given up their life" to that sick one. But that is not what our Lord meant when He said, "the good shepherd *giveth* his life for the sheep." True, He devoted His life to the sheep, but the word *give* refers to the act of atonement; the death that He died on the cross; a single act.

That is clarified and made plain by our Lord in the 17th and 18th verses of this same chapter where He said, "Therefore doth my Father love me, because I *lay down* my life, that I might take it again. No man taketh it from me, but I *lay it down* of myself. I have power to *lay it down,* and I have power to *take it again.* This commandment have I received of my Father."

Christendom, during so-called Holy Week, annually contemplates afresh, the trial, the mocking, the crucifixion, the death, the burial, and the resurrection of the Lord Jesus Christ. These are the things involved in our Lord's "laying down" of His life and "taking it" again. It is the culmination of His ministry. In fact, it is the crux of His life. "The Son of man came not to be ministered unto, but to minister, *and* to give his life a ransom for many." "It is the blood that maketh atonement for the soul." It is our Lord's blood which the Scripture speaks of as "precious" because it was spilled to make atonement for the human soul.

We are all aware that a vociferous branch of a sickly trivial Protestantism has sought to court a smug, shallow thinking, pharisaical intelligentsia with the suggestion that "Christianity is *a* way of life." But over against that vague nothingness, is the clear uncompromising word of our Lord Jesus to the Pharisees of His day, "I said therefore unto you . . . if ye believe not that I am he, ye shall die in your sins." Christianity, to use the words of a keen observer, "calls sinners, saves sinners, heals sinners." Christianity is a Gospel "for sinners only." Would God that modern man would cease his "frantic effort to belittle the reality of sin," and do as a true physician always does, "face facts, not run away from them!"

Other Sheep

Now for our consideration of this seemingly irreconcilable statement of our Lord. Let's look closely at what He said. "And other sheep I have, which are not of this fold." When we began our study in this chapter, we called attention to the fact that our Lord approached the sheepfold and entered in by the door. The sheepfold was Israel. He went into that fold and took out His own sheep, and they in turn entered through Him into what our Lord called "the more abundant life." In the oriental sheepfold there may be more than one flock. Frequently there are several flocks. Our Lord went into the sheepfold of Israel and called out His own sheep by name. That's an historic fact. But here our Lord indicated that He has a further ministry, that He has some "other sheep" which are not of the Israelitish fold. Did you note He called them "sheep," not goats or dogs? He was of course referring to the Gentiles; to those outside the camp of Israel; strangers to the covenants of promise, who previously were without God and without hope in this world, who would hear His voice.

Note the strong words our Lord used concerning those sheep. He said, "them also I *must* bring, and they *shall* hear my voice . . ." There are literally millions who rise up this day and acknowledge that they have heard the voice of the Good Shepherd—that they have heard the voice of the Son of God and having heard His voice, they live. They have been made members of His body. They have been made one with Him. Our Lord said concerning them, "and there shall be one *flock* and one shepherd." Our Authorized Version reads, "one *fold* and one shepherd" but the Greek word is emphatic, it is "one *flock* and one shepherd." In the early part of the verse, the word *fold* is used, but in the latter part of the verse, the word *flock* is used, which is something quite different.

Some may be surprised at the statement I am about to make. Our Lord never founded modern Christendom as we see it today. Christ founded the Church which is His body of which He is the head. He said concerning that Church "the gates of hell shall not prevail against it." It is self evident that our Lord could not have founded the almost fifty-seven varieties of denominations and churches that we have in this world today. Furthermore, an examination of the New Testament would clearly indicate how far afield is present ritualistic Christendom from the Church of the New Testament. That our Lord was not *un*aware of what would take place is clearly evident from the several parables found in the 13th chapter of St. Matthew's Gospel, for instance, this one: "The kingdom of heaven is likened unto a man which sowed good seed in his field: But while men slept, his enemy came and sowed tares among the wheat, and went his way." Notice where the enemy sowed the tares: "among the wheat," right in the very field where the good seed was sown. Our Lord continued and said,

> "But when the blade was sprung up, and brought forth fruit, then appeared the tares also.

> "So the servants of the householder came and said unto him, Sir, didst not thou sow good seed in thy field? from whence then hath it tares?
> "He said unto them, An enemy hath done this. The servants said unto him, Wilt thou then that we go and gather them up?
> "But he said, Nay; lest while ye gather up the tares, ye root up also the wheat with them.
> "Let both grow together until the harvest; and in the time of harvest I will say to the reapers, Gather ye together first the tares, and bind them in bundles to burn them: but gather the wheat into my barn."

See how clearly our Lord revealed what would take place and *who* would sow the spurious wheat. Who is the enemy? There is no doubt about it; it is Satan. Our Lord said so, for later in that same chapter we learn that

> " . . . his disciples came unto him, saying, Declare unto us the parable of the tares of the field.
> "He answered and said unto them, He that soweth the good seed is the Son of man;
> "The field is the world; the good seed are the children of the kingdom; but the tares are the children of the wicked one;
> "The enemy that sowed them is the devil; the harvest is the end of the world; and the reapers are the angels.
> "As therefore the tares are gathered and burned in the fire; so shall it be in the end of this world.
> "The Son of man shall send forth his angels, and they shall gather out of his kingdom all things that offend, and them which do iniquity;
> "And shall cast them into a furnace of fire: there shall be wailing and gnashing of teeth.
> "Then shall the righteous shine forth as the sun in the kingdom of their Father. Who hath ears to hear, let him hear."

So it is not surprising to find the good and the bad in every field; and to find right in the midst of professing Christendom that which is sown by the enemy of our souls. If it were otherwise, we would have a right to question. But the very chaotic condition of Christendom today is just one further evidence of the inspiration of the Scriptures; of the deity of our Lord Jesus Christ; and the truth of His word. But in the midst of all this contradictory element in the professed Christian Church, there has never been more than "one flock and one Shepherd." The Shepherd has been the Lord Jesus Christ, and the flock has been the sheep of His pasture.

The Oneness of the Flock

I think I am qualified to discuss this subject for it has been my happy privilege to have had the opportunity to minister the Word of God in churches of various denominations. I am aware that some branches of Christendom make much of what they call "Apostolic succession" and they jealously guard priestly and ministerial functions against any who have not had this successive "Laying on of hands." And yet, no less a Church dignitary than St. Peter wrote by infallible inspiration that all believers are "a royal priesthood" with all the rights and privileges of a chosen generation to "shew forth the praises of him who hath called (us) you out of darkness into his marvelous light." Some of God's greatest men have been "unordained laymen." Witness John the Baptist. He was ordained by God, and that's the ordination that really counts. Do not assume that I am voicing objection to ordination. I believe that everything should be done decently and in order. The Bible has something to say about men set apart for the ministry of the Word. From my own experience, covering many years and in many places, I *know* that there is only *one flock* and *one shepherd*. Irrespective of what part of the fold or branch of the Christian Church, a sheep may be in, one knows a sheep as soon as he meets one.

I shall never forget the visit to our home of the late Anglican Bishop J. Taylor Smith, a man whom I greatly loved. My little youngster was then less than a year old. As he came into her room where she was romping in her playpen, he put his big hand on her head, and with a quiet dignified voice that still echoes in my ears said, "God bless you my dear!" I turned to that distinguished Churchman and said, "Bishop, I am a non-conformist of the non-conformists, but I assure you my little girl will never forget that she received a blessing from an Anglican Bishop." The Bishop and I had choice fellowship together about the Person and work of our Lord Jesus Christ. Never once did we have any discussion of denominational creeds, but we had wonderful unity and fellowship together.

More and more during the past few years it has seemed to me that denominational barriers are being broken down as true Christians (men and women who have been born again by the Spirit of God) have become increasingly conscious of their relationship to the Lord and of their oneness with every other believer. They have recognized the voice of the one true Shepherd and unitedly have rejoiced in the mutual faith one of the other.

It has been my pleasure during the last four consecutive years to participate in the Founder's Week Conference at the Moody Bible Institute, a place that I love. It is one of the great if not the greatest Institution for the training of Christian workers in this country. Dr. Gray, the former President of that Institute, was a member of the Reformed Episcopal Church. Dr. Houghton, who is now President, is a Baptist. On the staff are such men as Dr. Wilbur M. Smith, a Presbyterian, and Dr. Max Reich, a Hebrew Quaker. You never saw such a variety of denominations under one roof! Probably one could find a dozen or more denominations represented on the staff of that Institute. I have no idea how many denominations are represented in the student body! But never once has there been a discussion of denominational differences at the annual conferences. There has been united fellowship about the Person of the Lord Jesus Christ and His precious Word.

The Unity of the Spirit

But someone may ask, "Why is it that all Christians do not see eye to eye on every little thing?" That's easy. In our first birth God never made any two of us exactly alike even if some were born twins; neither has He done so in our second or new birth. But we all have the family trait, "we love our Lord Jesus and His Word." God did not make us automatons, but intelligent agents with our own wills which may be yielded to His will. God did not make even two blades of grass alike but each blade is a member of the grass family. He has not made two flakes of snow alike, but each flake is white.

Along this line, let me quote from an article that appeared in the Moody Church News, the official organ of the Moody Memorial Church of Chicago of which Dr. H. A. Ironside is pastor. It describes a unique prayer meeting, and reads as follows:

"On Lord's Day afternoon, February 25th (1940), a very unique and blessed prayer service was held in the Moody Memorial Church in Chicago, under the auspices of the Great Commission Prayer League. It was convened in order to intercede with God on behalf of a war-torn world.

"The President of the Moody Bible Institute, Dr. W. H. Houghton, acted as chairman in the absence of Dr. E. M. Wadsworth, who was engaged in a conference elsewhere. The pastor of the church gave a brief message based upon the exhortation in I Tim. 2:1, 2, to 'pray for all men, for kings, and for all in authority,' that things may be so ordered 'that we may lead a quiet and peaceable life in all godliness.'

"Prayer was offered by representative believers from many different national and even racial groups. There was Finnish, Norwegian, Swedish, Russian, German, British, Lithuanian, Chinese, Hungarian, Jewish, and other groups represented. A marvelous spirit of unity was manifested. It was touching to hear Finns pray for Russians, and Russians for Finns, Germans for British and British for Germans. It indeed was a wonderful exhibition of the unity of the Spirit."

Was our Lord mistaken when He said, "there shall be one flock and one Shepherd?" There never has been more than one flock and there has never been more than one Shepherd! The important question therefore, is, are we members of His flock? Do we know the Lord Jesus as our own Shepherd? Have we come to experience His Salvation? Do we realize that it was for our sins that He died on the cross?

Walk Forty-Six

THE SUPERNATURALISM OF JESUS

THE Bible is occupied with two principal subjects, the Person and the work of the Lord Jesus Christ. In a very remarkable manner, we have both these subjects succinctly presented to us in a few verses in the middle of the 10th chapter of St. John's Gospel. Our Lord said,

> "Therefore doth my Father love me, because I lay down my life, that I might take it again.
> "No man taketh it from me, but I lay it down of myself. I have power to lay it down, and I have power to take it again. This commandment have I received of my Father."

That statement summarizes *the work* of our Lord Jesus Christ. It indicated, first, that He would lay down His life; in other words, He would die. Secondly, that He would do so in order that He might take it again; in other words, He would rise from the dead. Third, no man could take His life from Him; which is the same as saying His death would be voluntary. Fourth, He received authority to lay it down of Himself with equal authority to take it again; which means, that the death and resurrection of Christ were in the divine plan.

That brings us face to face with the ever persistent effort to get from under the responsibility for the death of Jesus of Nazareth. No less than two hundred and fifty thousand copies of a new book (The Nazarene by Scholem Asch) on this old situation have been sold recently. Men have attempted by every line of reasoning to set themselves right before God, giving very little attention to the more important matter of righting the wrong of Calvary.

With the passing of the years, the Person of Jesus Christ looms greater and greater. Even those who once despised His name, who stopped their ears at the mere reference to it, and spat on the ground every time they heard it, are now commencing to appreciate the ministry, the power, and the uniqueness of the Prophet of Nazareth. In every successive generation, an effort has been expended to do the same thing that Pilate vainly attempted, but still the stain of the blood remains.

Who crucified Christ? Who was responsible for His death? Israel has correctly reminded us that in the first place, they did not have the right to inflict capital punishment at that particular hour in their history, and that they could not crucify a criminal even if they had wished to do so. Crucifixion was not one of their forms of judgment. They also correctly tell us that it was a Roman form of punishment and that Pilate, the Roman Governor, gave the verdict that brought about His death. Beyond all this, however, there is that unimpeachable word of the Lord that can never be erased from the divine record which He gave in answering Pilate who reminded Him that he had delegated authority to either free or crucify Him. Our Lord said, "Thou couldest have no power at all against me, except it were given thee from above: therefore he that delivered me unto thee hath the greater sin."

Our Lord thus acknowledged that Pilate, by virtue of being the representative of the Roman Caesar, had authority from God to exercise judicial rights in the Empire, even to the extent of the taking of life. But note the latter part of that verse, "therefore he that delivered me unto thee hath the *greater* sin." Thus our Lord did not release Pilate from responsibility but at the same time, He placed the greater responsibility upon those who had delivered Him into the hands of the Roman Governor. But back of this, which is merely a question of the degree of judicial guilt, is the outstanding fact that it was my sin and your sin which in the final analysis put Jesus Christ to death, so that not one single one of us can be released from the responsibility of the blood-guiltiness of the Lord Jesus Christ.

The Divine Plan

But over and above the human guilt, there was a divine plan, revealed not only by the writers of the Old Testament, but also by our Lord Jesus Christ, that He had come for the express purpose of dying, and that no man could possibly take His life from Him. He would voluntarily lay it down of Himself. He would do so in order that He might rise again from the dead. This voluntary aspect of the death of Christ is graphically portrayed in the opening verses of the 18th chapter of St. John's Gospel where we have the record of what took place on the night of His betrayal. We read these words, "When Jesus had spoken these words, *he went forth* with his disciples over the brook Cedron . . ." Again in verse 4 of that same chapter, "Jesus therefore, knowing all things that should come upon him, *went forth,* and said unto them, Whom seek ye?" When the Roman cohort with the officers from the chief priests and Pharisees, together with Judas came toward Him, Jesus *went forth,* a voluntary act, *He went forth.* He laid down His life.

We learn from the Epistle to the Hebrews that He did this in order to "deliver them who through fear of death were all their lifetime subject to bondage." Then again in the Epistle to the Philippians we read, that our Lord "humbled himself, and became obedient unto death, even the death of the cross. Wherefore God also hath highly exalted him, and given him a name which is above every name: That at the name of Jesus every knee should bow, of things in heaven, and things in earth, and things under the earth; And that every tongue should confess that Jesus Christ is Lord, to the glory of God the Father." The whole summary of the life which our Lord lived on this earth can be brought down into the one great fact of His death on the cross, followed by His resurrection. That's why He came. It is that fact which makes possible the Gospel, the Evangel, the Good News which redeems guilty sinners.

We still hear much these days about having "Jesus as our example" or as "our ideal" or attempting to live "the Jesus life." But as another aptly said, one cannot avoid the conclusion after an examination of the Four Gospels that, "There is no sign that the first disciples were overcome by the 'inner life of Jesus.' For years they had indeed been under the influence of this life, but when it came to the end their belief collapsed. What does this prove? Surely that the glory of 'Jesus' inner life' had not the power to uphold. Their belief was first perfected by the assurance given them by the empty grave, and by the Pentecostal gift of the Holy Spirit. In other words, not by the influence of the personality of Jesus, wonderful as that is, but by His divine majesty."

In fact, as one studies the Acts of the Apostles, it "becomes clear that even the Early Church knew nothing of a belief in Jesus which may be described as 'following Jesus of Nazareth'; it knew only a prayer-relationship with the exalted Christ."

That's the Gospel. It is not an attempt to follow in His steps to seek Him as an example, but to revel in His death and resurrection the cornerstone of His work, and to rejoice in continuous fellowship with Him as the risen Lord in the Glory. It has been well said, "If Jesus is only an example, then He is there ultimately so that we may recognize our sin. But this is no evangel." So much for the work of our Lord.

Now something of His Person. In 1933 there was published in England, a translation of a very remarkable book written by one of Europe's outstanding scholars, Dr. Otto Borchert. For sixteen years this scholar sought a publisher for his work. It had been offered and rejected no less than ten times. Those publishers correctly concluded that this gentleman's work was contrary to the popular notion of the day but "with the disillusionment brought about by the Great War and the subsequent Peace, it found its public and its message went home." Many editions of the original German book have been exhausted and it has been translated into Dutch, Danish and Swedish, and finally into English. The title given to the original work by its author is particularly impressive "Der Goldgrund des Lebensbildes

Jesu" which is somewhat spoiled by the English translation "The Original Jesus."

Anyone who has done any thinking knows that in the later nineteenth century there was a tendency to suppose that "The Jesus of History must have been a purely human and non-supernatural person . . . but this view is now almost everywhere abandoned." William Temple, the Archbishop of York has made this striking comment: "Why anyone should have troubled to crucify the Christ of Protestant liberalism has always been a mystery. It is now recognized that the only Christ for whose existence there is any evidence at all is a miraculous figure making stupendous claims."

Dr. Borchert, in a chapter devoted to a discussion of the fact that the Jesus of the Scriptures is a contradiction of our ideas and the ideas of His time, makes this interesting observation: "It has indeed been reserved for one of our contemporaries to give voice to the most unheard-of, monstrous sentiment of all in this respect. The head doctor of a provincial lunatic asylum has dared to give it as his opinion that, 'from the point of view of a Psychologist' Jesus was insane."

Much as I have enjoyed that scholar's work, Dr. Borchert is wrong. It was not left to our generation to be the first to conclude that Jesus was insane. It was the verdict given, more than once by some who lived and saw Him in the flesh. Notice what John says in this 10th chapter of his Gospel. We should bear in mind that our Lord had just restored the sight of a man who was born blind; He had accepted the worship of this former beggar, and He had presented Himself as the Good Shepherd that giveth His life for the sheep. In verses 19, 20, and 21, we read these arresting words on the *Person of Jesus*.

> "There was a division therefore again among the Jews for these sayings.
> "And many of them said, He hath a demon, and is mad; why hear ye him?
> "Others said, These are not the words of him that hath a demon. Can a demon open the eyes of the blind?"

In another passage it was suggested that our Lord was "beside Himself" which of course is just a polite way of saying He was insane. Mark you, these words came not from the people. The common people heard gladly. The publicans and sinners clung to His very robe and listened with rapture to His words. But it was the Pharisees, the religious leaders who said, "He hath a demon and is mad; why hear him?"

It is extremely noteworthy that it was the words Jesus spoke which infuriated the Pharisees. The same condition exists today. It is not what Jesus *did*. All concede and acknowledge the uniqueness of His life; but it is what He *said*. We come therefore to a place in our consideration of the *Person* of Jesus Christ where we are faced with the suggestion from the one side that He was demon possessed and insane; and from the other side, that He *is* the glory, the visibility, the effulgence, the incarnation of the eternal God.

About the easiest way to dispose of someone whose logic is unanswerable is to suggest that he is beside himself, and when the matter cuts deeply into the conscience, then the decision is usually accompanied with much "noise." Festus tried that method on the Apostle Paul when he said with a loud voice, "Paul, thou art beside thyself; much learning doth make thee mad." Paul rightly answered, "I am not mad, most noble Festus; but speak forth the words of truth and soberness."

If the Prophet of Nazareth is only a man, then His claims must be dismissed and we are obliged to conclude with the Pharisees that He hath a demon and is mad, for no rational man would ever make the statement, "I am the resurrection, and the life: he that believeth in me, though he were dead, yet shall he live: And whosoever liveth and believeth in me shall never die." But if He is the Son of God, then the words are not only logical and belong on His lips, but they are gloriously true.

Just what did our Lord have to say about Himself? What are the words to which the Pharisees referred when they said, "Why hear ye him?" Our Lord said ". . . He that *heareth my word,* and believeth on him that sent me, hath everlasting life, and shall not come into (judgment) condemnation; but is passed from death into life." Again He said, "The hour is coming, and now is, when the dead shall *hear the voice* of the Son of God: and they that *hear* shall live." Since that's the case, we ought to hear Him and not dismiss Him as the Pharisees did by suggesting that He had a demon.

From whatever angle one examines the words of our Lord or whatever subject one chooses to look into on which He spoke or touched upon, Our Lord's words were so unique as to fully justify the retort of the soldiers who returned to their superiors without their accused and said, "Never man spake like this man." His message was so profound that the learned were absolutely bewildered, and yet so simple that a little child could understand Him. Well might Napoleon have said, who had a great knowledge of human nature, "I know men; but He (meaning Jesus) was no man."

To the suggestion that our Lord possessed a demon and is mad others who were present and heard our Lord said: "These are not the words of him that hath a demon. Can a demon open the eyes of the blind?"

The only logical conclusion to reach is that which was expressed in the words of the writer of this Gospel when he said, "And we beheld his glory, the glory as of the only begotten of the Father, full of grace and truth."

Walk Forty-Seven

A PLAIN ANSWER TO A PERPLEXING PROBLEM

NOT very long ago it was my pleasure to listen to a masterful address on the Gospel of St. John delivered by Dr. William Evans of Los Angeles. In connection with John in contrast to the others he said that in Matthew, Mark and Luke, "we find our Lord Jesus in His overalls," that is, He is working, constantly working. He is busily engaged in the market places or by the lake-side with the fishermen. But in John's Gospel "He has on His Sunday clothes." He is seen mostly in the Temple and particularly, at the feasts of the Jews.

In chapters 7, 8, 9, and about a half of the 10th chapter, we have a record of what took place in Jerusalem at the feast of Tabernacles or immediately after. The feast occurred during the month of October. Commencing with the 22nd verse of the 10th chapter in which our present study is found, we learn that our Lord was still at Jerusalem. But the time was a little later—at the Feast of Dedication. That feast took place on December 25th, rather striking, isn't it, seeing that Christendom celebrates that day as the birthday of our Lord. It's singular that the Word of God should have added, "and it was winter." John brings the matter down to the minutest details. He said, "Jesus walked in the temple in

Solomon's porch." It was a part of the Temple that had not been destroyed at the time of the Babylonian invasion. He who was greater than Solomon, walked in the Temple in Solomon's porch. We read: "Then came the Jews round about him, and said unto him, How long dost thou make us to doubt? If thou be the Christ, tell us plainly."

One can almost see the perplexing expressions upon the faces of the people. It is quite evident that it was the same group who had followed our Lord when He found the young man whom they had excommunicated from the Temple. In other words, they were the same Pharisees who had listened to His discourse on Himself as the Good Shepherd. Despite the plainness of the Master's words, those Pharisees were hopelessly bewildered. "How long dost thou make us to doubt? How long dost thou keep us in suspense? If thou be the Christ, tell us plainly." No more important question can occupy the mind of man. It is still the paramount problem even though our Lord walked this earth almost two thousand years ago.

Some may dismiss this matter by shrugging their shoulders and saying, "What interest is it to us what took place nearly two millenniums ago? Why should we be occupied with 'this Man' who lived for thirty-three years, thirty of which we have little or no knowledge; who at the end, died like a criminal outside the gates of Jerusalem. We find too many acute problems to consider which are of pressing importance at this moment. Why should we be concerned about this Man?"

If those questions are honestly asked, they deserve an answer. To the Pharisee's question our Lord gave a rational answer, despite the fact that He knew that the question was not asked from an honest inquirer's viewpoint.

The Powerful Influence of Jesus Christ

Notwithstanding the fact that our Lord ministered within the confines of a very limited area for only a period of three years (possibly not quite that long), it is startling that His influence upon this world should have been and still continues to be supreme. For instance, take the matter of the manner of reckoning of time as one little evidence of the tremendous influence exercised by the Prophet of Nazareth upon the life of the world.

It would be utterly impossible to reconcile any event in ancient or modern history and we would be hopelessly at sea, were it not for the Christian reckoning. Dr. W. M. Christie, one of England's great scholars, to whom we have previously referred and who has lived in Mt. Carmel in Palestine for more than forty years, has correctly suggested that "every attempt of mere man to create an era or stamp his date on the world's history has failed. Only in the era of Jesus Christ is any stability found. Everything must be reckoned in terms of Him. He even sets kings in their own place." Being an Englishman Dr. Christie pictures a court scene, and points out that "A sharp advocate quotes a law of say xxvi Victoria, but the moment he has done so, we see his lips moving and also the lips of those around him, counting out what they can only understand, the date of our Lord Jesus Christ. He alone takes His place in the center of the world's history. Our Jewish friends who have used their present calendar since about 1400 A. D. have used the date of October 7th, 3761 B. C. as the basis of their reckoning, but even now that calendar to them is little more than a mere curiosity, for Jewish newspapers printed in Jerusalem *today* have the Christian dating *only*." Dr. Christie has well added, "We date back as we date forward from Him. He is the key to the understanding of all history. He alone can say 'Time centers all in Me.' Take His name and His era from the world, and all is confusion. Without His light all is darkness."

Yet here were some who came to Him while He was walking in one of the porticos which was a part of His Father's house, and asked, "How long dost thou keep us in suspense? if thou be the Christ, tell us plainly." To this perplexing question our Lord plainly answered:

" . . . I told you, and ye believed not: the works that I do in my Father's name, they bear witness of me.
"But ye believe not, because ye are not of my sheep, as I said unto you.
"My sheep hear my voice, and I know them, and they follow me:
"And I give unto them eternal life; and they shall never perish, neither shall any man pluck them out of my hand.
"My Father, which gave them me, is greater than all; and no man is able to pluck them out of my Father's hand.
"I and my Father are one."

Let's stop there, seeing that our Lord was rudely interrupted by an angry group who "took up stones again to stone Him." In our previous study we called attention to the fact that all are agreed that the life and accomplishments of our Lord Jesus Christ are absolutely unique. The most confirmed critic recognizes the beauty of His life, the power of His influence, and the matchless glory of His high principles, but we part company on what He had to say about Himself.

What Jesus Said of Himself

It has sometimes been suggested that theology has deified Jesus. It has also been asserted by some who ought to know better, that Jesus never claimed to be God, that it was left to His followers to do so. Theologians, it has been charged, devised a system of theology called Christianity wherein they made Him to be the Son of God. They take pains to tell us that the title that Jesus used most frequently in speaking of Himself, was "The Son of man." But whether or not religious liberalists in the Church, or agnostics and atheists outside the church, are now able to comprehend what Jesus had to say about Himself, it is quite evident from the record that *the people who heard Him* had no difficulty in understanding His plain meaning.

Before we look at what He had to say about Himself as recorded in this particular portion of Scripture, it may be thought provoking to say the least, to enumerate a few things that Jesus said about Himself which are to be found in other parts of Scripture. We should preface these quotations with the statement that if He were only a man, He was the most brazen egotist that ever lived. Here are a few of them:

He declared that He was above the law, when He said, "ye have heard that it was said by them of old . . . but *I* say unto you. . ." He said He was "greater than the Sabbath . . . greater than the Temple . . . greater than Jonah . . . greater than Solomon," and when asked by His critics, "Art thou greater than our Father Abraham?" He answered, "Your father Abraham rejoiced to see my day, and he saw it and was glad. . . Verily, verily I say unto you, Before Abraham was, I am." He said He was the light of the world, the bread of God, the way, the truth, and the life. On several occasions beside the reference to Abraham, He insisted that He was the incomparable "I Am"—the very title God used when He answered Moses; who asked His name and He replied "I Am."

One may reject our Lord's claims and think what he will regarding them, but it can never be truthfully asserted that *He* did not claim to be the Son of God. Furthermore, He accepted worship as God.

Our Lord revealed why the Pharisees did not believe. He said, "Ye believe not, because ye are not of my sheep, as I said unto you. My sheep hear my voice, and I know them, and they follow me." He thus reminded them of the setting that He had previously presented of the sheepfold and how He had entered into it and called out His own sheep by name. But here was a group who also *followed* Him, yet were not His sheep, in other words, they did not belong to Him.

Well, says someone, then it is a case of "elective predestination!" Whether that be so or not, I would remind you that our Lord did not relieve those men of responsibility for their rejection of Him. Let's not forget that it is more than a mere possibility that they were not members of His sheep because they *believed* not. And furthermore, because they *would not* believe. Indeed that is exactly what our Lord told them as recorded in the 5th chapter of John's Gospel where we read:

> "Search the scriptures; for in them ye think ye have eternal life: and they are they which testify of me.
> "And ye will not come to me, that ye might have life.
> . . . . . .
> "How can ye believe, which receive honour one of another, and seek not the honour that cometh from God only?"

And what's more, He also said if they had believed Moses, they would have believed Him, for Moses wrote of Him.

Now notice what our Lord gives to those whom He calls His sheep.

> "My sheep hear my voice, and I know them, and they follow me:
> "And I give unto them eternal life; and they shall never perish, neither shall any man pluck them out of my hand.
> "My Father, which gave them me, is greater than all; and no man is able to pluck them out of my Father's hand."

Our Lord offers to His sheep salvation, not probation! He did not offer life for a "limited period" but He gives eternal life. His sheep are protected by His greatness and the power of His hand, and the power of His Father's hand, so that no man is able to pluck a sheep of His flock out of the hand of the Lord nor from the hand of His Father. That's salvation and salvation is the work of the Lord!

The Stones and the Testimony They Give

We should note what caused the trouble that feast day. Our Lord added, "I and my Father are one." Immediately the group "took up stones again to stone him." For a moment they were restrained by His words as He addressed them, "Many good works have I showed you from my Father; for which of those works do you stone me?" They answered Him, and one can delineate clearly the lines of anger that were indelibly stamped upon their faces, "For a good work we stone thee not; but for blasphemy; and because that thou, being a man, makest thyself God."

It cannot be made too clear that if Jesus were only a man, those Pharisees were justified in their rebellion against Him, for those to whom He addressed Himself plainly understood His answer to their perplexing question. The noteworthy feature is that while they came to Him for enlightenment, asking "Art thou the Christ?" when He answered them plainly, they took up stones to stone Him. Why did they take up stones? Incidentally, from where did they get the stones, for they were all in the Temple at the time? People usually do not find stones in Church.

Let's answer the second question first and we will discover another of those delightful, undesigned coincidences in the Scripture confirming the infallibility of the Bible. On two other occasions they took up stones to cast at Him and on each of the three times, He was in some part of the Temple, in the Cathedral if you please. For illustrative purposes only, let me present a current illustration. One would find it rather difficult to reconcile stone-piles in a cathedral court if for instance he attends St. Patrick's Cathedral in New York. There have been no loose stones around there for a good number of years. But if one attends the Cathedral of St. John the Divine in New York, he knows there have been a lot of stones around there for a long time, for the Cathedral has been in building forty-nine years and is not yet finished, and even today one finds heaps of stone around the place. The same was true in respect to the Temple "in the days of Christ and the Apostles." For "there was building in progress everywhere. The Herods were reconstructing many of the old cities and giving them names in honor of the Cæsars. The work on the Temple was practically continuous, sometimes as many as eighteen thousand workmen were employed." It is Dr. Christie, an authority on Palestine, who quotes these figures and who adds, "The question has been raised as to how it was possible for the people to take up stones for the purpose of stoning the Lord Jesus in the Temple area with its paved courts and absence of anything extraneous to its particular purposes. But we have the answer here. These courts were generally a great hive of busy laborers, and there were great heaps of stone and all sorts of building material at hand till the year *62 A. D.* when the work was concluded." Critics of the Bible, let those stones silence you for a while!

But why throw stones at Him? The people who did, gave the answer. They said, "For a good work we stone thee not." In other words, we recognize and even appreciate the good works that you have done, but that is no excuse for what you have said. We therefore stone you first, "for blasphemy," and second, "because that thou, being a man, makest thyself God." But what if the man *is* God manifest in the flesh? Then He is worthy to be worshipped; then He is equal with God; He is indeed God. It is the declaration of the New Testament that God clothed Himself in a body fashioned by His Holy Spirit in the womb of a virgin and revealed Himself to men so that He could die on a cross and make atonement for their sins, and thereby open up the avenue of approach by guilty sinners into the presence of a holy God.

Walk Forty-Eight

THE FINAL APOLOGETIC OF JESUS

IN our last study, we considered the three occasions recorded in St. John's Gospel, when the people picked up stones to stone our Lord. On each the action was called forth because of the claims that He made in respect to His relationship to His Father. It is noteworthy that at no time did they actually throw the stones. They merely picked them up. Evidently some unseen power prevented them from throwing the stones. Others may believe whatever they please as to what was the cause, but I prefer to believe the Bible record, that they could not because no man was capable of taking our Lord's life.

Now let's examine our Lord's defense of His claim. The Jews said, "For a good work we stone thee not; but for blasphemy; and because that thou, being a man, makest thyself God."

Commencing with verse 34, we read:

> "Jesus answered them, Is it not wrttten in your law, I said, Ye are gods?
> "If he called them gods, unto whom the word of God came, and the scripture cannot be broken;
> "Say ye of him, whom the Father hath sanctified, and sent into the world, Thou blasphemest; because I said, I am the Son of God?
> "If I do not the works of my Father, believe me not.
> "But if I do, though ye believe not me, believe the works: that ye may know, and believe, that the Father is in me, and I in him.
> "Therefore they sought again to take him: but he escaped out of their hand."

There are those who suggest that this answer by our Lord justifies the conclusion that God is the father of all men and that our Lord's coming was for the purpose of stimulating the inherent spark of divinity in each individual's life, thus bringing all men into a full consciousness of their sonship with God. Let's test that idea by an appeal to the Scriptures.

Who Are The "Gods"

As usual, our Lord always fell back upon the written Word. There can be no other court of appeal! "To the law and to the testimony: if they speak not according to this word, it is because there is no light in them." In other words, everything should be weighed by what the Bible has to say on the subject, and if there is any disagreement, it is because those who disagree with the Bible, have "no light in them." Our Lord referred to a verse of Scripture, "Is it not written in your law, I said, Ye are gods?" The passage is from the 82nd Psalm. We should read the Psalm in its entirety in order to get the setting in which this particular quotation is found.

> "God standeth in the congregation of the mighty; he judgeth among the gods.
> "How long will ye judge unjustly, and accept the persons of the wicked? Selah.
> "Defend the poor and fatherless: do justice to the afflicted and needy.

> "Deliver the poor and needy: rid them out of the hand of the wicked.
>
> "They know not, neither will they understand; they walk on in darkness: all the foundations of the earth are out of course.
>
> "I have said, Ye are gods; and all of you are children of the Most High.
>
> "But ye shall die like men, and fall like one of the princes.
>
> "Arise, O God, judge the earth: for thou shalt inherit all nations."

It is apparent that the subject of the Psalm is the judicial position occupied by those who are called "the mighty" or "the gods" whose business it is to execute judgment in the earth. The principle enunciated in the Psalm is in accord with the teaching of the New Testament Scripture as well. In the 13th chapter of Paul's letter to the Romans, we read (this of course was addressed to those who had already received Christ):

> "Let every soul be subject unto the higher powers. For there is no power but of God: the powers that be are ordained of God.
>
> "Whosoever therefore resisteth the power, resisteth the ordinance of God: and they that resist shall receive to themselves damnation.
>
> "For rulers are not a terror to good works, but to the evil."

Paul went on to say that the ruler "is the minister of God, a revenger to execute wrath upon him that doeth evil." Twice over in one verse, Paul insisted that rulers are "ministers of God." To resist them in the discharge of their divine prerogative is to resist the ordinance of God. This of course does not mean that when a ruler arrogates to himself powers that were never given to him, a Christian should bow to such arrogances, for Peter and John answered a council which did so by saying, "Whether it be right in the sight of God to hearken unto you more than unto God, judge ye." Rulers in their regular discharge of governmental functions stand therefore as representatives of God. Would God, more rulers would recognize this fact!

Now the writer of the 82nd Psalm, speaking on behalf of God, said: "You mighty in the earth, you that judge as my representatives, as gods in the earth; defend the poor and the fatherless; do justice to the afflicted: deliver the poor and the needy; remember, you stand as gods and all of you are children of the most High."

Children of God

As the most High God is the *possessor* of heaven and earth, so in a sense all men are "children of God." They are children of the most High. But notice the contrast that our Lord drew. He did not draw a comparison. We miss the point entirely if we assume He did. "Is it not written in your law ... *Ye* are gods?" But our Lord added, Since He (God) called them gods, "Say ye of him, whom the Father hath sanctified, and sent into the world, Thou blasphemest; because I said, *I am the Son of God?*" Our Lord therefore, did not place Himself on the level of man nor even on a level of "the mighty" among men. He said, "I am the son of God" which claim is as far apart from the position of "a god" as heaven is higher than the earth.

Now let us consider further this subject of God's relationship to the whole world. Will anyone be so naive as to suggest that God is uninterested in the things that are taking place in this world today? Is any man so devoid of a sense of the justice and righteousness of God as to believe that God will not bring to His bar of judgment the men who have been guilty of the atrocious acts of invasion that have taken place this past week? I tremble at the day when those men will stand before the bar of God's justice when God will demand of them an accounting for their wicked works.

God "hath made of one blood all nations of men for to dwell on all the face of the earth." Furthermore, God "hath made the world and all things therein." The Apostle Paul, when he preached on Mars Hill, called attention to the fact that this foundational truth was recognized even by one of the Grecian poets who said, "For we are also his offspring." The Apostle added, "For as much then as we are the offspring of God, we ought not to think that the Godhead is like unto gold or silver, or stone, graven by art and man's device." But between being "a child of God by faith in the Lord Jesus Christ" and being "His offspring" by virtue of having been made by the breath of His mouth, is the difference between being lost in eternity in a conscious possession of an *endless life,* and being in the presence of God, enjoying His fellowship, and the communion of the Spirit of God in a conscious bliss, enjoying *eternal life*. It is the clear, unequivocal testimony of the Word of God that, "as many as received him, (Christ) to them gave he power (authority) to become the sons of God, even to them that believe on his name: Which were born, not of blood, nor of the will of the flesh, nor of the will of man, but of God." This is the thing for which our Lord Jesus came into this world—to give life from the dead—to give new birth—to give eternal life.

As in the case of being an "offspring" of God and "a child" of His, there is a wideness like the wideness of the sea—so in the case of "a child" of His and "the Sonship of Christ," there is an infinite gulf of deity that separates us.

Our Lord said to the Pharisees, "If I do not the works of my Father, believe me not. But if I do, though ye believe not me, believe the works: that ye may know, and believe, that the Father is in me, and I in him." No man had ever made such a statement—"The Father is in me, and I in him." Incidentally, it is said of believers in the Lord Jesus Christ that they are "in Christ" and "Christ is in them," but it is never said that they are "in the Father" and "the Father in them." It is Christ alone who can say "The Father is in me, and I in him." It is true that our life "is hid *with* Christ *in* God," but it is written that "When Christ, who is our life, shall appear, then shall ye also appear with him in glory." God has had and only has one Son, but as the result of His coming into the world, He has begotten unto Himself a whole race of people who are children of God by faith in the Lord Jesus.

This apologetic of Christ did not satisfy the Pharisees, for "they sought again to take him:—but as usual "Jesus escaped out of their hands." Dr. A. T. Robertson beautifully put it when he said, "Overawed, but still angry, the stones fell to the ground, and Jesus walked out."

A Retreat Before the Advance to Calvary

As we examine the closing verses of this 10th chapter we find that our Lord retreated for a quiet visit to a little oasis in the desert of this earth. Our Lord had been in Jerusalem for some while past. During His visit there it had been exceedingly hectic. His soul had been in travail; there was controversy wherever He went. The Pharisees never left Him alone. They hounded Him with the idea of getting something that would offer an excuse to hail Him before the Roman governor. But now He left the city having escaped out of their hands. Commencing with verse 40, we read:

> "And (He) went away again beyond Jordan into the place where John at first baptized; and there he abode.
>
> "And many resorted unto him, and said, John did no miracle: but all things that John spake of this man were true.
>
> "And many believed on him there."

There in that quiet place beyond Jordan He abode, and *many people* came unto Him. How evident it is that the common people heard our Lord gladly. But observe that it was the magnetic power of the Person of Jesus that drew the multitude from the various cities to this oasis beyond Jordan, the place where John previously baptized and ministered. Supreme above all is the blessed Person of our Lord Jesus. The multitude recognized Him, and what's more, they rejoiced and revelled in His presence. There is something about the Person of our Lord that captivates the hearts of men who remain sufficiently long in His presence to hear His gracious words; which attraction cannot be matched by the drawing power of blood ties, country ties, family ties, or any other ties. The Bible calls it the love of God in Christ Jesus. He is the revelation of the very heart of God, of the very bosom of God. Those who listened to His words were not driven out of His presence but rather, they bowed before Him and rejoiced in His presence.

It is written, "many resorted unto him." The same is true now. Out of every country and tribe and nation and tongue, irrespective of the differences of language and of form and of color, men who have heard Him find a fellowship with Him and in Him that gives them a consciousness of His peace which is beyond the possibility of the human mind to comprehend or the human tongue to describe. What's more, they recognized in the bosom of our Lord the heart of a man.

The Power of a Ministry

Dr. S. D. Gordon tells of a minister whom he knew down in the Southland "whose public service took him to all parts of our country. He had been reared in the South and knew the colored people by heart, and loved them. And when he returned to his Southern home town, he would frequently preach for the colored people. He was preaching to them one Lord's Day with the simplicity and fervor for which he was noted.

"At the close among others, one big black man grasped his hand hard as he thanked him for the preaching. And then with his great child-eyes, big and aglow, he said, 'Youse got a white skin, but youse got a black heart!' But you know what he meant—you have a black man's heart, you have a heart like mine; your heart makes my heart burn."

That's exactly the experience the two disciples had on their journey from Jerusalem to Emmaus as our Lord joined them. Their hearts burned within them as He spoke to them about Himself. When He speaks, the heart always throbs with burning delight!

Now one further thought ere we leave this tenth chapter. Here is a touching but powerful comment on the ministry of John the Baptist: "John did no miracle." The Bible acknowledges that John never presumed to have the power to accomplish miracles. But said the people as they remembered what John said about the Lord Jesus: "All things that John spake of this man were true." There is nothing so fruitful as a ministry devoted to preaching Christ. A natural man may cry out for a sign but a spiritual man will always crave "the Word." John had evidently presented a true picture of the Lord Jesus. When Jesus came, they looked at the "blueprint" that John had drawn of Him; then they looked at our Lord in His own Person. They found that the "blueprint" and the Person were the same. Would God that it could be said of every preacher! When such a ministry is performed, the result will always be exactly the same as that which took place on this occasion, even though John the Baptist was already in the grave: "Many believed on him." There is a fruit that accompanies the preaching of the Lord Jesus that is as sure as when a seed is planted in the earth and watered by the rains from heaven and nurtured and warmed by the sun. It is inevitable as a God-sent man preaches Christ and Him crucified that men will fall in love with the Lord and bow in obedience before Him.

Walk Forty-Nine

HOW GOD MAKES OUR DISAPPOINTMENTS HIS APPOINTMENTS

WE are about to consider what is universally recognized as the outstanding miracle in the miracle-ministry of Jesus of Nazareth. It was the climax of His ministry as far as miracles are concerned; it crowned His public ministry. It was the last great miracle that He performed. Strange as it may seem, it led to His final rejection by the Sanhedrin and to His crucifixion; not because the miracle lacked evidence and support, nor because a fraud had been perpetrated by some hokus-pokus incantations usually muttered by sorcerers, but by the unanswerable testimony that the miracle itself bore to the Person of Jesus Christ.

It has been reported that Spinoza once said, "That if he could believe the raising of Lazarus, he would tear to shreds his system and humbly accept the creed of Christians." Undoubtedly the noted philosopher was sincere in his view, but the fact of the matter is he would have been incapable of doing so, seeing that faith is not born of reason. Men do not bow before the Lordship of Christ as a result of a mental assent to the historic facts of Christianity! Nevertheless, faith is not an unreasonable thing, nor has the Lord ever asked us to throw our reason to the winds. He has several times invited us to reason together with Him.

This is a wonderful chapter of Scripture. We see our Lord in His majesty and glory, in the perfection of His Deity, and the power of His voice; while at the same time we note the tenderness of His heart and the limitations of His flesh, the sympathy of His being which expressed itself in tears, and the anger of His indignation against the fruit of sin. We see the faith and devotion of two humble believers; then the shaking of their faith; followed by the disappointment and trial that they experienced, and finally, their appreciation that He was more than able for every emergency. We find gladness and sorrow, clouds and sunshine blended as they are nowhere else to be found. Here is the answer to the insoluble questions of life and death!

Rational Assent vs. Faith

Before taking up the record, let me discuss further the subject of rational reason which expresses itself in assent, and the matter of saving faith. There is a vast difference between the two. I do not suppose there is a single event in history except the resurrection of our Lord Jesus Christ, more fully attested than the fact of the raising of Lazarus from the dead. Both friend and foe of our Lord were present. It could not be refuted. The enemies of our Lord did not attempt to deny the miracle. Even the chief priests and Pharisees when they met together in council said: "What do we? *for this man doeth many miracles.* If we let him thus alone, all men will believe on him: and the Romans shall come and take away both our place and our nation." They gave rational assent to the physical factors of the miracle but they did not have saving faith. Miracles may sustain and confirm faith, but they do not produce saving faith, seeing that saving faith involves embracing the teaching of Scripture concerning sin and the Person and work of Jesus Christ.

A book that has been a great blessing to my heart is entitled "Cardiphonia." It was written by John Newton, one of the great English preachers during the American Revolutionary period. In one of his letters to a young English curate who found himself in a maze of spiritual darkness, unable to comprehend the great fundamental doctrines of the New Testament Scriptures, John Newton wrote: "I believe fallen reason is of itself utterly incapable of assenting to the great *truths* of revelation. It may assent to the terms in which they are proposed, but it must put its own interpretation upon them or it would despise them. The natural man can neither receive nor discern the things of God: and if any one would be wise, the apostle's first advice to him is, Let him become a fool that he may be wise; for the wisdom of the world is foolishness with God."

The rational assent to the historic record will never lead a soul out of darkness into light, but faith which is also a gift from God, bows before the glorious Person of Christ and cries out, My Lord and my God!

Now let's look at the record. Notice the opening verses:

> "Now a certain man was sick, named Lazarus, of Bethany, the town of Mary and her sister Martha.

"(It was that Mary which anointed the Lord with ointment, and wiped his feet with her hair, whose brother Lazarus was sick.)
"Therefore his sisters sent unto him, saying, Lord, behold, he whom thou lovest is sick."

Those three verses not only contain some deep Biblical truths, but also present a glorious picture. In the first place, the man was sick. That's not an unusual thing. Sickness has been one of the common experiences of men, despite the attempt of some to suggest that sickness is unreal, an error of the mortal mind. In this case, the man's *mind* was not sick, it was his *body*. The man's name is given as Lazarus; he lived in Bethany. Lazarus means "whom God aids." He lived just two miles from Jerusalem. We learn from the Scriptures that it was a place to which our Lord frequently resorted, and where he felt at home. Evidently the two sisters who lived with their brother, were such outstanding characters that they wrote their names indelibly upon the town so that it was impossible to think of the town apart from them. The Scripture says, "Bethany was the town of Mary and her sister Martha." What influence those two young ladies exerted in that town!

The Unfailing Physician

The Apostle John is careful to tell us some details regarding Mary. "It was that Mary which anointed our Lord with ointment, and wiped his feet with her hair, whose brother Lazarus was sick." Mary had no misgivings about her brother's situation. She knew it was sickness. She, together with Martha, when they realized the character of the illness, sent a messenger with a brief note addressed to the Lord which to my mind is the most perfect expression of faith and confidence possible to find anywhere in Scripture. They simply said, "Lord, behold, he whom thou lovest is sick." They knew Christ. They knew not only His power, but His love and His devotion to their brother Lazarus and to them. They had such deep confidence in Him that they did not ask a single thing from Him. They did not say, "Lord, hurry, please come to our brother, do something to deliver us out of our present circumstances." No, they did not ask anything. They simply said, "Lord, behold, he whom thou lovest is sick."

It was sufficient for those sisters to rest in the knowledge that their Lord knew the situation. Some of us have had family physicians whose devotion has been one of the many fine things characterizing their great profession of medicine. We have had confidence in them. In some cases, all that was necessary was to simply acquaint the doctor with our situation and he would drop everything and come to our homes. It is amazing what confidence we have in doctors and how willing we are to put our most cherished possession in their hands.

In that connection, here is a letter written by John Newton to a man who lay ill of "a tumor," who had been operated on by a surgeon but was still in deep pain and distress. Newton wrote a few words of encouragement to him.

> "I hope to be informed in due time, that the Lord has given you full health and cure. He has preserved me hitherto from the hands of surgeons; but I feel as if my flesh would prove, as you say, a very coward, were it needful to submit to a painful operation. Yet I observe, when such operations are necessary, if people are satisfied of a surgeon's skill and prudence, they will not only yield to be cut at his pleasure, without pretending to direct him where, or how long he shall make the incision, but will thank and pay him for putting them to pain, because they believe it for their advantage. I wish I could be more like them in my concerns. My body, as I said, through mercy, is free from considerable ailments, but I have a soul that requires surgeon's work continually;—there is some tumor to be discussed or laid open, some dislocation to be reduced, some fracture to be healed almost daily. It is my great mercy, that one who is infallible in skill, who exercises incessant care and boundless compassion toward all his patients, has undertaken my case; and, complicated as it is, I dare not doubt his making a perfect cure. Yet, alas! I too often discover such impatience, distrust, and complaining, when under his hand—am so apt to find fault with the *instruments* he is pleased to make use of—so ready to think the salutary wounds he makes unnecessary, or too large; in a word, I show such a promptness to control were I able, or to direct his operations, that, were not his patience beyond expression, he would before now, have given me up. I am persuaded, no money would induce Mr. ———— to attend upon a patient who should act towards him as I have towards my best Physician. Sometimes I indulge a hope that I am growing wiser, and think surely after such innumerable proofs as I have had that he does all things well, I shall now be satisfied to leave myself quietly and without reserve to his disposal. A thousand such surrenders I have made, and a thousand times I have interpretatively retracted them. Yet still he is gracious. O, how shall I praise him at last!"

The Physician's Devotion

Mary and Martha had such absolute trust in the Lord that they rested confidently in the fact that He knew of their trial. Notice what happened when Jesus heard about it. Addressing the messenger and His disciples, He said, "This sickness is not unto death, but for the glory of God, that the Son of God might be glorified thereby." What a remarkable revelation, that any man could be called upon to endure sickness for the glory of God and that the Son of God could be glorified thereby! That's something new. That puts the trials and disappointments of life upon a level that is divine. That indicates that God has a purpose to make all grace abound, even when sickness and sorrow and disappointment enter a life and a home of one of His own. It may be difficult to recognize it at the time, for it is contrary to our ideas. We are so apt to think that the Son of God is glorified when we are up and about, feeling splendidly and having no cause for complaint but rather with a word of thanksgiving on our lips. Yet, here the Lord said it *is* possible, and in one specific case it *was so,* that sickness can be for the glory of God. Since that was true in one case, who will question the fact that it may be true in any number of cases. Of one thing we are sure, we have the testimony of the Word of God that all things work *together* for good to them that love the Lord.

It is interesting to note that the Scripture is careful to tell us of the love that Mary and Martha had for the Lord, and the love and devotion that the Lord had for them. Verse 5 reads: "Now Jesus loved Martha, and her sister, and Lazarus." Careful Bible students have recognized that a knowledge of the Greek text frequently lends an added beauty to the divine record which is lost in our English translation. We have such a case in the 21st chapter of this Gospel, reporting the conversation between the Apostle Peter and our Lord. Three times over the Lord asked Peter if he loved Him. Three times Peter answered ". . . Yea Lord, thou knowest that I love thee." The fact of the matter is that on two of the three occasions our Lord used a different word than did the Apostle. He used the Greek word *Agapao,* but Peter continued to respond with the use of the word *Phileo.* Finally, our Lord stooped to Peter's level by using the word *Phileo* and in doing so He broke the Apostle's heart. We lose that touch in our English translation.

The word *Phileo* is a verb which "describes affection and emotion in its fulness." *Agapao* "has an entirely different significance." It means love, but "it is the love of intelligence, of judgment and consideration." Dr. Goodspeed interprets the word *Agapao* by our English word "devotion."

It therefore gives an added touch to this record of the 11th chapter when we understand that in the message of the sisters to our Lord ". . . he whom thou lovest is sick" they used the word *Phileo* whereas John, in describing the Lord's love of Lazarus and his sisters Martha and Mary, used the word *Agapao,* which means devotion. Our Lord had a deeper love for that family than even the sisters recognized. He was *devoted* to them. He was so *devoted* to them that though He knew Lazarus was sick and knew that he would die, He remained where He was for two additional days. He did not visit them; He did not go out of His way hastening to their home to minister to them. The fact of the matter is upon the death of Lazarus, *their* friends came to comfort them but the Lord stayed away. He was so devoted to them that He knew the best thing that could happen to them was to experience that hour of disappointment. Were we to ask those three, was it worth it, are you happy that you had to go through that experience? I have no doubt that each one would respond with a hearty "Amen."

It is also apparent from the record that our Lord permitted the household to have that disappointing experience in order to teach a lesson to the disciples. In other words, one family suffered for the benefit of others. Is it any wonder that the Scripture says, "We know that all things work *together* for good to them that love God." There isn't an experience, a disappointment or a trial that visits a believer but it has passed the Divine Will. The Lord recognizes that it is the best thing that could happen for our own benefit and enjoyment.

SICKNESS AND FAITH

There are some who have a mistaken notion as to what constitutes faith, and what causes sickness. Even some Christians arrive at the erroneous conclusion that when sickness touches the body of a believer it is because that believer has himself or herself sinned in some way. Therefore, all sickness and disease to them is punitive. They also conclude that if the sufferer will repent of his sins he can demand that God heal him. That demand is to them an expression of faith.

In the first place, this incident settles the question of whether sickness is always the result of sin. There is no mention in this chapter that Lazarus sinned. To the contrary, he was visited with illness in order that God might be glorified thereby. In fact, the Scripture goes so far as to say that God can use the wrath of man to praise Him. No, sickness is not always the result of sin in an individual's life. It may be, but it is not always so. It may even be for the purpose of the glory of the Son of God.

Now then, what is faith? I am referring to believers who have already received the testimony of God concerning His Son. Faith does not express itself in *demands* upon God. Faith bows in obedience before the divine will. Faith looks up into the face of the Son of God and says, "Though he slay me, yet will I trust in him." In his despair a believer may cry out to know the reason why, but that is because he is unable to fully appreciate and understand and see the purposes of God now. But faith throws itself unencumbered upon the mercy of God and trusts Him implicitly. Incidentally, that's exactly what faith also is in the matter of salvation. Faith is not a mental assent to historic truth, but faith is casting one's self upon the mercy of God, believing the testimony of God concerning the blood as an atonement for the sins of the individual as well as the world. Faith revels in that display of His love!

Walk Fifty

CONQUEROR OVER DEATH AND DECAY!

CONSIDERING the devotion that the Lord had for Mary, Martha, and Lazarus, one would suppose that He would either have headed for Bethany, or done what He did in the case of the nobleman's son who was sick to the point of death, whose father begged our Lord, "Sir, come down ere my child die." Our Lord did not go then either, but He said, "Go thy way; thy son liveth." Call it absent treatment if you will, but He did not even use that method in the case of Lazarus, for His thoughts are not our thoughts, nor His ways our ways!

The fact is that Lazarus probably was dead even at the time the messenger arrived to tell our Lord of his illness. Why didn't He do something? He didn't even attend the funeral service. As far as we know, He sent no message of condolence to the bereaved sisters. He abode two days still in the same place where He was. What's more, He said to His disciples, *"I am glad* for your sakes that I was not there . . ." Glad? Yes! As far as I know that's the only time the expression is used concerning our Lord. Imagine the Son of God being *glad* because He was not in Bethany to prevent the death of a friend, or to relieve the sorrowing and disturbing thoughts of two sisters who loved Him even unto death. Yet here it is written in the 15th verse, "And I am glad for your sakes that I was not there, to the intent that ye may believe; nevertheless let us go unto him." He did not say, "let us go unto Bethany," but, "let us go unto *him."* Our Lord knew what He intended to do.

The disciples were intent on preventing the Lord from going to Judea. They reminded Him that the Judeans of late sought to stone him. Why go there? To this our Lord responded "Are there not twelve hours in the day? If any man walk in the day, he stumbleth not, because he seeth the light of this world. But if a man walk in the night, he stumbleth, because there is no light in him."

Dr. A. T. Robertson directs attention to the fact that, "The ancients had poor illumination at night as indeed we did before Edison gave us electric light. Pedestrians, in the ancient days, actually used to have little lamps fastened on their feet to light the path." Our modern warfare which requires a blackout at night would indicate that we haven't advanced very much! Indeed, to date in Great Britain, more people have died from accidents due to the blackouts, than soldiers on the field of battle. How true it is "man has the capacity for light, but is not the source of light."

After the idea had an opportunity to sink into the minds of the disciples, our Lord added, "Our friend Lazarus sleepeth; but I go, that I may awake him out of sleep." Again the disciples thought they knew better than their Lord, so they suggested, "Lord, if he sleep, he shall do well." They were reminding Him that since Lazarus was asleep it was evident that the crisis had passed. You who have watched over the sick-bed of loved ones know what a great relief was experienced when you knew the crisis was past. I shall never forget an experience I witnessed along that line some years ago. A friend of mine was ill with pneumonia. It was the night the crisis was to take place. I visited the home that evening with another friend. About 10 o'clock the young husband began to perspire. My, how the perspiration rolled off him and how careful all were that he should not get into a draught. And then, after successfully changing his linens, the perspiration ceased. He turned his head on the pillow and went to sleep. What a relief to that young wife who waited on him incessantly. So the disciples said, Lord, if Lazarus is asleep so much the better; there is therefore no necessity for you to go to Judea and jeopardize your own safety. Then said our Lord plainly, "Lazarus is dead"; and in the same breath He added, "And I am glad for your sakes that I was not there, to the intent that ye may believe; nevertheless let us go unto him."

Martha's Approach

Thomas, who could never be charged with looking on the bright side, turned to his fellow disciples and said, "let us also go, that we may die with him." One thing is sure, our Lord could never get much comfort from His disciples. They treked their way to Bethany and when they were near to the town, someone told Martha that "Jesus was coming." She immediately rose up, left the house and went to meet our Lord, while Mary sat still in the house; typical of Martha, for it certainly fits into her character as we know it from the Scriptures. Martha did not wait for the Lord to say a word to her, either of greeting or consolation, but she blurted out as only a Martha can do, "Lord, *if thou hadst been here,* my brother had not died." She was unaware that our Lord had told the disciples *He was glad He was not there.* There can be no doubt that had He been in Bethany, there never would have been a funeral. He broke up every funeral procession.

For a long time I labored under the impression that Martha's comment was in the nature of a rebuke, thus putting the responsibility upon the Lord, as if to say, "Lord, you were late. Had you come when you received the message; had you spoken the word, *you* could have prevented this. You therefore are responsible." At least that is what *I thought* Martha meant!

Many of us, saint and sinner alike, have blamed God for disasters that have taken place because our limited knowledge made us unaware of the movements behind the scene and the purposes in the eternal councils of God. I had to go through the experience of losing my own mother before I understood Martha's words. Incidentally, Mary said the same thing when she came, in answer to the Master's call. When she met the Lord she did the very thing you would expect a Mary to do, she *fell down* at His feet saying, "Lord, if thou hadst been here, my brother had not died." I am thoroughly convinced that neither of the two sisters had a thought in their minds of criticism or rebuke or disappointment in their Lord, but their remark was a beautiful expression of faith and confidence. *If* their Lord had been present, death would never have dared to enter their home! Death flees in the presence of the Author of life. If my Lord had been here, physical death would never have entered into our home.

But someone may ask, Why the necessity for all this? Why did He not speak the word and prevent the experience of death? Why did He not relieve the suffering of heart and anguish of mind on the part of the two bereaved sisters. Why? Because He knew that those disciples after His return to the Father's House would suffer trials and disappointments, and would sometimes find the heavens silent. He wanted to teach them that even if He were silent, if the heavens seemed to be made of brass, He was not unmindful of every detail that was taking place in their lives. Such experiences would thus give them the incomparable privilege of remaining faithful unto Him under trial.

Martha seemed to clutch at a ray of hope. She vaguely hinted to the Lord that there was still a possibility of doing something, for she added, "... even now, whatsoever thou wilt ask of God, God will give it thee." Our Lord answered, "Thy brother shall rise again." Martha said, "I know that he shall rise again in the resurrection at the last day." Then came this wonderful declaration of our Lord, "I am the resurrection, and the life: he that believeth in me, though he were dead, yet shall he live: And whosoever liveth and believeth in me shall never die." Addressing a challenge to Martha, He said, "Believest thou this?" Incidentally, how poverty stricken would this poor world be, if it were not for the experience that brought forth this declaration of Christ. At every funeral service that it has been my lot to attend, I have heard that passage of Scripture quoted. It is an incomparable word, an awe inspiring word! It answers the questions of our minds. It stills the storms of our hearts.

Martha was not quite able to take in all that our Lord said, so she took refuge behind what she *did know* and believe, by answering, "Yea, Lord: I believe that thou art the Christ, the Son of God, which should come into the world." Then she left, as our Lord had asked her to call Mary.

"Jesus Wept"

There were some Judean friends in the Bethany house who had come to comfort Mary and her sister Martha. When they noticed that Mary rose up hastily and went out, they followed and said, "She goeth unto the grave to weep there." *That's a poor place to go to weep.* Mary went to the only *Person* in the world who could understand tears; she went to the Lord Jesus. She fell down at his feet and weeping said, "Lord, if thou hadst been here, my brother had not died."

The tears of Mary and the lamentations of the Judeans who came with her, caused our Lord to groan, or as Dr. G. Campbell Morgan puts it, "He was moved with wrath within His spirit, and troubled Himself" so that our Lord asked, "Where have ye laid him?" Incidentally, as Dr. Morgan correctly observed, "This is the only occasion in all the record, of Jesus asking anyone for information." They said unto Him, "Lord, come and see." And then we have that marvelous touch of compassion expressed in two words only, comprising "the shortest verse in the Bible, but no verse carries more meaning in it— 'Jesus wept.'" Once again our English translation obscures a precious thought which is apparent in the Greek text. The Judeans who came to Mary's house to weep, probably also included what were commonly called professional mourners. They moaned aloud. The word that is used to describe their weeping clearly infers that idea. But in telling of the tears of our Lord and the fact that He wept, the Scripture does not use the same word. It uses a word which describes the quiet flowing of tears.

Usually it is not the people who cry the loudest and moan the most boisterously who suffer the deepest; but rather those who do not show on the outside their deep inward sorrow of heart. Even the Judeans who wailed so loudly recognized the love behind the tears of Christ, for they said, "Behold how he loved him! And some of them said, Could not this man, which opened the eyes of the blind, have caused that even this man should not have died?" The Scripture tells us that again our Lord groaned within Himself and cometh to the grave.

Undoubtedly the home of Mary, Martha and Lazarus was more than of moderate circumstances. It appears that the grave was close by and may even have been in a garden connected with their own home. "It was a cave, and a stone lay upon it. Jesus said, Take ye away the stone. Martha, the sister of him that was dead, saith unto him, Lord, by this time he stinketh: for he hath been dead four days." I wish we had a candid picture of the expression on Martha's face. She knew that decay had set into that human body in four days. She knew the stench that would come from an open grave. The idea of removing the stone shocked and surprised Martha. Therefore, in her answer, she as much as said, "Lord, do you know what you are asking? We ought not to push the stone aside; putrefaction has already set in. Lazarus has been dead four days!" But our Lord said unto her, "Said I not unto thee, that, if thou wouldest believe, thou shouldest see the glory of God?"

Crying With a Loud Voice

Then they took away the stone from the place where the dead was laid. We can readily picture the tense moment. Not a whisper was to be heard. One could hear a pin drop. And in that tense silence, our Lord lifted up His eyes and said, "Father, I thank thee that thou hast heard me. And I knew that thou hearest me always: but because of the people which stand by I said it, that they may believe that thou hast sent me." And when He had thus spoken, He did something which He never did prior to that hour. In the prophecy of Isaiah, Jehovah presents His servant, the Messiah, in these words: "Behold my servant, whom I uphold: mine elect, in whom my soul delighteth; I have put my spirit upon him: he shall bring forth judgment to the Gentiles. He shall not cry, nor lift up, nor cause his voice to be heard in the street. A bruised reed shall he not break, and the smoking flax shall he not quench: he shall bring forth judgment unto truth." In other words, our Lord would minister quietly, graciously and tenderly; but successfully. But here our Lord *cried with a loud voice,* "Lazarus, come forth." In that deathly silence when all was tense, the Son of God's cry was heard by every individual present, "Lazarus, come forth. And he that was dead came forth, bound hand and foot with grave clothes: and his face was bound about with a napkin."

Dr. Wilbur M. Smith tells this interesting story which Dr. Lincoln A. Ferris, pastor of the First Church of San Diego, Calif., gave from his own life. Dr. Ferris said, "For four years I lived in Dobbs Ferry, New York, the home of Robert Ingersoll. It was said that he (Ingersoll) used to tell this story: 'I was never nonplussed but once. I was lecturing one night and took occasion to show that the resurrection of Lazarus was a planned affair to bolster the waning fortunes of Jesus. Lazarus was to take sick and die. The girls were to bury him and send for Jesus. Lazarus was to feign death till Jesus should come and say "Lazarus, come forth." To emphasize the situation I said, "Can any man here tell me why Jesus said, 'Lazarus, come forth'?" Down by the door, a pale-faced white-haired man rose, and with a shrill voice said: "Yes Sir! I can tell you. If my Lord had not said 'Lazarus' he would have had the whole graveyard of Bethany come out to him."

Walk Fifty-One

THE IRRESISTIBLE FORCE OF A SILENT TESTIMONY

I HAVEN'T any idea whether a P. T. Barnum or a John Ringling lived during the Gospel period, but I do know this, that Lazarus, who had the unique experience of being in the grave four days, never *exploited his experience*. Barnum would have gone to the other ends of the earth if he could have gotten hold of a man who had spent four days in a grave and who was alive to tell the story. All through the ages there have been men and women who have willingly sold themselves to this world and who have had no qualms about *trading* on their supposedly unique experiences. But Lazarus was not of that type. It is an arresting thought, but it is a fact, that not one single word is recorded of anything that Lazarus ever said—but what a testimony that man exercised by simply being alive. We are so prone to exaggeration, to talk about ourselves, to extol our virtues, to minimize our sins and defects, because *we* want the limelight. The shocking thing is that there are some Christians who love the place of prominence. It was true, Lazarus was a drawing card. He also bore such an irresistible testimony for the Lord, to the power of His Word and to the glory of His Person, that the Pharisees were all for putting Lazarus to death as well as the Lord. That's bearing an effective testimony!

When a Christian lives a resurrection life before the world, that life in itself is a most potent testimony to the Person of Christ. We have snatches of that type of thing in the Acts of the Apostles where the people took note that the disciples had been with Jesus. There was something about their countenance and their behavior which stamped them as being separate from other men. They were different! So too was Lazarus. His silent but unanswerable testimony led many to a knowledge of the Lord Jesus. What's more, Lazarus never put on a theatrical exploit. He did not build a temple, nor did he call attention to himself, but he lived a life before men; a resurrected life, if you please.

The Grave Clothes

Now let's look more closely at the divine record of this event. No one knows for certain just how Lazarus was bound. All that we know is that he was bound hand and foot with grave clothes and that his face was bound about with a napkin. Some brilliant critics have suggested, "How could Lazarus come forth if he were bound hand and foot?" Sir, the Christ who could call a dead man back to life would hardly have any difficulty with the mere matter of grave clothes.

It is interesting to observe two things in connection with this record: first, what our Lord did; second, what our Lord commanded either the people or His disciples to do. He alone had the power to bring the dead back to life. It was He who cried with a loud voice, "Lazarus, come forth." But He did not remove the stone nor did He remove the grave clothes. He asked that the stone be lifted and He instructed the disciples concerning Lazarus, "Loose him, and let him go." It has sometimes been suggested that God helps them who help themselves. That's an observation that hardly has the backing of Scripture. But this we can say: there are certain things that our Lord gives us the privilege of doing, and indeed never relieves us from the responsibility of doing. He could have removed the stone, He could have loosed the grave clothes; but He did neither, because *we* could do both.

This particular miracle is the last of the seven signs recorded in St. John's Gospel. All seven bear their effectual testimony to the deity and glory of our Lord Jesus Christ. They were intended for that purpose. They were done, not to draw attention to those upon whom the signs were performed, but to the One who performed the miracles. There is a spiritual application in each instance. In this particular case, it is so evident that it hardly needs comment. All of us are or were dead in trespasses and in sins. Some of us have experienced life from the dead. We have been raised from spiritual death into newness of life with God. That's a miracle just as glorious and equally as pronounced as the raising of Lazarus. Only our Lord can raise a spiritually dead person unto spiritual life. But He has given to men of His own choosing, men whom He has gifted as pastors and teachers, to loose the grave clothes from a resurrected saint. It is the business of a man of God to loose a redeemed sinner from the grave clothes that bound him to this world. What a sight Lazarus would have been if he had walked around Bethany wearing grave clothes! A Barnum might have had him do something of that sort, but the Lord would not. It is just as much a monstrosity to see a Christian walking around garbed with the grave clothes of this world.

I recall with much pleasure a comment of saintly Bishop Moule, on a verse or two of the 6th chapter of Paul's letter to the Romans, wherein the Apostle said: "But God be thanked, that ye were the servants of sin, but ye have obeyed from the heart that form of doctrine which was delivered you. Being then made free from sin, ye became the servants of righteousness." Bishop Moule aptly remarked that there is no such thing as a no-man's land in the Christian's experience. We *were* the servants of sin. We *were* slaves to our sin. We *have* obeyed from the heart that form of doctrine which was delivered unto us. Incidentally, observe that it is obedience to a doctrine which brings release. Our Lord put it, "Ye shall know the *truth,* and the *truth* shall make you free." Now then, said the Apostle, "being made free from sin, ye became the bond-slaves of righteousness." It is obligatory on the part of an individual who has obeyed the Gospel to cease from sin, and become a bond-slave of righteousness. He has no business going around with the grave clothes about him. He is an enigma and absolutely of no value to God as far as a testimony is concerned, and certainly no value to this world, for the world does not place any stock in the life or the testimony of a worldly-minded Christian. It is a solemn command, "Let every one that nameth the name of Christ depart from iniquity."

Our Great Book

The Bible is the most interesting book in the world. Trite you say? Yes! But it is true! It is interesting not only from the point of view of what it does say, but also what it does not say. Here's a book declaring that it speaks in the name of God. Again and again the writers preface their words with the phrase, "Thus saith the Lord." It is a book that tells us how to be delivered from our sins; how to live in fellowship with God; how to avoid hell and how to get to heaven. And yet it gives us very little about heaven and very little about hell. There are many things we would like to know, but what the Bible gives is so definitely and plainly stated that only one who seeks to twist the Scriptures can miss its message. For instance, all of us would like to know whether the fire of which our Lord speaks in describing the suffering of the wicked dead out of Christ, is figurative or literal. But no one can say that the Bible is silent on the *fact* of the eternal torment of the wicked dead. There are many things we would like to know about heaven, as for instance, whether a little child will always be a little child and whether we will recognize each other in the relationships we now enjoy. There are so many questions we would like to have answered. But of this there can be no doubt, that heaven is the delightful abode of every believer in the Lord Jesus and that each will enter into the full possession of all the glories which our Lord purchased for us at the cross of Calvary.

The Bible was never written to satisfy curiosity. Wouldn't we like to know what Lazarus thought while he was in the grave? We would be interested to know what he said to his sisters after he returned to his home. Oh there are so many things that we would have asked Lazarus, but not a thing is recorded for us in the Scriptures. Curiosity may have killed a cat, but it never enlightened a saint.

The Lord only reveals to us that which we need to know. He never satisfies idle curiosity. On one occasion, the Pharisees answering, said, "Master, we would see a sign from thee. But he answered and said unto them, An evil and adulterous generation seeketh after a sign; and there shall no sign be given to it, but the sign of the prophet Jonas: For as Jonas was three days and three nights in the whale's belly; so shall the Son of man be three days and three nights in the heart of the earth."

Of course Lazarus must have talked about his experience, but it has pleased the Spirit of God not to allow you and me to know about it since the purpose of the miracle was not to exploit Lazarus, but "for the glory of God, and that the Son of God might be glorified thereby."

Tennyson grasped the idea when he wrote these words:

> "When Lazarus left his charnel-cave,
>   And home to Mary's house returned,
>   Was this demanded—if he yearn'd
> To hear her weeping by his grave?
>
> "Where wert thou, brother, those four days?"
>   There lives no record or reply,
>   Which telling what it is to die
> Had surely added praise to praise.
>
> "From every house the neighbours met,
>   The streets were fill'd with joyful sound,
>   A solemn gladness even crown'd
> The purple brows of Olivet.
>
> "Behold a man raised up by Christ!
>   The rest remaineth unreveal'd;
>   He told it not; or something seal'd
> The lips of that evangelist."

Now let's read the record of what happened after Lazarus was raised from the dead. Beginning with verse 45 we learn:

> "Then many of the Jews which came to Mary, and had seen the things which Jesus did, believed on him.
> "But some of them went their ways to the Pharisees, and told them what things Jesus had done.
> "Then gathered the chief priests and the Pharisees a council, and said, What do we? for this man doeth many miracles.
> "If we let him thus alone, all men will believe on him: and the Romans shall come and take away both our place and nation.
> "And one of them, Caiaphas, being the high priest that same year, said unto them, Ye know nothing at all,
> "Nor consider that it is expedient for us, that one man should die for the people, and that the whole nation perish not.
> "And this spake he not of himself: but being high priest that year, he prophesied that Jesus should die for that nation;
> "And not for that nation only, but that also he should gather together in one the children of God that were scattered abroad.
> "Then from that day forth they took counsel together for to put him to death.

> "Jesus therefore walked no more openly among the Jews; but went thence unto a country near to the wilderness, into a city called Ephraim, and there continued with his disciples."

The 45th verse is pertinent for it evidences the very things that I have attempted to say. This sign was not to focus attention on Lazarus but upon Christ, for we read, that "many of the Jews which came to Mary, and had seen *the things which Jesus did,* believed on him."

The Bitter Hatred of the Council

One would have supposed that such a miracle would have caused the chief priests and Pharisees who represented the ruling religious class to embrace and rejoice over the One who had come with power to raise the dead. But they were so blinded in their prejudice and hatred, that in despair they cried out, "What do we? for this man doeth many miracles. If we let him thus alone, all men will believe on him: and the Romans shall come and take away both our place and nation." Of course they did not realize that their rejection of Christ would lead to the very thing they feared. The Roman hordes did come. They took away both their place and nation.

There must have been much speech making at that council, but we have the record of only one. That was given by Caiaphas who was the high priest that same year. Some differences of opinion center around the import of the speech but the comment which G. Campbell Morgan gives on it may or may not be accurate but it is at least pointed.

"In all literature," writes Dr. Morgan, "there is on record no more clever and damnable speech than that! It was the voice of the politician at his worst who was not prepared to say with blunt brevity what he meant, but would clothe a dastardly intention in elegant phrases. Caiaphas began very cleverly. I never read it without thinking it is a wonderful way to begin a speech, if you are taking part in a debate, or are on a committee. He begins by saying, 'Ye know nothing at all.' That is the way to dismiss the previous speakers. Well, what do *you* know, Caiaphas? Now mark the elegance of the phrasing. 'It is expedient for you that one man should die for the people, and that the whole nation perish not.' That is all. A very brief speech. It simply meant: There is only one thing to do, kill Him, get Him out of the way at any cost. It would not do to put it like that, so he put it on the ground of political expediency and national well-being. It was a most dastardly speech, but it won on the human level. . . It is expedient! What deviltry can be done in the name of expediency!

"What was the counsel they took? They determined to kill Him. That is how it ended. 'From that day forth they took counsel that they might put him to death.' "

At the beginning of our Lord's public ministry the Holy Spirit drove Him into the wilderness to be tested by Satan. At the close of His public ministry, during which time every footstep was a benediction and every breath sweetened the air, it is arresting that He could no more openly walk among the Judeans, "but went thence unto a country near to the wilderness." I make no apology for the statement I am about to make. This world would never be experiencing its present turmoil and unrest, its war, deviltry, and devastation, were it not for the fact that this age, this generation, like every preceding age and generation has rejected the Lord Jesus Christ! But God be thanked that there are those in this world and in this generation who like that small group in every age and every generation have bowed the knee to the Lordship of Christ, and who rejoice in His salvation. They revel in His love and confidently and hopefully look forward to the day when He shall dash in pieces everything that oppresses, and from the city of Jerusalem He shall reign as the monarch of the world, the King of kings and the Lord of lords. God grant that the day be hastened. In the meanwhile it is the hour of opportunity and grace for the individual. To each of us is offered forgiveness of sins and redemption through His blood, by believing and receiving Him as our Lord and our God.